The ISLE OF MAN RAILWAY

Volume I

THE BRITISH NARROW GAUGE RAILWAY — No.2A

The
ISLE OF MAN RAILWAY

Volume I
An outline History of The Isle of Man Railway
including
The Manx Northern Railway and
The Foxdale Railway.
(Pre-1873 to 1904)

by
James I.C. Boyd

'Receipts may be predicted by the
rise and fall of the Barometer'

(Frederick Henry Trevithick: April 1875)

THE OAKWOOD PRESS

© Oakwood Press and James I.C. Boyd 1993

First published 1962 as one volume

ISBN 0 85361 444 X

This edition to be published in 3 volumes

Printed by Cambrian Printers Ltd, Wales
Typeset by Gem Publishing Company, Brightwell, Wallingford, Oxfordshire.

All rights reserved. No part of this book may be reproduced or transmitted in any form or by any means, electronic or mechanical, including photo-copying, recording or by any information storage and retrieval system, without permission from the Publisher in writing.

Published by
The OAKWOOD PRESS
P.O.Box 122, Headington, Oxford.

Contents

Abbreviations	4
Foreword	4
Modus operandi	5
Manx Government and Railway Legislation	5
Preface	6
Introduction – Personal Relations	8
The Island before a railway	11
Attempts to build a railway	17
A railway is born (1820–1871)	27
'A cheap narrow-gauge railway'	35
Historical Chronology 1872–1904	35
The Vignoles, Rixon, Mackenzie & Watson Reports: 1873	43
Acknowledgements	255
Sources	256
Bibliography	256
Index	256

Abbreviations

Beyer, Peacock & Co. Ltd.	BP & CL
Douglas & Laxey Coast Electric Tramway Ltd.	D & LCETL
Douglas, Laxey & Ramsey Railway Co. Ltd.	DL & RRCL
Douglas, Laxey & Snaefell Railway.	DL & SR
Douglas Southern Electric Tramways Ltd.	DSETL
Foxdale Railway.	FR
Great Western Railway.	GWR
Institution of Civil Engineers.	Inst CE
Institution of Mechanical Engineers.	Inst ME
Isle of Man Mining Co. Ltd.	IOMMCL
Isle of Man Railway Co. (Ltd.).	IOMR
Isle of Man Steam Packet Co. Ltd.	IOMSPCL
Isle of Man Tramways & Electric Power Co. Ltd.	IOMT & EPCL
London, Midland & Scottish Railway.	LMSR
London & North Western Railway.	LNWR
Manx Brick & Tramway Co. Ltd.	MB & TCL
Manx Electric Railway.	MER
Manx Northern Railway.	MNR
Member of the House of Keys.	MHK
Midland Railway.	MR
Speaker of the House of Keys.	SHK

Foreword

The name Man is derived from the Celtic, for District. The Island is 31 miles from north to south and 13 miles wide at its broadest part; exact agreement about its area is not reached by scholars; it is about 220 square miles. Until 1266 it was part of the Kingdom of Norway; at that time Magnus, King of Norway, ceded his rights to Alexander III, King of Scotland, after whose death the inhabitants placed themselves under the protection of Edward I of England. By him and his successors, temporary grants were made to English nobles under the title of 'king' and the Earls of Derby ruled it from 1405 to 1651. It was then taken from them by Parliament owing to the Royalism of the then Countess, and restored at the Restoration; in 1735 it passed by descent to the Duke of Athol. In 1765 it was purchased by the British Crown, but full rights were not obtained until 1829.

The Island retains a semi-independence. It has its own Governor, its own Parliament (The Tynwald). Popular election was introduced in 1866. The laws are promulgated on Tynwald Hill in Manx and English but the Celtic dialect is rarely found. St Patrick traditionally founded the bishopric of Sodor and Man, consisting now of the Isle of Man alone, but originally including the Hebrides or Southern Islands of Scotland (as distinct from the Orkneys or Northern Islands of Scotland).

Apart from the northern plain, the country is very hilly, Snaefell in the northern part being the highest point (2,036 ft).

The former Arms were a ship with sails furled and motto '*Rex Manniae et Insularum*'. At the Scottish conquest they were changed to Three Legs, clothed at the thigh and spurred; motto '*Quocunque Jeceris Stabit*'.*

The recurring connections between the railway of the past, as well as the railway of the present, and the history and traditions of the Island – not least in the names carried by its locomotives and the Arms of the Railway Company – are clearly apparent.

---

*'Which ever way you throw me, I stand upright.'
Note: The reference to an Act in this volume refers to an Act of Tynwald unless stated to the contrary.

Modus operandi for this publication

The basic history of the Isle of Man Railway herein, is covered by a Chronology. All subjects appear by date within that Chronology: extended information on any particular subject (e.g. Operating, Route, Locomotives etc.) is to be found in additional volumes.

The Reference Library of The Manx Museum possesses an extensive collection of material: primary sources in this collection are the basis of much of the material herein. Not all secondary sources have yet been accessioned, and not all material has warranted full disclosure: where appropriate the Reference Library reference number is quoted as a footnote.

Manx Government & Railway Legislation

Government is by The Court of Tynwald, claimed to be the oldest legislative body with a period of continuous history in the world. A Legislative Council and a House of Keys together form the Court. Prior to 1866 when the capital was moved from Castletown, the House of Keys was self-electing: since then it has consisted of 24 elected members sitting for five years. In 1874 it moved from Castletown to Douglas.

The Sovereign is Lord of Mann, and her representative is the Lieutenant-Governor.

As regards railway legislation, although the Council and Keys sit as one body, each votes separately and all Bills must pass through both branches before signing. Duties and direct taxes are imposed, and all expenditure approved here.

Manx railways are subject to insular regulation and not to Westminster. From time to time however, persons from outside the Island may be formally invited to advise etc.; an example of this from the past has been the appointment of an Island railway inspector from the English Railway Inspectorate (the appointment is made by the Governor).

It will be clear from this history that the Boards of the railway companies considered here have found that the powers of the Governor have often proved to be an interference not altogether helpful to their commercial well-being and that when the assistance of Tynwald would have been to the advantage of public transport (including tourism) by railway, that body has proved tardy and even deliberately ready to ignore constructive suggestion.

By and large, relations between railways and the knowledgeable who operate them, and members of government who have been unwilling, unable and even (so it is alleged) unfit to concern themselves with railway problems, are not a recent circumstance; evidence herein will show they date back to the 1850s. This state of affairs has never been more clearly shown than in the past two decades. The Manx are, by their own admission, a proverbially cautious people.

Preface to the Fifth Edition

The First Edition of THE ISLE OF MAN RAILWAY appeared in 1962 and the subject has remained one of constant interest ever since. New editions, revised and enlarged were completed with the fourth in 1977 and this has been long out of print. It might be thought that this would suffice, but a new surge of demand has arisen since The Isle of Man Railway Co. went into liquidation in 1978; although only a truncated part of the original railway system survives, there is now hunger for a fuller history and this is made possible by the changed circumstances of the present.

Although the sources of information listed herein may seem adequate enough, it is a matter for despair that for two decades at least, the security of the Company's records has been appreciated by few in the Island which has no legislation for the safe keeping of insular documents. At one time material was being sent to the Prison for burning or thrown down disused mine shafts and since then what has been described to the Author as a form of pillaging with the connivance of authority, has removed paperwork into England – albeit this has survived whereas it might not have done otherwise. Some 'custodians' of this paperwork are not prepared to reveal its extent nor if, by a show of goodwill, they intend to place it in a place of public scrutiny.

This being explained, some balance is redressed as (compared with the meagre information grudgingly permitted to the Author in the late 1950s) what remains is a treasure trove and it may be hoped that an enlightened Legislature will shortly arrange for it all to be accessioned and made available for public research. In view of increased wealth of resource, no attempt has been made to follow the pattern of the previous editions; certain inaccuracies which appeared in consequence of the frailty of memory of my informants have been corrected.

Since 1977 – when the last edition appeared – the Isle of Man Railway has lost two-thirds of route: only Douglas–Port Erin remains and even as I write, its future is not assured. Not only the Railway but the whole aspect of the Island has changed dramatically in the last fifteen years. Its roads are cluttered with cars and heavy lorries – many of the latter conveyed to the Island by car ferry, and the unsuited road surfaces are torn apart. The tourist trade, on which so much of the Island's economy depended and the railways which served it, has suffered considerably. Allegedly high fares charged by The Steam Packet Company are blamed for this but the lure of the Mediterranean's more reliable weather and inexpensive holiday packages by air must also have played a part. The former importance of tourism has been dimmed by the Island becoming a residential Tax Haven and a base for 'laundering money': in consequence, large company-owned limousines posture on narrow roads as unhappily as do their non-owners' life-styles rub shoulders with the islanders' modest saloons and limited incomes – and hostility festers.

As just stated, what is now the 'steam railway' (as opposed to the 'electric railway') has as yet been accorded no certain future by Government while centres of fiscal manipulation can move away to more advantageous shores as quickly as they came. Yet, even now the Island can take steps to prevent the loss of its precious assets – historic industrial features no less – and control the despoliation of its countryside by inappropriate development; if so it will always remain what a century ago it claimed to be, 'The Gem of the Irish Sea'.

August 1992
Colwall,
Herefordshire.

Personal Relations

I have written elsewhere that my mother's family first visited the Isle of Man before the turn of the century. Throughout the summers which spanned the two World Wars, my own family and relatives continued to do the same; it was a habit we shared with many north-country people. Not that the Isle of Man was the principal venue for holidays in our part of Lancashire and Cheshire – rather most people went to Blackpool or North Wales or the Lake District (the snobs to Bournemouth) and a few adventurers to the Continent. I came to know North Wales and its railways at a later stage, and throughout my childhood lived among those drab and uncolourful railways which served the Greater Manchester district. A boarding-school period broadened my horizons to the Great Western Railway and the Somerset & Dorset – but our annual August sojourn in the Isle of Man was a recurring Elysium.

It began each year shortly after the VIKING had berthed at Douglas pier; she was the fastest ship in the Isle of Man Steam Packet Company's fleet, and sailed from Fleetwood mid-morning each day (allowing tantalising glimpses of the Knott End train shunting at its terminus on the far side of the Wyre). Between Douglas pier and the railway station we often patronised a horse-drawn cab, surrounded by the minimum amount of luggage my parents considered necessary for a four-week stay – a formidable collection! As I rushed off the cab and across the circulating area at Douglas station, that unchanged scene broke upon and delighted me ... year upon year. The smell of coal smoke among those unexpected palm trees beside the line; the low rakes of variously coloured carriages which drooped heavily along the platform edges, their bowed bodies putting one in mind of cows anxiously awaiting milking time. Up and down between them, with apparent freedom of movement or utterly without mission, those most gorgeous bright green engines flitted to and fro, with shining brass and copper work, their side rods flashing in the sun (it was always sunny, of course), and with shiny brass numerals on their chimney sides. They had just been waiting for my return; 'I'm No. 5, remember me from last year?' Upon their front buffer beams they sported a curious miscellany of tinware ... jugs, cans, teapots or feeders, each with its own blend of lubricant, and when, after fussing about the yard until exhausted, an engine wilted before the water crane, the driver would swing down from the cab, walk to the front end and, selecting the brew of the moment, address himself to various parts with an oil can filled from that medley of receptacles.

We left Douglas (after anxious reassurance that our luggage was safely stowed in the van) on the Port Erin boat train at 2.30 pm from Platform Two. Simultaneously a North Line train would be booked to leave for Peel and Ramsey (both portions generously labelled by long boards, which were hung from the van grabhandles). This was our introductory thrill – Manx drivers invariably blew the condensate from the cylinders for quite some distance from the start, and if the two trains left at the same time, as was often the case, the draincocks threw up a cloud of steam well-peppered with small clinker, which each spouting cylinder grouted from the 'ballast'. The trains would lurch side by side, swaying, rolling, enveloped by steam, and we would hang out of the open windows regardless of parental tugs at the seats of our shorts. The north train always won the race, for ours had to begin the formidable Port Soderick bank, which soon slowed us to walking pace. In the slightly calmer conditions which ensued, my mother would tell us (she did so every year) that our engine was the KISSACK, and she had been at Wintersdorf School, Southport, with his daughter. She also reminded us that the flowery banks of the slopes of the Nunnery Cutting which now enveloped us, had been seeded by the Reverend So-and-So, who threw out more seeds every year he came. We half-listened because it was polite to do so, but the personal sound of a Manx bogie coach was more to my hearing, and fortunately it is one which can still be enjoyed. The coaches, with their bare seats, bare floors and lamp bowls half-full of rainwater, made a low growling roar as they were tugged unwillingly and painfully by the labouring engine over those hard flat-bottomed rails; the chains which held their bogies, the linkage of the couplings, brake gear and droplights all rattling in various cadenzas of sound . . .

My day began in one of those back bedrooms on the seafront at Port St Mary. Through the brass bed-end I could see the railway in its whole sweep from Colby to Port St Mary. I had only a vague idea of the times of trains, but long before they came into view I could hear their individual whistles borne by the breeze along the fields by the shore. The earlier engines had a high-pitched shriek; the later ones were more dignified. The brass dome of the train from Colby would catch the morning sun and glint across the cornfields already half-harvested. You could tell exactly where it was, as it whistled for every lady crossing keeper to close her gates to the road.

Often No. 16 was the 7.15 am ex-Port Erin Boat Train engine and the load would be ten bogies. I could hear the singing and shouting from those people who were departing, and even more so from those who did not have to leave; seeing the Saturday morning Boat Train away was a ritual for those who met each, but only once a year. In the Douglas direction, the practice of the guards waving their white and green flags and the answering whistle of the engine was performed right beneath my window.

It will sound sacrilegious to add that I spent quite a lot of my time on, but not riding upon, the Isle of Man Railway in those days. Nor was I there to see the trains; like many another, I sought the long grass and ill-frequented cuttings of the line where I might find butterflies to add to my collection, and which would make me the envy of my school friends who had to spend their holidays in England. The Isle of Man, no matter in what subject, was a youngster's paradise, and I grew up with a strong affection for its countryside and the railway which served it.

In another age and in quite differing context Psalm 119 was written thus: 'I have had as great delight in the way of thy testimonies as in all manner of riches'. So it was between me and the Isle of Man railways.

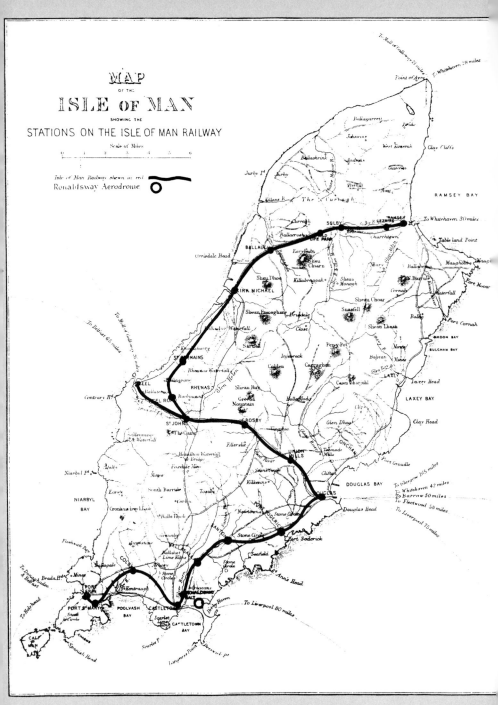

Nineteenth Century promotional map.

The Island before a railway

'Go Abroad to the Isle of Man' has long been a favourite cliché of holiday advertising for the Island. And 'going abroad' it has been for millions of English, Irish and Scottish people who feel that a holiday is never complete unless they cross a considerable expanse of water to begin it. Not for them the easy access of the French coast, a stone's throw from Kent; nor the close proximity of Ulster to the Scottish coast. It must be a 'proper sail to get there' and with Douglas about three hours sailing time from the Lancashire coast, it is natural that north-country people know the Island most intimately.

To appreciate the story of the Isle of Man Railway, the Island backcloth is an essential ingredient, so that a preliminary appraisal of the country will be appropriate.

> Man is an island in the Irish Sea, distant from St. Bee's-head, in Cumberland, thirty nautical miles; from Barrow-head, in Scotland, sixteen miles; from Strangford, in Ireland, twenty-seven miles . . . Its length rather exceeds thirty miles, and its mean breadth ten.
>
> Etymologists are not agreed respecting the derivation of its name . . . Some suppose it to be derived from Mona, a word which they imagine . . . to have been used by Caesar to denote this island. Mona and Monoida are classed by Ptolemy under the head of Irish Island . . . and the Mona of Tacitus is undoubtedly Anglesea; . . .
>
> Perhaps the words 'Mona' and 'Man' may both of them be derived from the ancient British word 'mon' (accented grave in Owen's dictionary) and signifying 'what is isolated' . . .

So begins an account of the Isle of Man as set down by George Woods in the first years of the nineteenth century at a time when the Island was a backward and primitive country. It was considerably behind England in its development, lacking in roads and trade, the men given to overdrinking and the women doing most of the farm work. Most of the men worked with the herring industry and tended the land only when fishing did not call them; a few small concerns had worked the lead and other mineral deposits, but at the time of Woods' visits, many of the mines were ill-managed and flooded. Of woodlands there were none, except where they had been planted; there was little or no industry apart from brewing, the products of which were consumed by the aforesaid fishermen.

Fifty years before railways were introduced to the Island, there were but three carriage roads: Douglas to Castletown; Douglas to Peel and Castletown to Ramsey (the last named being the last constructed); apparently the Island west of Castletown was unworthy of a carriage road. Woods mentions that in 1760 these roads were dangerous to horsemen in winter, and for carriages even in summer, but that 'they are in an improving state'.

Turning to the manufacturing side of the Island before the coming of the railway; it was shortly after 1800 that the first mill was erected at Nunnery and this may still be seen on the left hand of the railway immediately on leaving Douglas station. Until this time, there were insufficient mills to grind wheat, which had to be exported and the flour imported. Of factories, other than breweries, there were 'tan-yards, candle and soap manufactories . . . malting and brewing being uncontrolled, ale and beer may be made for considerably less than half the price they cost in England . . . these last trades . . . are probably the chief in the Island; and judging from the quality of the ale, and the number of people who daily get intoxicated with it (particularly in the fishing season), the business of brewer must be extremely profitable . . . half the inhabitants die of "grog consumption" . . .' None of these products was made in sufficient quantity to export them, but carriage of skins and hides, flour, wheat, stone for buildings (the only brick works was an inferior one near Douglas), casks of beer or herring, seaweed and coal, were among the commodities which the inadequate roads had to carry. In the middle of the nineteenth century, woollen mills had sprung up and there was some weaving on hand looms, but the price of importing coal and carrying it in the Island was a restrictive factor.

Before the coming of the railway the population was relatively small; in the eighth century there were less than 300 families, which grew to 1,300, but 'scarcely half that number' in 1854. By 1792 the Douglas area had 5,000 inhabitants and next came Castletown area with 3,300. At this time and until 1866, Castletown was still the capital of the Island, after which Douglas took the title. By 1900 the total population was over 54,000 and today is rather less than that.

There are no snakes; the Manx puffin is now extinct; railway embankments are a paradise for the entomologist. Frost and snow come rarely and do not last long; the summer's heat is tempered by the sea's proximity and for the same reason, winter gales may blow frequently and for long duration.

Before the development of the railway ports (Fleetwood, Heysham, etc.) the Island looked to Liverpool or Whitehaven for its imports, coal in particular. Until the Act of Revestment in 1765, the chief business of the Island was smuggling, said to exceed £350,000 per year and was reputedly encouraged by the Duke of Athol. Many thereby became rich, but after the Act they had to exchange an irregular and idle life to become fishermen or farmers, or emigrate to America.

As the time of the railway approached, considerable improvements had taken place. Herring fishing had become the chief commerce and the summer visitor had begun to take advantage of that Victorian institution, a middle-class vacation. Transport (for visitors the Irish jaunting car was used) was virtually non-existent once the Island was reached, and severely limited the opportunities which prominent Islanders felt should be broadened by the building of a railway system. Furthermore, once the environs of the four main towns, Douglas, Castletown, Peel and Ramsey, had been left, there were primitive conditions little better than those found by Woods. A railway, giving access to the smaller towns, would oblige them to improve their amenities if they too, desired to attract visitors.

It is significant that not until the British Crown obtained full rights over the Island in 1829, did any murmur of transport promotion take place; it is remarkable nevertheless that, at a time so early in railway development, such a thing should be mooted for the Island. This may well have been due to the close ties with Liverpool which, at that time, was excelled by no other English city for 'railway-mindedness' as it was about to be connected with Manchester by 'the world's first passenger railway'. It was not a *railway* at this juncture however, but, more important, the promotion of a steamship company in December 1829 (this was later to become The Isle of Man Steam Packet Company, still a vigorous undertaking). Most visitors who reached Douglas were, however, dissuaded from going further when they saw the rude equipages which were all the Island had to offer. It was the solution to this impasse which is the subject of this book.

We may complete this pre-railway era review with a few helpful facts to assist our image of the situation as the 1870s began.

The population of Douglas was then 14,000 and elsewhere was negligible in comparison; the principal aim of a railway would be to carry summer visitors as Island traffic alone could not justify the cost of a railway. Most visitors would be based in Douglas and a railway would have to woo them into exploring the-then somewhat backward remainder of the Island, albeit with a beauty of its own: it would also have to compete with 600 'Hackney Cars' which already clamoured for this business.

Whitehaven as a place of shipment for the Island, has been mentioned but it was not suitably placed for tourist business. This was based on Liverpool. In winter IOMSPC sailings were thrice weekly but in summer up to five times daily. Ships brought an average 800 persons per sailing: in the period June–November 1872 upwards of 130,000 had landed at Douglas, some from a daily service from Barrow which only operated during the summer.

The importance of provincial ports was a governing factor in laying out a railway – Douglas was pre-eminent but Castletown and, less so, Peel played their part: Ramsey harbour was mainly concerned with the coal trade whilst the others imported provisions (tea, sugar, tobacco), coal and lime. Castletown was the centre of agricultural imports. There were 600 sailing vessels engaged in fishing, 300–400 based on Peel and the remainder on Port St Mary. Peel was a useful anchorage; in certain weathers it is preferred Douglas and a breakwater was built to improve it, while the same was done at Port St Mary. With well-intended zeal the promotion of a Port Erin breakwater at a cost of over £80,000 was but a first stage to making a 'deep-landing pier for steamers ... about £6,000 has been voted for the purpose' (1873). The IOMR would duly link five of these six ports.

The foregoing shipping notes should not be taken as finite; all ports had some general cargoes and the importance of one against another varied according to season, weather and economics. The IOMR promoters recognised that Castletown was second to Douglas in terms of shipping being, for the mariner, a more desirable haven from England than the passage round the Calf of Man to Peel. During 1872 the promoters evinced some useful facts about Castletown; 806 vessels of 20,040 tons burden had entered the harbour, of these, 167 brought 7,319 tons of coal and 27 brought 1,755 tons of general cargo. The coal was consumed in the country districts through which their railway would pass; 580 tons of goods went to Peel and 150 tons to Port St Mary. The local brewery also sent '150 tons* of beer' into the countryside. Eighty-nine vessels had carried away 3,591 tons of farm produce and vegetables, and 'a large quantity of lime'. From this evidence the promoters saw the best site for a station was on The Claddagh, with a Harbour Tramway to support it; should the original intention to place the

---

*Should this be 'tuns'?!

station at Ballalough be carried through, goods traffic would remain with the horse and cart as at present. Passengers too, would be at a disadvantage as Ballalough was some distance from The Green and King William's College; the College Principal welcomed the railway – it would bring an increased number of day boys from the Douglas area.

Evidence of local enthusiasm appears in that some Castletown residents were ready to come forward and set up a Company to build such a Tramway, and work it or lease it to the intended Railway Company.

And no less might be expected of the inhabitants of the former capital of the Island . . . !

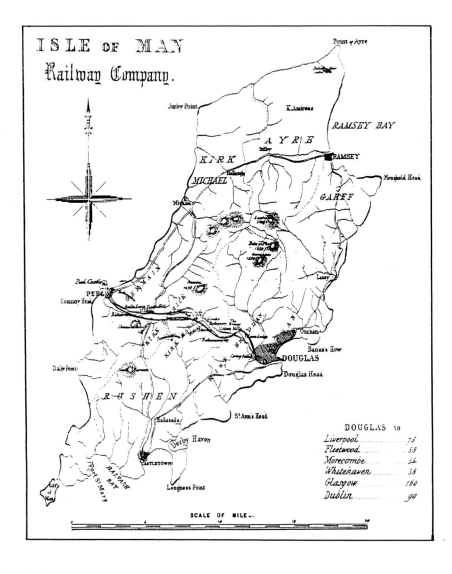

ISLE OF MAN RAILWAY COMPANY.
Limited.

CAPITAL £90,000, in 18,000 Shares of £5 each.—Deposit 10s. per Share.

Directors.

THE RIGHT HON. LORD VISCOUNT RANELAGH, 7, New Burlington Street, CHAIRMAN.
LIEUT.-COL. AUGUSTUS WILLIAM HENRY MEYRICK, 43, Grosvenor Street.
CAPTAIN EDWARD CHETHAM STRODE, South Hill House, Shepton Mallet, Somersetshire.
CHARLES APPLEYARD, Esq. 1, New Square, Lincoln's Inn,
WITH POWER TO ADD TO THEIR NUMBER.

Solicitor.
CHARLES APPLEYARD, Esq. 1, New Square, Lincoln's Inn.

Engineer.
CAPTAIN WILLIAM S. MOORSOM, 17A, Great George Street, Westminster.

Brokers.
Messrs. PEPPERCORNE, 2, Royal Exchange Buildings.

OFFICES: No. 1, NEW SQUARE, LINCOLN'S INN.

This Company has been initiated for the construction and maintenance of a Railway in the ISLE OF MAN, hitherto without that valuable and almost indispensable means of transit.

The Island is advantageously situated for commercial and general purposes, being only a few hours sail from the coasts of England, Ireland, and Scotland, and at all times easy of access therefrom.

The country possesses great agricultural capabilities, and is celebrated for its extensive Cod and Herring Fisheries; its valuable mines of Lead, and other minerals; and as an almost unrivalled resort for tourists and others—more than 50,000 persons having landed at Douglas alone in one season; whilst the numbers that have landed at Castletown and Ramsey are also considerable. The cost of living is inexpensive, as, from the light duties upon imported articles, and the abundant produce of the country, provisions, and all the necessaries and luxuries, of life may be obtained at moderate prices.

The climate is delightful and salubrious, and on that account highly and deservedly esteemed as one of the favourite watering-places of the North of England; the scenery is highly picturesque; and the Island abounds in valuable indigenous materials, such as limestone, marble, slate, red sand-stone, and other products which it is unnecessary to specify. The principal towns of the Island are DOUGLAS, PEEL, CASTLETOWN, and RAMSEY; DOUGLAS being the chief port and commercial emporium; CASTLETOWN the seat of the Local Government; and PEEL the town from whence the fisheries are principally conducted, and the place of general attraction to tourists and others visiting the Island. The recent Government Commission has recommended that harbours shall be constructed at DOUGLAS and at PEEL.

The map herewith will show the form, extent, localities, &c., of the ISLE OF MAN more clearly than any descriptive statement would do; and the positions and the distances of several ports and places on the adjacent coasts of ENGLAND, IRELAND, and SCOTLAND, will also be found exhibited thereon.

2

The Railway to be constructed will extend from DOUGLAS to PEEL, about twelve miles in length, with intermediate stations ; and the population of the Island, which will be directly accommodated by the Line, will comprise about 30,000 persons.

The course of the projected Line will be found traced, *in red,* upon the map above referred to.

The requisite surveys have been effected, the plans and sections prepared, approved, and lodged ; and, in accordance with the terms of a contract with Messrs. Carlisle & Co., prepared by the Engineer of the Company, the construction of the Line and Stations, with complete working stock ready for traffic, will be effected at the rate of £6,500 per mile, exclusive only of the purchase of land, which is in progress.

It is confidently anticipated, from statistics which have recently been collected with considerable care on the spot, that, from the Traffic arising chiefly from Passengers, and also from the carriage of minerals, fish, other articles of commerce, and agricultural produce, a revenue will be derived amounting to not less than £12,000 per annum.

The Act of the Local Government of the Island, which is in progress, and to which no opposition presents itself, will comprise all the requisite provisions and conditions for the conduct and management of the Company, Stations &c.

Above two-thirds of the Shares are already taken, and for the remainder, applications may be addressed to the Directors of the Company, in the form annexed, at the Offices of the Company, No. 1, New Square, Lincoln's Inn W.C. ; or to Messrs. Peppercorne, Brokers, No. 2 Royal Exchange Buildings, London. E.C.

Prospectus – 1857 Scheme (Page 2.

Attempts to build a railway

In 1824 a canal linking Douglas & Peel was mooted: in 1838 the folly of a railway of the same intent was ventilated in the Press. There were several attempts to build an Island railway before success was achieved, but a full account would prove to be tedious. A simple list is sufficient to begin:

1	9th September, 1845	ISLE OF MAN RAILWAY COMPANY
2	26th September, 1845	GREAT MANX RAILWAY
3	January 1857	ISLE OF MAN RAILWAY COMPANY LTD.*
4	September 1860	Revival of 1857 Scheme
5	February 1862	DOUGLAS–PEEL RAILWAY COMPANY LTD. Scheme[2]
6	April 1862	ISLE OF MAN EXTENSION RAILWAY
7	1864	ISLE OF MAN RAILWAY – Douglas & Peel Railway[3]
8	September 1867	Furness Railway proposition
9	September 1868	Attempt to revive 1864 Scheme

As certain of these plans led to the ultimate railway, a closer look at each makes for interest.

1. ISLE OF MAN RAILWAY COMPANY†. In July 1845 THE RAILWAY REGISTER and others noted among the revised schemes for new railways, the provisional registration of same with a capital of £500,000 in £20 shares. Standing Orders 'at the Court of Tynwald holden at Castle Rushen, the 14th November, 1845' later provided for the building of such a railway.‡ The provisional committee# was a mammoth one, with thirty-eight members in the Island and almost as many in London. The routes to be taken proved to be the historic ones to Peel, St John's to Ramsey, and to Port Erin: the main line was to Peel and other lines were described as 'branches'. Old spellings appear, such as Ballassalla and Port le Mary.

The scheme was a child of the Railway Mania period, and no more is heard of it.

2. GREAT MANX RAILWAY. Within days of the foregoing a GREAT MANKS RAILWAY (an ancient form of spelling) was provisionally registered, a title hurriedly amended to the contemporary form; it was 'to serve Douglas, Peel, Castletown and Ramsey' and disappeared as quickly as it arrived.

3. ISLE OF MAN RAILWAY COMPANY LTD. News of this promotion appears in the MONA'S HERALD 14th January, 1857 concerning an application to Tynwald for a railway between Douglas and Peel. The course was much along the proposed route of 1845, but the idea died. The capital proposed was £90,000 in £5 shares and the engineer, Capt W.S. Moorsom. Contractors would be Carlisle & Co.

---

*Manx Museum: MD 332/98i and MD 332/98e
[2]Manx Museum: R/188
[3]Manx Museum: R/186
†Parliamentary Paper: Joint Stock Companies registered under provisions of Act 7 & 8. Vict. cap. 110 1846 (504) XLIII 55
‡Manx Museum: B 1192, D 151/IX
#Chairman: Captain Bacon of Seafield, IOM

4. A re-incarnation of the 1857 scheme was foreshadowed in September 1860:

> Some time since (1856) we stated the agent of parties in London was over here and surveyed the line of country between Douglas and Peel with a view to forming a line of rail between the two towns . . . application will shortly be made to Tynwald to form a Company to carry out the same . . . three engineers from London have been for some time on the Island.

The MONA'S HERALD was sceptical . . .

> The railroad to Peel once more . . . this is about the sixth time the periodical fever has come over the Island . . . new companies have come up one after the other . . . shares are bought on the market and a few bottles of wine imbibed in baptism of the enterprise . . . we have very little expectation of seeing a Manx railway constructed by speculating geniuses from England . . . a Prospectus has been issued . . . 12 miles long. The estimated cost is £90,000 and the yearly receipts are estimated at £12,000.

There was much said against the building of any railway at all, especially by the landowners,* and nothing transpired.

5. DOUGLAS & PEEL RAILWAY CO. LTD. Another similar scheme about which a Prospectus† was published and a set of Plans and Sections were deposited. William Gravatt CE, FRS, was the appointed Engineer, whilst the promoters' other interests included the IOMSPC and the Foxdale Mining Co. The line's course would have virtually been identical to that adopted for the Isle of Man Railway of 1870, with termini at the same locations. Its length would have been 11 miles 1 furlong 5.5 chains and the route would fall towards Peel for 9½ miles at 1 in 105, passing by the river at Glenfaba, which would be diverted for the purpose. This was another non-starter. The Foxdale Mines' traffic was considered and the papers reported:

> We do not know precisely what is now paid for cartage by this Company to get their ore eight miles across country to Douglas . . . a tramway of course will be laid from the mines to St. John's, where the ore will meet the rails.

There was also a newspaper editorial reading:

> THE RAILROAD
>
> There have been repeated attempts to survey the Douglas–Peel railroad but stakes erected in July had been pulled up by the Manx farmers before the next Spring; they were re-staked the next Summer and obliterated the next Winter. The evidence of various odd schemes takes the form of a line of double row pillars at intervals of 8 feet.

In March 1862, the same paper's editorial commented that the towns of Douglas and Peel must be famous for the number of railway projects begun . . . failure was said to be due to the greediness of the landowners. The capital proposed was £75,000 in £10 shares.

6. ISLE OF MAN EXTENSION RAILWAY. This proposal first made the headlines in April 1862. Its prospectus showed the intention of adding branches to Castletown, Ramsey and Foxdale to the previous promotion of

---

*Manx Museum: MD 332/98g. (Lady Buchan's land)
†Copy in Tower Collection dated 1862.

the Douglas and Peel Railway Co. Ltd. The paper received an anonymous letter explaining why the last scheme had failed . . .

> the President of the Society of Engineers surveyed the line, prepared plans (etc) . . . a contractor collected the necessary plant . . . at the last moment a stop was placed on the proceedings . . . the reason given was the obduracy of the landowners and the outrageous prices asked for the land; also it was expected that the House of Keys would object.

It would be different this time:

> . . . landowners and farmers all along the route are all in favour of the project . . . but the public have been humbugged so many times over this small job that we have lost all confidence . . . we shall remain unbelievers until we hear the whistle and see the cars rattling along the rails . . .

wrote the HERALD.

> The profile of the Douglas–Peel railway is almost complete . . . an additional staff of assistants arrived on Saturday. (23rd April, 1862).

Yet once again it all vanished without notice.

Not a lot of activity followed this; though not stated at the time, future events were to show that Island folk were not anxious to take up a financial interest in the affair. The silence was occasionally broken by such letters as this which appeared in the MANX SUN:

> . . . for about twelve months of the year the Douglas–Peel Railway might get somewhat to do in the way of passenger traffic . . . during the season it would be employed in the conveyance of herrings for export; these two temporary sources of revenue would hardly make it a paying concern . . .

Such comments carried some weight, whilst other newspaper articles stressed the advantage of a railway:

> . . . the need required for the populous district of the Foxdale Mines alone would be very great. At present the ore has to be carted from thence, a distance of nine miles to Douglas, and the whole of the coals for working the mine and the use of the population there, and most of the groceries and necessities are carted from Douglas. A short tramway to Foxdale would secure all the traffic of the neighbourhood, and would in all probability cause the valuable granite quarries at Barrule to be worked to profit . . .

Letters to the newspapers were frequent; there were references to the 'elusive mirage of the Douglas & Peel Railway which has so often dazzled to deceive . . . but this time we hoped would assume the more pleasing form of reality'. Another writer congratulated the Island on the loss of the scheme and trusted it would result in more attention being paid to a 'paying and very cheap system . . . the Fairlie system of railway working of very narrow gauge (rather than) lines of ponderous construction and broad gauge . . .'

We may move for a moment to a background to these proposals. In 1859, 1863 and 1872 the Tynwald Court had addressed itself to the possibility of railways and Standing Orders were framed in anticipation of Railway Bills; another concerned accidents, stating that if one should occur, 'the facts must be immediately telegraphed to the Governor'. A severe penalty would follow for neglect of so doing.

Before examining railway matters any further, it is essential to emphasise that the life of the Island depended entirely on sea communications, and its internal transport was related to the coming and going of ships. In 1870, despite the threat of rail competition, two road coaches plied between Douglas and Peel; these were named FENELLA and RAILWAY. They ran daily (Sundays excepted) leaving the Marine Hotel, Peel at 9 am and 'returning from Douglas on the arrival of the steamers'. No better example of the dependence of the Island – mainly on the Isle of Man Steam Packet Co. – could be instanced.

Harbour improvements had begun about 1845: later proposals were encouraged by a scheme which the new Governor, Henry Brougham Loch,* initiated in 1863 and by October 1864, a fine breakwater was under construction at Port Erin whilst improvements of similar nature were being undertaken at Douglas, Ramsey, Peel and Castletown. [Even today the ports of the Island are no mariner's paradise in bad weather, and Douglas can at times be unapproachable; in such conditions boats make for Peel.] The Port Erin scheme came to notice in THE ENGINEER for 11th August, 1865 . . .

> Since the commencement of the Undertaking in October 1864 . . . three lines of tramways have been laid and two powerful locomotive-cranes are in operation. The cost is £60,000.

It was the Port Erin work which brought a steam locomotive to the Island for the first time. The breakwater there was planned boldly and constructed ambitiously, requiring twelve years to complete with many ancillary buildings and temporary structures having to be provided. A large quarry – still much in evidence today – provided the filling-in materials. The year 1876 saw the work complete at a cost of £83,000, a considerable sum in those times. It will be noted that the breakwater scheme was closely linked with the proposition for regular steamship services and the later IOM Railway felt fully justified in extending their South Line beyond Castletown to reach what they felt would be a most valuable terminus. Without the building of the new breakwater, the extension would have been a speculative one, as both Port St Mary and Port Erin were hardly more than fishing villages. There were interruptions in the construction and critics of its conception: on 20th January, 1872 the SUN said it was a blunder in every way. In 1881, a frightful westerly gale hammered the breakwater and it cracked, the lighthouse was thrown into the sea and its blocks scattered like a child's building bricks. Destruction was completed by another gale and on 22nd December, 1884 the work was utterly smashed. The possible objective of the South Line of the future Isle of Man Railway lay in ruins – and does so to this day.

Meanwhile a contemporary account of Port Erin travel reads:

> I remember a ride one evening from Port Erin to Douglas. The road was thick with coaches, all choked with pleasure-seekers returning to their lodgings in

---

*Henry Brougham Loch (1827–1900). 1st Baron Loch of Drylaw.
Gazetted to Bengal Cavalry 1844; served in Crimean War; to China Embassy 1857 – imprisoned and tortured – returned to England 1860. Private Secretary to Sir George Grey. Governor of IOM 1863–82. Knighted 1880. Governor of Victoria 1884–89. Peerage 1895.

Douglas after a drenching day. They were still wearing the clothes that had been wet through that morning: their boots were damp and cold; they were chill with the night air: but they did not grumble ... rattling through Castletown they shouted with chaff at some redcoats who were lounging by Castle Rushen and when darkness fell, they dropped asleep. The horses' hoofs splashed along the muddy roads and every driver cracked his whip amidst a chorus of stertorous snores. (*Sir Hall Caine*)

7. ISLE OF MAN RAILWAY (Douglas & Peel Railway). The correct title for this further intent is that in parenthesis, but reference was made using either title. The proposed undertaking of 1864 was by Samuel Gibbon Getley, MP for Belfast (and three times its Mayor), with William McCormick, MP for Londonderry and with Engineer G.W. Hemans. It was widely advertised in the Irish papers during March 1864 and in September found a staunch Manx supporter in Thomas Corlett Jackson of Crosby. The Court of Tynwald at Castle Rushen made an Act on the 11th April, 1865; the capital was £100,000 in shares of 10/- each, with borrowing powers up to £50,000. Passing the Legislature of Tynwald Court at St. John's on 5th July, 1865, gangs of labourers were set to work to cut demarcation ditches. But even as early as the following November, rumours of abandonment had been denied. The newspapers printed invitations for share applications and the promoters boasted about the quality of local slate being equal to the Welsh, and that there was granite to be had at St John's.

This time, provision was made to fine anyone found 'pulling up stakes or removing poles, £2 for every such offence'. Fares could not be charged if milestones or mileposts had not been set in place, or if the list of tolls was not displayed at every station; engines would be obliged 'to consume their own smoke'. The Lieutenant Governor was to appoint an Engineer to inspect the railway; a certificate would be issued by the former after which public transport would be permitted, subject in the first place to the Engineer being satisfied. Offices were in Liverpool and a census of Island traffic had proved that a railway would be profitable. The Manx Government, cautious of the scheme, stipulated that £9,000 be deposited as security against damage whilst surveys were being made, it being said that there had been considerable liberties taken on private property by surveyors for the projected railways. Some money was deposited with the Government but the project ultimately failed and there was litigation over the disposal of the deposited cash.

Of the plan itself, the Deposited Plans surviving* have 'Isle of Man Railway Co. Ltd.' attached to them by gummed label, thus creating the error over the proper title and suggesting this and previous schemes were carefully scrutinised before the 1870 promotions were advertised.

The Douglas terminal would have been more southward than was ultimately the case; this would be achieved by diverting the river. However, by and large the expected route to Peel would be taken, the steepest part being a 1 in 100 climb from Douglas to a summit of 280 ft. At Peel too, the terminus would have been more to the south of the latter-day station. In this case the Glenfaba River was not to be diverted, but crossed twice on girder bridges.

---

*Manx Museum: R/186

The Getley plan was in limbo for many months, and speculation as to its progress or otherwise was rife. Opinions against any railway waxed strongly for there were few in the Island who had any experience of railways at all: one such was 'a great number of railway travellers now carry keys to unlock and lock railway carriages so that they may let themselves out in cases of great emergency . . .' This did not inspire confidence. By November the rumour of abandonment was being refuted . . . 'such statement is entirely false . . . we are requested to give an immediate contradiction. The application for the return of the deposit is only the usual step preparatory to the commencement of the works', wrote J.J. Ridley, Solicitor to the IOM Railway Co. at Westminster. On 18th September, 1867 came the announcement: 'The Chancellor of the Duchy of Lancaster has fixed 20th September for the appointment of an official liquidator for this Company'. (The appointment was at the District Registry, Liverpool.)

8. Of all the preposterous ideas, the award must go to THE KENDAL MERCURY for 28th September, 1867 wherein a bold article advocated a branch of the Furness Railway being built on the Island – railway ferries from Barrow perhaps?!!!

A fascinating retrospection in the ISLE OF MAN EXAMINER on 27th December, 1929 recalls how the House of Keys obstructed railway schemes. It commented on the suspicious nature and diffidence about embracing modern invention which was a characteristic of the time (and hinted that it still existed). There had been an enormously-lengthy Keys' discussion after Getley had deposited £9,000; 'The Snails of Mona'. Lord Loch, the Governor was not blameless either.

9. There is report that certain of the frustrated Belfast promoters had returned to re-incarnate the Getley railway in September 1868 – at the period of the Furness Railway hint – and 'surveyors are already operating' (MONA'S HERALD 30th September). Perhaps linked to this, that paper had on 11th November; 'all landowners save one are in favour and to meet the requirements of mines, quarries etc. the gauge will be 3 ft 6 in. instead of 4 ft 8½ in.'.

A letter survives from a would-be contractor:*

Mount Vernon.
24 Octr. 1868.

Dear Sir,

I herewith send you on the other side a statement of what we could construct the Douglas and Peel Railway for and feel assured with a good committee it would be a success at that price and with 5 per cent guarantee.

I am Yours,
faithfully,

John Pilkington

MEMORANDUM OF THE UNDERTAKING OF THE ISLE OF MAN RAILWAY

Messrs Pilkington & Quill will undertake to construct the line from Douglas to Peel with works and stations complete. The line to be a single one, and double at

---

*Original in Tower Collection

stations, 3 ft 6 in. gauge and 50 lbs. per yard rails, with rolling stock sufficient to work the line consisting of engines, 1st, 2nd and 3rd class carriages and waggons for the sum of . . . £59,000 . . . and will further undertake to work the line, keep in repair, and give guarantee of 5 per cent per interest to the shareholders.

The above sum does not include the price of the land, which may be purchased by the Directors from 100 to 150£ per acre or about £8,000 including sundries.

Isle of Man Railway Company
December 1859

We the undersigned being Directors of the Isle of Man Railway Company do hereby declare that the money required by the standing orders of the Tynwald to be deposited for the purpose of procuring the Act necessary for the making the proposed Railway from Douglas to Peel in the said Island will be duly deposited and that the said act will be duly applied for on the conditions only that the owners of the major part of the land on the line of the proposed Railway shall agree to sell to the said Company so much of their land as may be required for the purpose of the said proposed Railway at its present actual saleable value

Signed —
Ranelagh
E. Cheetham Strode
Charles Appleyard
J. D. Barry
Augustus Wm Meyrick

Isle of Man Railway Scheme (January 1857): Deposit of Money.
[Manx Museum: MD 332/98i]

FORM OF APPLICATION.

TO THE DIRECTORS OF THE

ISLE OF MAN RAILWAY COMPANY.

GENTLEMEN,

Having paid to Messrs._____

£_____, being 2s. 6d. per Share on _____ Shares in the above Company, I request you will allot me that number of Shares, and I agree to accept the same, or any less number that may be allotted to me; and I agree to pay the Balance of 7s. 6d. per Share, the Deposit thereon, the Calls when made, and to sign the Deed of Settlement when required.

Dated this_____ day of _____ 1860.

Christian and Surname (in full) _____

Residence_____

Business or Profession (if any) _____

Application Form – 1860 Scheme.

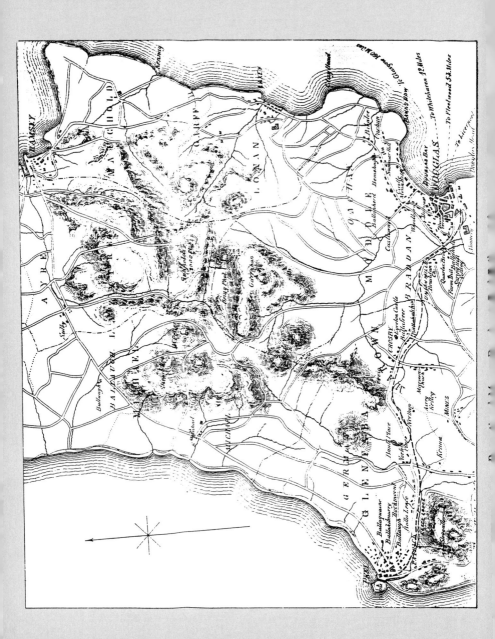

A railway is born
(1870–1871)

On 21st April, 1870, following preliminary probings, a meeting was called in St James' Hall, Douglas, at which all interested persons were invited to attend with a view to projecting a railway which would not suffer the indignities of earlier ventures. Agreement was reached to form a company and link the four main towns on the Island by railway – Douglas, Peel, Ramsey and Castletown. At a later date the Castletown line might be extended to Port Erin in connection with the harbour works building there, on the completion of which a regular steamer service would ply to Holyhead.

An updated Estimate† prepared by the Clerk of Roles (sic) Castletown, quoting English and Scottish railway statistics

> ... constructing and stocking line @ £4,200 per Mile ... 40 Miles say £170,000 ... the Isle of Man contains 54,269 inhabitants ... carriage of lime to Douglas and the North side of the Island from Ballasalla, the coal and other goods ...

and following the beforementioned April meeting, a Draft Prospectus† was prepared on 10th June by George Frederick Armstrong, CE, FGS, FSA (37 Norfolk Street, Strand) and submitted to 'The Members of the Preliminary Committee of the Isle of Man Railway Company' on 24th June. The connecting of the four principal towns was intended, with extensions to Port St Mary and Port Erin. Following experience in Norway, Sweden, Queensland and India, Armstrong chose the 3 ft 6 in. gauge which would meet the requirements of the 100,000 annual tourists better than the six hundred Hackney Carriages, which only held 7 persons who were charged at an average of 1/6d. Great stress was laid on lime and coal traffic, together with the output of the Foxdale lead mines which was currently carted to the coastal ports and the return trip filled with coal, no less in exported grain and cattle. Average cost would be £4,000–4,500 per mile and landowners were prepared to take shares in exchange for surrendered property. Locomotive coal would be obtained from Cumberland, 30 sea miles away.

Armstrong sent a letter† with recommendations as to how to raise finance, the enlisting of Brokers, and to put the Prospectus in the newspapers whilst the money market was favourable. He was prepared 'as a *temporary arrangement* only, for this office to be used as the office of the Company.'

Without delay, a suitable sum of money was raised with which to carry out surveys of possible routes, James Armstrong, MICE, President of the Institution of Civil Engineers carrying out this work and reporting that such railways could be entertained.* As soon as sufficient financial support was promised, the 'Isle of Man Railway Company Ltd.' was registered on 19th December, 1870: (under an Act of 1880 the Company was permitted to omit

---

†Originals in Tower Collection
*His expenses were not agreed-to by the IOMR Board until 5th February, 1873!

'Limited' in reference). The capital was to be £200,000 and the Engineer appointed was Henry Vignoles, MICE.[‡]

On 3rd January of the following year, George Henry Wood (who had been associated with the promotion of the Company), was appointed Provisional Secretary and Vignoles went to work on his own survey, which was completed in April along with a Report. Vignoles had made it his business to inspect the 1 ft 11½ in. gauge Festiniog Railway in North Wales which was at this time the leading narrow gauge concern: he would doubtless have been advised by Charles Spooner, Engineer of that undertaking, not to adopt so narrow a gauge as that used at Festiniog. He would also be influenced by Robert Fairlie, whose connections with the narrow gauge were then at their height, and who advocated the 3-foot gauge as the most suitable dimension for narrow gauge promotion. It comes as no surprise that Vignoles recommended this gauge for the Isle of Man, and that it was adopted. The Report goes '... I am convinced that ... with a 3-foot gauge (it) may be worked at 40 or 43 per cent of the receipts, and that the greatest economy would accrue from using rails weighing 45 lb. per yard.' (Vignoles' attempt at accurate costs was followed by an estimate of dividend in the Prospectus; it was anticipated that a 12½ per cent dividend should be available from the issue of 40,000 shares at £5 each with earnings of £30 per mile per week. It was assumed that working expenses would be 50 per cent of receipts.)

Concern was soon expressed as to the position of landowners whose property the railway might traverse, and the following was a typical newspaper comment of January 1871:

> Information is that it is not the intention of the promoters of the BILL now about to be applied for, for the purpose of the proposed railways, to ask the Legislature to deviate from the provisions of that Act, unless where the same may be found impracticable ... a portion of that Act provides that 'the Railway Co. shall make and at all times maintain for the benefit and accommodation of the owners and occupiers of lands adjoining the railway, proper watering places for cattle, where, by reason of the railway, the cattle ... shall be deprived of access to their former watering places ...'[*]

[‡]Henry Vignoles, born 16th November, 1827, third son of Charles Blacker Vignoles, at that time carrying out Government surveys in the Isle of Man. Placed under the care of Dr Garvey, Master of a boys' school in Douglas. Removed to Liverpool, where his father was engaged under George Stephenson on the Liverpool and Manchester Railway. Removed later on to Dinting Vale, near Glossop, in Derbyshire, his father having been appointed Engineer-in-Chief to the Sheffield and Manchester Railway. In 1840–41 sent to Repton School; from Repton to Manchester Grammar School.

In 1843 Vignoles sent to Ireland to join his eldest brother Charles, who had been appointed Engineer to the Shannon Commission. In 1846 accompanied his father to Warsaw and ultimately to St. Petersburg. On leaving Russia, Vignoles appointed co-resident engineer with his brother Hutton on the Frankfurt, Wiesbaden and Cologne Railway; and in the next year, 1854, he became Chief Resident Engineer on the Western Railway of Switzerland. In 1858 appointed Chief Resident Engineer on the Bilbao and Tudela Railway through the Cantabrian Pyrenees; afterwards head of his father's staff in railway construction in Poland: last professional work was the railway from Douglas to Peel, and Douglas to Port Erin, the first railway in the Isle of Man. He died on 16th June, 1899.

[*]Standing Orders on Railways Bills – Committee appointed to revise same; 9th February, 1871. [Manx Museum: B192x/1x.]

The MANX SUN (4th February, 1871) said:

> Various submissions have been made on the subject of land values along the route of the proposed Douglas–Peel railway. It may be pointed out that land cut by the line and compensated for must first be allocated a linking bridge and even then small parts of estate severed from remainder are left with little worth. It is pointless to be compensated on the basis of the value of a narrow strip of land taken by the Railway.

The same paper carried this Notice on 13th February, 1871:

Isle of Man Railway Co. (Limited).

Capital £200,000 in
40,000 shares of £5 each.

Provisional Committee:

Mark H. Quayle	Clerk of the Rolls	IOM
James Gell	Attorney General	IOM
Major J.S. Goldie Taubman	The Nunnery (Speaker: House of Keys)	
Edward M. Gawne	Kentraugh (former Speaker: House of Keys)	
Rev. William Bell Christian*	Milntown, Ramsey	MHK
W.B. Stevenson	Balladoole	MHK
M.W. Goldie	Slegaby	MHK
W.F. Moore	Cronkbourne	MHK
Thomas Moore	Billown	MHK
Evan Gell*	Whitehouse	MHK
J.C. Goldsmith	Ramsey	MHK
Wm. B. Jefferson	Ballahat	MHK
F.L. Gelling	Castletown (Advocate)	
John Thomas Clucas*	Sunnyside (Advocate)	
Engineer	Henry Vignoles, MICE, 21 Luke Street,. Westminster.	
Secretary	G.H. Wood.	
Registered Office	(Temp.) Athol Street, Douglas.	
	[in 1873, St. George's Street, Douglas.]	
General Superintendent	[1873 F.H. Trevithick.]	

Extracts from Prospectus stated:

> The Coy is formed for the purpose of connecting the four towns of the IOM Douglas, Ramsey, Peel & Castletown by a three-feet gauge railway, similar to that already in use in Sweden, Norway, Queensland and elsewhere. It is also proposed to extend the line to Port Erin and Port St. Mary ... There are several mining districts of the Island near the line of rail ... and a large income may safely be relied upon from the traffic of these mines.

Vignoles' First Survey and Report was dated 20th April and addressed to the Provisional Committee in the Isle of Man, who had commissioned it in the previous January through its member Mr J.T. Clucas: three railways were recommended:

1. Douglas to Peel via Crosby and St John's   11 miles
2. Douglas to Port Erin via Crogga Glen, Ballasalla, Castletown and Colby   15 miles
3. Peel to Ramsey via Kirk Michael, Ballaugh and Sulby   16 miles

making in all,   42 miles

---

*each embraced by the later Manx Northern Railway undertaking.

Of the first line Vignoles remarked:

> ... this line nearly follows that proposed by Mr. Hemans in 1864 except for a short distance near the Union Mills ... from St. John's to Peel I found it desirable to deviate from the projected line of 1864 which kept in the valley and terminated at a very low level near the Port of Peel ... it was in my opinion, absolutely necessary to lay out the line with the view to its continuation from Peel to Ramsey ... consequently, the line from St. John's to Peel the line as now proposed keeps on high ground.* By this arrangement, in future working, the same train which goes from Douglas to Peel will continue the journey from Peel to Ramsey. ... To facilitate the future working I also decided to lay out the line in such manner that there shall be no shunting, backing or turning of engines necessary at Peel: this is effected by curves of easy radii for a narrow gauge railway. ... I did not overlook the probable importance of a fish trade at Peel ... should the fish trade eventually require a short branch line or tramway, this could be made for a limited amount.

Vignoles felt however, that a wire tramway would be sufficient, but recommended a decision be deferred until after the opening of the main line when the fish traffic requirements would be clearer.

Some members of the Committee thought it would be better to 'connect Port Erin and Castletown with Douglas and Peel by building a line via the Foxdale Mines'. Capt. Goldie suggested that the extremities (Port Erin and Ramsey) should be linked by a direct line, and be able to tap the Foxdale traffic. Vignoles thought such arguments were sound but were outweighed 'by the difficulties and expense that such a route would have when viewed from an engineering point of view.'

Vignoles had considered other routes but by taking the Port Erin Line through Crogga and Ballasalla, it would pass through a region most likely to pick up tourist traffic – it was considered that traffic between Ballasalla (lime) and Douglas was too valuable to lose. As to Foxdale Mines business, Vignoles said it would (in time) be dealt with either at St John's on the Peel Line, or Ballavale on the Port Erin Line 'should the Mines warrant the expense of a tramway it could be constructed from near St. John's; the cost of working it by steam or horse would not be great as the traffic would be mainly downhill.'

How far-seeing and wise would Vignoles' judgements turn out to be!

The Report mentions the earlier Port Erin route survey by James Armstrong which Vignoles felt was open to opposition by the owner of the Nunnery Estate; even following the Kewaigue stream to avoid it would be inadvisable as the Kewaigue road would have to be crossed on the level instead of by bridge: also the former course would be more expensive and graded at 1 in 44.

As to the Ramsey Line from Peel, immediately after leaving Peel 'the line was to turn eastward and then northward through a dip or saddle some way from the coast'. Before reaching Glen Broigh (sic), it would 'turn westwards again and cross the main road at a point near the second milestone from Peel, then, winding round the base of the hill ... continue to Glen Broigh which is crossed at a point where the ravine is narrow' by means of an embankment. Between Glen Broigh and Glen Cam the line was to lie

---

*Peel station would have been 105 ft asl.

IN THE COURT OF TYNWALD.

ISLE of MAN RAILWAYS

Incorporation of Company; Powers to make Railways to connect the Towns of Douglas, Peel, and Castletown, and Port Erin, and the adjacent Villages; to Purchase Lands and Houses by Compulsion; to Levy Tolls, Rates, and Duties, &c.

NOTICE is hereby Given, that application is intended to be made to the COURT of TYNWALD for leave to bring in a Bill to incorporate a Company (hereinafter called "the Company"), and to confer upon the Company all necessary and proper powers for effecting the objects hereinafter mentioned, or some of them; that is to say:

To make and maintain the Railways hereinafter described, or some of them; together with all necessary and convenient Stations, Approaches, Bridges, Roads, Communications, and other Works connected therewith; that is to say:

RAILWAY NO. 1.—DOUGLAS TO PEEL.—A Railway 10 miles, 7 furlongs, and 3½ chains, or thereabouts, in length, commencing at or near the foot of Bank Hill, near Douglas Bridge, in the Town of Douglas, in the Parish of Onchan, and terminating at Peel, in the Parish of German, in or near a field (numbered 1,709) on the deposited Plans hereafter referred to) belonging to LEONARA WATTLEWORTH, and in the occupation of WILLIAM QUAYLE, which said intended Railway will pass from, through, in, or into the several Parishes, Towns, or other Places following, or some of them, that is to say—Douglas, Onchan, Braddan, Marown, German, Patrick, and Peel, in the Isle of Man.

RAILWAY NO. 2.—DOUGLAS, CASTLETOWN, AND PORT ERIN.—A Railway 14 miles, 6 furlongs, and 4 chains in length, or thereabouts, commencing in the Parish of Onchan by a junction with the lastly-described Railway ("No 1") at a point 3 furlongs and 5¼ chains, or thereabouts, from the commencement thereof, in a field called the Hill's Meadow, near to, and adjoining, the River Douglas (No 2,477 in the Plans hereinafter referred to), and belonging to HENRY BLOOM NOBLE, EDWARD CAIN, ARCHIBALD CLARKE, ANN BRIDSON, ELEANOR GELLING, and GILBERT TORRANCE, and in the occupation of JAMES BELL, and terminating at Port Erin, in the Parish of Rushen, in or near a field adjoining the main road from Douglas to Port Erin (numbered 1,248 in the said Plans), belonging to WILLIAM HENRY GAWNE, and in the occupation of JOHN GEARY, 4¼ chains, or thereabouts, from the front door of the Falcon's Nest Hotel, at Port Erin aforesaid, and which said intended Railway will pass through, in, or into the several Parishes, Towns, and other Places following, that is to say—Onchan, Braddan, Santon, Malew, Castletown, Arbory, and Rushen, or some of them, in the Isle of Man.

To purchase and take by compulsion, and also by agreement, Lands, Houses, Tenements, and Hereditaments, for the purposes of the said intended Railways and Works, and of the said intended Bill, and to vary, repeal, or extinguish all existing rights and privileges in any manner connected with the Lands, Houses, Tenements, and Hereditaments so purchased or taken, or which would in any manner impede or interfere with any of the objects or purposes of the said intended Bill, and to confer, vary, or extinguish other rights and privileges.

To alter, divert, cross, or stop up, whether temporarily or permanently, all such public and other Roads, Highways, Streets, Paths, Rivers, Bridges, Aqueducts, Canals, Pipes, Sewers, Streams, Watercourses, Railways, and Tramways, within the aforesaid Parishes, Towns, and other Places, or any of them, as it may be necessary to alter, divert, cross, or stop up for the purposes of the said intended Railways and Works, or any of them, or of the said intended Bill.

To levy Tolls, Rates, and Duties upon or in respect of the said intended Railways and Works, and from time to time to alter such Tolls, Rates, and Duties, and to confer, vary, or extinguish exemption from the payment of such Rates and Duties.

To deviate laterally from the Lines of the intended Works to the extent shown on the Plans hereinafter mentioned or described in the said intended Bill; and also to deviate vertically from the levels shown on the sections hereinafter mentioned.

And Notice is hereby further Given, that Plans and Sections of the said intended Railway and Works, and of the Lands and Property as proposed to be purchased and taken as aforesaid, together with a Book of Reference to such Plans, will be deposited for public inspection at the Rolls Office, in the said Isle of Man, not less than one calendar month previous to the hearing of such application; and that a copy of so much of the Plans, Sections, and Book of Reference as relates to each Parish in or through which the said Railways and Works, or any part of them, are or is intended to be made, together with so much of the Standing Orders as relates to the deposit of Plans, Sections, Books of Reference, and other Books and Writings, or Extracts or Copies of or from the same, will be deposited for public inspection, in the case of each such Parish with the Schoolmaster thereof, at his residence, not less than one calendar month previous to the hearing of such application.

And take Notice, that such intended application is appointed to be heard by the COURT of TYNWALD, at a TYNWALD COURT, to be held in DOUGLAS, on the 16th day of NOVEMBER next, at 11 o'clock, a.m.

Dated this 5th day of October, 1871.

A. W. ADAMS,
RICHD. SHERWOOD, } Advocates for the Bill.

James Brown & Son, Printers by Steam Power, "Times" Office, Athol-street, Douglas.

Ramsey Isle of Man Oct 23d 1871

To the Secretary of the
Isle of Man Railway Co Limited
Athol St. Douglas. IoM

Sir,
As it appears that your Board of Directors have treated our Notice of withdrawal (under the altered circumstances) from your Company with contempt — We the undersigned now give you notice, and request you to lay the same before your Board of Directors of our intention to petition and employ Counsel against your application to the Court of Tynwald on the 16th day of November next, unless prior to that date our names be removed from the Register of Shareholders and the Cash paid on account be returned, or an official promise to do so given to us in writing.

We are, Sir,
Your obediently

Daniel Cashin, Bank Agent
Wm Hampton, Post Office
W.J. Russell, Grocer
Thos R Corlett Junr, Law Student
John Chamothe, Advocate

Protest from Ramsey Shareholders: 1871.

between coast and main road; Glen Cam would be crossed by embankment and the main road at Ballaquine 'to avoid crossing the objectionable ravines of Glen Moar (sic) and Glen Wyllin where their widths and depths are so great that it would have been necessary to construct expensive viaducts in both cases upwards of 100 ft high and 500–600 ft long'. By keeping inland as far as possible, Vignoles intended to cross these glens 'at points where their widths are contracted and where embankments would be feasible'. After passing Glen Wyllin the line would have turned slightly westward and crossed the main road 'about the middle of the village of Kirk Michael'; after passing to the west of Bishop's Court and east of Orrisdale, from Ballaugh the line would have followed the course of the Sulby River to Ramsey.

As to gauge, Vignoles had acquired 'detailed information' from other narrow gauge railways (the Festiniog Railway in particular) and decided upon 3 feet. He considered 45 lbs/yard rails sufficient 'the weight of rails used in Norway and Queensland* is only 40 lbs. I consider this too light'.†

The Report included a list of seven 'suitable stopping places and twelve stations' (there being a distinction): buildings to be constructed in substantial 'rubble masonry with zinc or slate roofs' were 'passenger stations, goods sheds, engine sheds, tank houses and large workshops at Douglas'. Three miles of sidings were envisaged and the stopping places would have 'a small house to serve as waiting room and ticket office'. The stations recommended were:

Douglas	Port Erin	Crosby
Peel	Ballasalla	St John's
Ramsey	Port St. Mary	Kirkmichael (sic)
Castletown	Colby	Sulby (Sulby Bridge as built)

and stopping places would be:

Arbory (Ballabeg as built)	'Between Glen Cam & Glen Shelton'
Ballavale (Santon as built)	(St Germain's as built)
Crogga (Port Soderick as built)	Kella (Sulby Glen as built)
Union Mills	Ballaugh

In retrospect, Vignoles' suggestions were carried through very closely by the Isle of Man Railway, but when the Manx Northern Railway (St John's–Ramsey) was built much of his scheme was disregarded.

Looking ahead, the first General Meeting was held in Douglas on 14th June, 1871 but it was clear from this that, despite a rosy forecast, people were not over-anxious to part with their money, and resources became stretched at the outset. On 14th December, 1871, G.H. Wood, Secretary of the Isle of Man Railway, was obliged to publicise the intention of altering the Company's constitution, abandoning the Ramsey project and reducing the capital to £120,000; these changes were effected. There was, in fact, a real scarcity of hard cash within the Island at the time – it was the visiting tourist industry which was later to improve living standards. Meanwhile, Major J.S.G. Taubman (Speaker, House of Keys) was appointed as the first Chairman.]

---

*existing systems of 3 ft 6 in. gauge.
†Manx Museum: MD348/1 re opposition to gauge. (June 1871)

This was followed by a lull until on 14th October the SUN published a note on the two authorised Railways:

> *Railway No. 1* Douglas–Peel 10 miles 7 furlongs 3½ chains, commencing at or near the foot of Bank Hill, near Douglas Bridge in the town of Douglas in the Parish of Onchan, and terminating at Peel in the Parish of St German . . .
>
> *Railway No. 2* Douglas, Castletown & Port Erin 14 miles 6 furlongs 4 chains, commencing in the Parish of Onchan by a junction with Railway No. 1 at a point 3 furlongs 5½ chains from the commencement thereof . . . and terminating at Port Erin in the Parish of Rushen, in or near a field adjoining the main road from Douglas to Port Erin . . .

No authorisation was given for a line to Ramsey.

All seemed set for a brighter future but the matter of financial support was critical for success: 1871 ended with money an elusive element.

Historical Chronology 1872–1904

1872

'A cheap narrow-gauge railway'

[It will be noted that 3 ft gauge railway development was not confined to the Isle of Man alone, for a Ballymena, Cushendall & Redbay Railway was promoted on 18th July 'gauge, not wider than 3 nor narrower than 2 feet'. It opened to the 3 ft gauge but was 'overtaken' by the Glenariff Land & Development Co. whose mineral line opened in 1873–4.]

An enthusiastic correspondent to the TIMES on 6th January, 1872 concluded:

> ... a brighter era never dawned on our little Island than that which we with pleasure now anticipate, namely, the cutting of the first sod and laying the foundation stone of the principal station to this railway in Douglas by our good-living and excellent Mrs. Loch, wife of our present respected Governor. So may its fair inauguration prove its successful issue ... 'An Old Resident'.

and on 13th January, 1872 the same paper reported:

> ... several English contractors are preparing to tender for the construction of 26 miles of railway for a single line with sidings upon a gauge of Three Feet.

To stoke up more enthusiasm for the railway project the newspapers gave the matter no rest. The whole of the Prospectus having being presented, and parts of it rehashed at intervals to keep the pot boiling, is evident from the edition of the SUN on 20th January, 1872 and the full advertisement 'TO RAILWAY CONTRACTORS' in THE TIMES the previous week;* this began:

> The Directors of the IOMRCo are desirous of receiving tenders from contractors for the construction of about 36 miles of railway with sidings to a gauge of Three Feet ...

the original being dated December 1871.

This press recital was broken by the anger of Ramsey now certain it would be dropped from the scheme. This anger was heightened by the forthcoming opening of the New Landing Pier and the laying of the inaugural block of the Battery Pier at Douglas (taking place in July 1872). Ramsey considered it had been slighted by both sea and land; whilst a handsome sum had been spent on the new seaworks at Douglas, another was being wasted at Port Erin 'a place of no significance compared with Ramsey' where £50,000 had been squandered on Goode's design of breakwater, encouraged by the 'Lt. Governor H.B. Loch in whom nobody has any confidence'. Furthermore; a 'Landing Pier' at Port Erin had just received the backing of a petition on behalf of the IOMR – as if enough was not enough. Now, for a more paltry sum, Ramsey would have no railway and worse, a mere £2,000 had been granted to it for a landing pier whereas Port Erin would receive a further £7,000. 'The busy and populous town of Ramsey ... was of little importance in the eyes of the Court, but the claims of that little fishing village of Port Erin where so much money has been thrown away already ...' Those wishing to land or embark at Ramsey still had to wade through the breakers!

*the English newspaper

Castletown residents were not best pleased with the site chosen for their station at Malew Road; it was not convenient, so they submitted a Memorial to the Directors on 25th April and urged them to move it to the upper end of The Claddagh; their request was met on condition that the necessary connecting road 'would be formed by the Memorialists'; this was done. The Minutes noted that 'the line was deviated at serious cost' with the purpose 'to have better connection with the harbour and assist the fishing industry'. Oddly, a rail connection to the harbour was never provided.* A modification at Quarter Bridge was to give a better road level crossing.

As noted, shortage of finance became so embarrassing that the Special Meeting on 16th January, 1872 had announced that the Ramsey Line would be abandoned and without further funds, Peel and Port Erin Lines could not proceed. Vignoles said a line to Ramsey would cost £1,000 more per mile than the one to Peel.

> It must be remembered that the line to Ramsey was not being forsaken; all that they were intending was to make a start with what they considered that portion of the original scheme from which a return might be immediately looked for . . . It must be apparent that if these resolutions were not adopted . . . the whole scheme would collapse and they would have no railway at all.

Though capital was reduced to £120,000, borrowing powers were increased. The local Press was quick to point out the miserly contribution of the Manx towards their railway (a figure given as a mere £30,000) so sights were then set on England to attract persons of wealth to the scheme. John Pender (later Sir John Pender, MP, a railway financier) was won over and accepted a seat on the Board in May 1872 – he later became Chairman with Taubman as Vice-Chairman.† With his influence, other leading financiers with railway interests gave their support too: these included the Duke of Sutherland,‡ whose activities at that time were legion among railway schemes, and George Sheward[#] who was on the London & North Western Railway Board together with His Grace. [The foregoing gentlemen had been wooed by A.W. Adams (Advocate for the Company).]

On 11th May, 1872 the SUN broke the news:

> Adams (Advocate) has arranged with His Grace Duke of Sutherland and John Pender (persons whose rank and position form a guarantee that the undertaking

---

*'The Claddagh' is the area around the Silver Burn between the present-day Alexandra Bridge and Swing Bridge.

†John Pender (1815–96). A pioneer of submarine telegraphy who began his career as a textile merchant in Manchester and Glasgow and became a director of the first Atlantic Cable Co. in 1856. He was joint founder of the Anglo-American Co. in 1865 and had many other business interests. Liberal MP for Totnes 1865–66, and for Wick Boroughs 1872–85 & 1892–96. KCMG 1888; GCMG 1892.

His other directorships at this period included: a) Eastern Extension, Australasia & China Telegraph; b) Girvan & Portpatrick Junction Railway; c) Oude & Rohilkund Railway (India).

‡George Granville William Sutherland Leveson Gower KG Third Duke of Sutherland. 18th December, 1828–22nd September, 1892. MP for Sutherland 1852–61. Director of LNWR 1852–92 and in early life spent much time in that Company's Wolverton Works. Director of Inverness & Aberdeen Junction Rly and Highland Rly. Supporter of Fell System on first Mount Cenis Rly and promoter of Shanghai–Woosung Line, first railway in China.

Made Honorary Member of Institution of Civil Engineers 2nd May, 1865.

#George Sheward. Directorships in 1875 included: Tasmanian Main Line Railway (Chairman): Buenos Ayres & Campana Railway (Chairman): North Western of Montevideo Railway: West London Extension Railway: Isle of Wight – Newport Junction Railway.

will now go on) to take heavy financial stake and personal interest in the management of the Company. The latter is the member for West Burgh; they will take seats on the Board. It is suggested that the Duke of Sutherland or the Earl of Derby should be invited to cut the first sod.

Sheward was also a director of the West London Railway, Chairman of the Sambre & Meuse Railway in Belgium, and also of the Windsor & Annapolis Railway in Nova Scotia. He was Chairman of the English & Foreign Credit Company, a useful connection for the Isle of Man! With these healthy links, and that also of the Hon H.F. Stanley, MP, of Witherslack, Carnforth, most of the remaining shares were quickly taken up, and after 4th May, 1872 the TIMES regular advertisement inviting the public to take up shares disappeared.

A Memorandum of Association and Articles for the IOMRCoLtd was adopted on 4th September by which the capital was restored to £200,000 which included an issue of £40,000 in debentures. (A list of twelve subscribers to the scheme had been published on 2nd May, 1870.) It was agreed that the year be computed from 12th June, 1872.

All was now clear for further progress. The Duke of Sutherland was given the Chair which he held for seven years – he was succeeded by Sir John Pender who held it for the following seventeen years and so materially strengthened the undertaking.

Earlier in 1872, advertisements had appeared inviting tenders for the construction of the Peel and Port Erin* lines and, after four had been received, the Press reported on 6th April, 1872 that Messrs. Watson & Smith of Bishopsgate Street, London, had been given the work of building both lines.† A far-reaching step was taken in the following August when the tidal swamp near Peel harbour was purchased for the new terminus.

> The directors this week have concluded a contract with Messrs. Watson & Smith of London ... for the formation of the Isle of Man Railway ... have engaged to complete and open the line from Douglas to Peel on or before 1st June, 1873 and

---

*then but a handful of houses.
†John Watson & John Bevan Smith, Ethelburga House, 70 Bishopsgate Street, London.

John Watson became railway contractor in 1855 trading as John Watson & Co. Work included Vale of Towy Railway; in the late 1850s he built the first section (12 miles) of the Bahia Railway.

Then joined by brother-in-law James Overend; they received the tender for Swansea–Carmarthen Extension Rly. in March 1862 and the Mid-Wales contract. Overend retired in 1865, Watson continuing on his own until 1869, working on Tottenham & Hampstead Junction, and Newry & Armagh lines.

He was joined by John Bevan Smith after 1869 until February 1875, when he filed a petition for bankruptcy. He was joined by W.J. Smith in February 1875 and the firm was reconstituted as Watson, Smith & Watson which carried out further railway contracts and did consultancy work. They went bankrupt in 1885.

Known locomotives included:

0–4–0ST 8½ × 10 in. cylinders built by R. & W. Hawthorn Ltd., Forth Bank Works, Newcastle on Tyne. There were two consecutive engines, Maker's Nos. 537–538 with 1 ft 8 in. diameter driving wheels and of 3 ft gauge owned by Watson; one is said to have carried the name MONA and been at work in the Island by January, 1873. It was withdrawn at the end of the contract and stood on the site of the present Douglas station when Peel and Port Erin lines were complete. Its fate is not known, nor whether its sister engine was also in the Island. (It is suggested that it may have been Maker's No. 1045 of 1858 supplied to Mr. Graham of The Neath Abbey Coal Co. Ltd., 'about 2 ft 8 in. gauge' and named IRON DUKE. It had 8 × 16 in. cylinders and 2 ft 4 in. diameter wheels; the difference in dimensions may rule out this supposition.)

(Notes kindly supplied by Frank Smith of Bolton)

that to Castletown, Port St Mary and Port Erin on or before 1st June, 1874, work on both lines expected to commence immediately ... engineers expected within a few days to stake out the line.

Watson & Smith soon began to make their presence known. Initially they would be paid in cash and £5 shares less 5 per cent retention. In a community hitherto almost immune from the spectacular, the advent of a firm of railway contractors, plus the necessary machinery, transport and navvies, caused an entire collapse of normal living. Labour costs were at once measured by what Watson & Smith were paying; carts and horses were hired out to them to the neglect of the farmlands on which they were wont to work; local labour left their employers and went to work with the contractors for what they perceived would at least be two or three years of regular and certain employment with a good rate of pay. The local newspapers were quick to point out that Messrs Watson & Smith had almost monopolised the Island.

In the flat marshy ground alongside the ropeworks at the south of Douglas, the Rivers Dhoo and Glas made confluence and flowed out in one stream as the River Douglas (the original mode of spelling is clearly apparent). Navvies began to turn this waste ground (known locally as 'The Lake') into a railway terminus. The course of the rivers was altered above the marsh to make it easier to fill in.

There was now talk of an opening and the SUN on 8th June, 1872 had:

> We hear that the ornamental barrow and spade to be used at the turning of the first sod of the Island railway arrived here on Wednesday but for some unexplained reason everything connected with the railway, even to the date of the opening of the work, is veiled in profound mystery ...

to which the Secretary (G.H. Wood) replied:

> Gentlemen, I am instructed to inform you that on Saturday last the directors of the IOMR Co. Ltd. concluded they cannot make any display on the occasion of the cutting of the first sod of the IOM Rlys. but they hope to do so at some future time ... directors ... regret that they are compelled to come to this decision but considering the wishes expressed by the principal shareholders in England, they have no alternative ...*

Some had hoped a royal personage would have done the honours at such an opportunity, but even the Duke of Sutherland was prevented from cutting the first sod: so it was after an informal occasion that work began in June 1872. It was controlled by Henry Greenbank, MICE, Vignoles' resident Engineer who, in 1878 was to become the Company's Engineer in succession to Vignoles and retain the position until his death in February 1922, a remarkable term of service.

The SUN (15th June, 1872) said:

> A meeting of shareholders was held on Wednesday when the number of directors was reduced from twelve to seven ... Mr Adams, (one of the solicitors to the Company) was 'sure that the line to Ramsey (which had only been temporarily abandoned) would be carried out when ... other contemplated lines were completed ...'

---

*With the lion's share of capital coming from London, the Company was now totally under English control.

Construction was not confined to Douglas alone, and each station site became a railhead for new work. Progress was inclined to be a little spasmodic at times, requiring all the ingenuity of the resident Engineer to ensure smoothness; the tendency to hold-ups in shipping deliveries during bad weather was the prime cause of this. Insufficient funds were to prevent stations and buildings of the nature Vignoles intended; instead, some wooden erections (including 'sentry boxes') had to suffice and refreshment facilities reduced. However, some crossing 'lodges' were to be built in stone.

It was 29th June, 1872 before the SUN kept its readers informed again:

> The ground has been broken in several places for this line . . . contractor is expected to start in earnest in course of a few weeks. The proposal is to employ local 'spade and barrow labourers': wages paid here are much lower than in England.
>
> A Schooner arrived here on Saturday night with material for the railway; the work is being rapidly pushed ahead from Braddan Church towards Peel . . .

said the TIMES on 29th June.

On 31st August following, the SUN gave indication of the lack of importance the Railway directors now gave to a Ramsey project:

> It will be well known that in connection with the higher level required for the contemplated line of the railway to Ramsey and the north, the station at the Peel terminus had been fixed to be very inconveniently placed at the upper end of the town, a long way from the quays. As might be expected, this occasioned great dissatisfaction to the trading portion of the community and in answer to urgent remonstrances, the directors have ordered their engineer to select the best line from St. John's to Peel, irrespective of the line to Ramsey . . . consequence line will now run by Glenfaba Mills, through the Close Chairn fields to the top of Peel Harbour where fish can be loaded direct from the boats instead of being carted through the town to the station.

Evidence of the stringent economies necessary at this period, and that 'there would be no surplus for the erection of expensive terminal edifices', comes from a station list of October 1872:

Douglas	1st Class station	Wooden building
Peel and Port Erin	2nd Class ditto	Wooden buildings
Castletown, Ballasalla, St John's	3rd Class ditto	Wooden buildings
Crosby, Colby, Port St Mary	4th Class ditto	Wooden buildings
Union Mills	5th Class ditto	Wood and corrugated iron building

Santon and Port Soderick (Ballashamrock or Crogga as sometimes known) had also been agreed upon as stopping places but their position and nature had not been resolved. On the Peel Line, level crossings had stone lodges; on the Port Erin, small wooden huts (a 1973 survivor was at Mill Road crossing, Castletown). On second thoughts, the stone station buildings at Castletown and Port Erin were given an extra wing to enable them to be used as Station Masters' accommodation in the future as money was not available to give them full living quarters at the start. Possibly the 1872 list was amended in the case of these two stations as 'materials of the neighbourhood' (stone) was used instead; they were later described as 'permanent'. At other places it was necessary to use wood and corrugated iron 'in the style . . . at the Union Mills station' – the best that could be then afforded.

Reverting once more to those personalities who were to have a long influence on the prosperity of the Company, it should be added that at the time Wood was made permanent Secretary, William S. Mackenzie was appointed General Superintendent. A General Purposes Committee was formed to administer locally; it became the only administrative body after 1905, meeting almost weekly from the start.

Although the Island was almost free of industrial sites (mining apart), there had long been places where clay pits, quarries, lime works and the like had existed, simply to meet domestic requirements: there were also foundries, saw mills, partially allied to shipbuilding and repairing. The brickworks at Peel opened in 1866 and that at Ballaharra near St John's had been in operation since before 1872. However, the promise of railway construction brought renewed interest in what might prove to be coal mining on a commercial scale to which the SUN made several references:

> 4th May, 1872 – COAL MINING AT DERBYHAVEN. A preliminary meeting to form a company to be called the Isle of Man Coal & Mineral Co. Ltd. was held at Creer's Market Hotel. Borings are near Derbyhaven.
>
> 25th May, 1872 (Letter) – There can be no objection to a party of gentlemen amusing themselves by making a boring in search of coal at Derbyhaven at their own expense. But as I read the Secretary's Statement, it was contemplated that this amusement should be enjoyed at other people's expense . . .
>
> 31st August, 1872 – Mr R. Cain, the contractor for building the Derbyhaven Breakwater, chose his quarry at Skillicore-voss on the lower carboniferous limestone near the mouth of the Santon River . . . he estimates the quantity of coal in the centre of the Breakwater to be at least 30 tons. The seams are thin and I am afraid they are the last of the formation in the Isle of Man.

(so wrote William Henry Cubbin.)

By November, increasing criticism of flimsy railway fencing was to be heard; claims were met for damage to crops by the contractors who were, incidentally, unable to proceed over Deemster Sir William Leece Drinkwater's land.* A loan from the Bank of Mona assisted them, together with Promissory Notes on Dumbell Son & Howard from the IOMR and in December it was discovered Watson & Smith had imported 50 tons of iron rails which were underweight as per contract (i.e. 40 lbs in lieu of 45 lbs); their excuse was that they intended to use them in sidings – the contract price was then suitably adjusted. A.W. Rixon the London Secretary was instructed to oversee the contractors, suggesting the London Directors were doubtful of Manx supervision.

In December the money problems continued – debentures could not be issued until one fifth of the share value had been paid up on at least 8,000 shares . . . this proved a stumbling block as some shares had already been given to the contractors, and in payment for land. Many *full* payments were as yet pending.

---

*Residence Kirby Park. He was the First Deemster (one of two appointed judges).

A typical attendance of the London Board (27th January, 1873) (last previous meeting 17th December, 1872) held at 18 Arlington Street,† London (Piccadilly), was:

Duke of Sutherland (Chair)
John Pender
Hon F.A. Stanley (*his first meeting*)
Major J.S. Goldie Taubman*
J.T. Clucas*
George Sheward

G.H. Wood (Secretary)*
W.S. Mackenzie (General Superintendent)*
H. Vignoles (Engineer)*

A.W. Rixon (London Secretary)

†Pender's residence.
*Island-based, and having to travel to London for meetings.

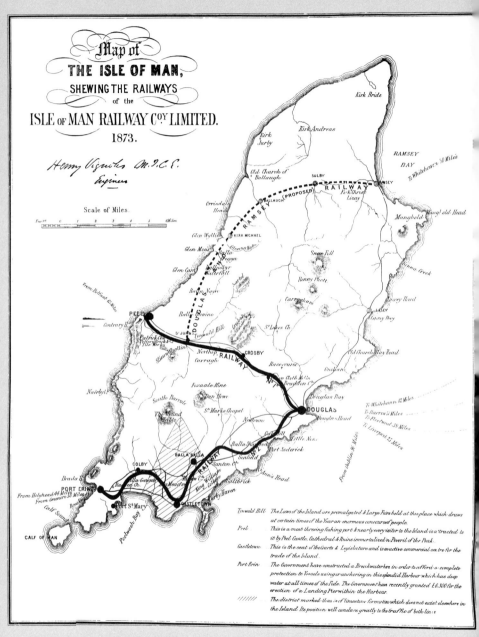

Promotional Map Signed by Henry Vignoles (1873).

The Vignoles, Rixon, MacKenzie & Watson Reports: 1873

The chronology may here be interrupted to give detail from the Reports of building and subsequent opening of the railway and explain the origin of many problems which were shortly to arise: (the occasional near-repetition of fact which follows in the next chapter is deemed to be acceptable.) This chapter sets down events as seen through the eyes of the General Purposes Committee and Board and, taken together with these Reports, it forms a complete picture of the situation as seen from two aspects and hints at the underlying animosity between Board, Committee, Engineer* and Contractor.

Insight into Watson & Smith's progress and other works comes from Vignoles' Reports of January, March, April, June, November and December 1873. The six months prior to January had been uncommonly wet, though Watson & Smith had been able to progress on the Douglas–Peel section to a state where completion of earthworks and bridge abutments/masonry would be ready by the end of March. The geology of some 5 miles between Union Mills and St John's made the ground so bad that work was abandoned after 'tipping horses stuck in the mud and were rescued by ropes . . . another was killed by wagons running over it whilst stuck in the embankment'.

By January diversion of the river at Douglas was complete, as were diversions of the road between Quarter Bridge and Braddan Bridge over Deemster Drinkwater's land.† Meanwhile the contractor's locomotive was working on an isolated 1 mile of track at Ballacraine (just short of St John's) and a cutting nearer Crosby was providing useful material for embankments with its 'gravelley material'.

Between Ballacraine and the terminus (Peel), all important earthworks were completed and another mile of isolated track was laid; the river had been diverted but the retaining wall between it and the railway could not be started as water levels were too high. Similarly, flood water at Quarter Bridge made it impossible to begin the river bridge there but the seven other bridge sites were ready to receive the wrought iron girders which were being made at Derby by Stacey, Davis & Co.‡ There were to be three road overbridges in masonry; Braddan, Union Mills and Glenfaba of which the latter two were finished.

To complete the track between Douglas and Peel, another 100 tons of rails were needed; 533 tons were already on the Island, 250 tons were lying at Fleetwood or at sea, and the remainder had been rolled but not despatched. The makers were Samuel Witham & Co. of Wakefield with every rail having

---

*The resident engineer, Henry Greenbank, was responsible to Vignoles on the site; the latter's Reports are headed 'Engineer's Office, London' or '21, Duke Street, Westminster'. Vignoles' personal visits to the Island were intermittent.

†The straightening of the road along this length is still evident, and is the scene of hold-ups in the morning rush-hour! (It forms part of the TT Course.)

‡Stacey, Davis & Co., The Phoenix Foundry & Engineering Works, Stuart Street, was one of Derby's former group of firms with emphasis on bridge building, though general engineering was also practised.

First noted in Wright's Derby Directory of 1874, they continued to appear as above in various directories and in 1880–81 as 'engineers & iron founders, iron bridge & roof builders, Phoenix Foundry, Nottingham Road.' Thereafter they became The Phoenix Foundry Co. They suffered from the lack of a railway siding facility and 'one impression that lingers is of the inspiring sight frequently seen in the early years when huge pieces of work were being drawn from the yard to the railway by long double teams of horses': DERBY MERCURY, 27th November, 1925.

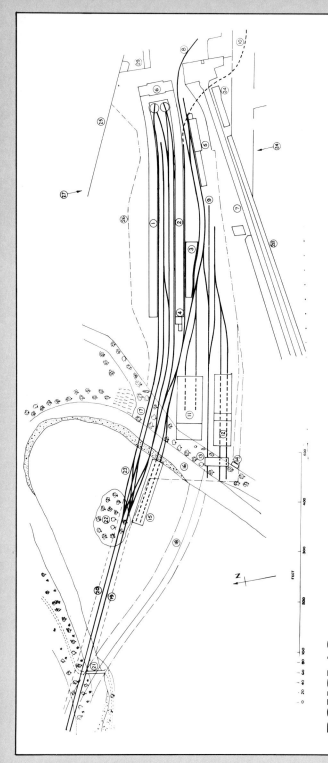

DOUGLAS: one of two undated plans for a terminus c.1870–1

1. Arrival platform/departure platform (Peel Line)
2. Arrival platform/departure platform (Port Erin Line)
3. Coal Stage
4. Water Tank
5. Goods Shed
6. Station building
7. Quiggin's Borewalk
8. Quay extension
9. Sunken siding
10. Alternative extension to Quay
11. Locomotive Workshop
12. Carriage Workshop
13. Traverser
14. Urinals
15. Carriage Shed
16. River
17. Hermitage Estate
18. Alternative course for line
19. Port Erin Line
20. Peel Line
21. Nunnery footbridge
22. Coppice
23. (Alterations on original design)
24. Quiggin's premises
25. Peel Road retaining wall
26. Boundary railway land
27. Peel Road
28. Quiggin & Co.
29. Stable

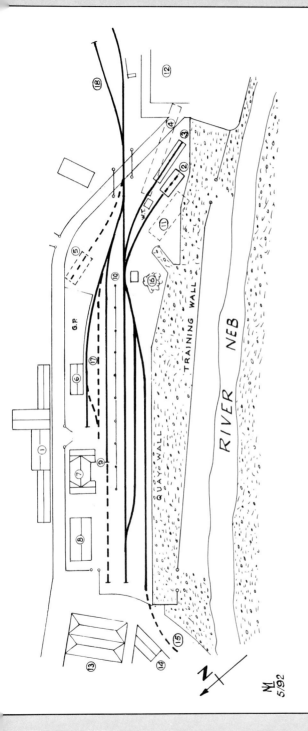

PEEL: pre-1907

1. Warehouses/Gas Works
2. Locomotive Shed
3. Carriage Shed
4. Site for larger Carriage Shed
5. Site for larger Locomotive Shed
6. Goods Shed
7. Station building
8. Refreshment Room
9. Original extent of departure line
10. Fence
11. Further alternative site for larger Locomotive Shed
12. Shipyard
13. Warehouses
14. Public House
15. Line to Quay (proposed)
16. Coal tip
17. Proposed run-round
18. Siding to brickworks

been inspected at the makers before acceptance.* They had received 7,625 sleepers and 4,000 were even now in a ship bound for Peel.

Of the features which displeased Vignoles, the fencing was the worst. Watson & Smith could not be blamed for it, he conceded: he (Vignoles) had been told to keep down costs by ordering cheap fencing 'for what he understood was to be a cheap narrow gauge railway'. Watson & Smith had adhered to the drawings but they were now putting in six wires and intermediate posts. They claimed they had not been paid for this extra work.

The contractor's locomotive working at Ballacraine was hauling rails, sleepers, etc.; it was a four-coupled tank engine with 8½ in. cylinders 'built by Hawthorn of Newcastle ... not yet in good working order as there are some missing pieces'.

Vignoles had done the drawings for the stations and invited tenders from builders on the Island, the work to be complete by the following June. He found that, with one exception, no Island builder could comply so enquiries were made in Liverpool and London. (Gelling & Kaye of Douglas had replied.)

Out on the Castletown Line the heavy earthworks between Douglas and Oakhill were progressing well, and when track was laid, earth from Oakhill cutting could be brought down to fill in the low ground at Douglas. Beyond Oakhill nothing had been done, but despite the hindrance of bad weather, theodolite and level work right into Port Erin had been completed, and stakes and chain pegs put into the ground.

By March Vignoles was able to write '3½ miles are ballasted, with the contractor's engine running over them'. He was now concerned with earning capacity: he was familiar with the Isle of Wight Railway,† then earning 'nothing'; he expected the IOMR to earn £30 per mile per week (there being no Government or local taxation which in England amounted to 5 per cent of receipts). 'When the line is developed I anticipate a dividend of 12% on share capital'. He reminded that the Barrow and Liverpool steamers were bringing in over 150,000 visitors in 1872, helped no doubt by the new Douglas pier. He was encouraged by 'the £60,000 voted to prolong the Douglas breakwater and £6,300 for a permanent landing pier at Port Erin', and deemed that the prospects were rosy. At present those arriving by such steamers

> would roam half the night in Douglas seeking lodgings, and after the arrival of the steamers ... it was impossible to procure sufficient cars or omnibuses ... to go to Peel or Castletown the same night.#

---

*Samuel Witham & Co. moved from Leeds and was established in Calder Vale Road, Wakefield in 1863. During the depression of the 1870s, the firm found itself in difficulty, and closed in March 1877. At the auction following, there were no takers for the business as a going concern, and the plant was sold off piecemeal.

Witham was Mayor of Wakefield 1869–70 and an Alderman of the Borough.

†There were many similar features with the IOWR, incorporated in July 1860 and extended during the following decade. Some financial aspects were also similar, as was the entire dependence on steamships. The IOWR benefitted from a tramway from pier to railway station at Ryde and might have been showing better returns but for the cost of two accidents: certain extensions had had to be abandoned due to cash shortages.

#And some maintain things are no better in 1993!

Throughout, Vignoles underlines 'the strictest economy' was being adopted, though it is nowhere stated precisely that the railway workshops were built in timber on masonry foundations, certainly every other building (save that and Douglas goods shed) was of timber and imported on a knock-down basis and erected on site. This proved to be unavoidable and was a very different picture from his Engineer's Report of 20th April, 1871.

His Report of 22nd April is full of optimism: the Douglas–Peel Line would be laid throughout within a week of the last rails arriving, but these were still on board a ship ex-Fleetwood 'and expected daily in Douglas'. Completion was dependent on these. Two engines were now on the Island – one was erected and working for the contractors whilst the third 'would shortly be shipped from Liverpool'; carriages and wagons 'come by every steamer, last Saturday's bringing one carriage and three wagons. This week two extra steamers leave Liverpool and I hope will carry more vehicles up to 16 ... by 26th.'

Vignoles foresaw that the 'repairing shops will be finished by the end of April. Douglas station, made in Liverpool, was shipped ten days ago and will not take long to erect'. He had hoped the railway would be ready to accommodate the Whitsuntide traffic, but it was now a forlorn hope. Whilst the weather continued dry, he was urging Watson & Smith to prosecute the Castletown Line – they had until July 1874 to finish it.

The Report of 19th June showed that girder bridges were then being painted and the crossing gates were going in. The Douglas buildings were ready and a steam pump was drawing water of better quality than the local supply from the Tube Wells. Telegraph poles were up and signal parts had arrived but none of the provincial station buildings was finished. 'The old building which has been converted into a carriage shed at Peel ... has been repaired (etc.) and the Peel Water Company would supply the water at the engine shed'.

The permanent way was still some way-off this definition and though nine miles had been ballasted, it was only 'in fair order' and there was insufficient length of sidings. Of the initial rolling stock, two 2nd class, and one saloon carriage were outstanding, together with four covered goods wagons. Vignoles was certain the opening could take place on 2nd July as proposed, and that the inspection would be satisfactory, being wholly satisfied with Watson & Smith's work. Due to the contractor concentrating on the Peel Line, the Castletown Line had fallen behind though Kewaigue Bridge was complete and that at Port Soderick under weigh but as yet, the girders for the Nunnery Bridge had not arrived. A common complaint from the contractor was that the Company had not acquired certain lands, with consequent delay to them.

When Greenbank sent a short report as requested on 17th July, he demonstrated that the position of the Castletown Line had improved but little, and he emphasised that to meet an opening date in July 1874 many more men would be needed; the cutting under the Castletown road near Ballabale was one of the heaviest on the line. Better fencing than on the Peel Line was erected for three miles.

Vignoles was over again in November and in company with Rixon made an inspection. The stock had been maintained in good order 'by the late General Superintendent':

> the fishing season being over 'the number of men is daily increasing ... the heaviest part of Railway No. 2 is remote from the working population who manifest a most extraordinary dislike to walking a few miles to their work, preferring to lounge about in idleness near their homes than to earn good wages by rising an hour earlier. I have rarely encountered in any country not excepting Spain and Russia, such an idle set of men as you see daily in Douglas and Peel during the winter months. The contractors have erected comfortable huts with bed clothes and bedding at various points in the least inhabited district but curious to say these are not half occupied ... there are about 350 men between Douglas and Port Erin.

The unsettled question of where Castletown station was to be sited* depended on the inhabitants building a road to the position they had preferred ... unless they did, the Railway would have a station 'in the fields'. Vignoles could not commence a stone station building until this was known.

Vignoles required extra stock for the South Line: two locomotives, five 1st class, ten 2nd class carriages with brakes, and two brake vans. He recommended his Plans for Douglas and Peel Quay Tramways should be followed up, but that at Peel to be left pending; that at Douglas would be limited at this juncture to a length of 500 yards to meet the needs of mineral, fish and coal traffic; tramway rails would be laid on longitudinal sleepers and the cost would be about £1,500. Later, the Tramway could be carried to the Steamboat Pier which would necessitate taking down and rebuilding the quay wall opposite the Royal Hotel, as beyond there the quay narrowed.

And what of Rixon's view of things? The following list is just a selection:

1. The consequences of Mackenzie's termination of engagement (sic).
2. The carriage of Mails.†
3. A siding for the brickyard (St John's).
4. The opening of through passenger traffic between Douglas and Ramsey via Peel.
5. Advertising on English stations.
6. Tramways on quays at Douglas and Peel and communication with the Landing Pier at Port Erin: 'Fish traffic will remain poor until such are built'.
7. The raising of additional capital to pay for the deviations at Castletown and Peel, and Rich's requirements.
8. The construction of the Ramsey Line.

Some decisions included:

For the time being, Greenbank to take over Mackenzie's duties.
Carriage of mail would bring in about £80 per annum.
The St John's Brickworks' products to be carried to Douglas from a siding yet to be laid.#
The telegraph, though working between Douglas and Peel, often out of order at intermediate stations.

---

*the accompanying Plan is missing.
†Manx Museum: see Government Office Papers re this traffic.
#Not yet opened but a pencil note adds 'put in points'.

One form a passenger service between Peel and Ramsey might take was, 'a one Horse Car to carry four passengers and the driver, larger vehicles being substituted in case the traffic was adequate for their support'. The mail might also be contracted for. (Obviously the patronage was not expected to be overwhelming!)

The Douglas Quay Tramway (sic) could be prosecuted; arrangements might be made for it with the Harbour Commissioners, the IOMR paying 2d per ton toll; Rixon did not think it expedient to proceed with the Peel Tramway or 'the extension of the line from Port Erin to the new Landing Stage'.

Vignoles' 11th December Report confirms that at Mackenzie's suggestion, new engines should have larger water tanks and coal bunkers and these would add £20 to the price of each.

Things were not quite so straightforward with the intended carriages, Metropolitan had to be informed of the best terms the IOMR could offer for payment but were castigated for poor paintwork on the last delivery. With the IOMR looking for lower prices, Metropolitan said that, on the contrary, all carriages would cost more due to higher costs for labour and materials . . . in fact, the previous 1st class vehicles had been made at a loss. Vignoles admitted a figure of £220 each for these had been a low one, as Metropolitan had inferred that seats and fittings had to be little better than 2nd class carriages on English railways whereas he had insisted on 'best horsehair cushions on springs, with high and well-stuffed backs . . . there was much grumbling on the part of the Metropolitan Company about this at the time but my wishes were carried out'. Metropolitan was also induced to repaint the exterior of all their carriage stock at their expense.

Vignoles conceded the Metropolitan vehicles were well and solidly constructed, though 'painting was not quite up to the mark'; he himself was partially to blame as the stock had arrived on the Island at too early a date. Furthermore, as the steamers could only take one or two at a time, he had to 'hurry away the carriages from Birmingham before the paint was properly dry'. Metropolitan's quotation was five 1st class @ £265 each; ten 2nd class @ £195 each; ten ditto with brakes @ £200 each and two brake vans @ £190 each = £5,655.

Out on the South Line construction, the fine weather had hastened the work; more men would have to be brought in as the fishermen from the south of the Island would go off to sea in the spring; presently 400–420 men were engaged. On the Peel Line, discussions with Captain William Kitto of the IOMMCL 'and Mr. Taylor (of the well-known firm of mining agents of that name)' gave rise to hopes to carry all their traffic using St John's as a base.* Also, the Manager of the Glen Helen Slate Quarries had been offered a site at St John's to store slates and there was potential in taking sand from there to Douglas for the building trade.

The foregoing Reports have not been the only ones to survive, for those of William S. Mackenzie, the General Superintendent exist also and are dated 22nd April (the same date as the last of Vignoles), 12th June, 17th July and 15th September. Not surprisingly, these duplicate and even triplicate what has been said by Vignoles or what follows.

---

*Kitto had advised on 19th December, 1870 that the average cost of cartage for the last five years had been £1337 4s. 4d.

Mackenzie (a bachelor) came from Waterloo, Liverpool. Wood had found him two-room lodgings in Douglas when he took up appointment in the first week of January at a salary of £400 per annum. Writing in his first (April) Report he warned that though the line should be ready for all traffic by mid-June, heavy goods could not be carried unless 'cranes, goods sheds and sidings are ready'. He also took trips to the mainland to check progress on the stock from Manchester (*twice*) and Birmingham. With Vignoles' approval, he had obtained furniture and clocks for the station from Douglas suppliers. He also found that the signals had not been erected.

To save expense, he considered that 'after the busy season, the number of staff might be reduced considerably'. He had engaged two enginemen ('one I have known many years and he can act as Working Foreman and Driver'): the other had been recommended by both Sheward and Joseph Bourne (Manager and Engineer of the IOWR). The first man was currently driving for the contractors but could be put into Company work at short notice. Mackenzie recommended Waterlow & Sons for the supply of seven ticket cases and the tickets themselves.

Apparently Wood had already drawn up a set of Bye-laws, of which Mackenzie approved. The Douglas station buildings contained no provision for general offices which Mackenzie deplored, and as the present rented accommodation* was insufficient, it would be essential to find larger premises once the railway was open.

On 12th June, he felt he should report again, 'prior to the Government Inspection'. He recounted that of the thirteen level crossings, (six over public highways) all had either a small stone building or a wooden hut for the watchman. Of the six, three might be worked by the adjacent station staff; two of the other crossings would have to be manned and at the last one he hoped to come to some 'arrangement with the farmer who lives near thereto'. He hoped the Governor would permit gates to be left closed to the roads.

To achieve locomotive economy the timetable had been planned so Douglas–Peel–Douglas could be worked by one engine; such an arrangement would dispense with intermediate Single Line Staffs and there would be only one Staff, 'Douglas & Peel'. When required, Staff & Ticket Working would be adopted, and the departure of trains would also be notified by telegraph. On weekdays five trains would run daily in each direction but only two on Sundays.

On 17th July he reported that driver S. Steele, taking the 9.00 pm to Peel, had hit and killed a cow at Ballywyllin, but the train was undamaged and went on to Peel. On another day the same driver, on the 6.40 am, found a horse on the line at 'Ballacraine road' but it jumped off over the fence. A short distance further on there was a cow on the line; he had already written to Greenbank about insufficient fencing. On 15th September he had to report a 'lurry' on the line near 'Kirk Braddan Bridge' when the 4.45 pm Down train was due. Apparently a ganger was doing a last-minute spot of ballasting and thought he had sufficient time to complete it. 'Mr Adams, the contractor's agent, will see that this does not happen again'.

---

*whereabouts not known.

Lastly, on 18th November Watson also reported his difficulties in obtaining labour, the exorbitant wages he was paying without success, and the very poor quality of labour compared with the initial period: he needed good weather and a strike-free period (there were other strikes on the Island at that time). He had experienced serious losses after signing the contract, due to increase in the price of rails, 'small iron', girders and so on. He hoped that the Board would recognise his losses and the cost of pushing forward work on the Peel Line during adverse weather as on 2,300 tons of iron he had lost at least £2 10s. 0d. per ton. The Peel Line cuttings had been prosecuted in adverse conditions no matter the cost – one of clay had cost more than if it had been cut through hard rock.

He looked forward to a benevolent Board agreeing to add another £5,000 to his contract . . . difficulties of raising money for people of moderate means was his excuse for seeking 'assistance now' and he suggested a financial arrangement by means of supplementary contracts (etc.) by which he would pay all interest on Shares and Debentures from the opening of Railway No. 1 to that of No. 2. The cost of an accident at Union Mills, involving a contractor's train and the £5,000 requested might be merged and form part of the contract amount of £40,000 in Preference Stock. (He was to meet the Board the following day.)

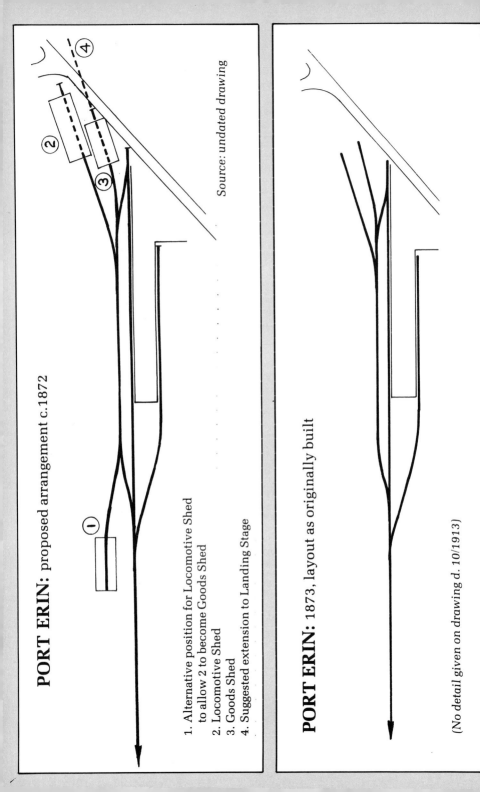

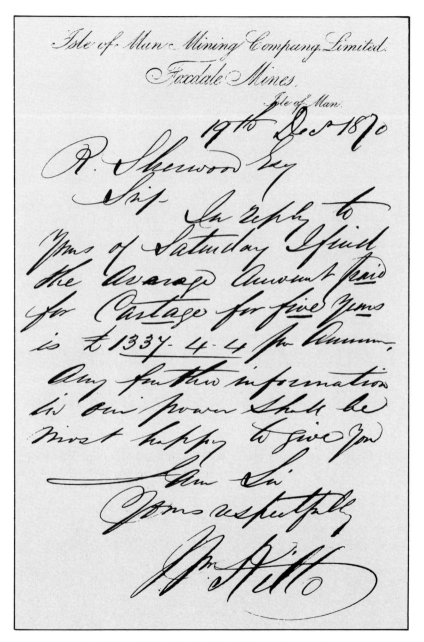

Isle of Man Mining Co. Ltd. Pre-Railway Cartage Expenses.

1873

In January, Greenbank complained that the pegs being used to stake out the Peel course were being removed, nonetheless the earthworks were in a forward state and soon 3½ miles of track had been laid. Although it was intended that the prefabricated timber station buildings should be made in the Island, this did not prove practicable and they were built in England, shipped in parts and erected with Manx labour. Messrs Gelling & Kaye of Douglas were engaged to erect Douglas station, the parts for which had arrived by mid-April and were soon erected.

Also in January, land valuations had commenced on the South Line and before long, earthworks appeared between Douglas and Oakhill. James Armstrong CE (who had surveyed for the railway in 1871 on behalf of the promoters) was paid £90 5s. 6d. for his work and then in March, further finance was authorised; 5% Debentures were issued and Watson & Smith agreed, on the day of issue, to be paid in them. Considerable sums were paid out to compensate landowners whose timber had been cut down.

During March The Isle of Man Race Co. applied for a 'platform' on the Douglas side of the river 'before coming to Union Mills' which could be used for summer athletic meetings when 5,000 people might be expected to attend.* Watson & Smith could build it for £71 10s. 0d. if the Race Company would build the approach road; this was approved and the project completed.

During February, 'two men were injured by a fall of earth near Ballacreggan on the Castletown Line . . .'; the event calls attention to the fact that Dr. Elliot (who attended the men) was appointed Surgeon to the Railway Company in view of his length of experience in the Laxey Mines.

Before March, Mackenzie had been sent to Manchester and Birmingham to make enquiries about the supply of locomotives and rolling stock and to meet the cost a revised Prospectus for 40,000 fully paid-up £5 Shares was approved by the London directors (the Duke in the chair) on the 24th March. Free Passes were given to the Lt. Governor Henry Loch, the Chairman, Vice-Chairman, directors, Vignoles and A.W. Rixon (London solicitor); the latter was 'Secretary' to the London contingent for the whole of its existence until 1905. These Passes were made of metal, with the Legs of Man on one side and the Company's name on the other: Passes were to become a frequent bone of contention. Shortly afterwards, the Company's shares were quoted on the London Stock Exchange.

---

*Horse racing in the Island took place at several venues – the most formal was at The Strang, in a field probably used for the Strang Fair (1816–34). The Isle of Man Race Co. held their first races here on 14th July, 1870, sponsored by Governor Loch, and the Company chartered a first-class steamer from Liverpool to convey the horses. The site of the Race Platform was probably on the east side of the line on the approach to Union Mills station. Jenkinson's Guide of 1874 refers to two grandstands holding 1,000 people in each and after the first year, the Races were extended to *two* days in August. [Ref: THE STRANG (John Keown) and HISTORY OF UNION MILLS (P.M. Lewthwaite)]
Wood's diary refers to them on 3rd August, 1902.
A possible location for the platform is Map Ref: 776362.
Another course beside the IOMR was at Belle Vue where meetings were held from the end of last century on a course provided to that end. This was the site of the International Exhibition of 1892. 'Racing degenerated to such low estate that the Course was closed and later became a municipal Sports Ground', [ISLE OF MAN (E.H. Stenning)] and is now an Athletics Ground known as The Douglas Bowl.

Peel station was in the news during March 1873:

> ... is erected on a piece of reclaimed ground adjoining Peel Quay. Like Douglas is, a wooden structure with a tiled roof. It is in the 'New English' style but extremely striking and tasteful in appearance... at a little distance is a goods shed ... Mr Wright from St Pancras station London, is appointed Station Master, Mr Williams at Union Mills, Mr S.D. Gibson at Crosby and Mr Grimmett at St John's.

Cash shortage being again evident, THE TIMES was used on 28th March, 1873:

> Subscriptions have been invited for £50,000 in £5 shares of the Isle of Man Railway Company (Limited) of which the Duke of Sutherland is Chairman. These shares form part of the authorised capital of £160,000 of which £70,000 has already been taken chiefly by residents in the Island. The undertaking comprises a line from Douglas to Peel which will be opened in June next and one from Douglas to Port Erin which will be opened next year the total length being 27 miles and the estimated cost per mile £8,000. It is stated that between the months of June and November upwards of 130,000 people chiefly from Lancashire and Yorkshire visit the Island.

The next excitement was a shipment of the first locomotive for the IOMR: the SUN's reporter was there (29th March, 1873):

> The first of three engines ordered for the Railway Company ... arrived per steamer on Thursday night. The engine is what is known as a tank engine ... it is of the outside cylinder class and has attached to the front wheels what is termed a bogie frame – commonly used in America ... the engine was visited at the Quay yesterday by very large numbers of the inhabitants and minutely inspected. A few days will be required to put the machinery together and she will then be removed to the line ... the 1,253rd engine manufactured by the firm of Beyer, Peacock & Company Limited.*

There was now plenty to see and the SUN kept the public abreast of such matters. On 12th April, 1873 it said:

> ... work pushed on with all speed ... plant arriving in considerable quantities ... during past week several iron bridges have been brought to Douglas by steamer, and a 6 ton vehicle, the first of five trucks which are to be furnished by the Metropolitan Railway Carriage & Wagon Company Limited, Birmingham, also arrived on Tuesday and another two were brought over to the Island by Thursday's steamer. The second engine is expected by today's steamer. The trading vessel PHYSICIAN, Jones, Master, from Granton, discharged a cargo of railway sleepers at Peel on 2 inst. ...

A letter from John Pender, 12 Arlington Street, London, to Alfred W. Adams (12th April, 1873) reveals progress:

> ... I am glad to hear the work is progressing so satisfactorily ... Watson seemed to think they might carry the Whitsuntide Passengers at the beginning of June, and that he expected within a week or ten days to run an Engine from Douglas to Peel. Has this been done yet?
>
> You are aware that the Duke of Sutherland and some of the Directors of the London & North Western Railway propose to visit ... 27th or 28th instant, their

---

*Beyer, Peacock & Co. Ltd., Gorton Foundry, Manchester. Founded May 1854 (Charles Beyer was Manager of Sharp Bros.). Richard Peacock MP joined him to form the partnership, being also the founder of the Institution of Mechanical Engineers in 1847. Ceased trading 1964.

Steamer calling at Peel and going round to meet them at Douglas . . .
Watson said there would be no doubt he would be able to take them along the Line with the Locomotive or Trucks . . .

By late April even more column-inches were given over to the Railway. On the 26th the SUN could write:

First of the three locomotive engines . . . has had her running powers thoroughly tested . . . the engine which is named the SUTHERLAND . . . arrived three weeks ago . . . since being fitted up the SUTHERLAND has assumed a neat and attractive appearance . . . the engineer and stoker are thoroughly protected from the effects of inclement weather . . . by a large iron cover, known to the initiated, we believe, as 'the house' (a purely Beyer, Peacock term. JICB) this also being an adjunct generally used and well-known in America. Nearly the whole of the engine is painted green . . . a large concourse of spectators assembled on the surrounding eminences at that part of the line where the trial was made – that passing Braddan Church and the first scream of the whistle brought a considerable number of onlookers. Mr Wilson (Locomotive Superintendent), at the close of the trial, expressed himself thoroughly satisfied with the result. Mr W.D. Wilson is a Manxman by birth belonging to the Parish of Kirk Santon, son of Mr. William Wilson a gentleman of considerable eminence as an engineer who was for some 25 years engaged on the Western Railway lines of France . . . Mr W.D. Wilson is appointed to the superintendence of the locomotive department of the Insular Railway was . . . similarly engaged in France and came to the Island from Gaston.

The next entry was:

. . . the second locomotive has lately arrived . . . to be known as the DERBY . . . the first passenger carriage arrived on Saturday evening last by steamer from Liverpool, it is marked SECOND CLASS and being apparently equal in comfort to the third class on a few lines on the other side of the water and inferior to carriages of that class on most of them, it does not admit of having much said in its favour. Several iron bridges have also arrived lately. A first class passenger carriage arrived by the steamer SNAEFELL on Thursday morning.

The 1873 Annual General Meeting announced two deviations – a diversion from the intended route at Peel, down to the harbour side instead of to a point further south, and another at Castletown to bring the route nearer to the town.

Within a year the Peel Line had advanced so well that an experimental run was made between Douglas and Peel on 1st May, 1873. The Island could afford to be well pleased with such progress.

[An amusing sidelight, which has no place in the IOMR official records, comes from a dispute between M'Kie, contractor for the North Wales Narrow Gauge Railways and that Company, when it was revealed that track materials were being shipped by M'Kie to the Island to recompense him for lack of funds from the NWNGR Company who, he alleged, were not assessing his work fully!]

Daniel Cregeen,* a Manxman working on the South Line for Henry Vignoles, became involved with landowners who, appreciating his origins, asked him to value land taken over for the Railway. Because of this he asked that he should be employed formally by the Company for such transactions. On 13th October John Adams for Watson & Smith wrote to Alfred Adams

---

*see also Laxey scheme 1882.

complaining: 'Brydson of Ballaquiggin has stopped us from entering his turnip field until these are valued ... and brought the work to a standstill'. The landowners' concern about their boundaries along the Railway was a universal complaint about the flimsiness of the fences put up by the contractor: once trains began to operate, their complaints appear to have been upheld by the number of pigs, sheep and cattle which found their way onto the line and were struck by trains. Such complaints were to extend for years rather than months, but Vignoles maintained that the fences were adequate, and the Board ignored the protestations. It does appear that the contract for the fencing was under-specified.

Vignoles was kept busy and accepted payment in Debentures; having been told there was insufficient money to provide platforms, he was instructed to order ten 'goods waggons' and erect a 'platform at Braddan Bridge'. To erect the timber stations, Braby & Co. of Douglas were appointed as sub-contractors to Watson & Smith, who were falling behind in construction due to heavy rain. Uniforms for guards of grey cloth with a red stripe, and corduroy suits for porters were ordered, so it is said, through the insistence of Mr Watterson (later, Station Master at Port St Mary), much to the Board's annoyance.

June saw several decisions which were not to be fulfilled and the first was to erect general offices on 'station ground' at Douglas (it would be 1887/8 before this was done). Secondly, there were to be tramways onto the quays at both Douglas* and Peel (this desirable objective never came to fruition): though there was a harbour tramway at Peel during the First World War, Douglas never enjoyed such benefit.

A nice entry in the Isle of Man Steam Packet Co. Minutes (2nd July, 1873) confirms the decision to charge £40 for the use of the steamer KING ORRY on 30th June when it was chartered by 'the Duke of Sutherland and party'. This decision followed a request from G.H. Wood, Secretary of the Railway, for a special steamer for the event; it was at that time decided the Packet Co. would charge only the working expenses of such a steamer but if that special ship should take passengers in addition to the party, only ordinary fares would be charged.

There was a muddle about payment for rolling stock from The Metropolitan Carriage & Wagon Co. Ltd., Watson & Smith being incorrectly debited with the cost of the first batch of stock which was not part of their contract. More muddle was apparent when a demand for English Income Tax was received at the London office. Customs & Excise requirements meant that lock-up warehouses were now built at Douglas and Peel to store dutiable goods.

On 9th June, the Governor had sent a telegram to the Secretary of the Board of Trade requesting the name of the Railway Inspector as 'Governor wished to communicate early with him on the subject'. He was given the name Colonel Rich ('his address is No. One Whitehall') and the Governor duly told the IOMRCo that Rich would be inspecting the line.† The Peel

---

*Vignoles' North Quay Tramway drawing of 1873: from the end of the South Line platform track, across the foot of Bank Hill to terminate opposite the Steam Packet Office with a loop opposite the Black Lion Hotel. Length: 33 chains 20 links.
†Manx Museum: 46/16. Col F.H. Rich (Board of Trade Inspector)
   Joined Royal Engineers 1840, became Lieut Colonel 1867 and Colonel 1873 Ref: RAILWAY DETECTIVES (Stanley Hall) [Ian Allan Ltd. 1990]. Became Chief Inspecting Officer 1885 on the death of Col W. Yolland, serving until 1891.

Line was complete but station buildings were unfinished and although the track was down, not all of it was ballasted. However, Douglas station (given priority) was complete. Out on the South Line the underline bridge at Port Soderick (the largest on the whole system) was occupying the contractors. They did request the use of the railway rolling stock but this was refused.

It so happened that a party of officials of the London & North Western Railway and Lancashire & Yorkshire Railway was crossing from Ireland following the opening of the Dundalk & Greenore Railway on 30th April. It seems that no time had been lost by these gentlemen in leaving the junketings and 'dejeuner' held in the decorated goods shed at Greenore, sailing the same evening for the Isle of Man. The Duke of Sutherland, George Sheward and others with financial interests in the IOMR were among them. Such an unexpected and impromptu visit, caused by circumstances which the Isle of Man Company could hardly have anticipated, caught the undertaking 'with its pants down'. The Duke having expressed a wish to see the progress of the work, a trial run was made on 1st May.

The SUN made much of the occasion, heading its article:

EXPERIMENTAL TRAIN, DOUGLAS–PEEL

The opening of the Dundalk & Greenore Rly. and the inauguration of a new line of steamers from Greenore to Holyhead had brought these gentlemen together on the previous day . . . advantage taken to visit the IOMR. (There was a steamer from Greenore to Port Erin, the LNWR's EDITH.) After refreshing themselves at The Falcon they drove to Castletown and Douglas. The party included several directors of the LNWR including Stephen Reay (Secretary) and Mr Webb, Chief Locomotive Superintendent. A train was waiting to convey the company to Peel, very great exertions having been made to have the line completed in time but in consequence of the vessel MARY ALICE laden with rails for the permanent way having been detained at Fleetwood for a week, the work of completion had necessarily been retarded (she had left that port on Friday last and had not on Wednesday arrived in Douglas where she was to discharge her cargo). It was consequently found necessary at the last moment to remove rails from the Douglas–Castletown line which had been laid down there . . . the last rail, we understand, had not been laid on the Peel line until about 8 o'clock that morning. As a test, an engine, 2nd class carriage and wagon were sent along the line to see all was right. A body of workmen occupied the wagon and several places which were found to have the appearance of weakness or awkwardness had the finishing touch given to them . . . In the carriage which accompanied the test engine were Mr and Mrs A.W. Adams, Mr Watson, Mr Vignoles and Mr Greenbank. All went pretty smoothly until St John's station when the carriage, which had had one of its axles twisted on being landed from the steamer, went off the rail through the distance between the wheels not corresponding with the gauge. It was shunted at St John's however, and allowed to remain there, the engine and wagon going only a little further on (Glenfaba Bridge) and then returning to Douglas without completing the journey to Peel, so that it might reach the latter place in time to meet the Duke and his party, which it was successful in doing . . .

The actual train by which the distinguished party travelled consisted of four wagons. Of these one was rendered considerably safer than the others by having an iron railing placed along the sides so as to prevent any risk from the sudden jerks expected and met with on the journey . . . crowd had increased to some 900 or 1,000 . . . train moved off with its load of about 80 passengers, cheering resumed, his Grace courteously lifting his hat and bowing in response.

The engine attached to the wagons was the first brought to the Island (the SUTHERLAND). The Duke travelled on the engine together with Col Rich, Mr Vignoles, Mr Greenbank and Mr Watson. The Superintendent of the locomotive department Mr W.D. Wilson had charge of the engine. The start was made at 2.15 pm and steam was put up soon after until a pretty smart pace was reached. The train was watched and cheered at every available point . . . a short stoppage was made at Kirk Braddan bridge where water was taken from a tank on the right hand side of the line . . . at Union Mills a merry welcome was given by the workers . . . St. John's was reached at 3.05 pm. Water was again taken here and after a stoppage of five minutes the train proceeded. On approaching Glenfaba Bridge to which the test train had not proceeded, the train commenced its journey on an untrodden path and the pace was accordingly reduced. This was fortunate, for shortly after passing under the bridge, the two front wheels of the engine went off the rails . . . Jacks had been brought along . . . and soon was made alright again. The passengers who had alighted, resumed their seats and after a stoppage of 20 minutes (3.35–3.55) the journey was continued (the gauge was tight by ⅜ in.). Peel was eventually reached a few minutes past four. Just as the entrance to the town was being made, the middle pair of wheels of the engine came off . . . occasioned by the newly laid rails being somewhat loose. The return journey started at 5.05 pm with contractor's engine MONA, terminus reached at 6.50 pm . . . over 1,000 persons waited at the station . . . the steamer sailed within a few minutes of arrival of the train at Douglas.

Some had opportunity to inspect the station and workshops, in particular 'three Abyssinian Tubewells which raise water into a tank by steam pump',* which gave independence from the Douglas Water Company.

Mackenzie reported on 12th June, expressing fears about the level crossing at Quarter Bridge 'there will be during the summer 100 vehicles and upwards using this road daily . . . however the crossing is well protected with signals on both sides these being distance (sic) signals . . .'† A modern touch was the provision of electric bells to stations on either side of it, Douglas and Union Mills. The proposed timetable was for five trains each way on weekdays and two on Sundays; this service could be worked by one engine and only one Single Line Staff (Douglas–Peel) was necessary. Extra trains would be controlled by Staff Ticket: a telegraph linked all stations (see Volume III for signalling etc).

There were shortcomings: seven items of rolling stock were outstanding and though 500 yards of sidings had been laid, more were needed to follow – in fact it would be the next November before the Peel Line was finished. Still in mid-June, little had been done on the South Line beyond Ballashamrock (later to become Port Soderick) but a month later earthworks had reached Santon.

The still-unopened railway was a magnet for children, so much so that Jno. Henry was employed as a constable 'for watching and keeping clear the railway on Sundays, and preventing fences being broken down by children'. In the last few days of the month a large supply of locomotive coal arrived through Thomas Heald of Liverpool (60 tons @ 17/6d. per ton). Additional expense was involved in 'carting, trimming, weighing and checking'. Days before opening, Mackenzie visited the thirteen Peel Line level crossings 'by car' and, if they were to be manned, appointed gatekeepers.

---

*stated as four originally.
†these signals were of disc type.

Introduced into all this was the matter of refreshment rooms on the stations and especially opposition to the sale of alcohol and Sunday Observance. Thus, the SUN on 3rd May, 1873:

> Tynwald Court. Mr Adams introduced a petition from the IOMRCo ... by the Taverns Act accommodation must be of a certain character and extent: e.g. if a mile or more from town there must be stabling. This clause was not at all suited to the refreshment rooms which the Co. proposed to establish. Also the Act stated a certain number of bedrooms must be provided ...

and its Leader on 10th May said:

> Signs are not wanting that the introduction of a Railway into the Island is not to be an unmixed good ... there has been great opposition to Refreshment Rooms and Sunday opening.

The Company's application to the Legislature for an Act for licence to serve intoxicants at Douglas raised a storm of protest among the considerable population who opposed intoxicants and gave the newspapers considerable correspondence.* In church, a sermon was preached on the wickedness of the Railway Board who proposed not only to run trains on a Sunday but quench the thirst of passengers as well. Despite a rough handling, the Bill was given assent. Both Peel and Douglas provided refreshments and at Peel the separate building, alongside the station itself, was larger if anything than its neighbour. However, when the old buildings at Peel were demolished during the rebuilding of the station, accommodation for refreshments was not re-provided, although that at Douglas survived as a useful amenity. The Company usually put the letting of the refreshment rooms to auction and the Peel rooms were let to Frank Cottier of the Peel Castle Hotel for £20 for the period 1st August–31st December, 1873.

Advocate A.W. Adams was not satisfied and wrote to Rowland Fisher (Vignoles' assistant) about Douglas station. Fisher replied:

> 17 Great George St., Westminster to A.W. Adams
>
> *4 September 1872.*
>
> Mr Vignoles has just handed me your letter as well as one from Mr Watson on the same subject viz: the alteration of the site of Douglas station in such a way as to provide for more extensive building operations ...
>
> ... our first consideration was to provide the best accommodation for the Line without reference to Shops although I always tried to have in mind the advisability for Refreshment Rooms etc. Mr Vignoles and I have completed everything on that understanding so that a contractor might commence work as soon as he had signed the Contract. To re-commence on your plan or suggestion, it appears to me, would be drifting somewhat from the Railway Company's work into one of speculation (and a very good speculation too I should think). It therefore occurs to me that I can hardly ask Mr Vignoles or the Coy. to pay the expense of new designs and a journey to the Island. At the same time if the Coy. think that their interest requires a design to be prepared on the basis suggested by you I would be most happy to undertake it. I have been thinking before I saw your letter of using this ground which would be somewhat of a compromise between the two plans ...

[Adams' letter to Vignoles has not survived but Vignoles' reply to him has done so: Vignoles admitted he lost his temper at the sight of it but added 'I

---

*'ale-harbours', 'brandy-booths' and 'rum-retreats' were among the definitions given by correspondents.

wish we were rich enough to carry out what you propose'. He had given Pender his word that the £10,000 would suffice for

> the absolute station requirements . . . I subsequently cut my coat according to the cloth . . . it will take the most studied scheming to build all our stations, engine, goods and carriage sheds, workshops and tank houses . . . (etc. etc.) and not exceed £10,000 . . . in all cases there will not be a farthing to spend on Buildings of a speculative character . . . if I build Douglas station on any other site . . . it will run us into great expense for Retaining Walls, etc . . . if I place our station right up against the wall of Bank Hill I should occupy ground which eventually may be more valuable for other purposes and it would not be possible to build on the ground where I now propose the Station afterwards, as it would be occupied with sidings, platforms, etc . . . it is very true that the station, as I propose it, does not occupy all that plot of ground which cost the Company upwards of £2,000 and I think it would be a great mistake to do so.
>
> It was necessary to buy this plot of land to avoid the Ropewalk Buildings – obtain an exit from our Railway to the Quays and avoid taking the frontage of Major Taubman's proposed new street, but that is no reason why we should build our station on the most valuable part of it – which at all times will be available for extensive buildings or even for sale.
>
> Later, it is quite possible speculators will be only too glad to buy the site for a Hotel or shops above the Company having offices & Refreshment Rooms below . . .
>
> Always yours sincerely,
Henry Vignoles. *

A third locomotive arrived in the first week of May '. . . which is to be named PENDER . . . remained on the quay until Wednesday (due to a 'broken trolley')'.

Ultimately Col Rich returned again and on the 26th June he examined the Douglas to Peel section and with reservations, agreed that public services might commence. On the next day (a Sunday) he made an early start from Douglas with an engine and fifteen four-wheel carriages, with a view to testing the haulage capacity of the engine. Breakfast was taken at Peel and the return run made in 35 minutes.

The following day another special train ran over the line, calling at each station to deliver furniture and stores and setting down the new employees at their appointed work places. Advertisements appeared in the Press calling attention to the desirability of closing those retail establishments owned by 'respectable merchants' on the occasion of the public opening!

It is a matter for national joy when on Tuesday, 1st July, 1873, the first official journey took place. The local Press emphasised that the event was not simply one for celebration by the proprietors, but cause for great satisfaction by all those who had the Island's welfare at heart. On arriving at Douglas station at 11.55 am, His Grace took his seat in the Director's Saloon, part of a special train of a dozen coaches plus one open wagon which carried

---

*What a valuable source of information is this one document which underlines the dominating influence of the Taubmans, the limitations of the Ropewalk (housing a concern occupying the same ground today) and as stated elsewhere, the sound sense of Vignoles and his perception of future requirements!

the band of the Royal Bengal Fusiliers.* Engine No. 1 SUTHERLAND was at the head, and on the smokebox it bore the legend 'Douglas & Peel United'. The band managed to play whenever they stopped at a station and the journey was completed without contretemps in 47 minutes.

At Peel a banner was spread across the line reading in Manx: 'Success to the iron road between Douglas and Peel', and in case the journey had proved a thirsty one for the large party, the contractors had laid on an ample supply of refreshments, not only for the favoured, but for all.

A second train, bearing those of lesser rank, arrived shortly afterwards and the first train then returned to Douglas without further ado. It required 27½ minutes for the journey, averaging almost 25 mph in a demonstration of speed and safety, whilst the second train followed it. Lunch was taken in the Volunteer Drill Shed. Close on 500 persons travelled that day, which ended with dancing and a firework display. Public service began the following morning and on 3rd July, the Duke sent the following telegram to the Manager: 'What did we take yesterday? Sutherland.' This telegram was preserved (together with a portrait of His Grace) in the Boardroom.

The flavour of this occasion† — though a little repetitive of the foregoing — is valuable as seen by the SUN's reporter:

> The large field to the north of the station was not as well-filled as on the trial day, probably because an admission fee of 6d. was charged . . . 400 persons were invited, therefore two trains ran. The Director's Saloon carriage used by Col Rich for his inspection, plus a few 1st class and sufficient of the others to make up a dozen carriages in all. In the centre of this train was an open wagon or cattle truck provided for the band, for whom it was thought necessary to provide an open-air seat. Engine was SUTHERLAND, and Mr A.W. Adams occupied the driver's box. SUTHERLAND was very neatly decorated with flowers and mottoes 'DOUGLAS & PEEL UNITED', 'SUCCESS TO THE IOMR', 'PROGRESS'. The second train was shorter, having ten carriages and a van, engine DERBY, decorated as SUTHERLAND with 'ELLAN VANNIN SON DA BRAGH' ('Dear Little Isle of Man for ever'). At 11.40 am everything was ready, signal was given by the station master . . . train glided easily and gracefully from the station, band started to play 'The British Grenadier', and continued at stations and other points along the line. The guard was Mr. George Hogg. . . . second train of eleven carriages left at 12.10 pm the cheering being rather more firm . . . guard J. Briers and driver Steele . . . first train reached Peel at 12.25 pm, second at 12.47 pm, being 45 and 37 minutes respectively . . . elegant lunch served in Refreshment Room of station at the cost of Messrs. Watson & Smith. The party then went to Peel Castle. At 2.05 pm the first train started on return journey, and arrived in Douglas in 27 minutes. The second left half an hour later, and did the journey in 22 minutes . . . A banquet followed at Munteer Drill Hall, Douglas.

A week later the SUN had another article:

> The success of the present Company is not due to one man nor to half a dozen . . . scarcely possible to know who deserves the credit . . . Hon Clerk to the Rolls

---

*The Royal Bengal Fusiliers was one of the old British regiments (previously in the service of the East India Company) which was taken over by H.M. Government in 1860 after the Indian Mutiny 1857–59. They wore a racoon skin fur cap (or busby) with white and grey plume on the left side with a large grenade badge in the front of the busby. Raised by Clive of India the Regiment was, together with other units in the service of the East India Co., transferred to the British Army in 1860 and came to England for the first time in 1871. Visiting the Isle of Man in 1873, it was a natural choice for the opening ceremony.

†also recorded by THE GRAPHIC for 12th July, 1873.

J.T. Clucas Esq: other leading men of the Island engaged an engineer Armstrong who made a careful survey . . . Henry Vignoles MICE was employed in January 1871 . . . Watson & Smith constructed at average of c.£8,000 per mile . . . Col Rich inspected on behalf of Board of Trade . . .

Douglas station is at The Lake, a large piece of reclaimed land forming one of the sides of Bank Hill, extending to the far end of Quiggin's Ropewalk. Passenger entry is by three flights of steps to Bank Hill, and to other traffic at the foot of them. The Ticket Office is built of wood in the Swiss style; its south wing is taken up by the station master's office (Mr Buckett's) and offices of the clerks. The north wing is the cloak and left luggage office, ladies waiting room and 'other convenient offices': the centre forms a large entrance and waiting hall. A double line of rails merges into a single not 300 yards from the starting point: passengers leave by platform on south side and arrive by that on the north. The goods depot is situated on the left of the line, and consists of a zinc-covered shed. To the right is the engine and carriage shed. Nearer the station is a large water tank, supplied by Abyssinian wells sunk by Mr Partridge; to the west is the space for coals; also mechanics' and blacksmiths' workshops.*

At present the Company have ready 3 locomotives and 30 passenger carriages (1 & 2) about 30 luggage wagons and cattle trucks . . . it is only fair to state to the public that the 2 class are inferior to those of 3 class used on most English and Scotch lines.

Apart from the Duke, the other directors at the time of opening were: J. Pender (Vice Chairman), Rev Christian, Hon F.A. Stanley, J.T. Clucas, G. Sheward, Major J.S.G. Taubman. On 19th July, 1873 traffic figures for the previous seven days appeared in the Press:

Passengers, parcels, fish, horses, carriages, dogs & cattle	£314 11s. 3d.
Merchandise & Minerals	3 12 0
Total for week	318 3 3
Grand Total	£674 17s. 1d.

There can have been but few railways whose anticipated results were more accurately forecast – in the first five weeks receipts averaged more than the estimated £30 per mile but this was summer and by the following March the figure was £7 per mile. These figures were quoted in the Press in answer to various attempts to belittle the success of the railway – these attempts were laid at the door of those whose living was obtained from the displaced road services, but they were ineffectual and soon ceased. Seven days after this an iron bar held in place by five large boulders was found on the track on the curve beside the brick works at Peel – perhaps angry road-car proprietors were attempting to derail the train? On 12th July the 1st class carriage left the rails.

Passengers did not always find things to their liking: smoking was taking place in non-smoking compartments and both sexes were travelling together in unlit compartments; some men were drunk. An aggrieved employee wrote to the newspaper alleging that railway servants were being forced to 'cover up' for the management, that the Saloon carriage would be attached simply for one person, that women of doubtful character were travelling on

---

*renewed in 1890s.

the footplate, that drunks returned from Peel to Douglas on Saturday nights and turned Douglas station into similar form of Liverpool's worst slums.*

The SUN (17th July) had notice of the issue of £13,000 5% Mortgage Debenture Bonds – being the second issue of that amount towards the £40,000 Mortgage Debentures authorized.

The TIMES for the 5th July presents a very full report of the opening; in summarising the work done by the contractors, a description of the original station buildings is given. Buildings at Douglas and Peel were of wood and 'English Bricks', supplied by Burby & Co. of Deptford whereas Peel station was a double-fronted building in weatherboarding, having zinc tiles in two shades of red laid in decorative diagonal lines. The design is described as Gothic and buildings at the intermediate stations, Crosby and St. John's were similar but Union Mills is not mentioned. The timber was painted in stone colour, with the framework picked out in Indian Red. The goods sheds were all erected by Gelling & Kaye, and they too had zinc tile roofs.

After the opening, the London directors became increasingly anxious about the state of the works on the completed Peel route and those incomplete on the Port Erin Line, but it was to be the following 23rd March when they demonstrated this by sending Sir Charles Hutton Gregory, KCMG, (a past President of the Institution of Civil Engineers) to inspect these lines and report on their solidarity.

At the General Meeting on 17th July, 1873 (the Peel Line having just opened) second thoughts prevailed about the junction between the Peel and Castletown Lines which would have continued as single tracks almost into the terminus. Instead, it was agreed 'to lay down a double line from the intended junction near Douglas, and so into Douglas station'. The Castletown Line

> crosses Douglas River on an iron girder bridge of three openings, each of 30 ft span. The old road through The Nunnery has been diverted and passes under the furthest arch of the bridge; then the line runs over the site of the old road and enters deepest rock cutting. The rock extracted here is 15,000 yards in extent . . . it dips and a long deep cutting on the seaward side of Oak Hill requires the removal of fully 60,000 sq. yds. of rock and soil, the largest cutting on the Castletown Line . . .
>
> As to Port St Mary . . . and the distant site of the station . . . it appears that the Company will neither do justice to the public or itself unless a direct communication with the village by means of a tramway, is effected.

July 1873 was a month which began happily enough but not for long. As beforementioned, during the first week a length of rail, 5 ft long 'was laid on the rails at Ballywyllin, fastened with large stones at each end'. A reward of £50 was offered for apprehension and conviction. Days later, Guard Hogg (he who had attended the Opening Train) was dismissed for drunkenness on the 5 pm Peel train. London required Greenbank to report on the Castletown length and its progress . . . 'if not satisfactory, why not?' Watson & Smith were in trouble because at St. John's they had dug a hole for ballast and failed to fill it up again. Their contract included the supply of rolling stock and stations (though these charges were later questioned) and they were called to account for what they had spent on stations, rolling stock, Railway No. 1 (Peel), and Railway No. 2 (Port Erin).

---

*SRN No. 27 gives further newspaper detail of this period.

Locomotive coal in those first days came from various sources; currently it came from The Westminster–Brymbo Coal & Coke Co.*. Fencing was still the subject of complaint, trains being held up frequently by animals on the line. The existing track near Glenfaba, Peel, was recommended for deviation to keep it further from the river, and the re-location of Castletown station had not been determined. Col Rich (in timely recommendation so it proved) advocated the Block System be introduced on the Peel Line.

The London directors wanted Excursion Tickets withdrawing and more Sunday trains put on – clearly they had little idea of the Island Sabbath. The Racecourse Platform had to be extended and to hoard the cash, second-hand safes were sent from London. Vignoles was again told to prosecute plans for quay lines at Douglas and Peel.

Frequently the London faction used the railway in the Isle of Wight as an example of what might be done on Man: they also wanted placards and advertisements on stations as on the 'Dingwall & Skye Railway'. The influence of the Duke was never clearer . . .

On 16th July, 1873, a contractor's ballast train (12 loaded wagons hauled by SUTHERLAND) entering Union Mills under a clear signal ran into the rear of a Douglas-bound passenger train (No. 3, PENDER, 11 passenger stock and a wagon of platelayers) in the station, which was by regulation required to collect passengers' tickets there.

The Up 'Distance Signal' (sic) would have returned to danger by a suitable weight but the Station Master had removed it as he thought the contractor's men were working the signals. He had no knowledge of a train following the passenger and had taken the weight off 'as he could not work the signal from the station'. It transpired that trains were being worked on a time interval of five minutes: it was said that 'the staff do not understand their work', and 'It would be better if the Staff & Ticket system were in use but even this would not have prevented the accident'. The ballast train was being worked (ad hoc) by the contractor's 'own engine' (sic) – apparently SUTHERLAND was on loan – but from that day all such ballast trains were suspended and passenger trains were now to be worked by Staff alone and no Tickets issued (as they had been on Tynwald Day, 5th July). Some said the ballast train was going too fast and the General Purposes Committee complained to the Manager that trains went too fast when making up time, as the line was as yet unfinished; the telegraph was not yet working and there was a severe lack of proficient employees. The Guard's Log, in the van hit by the ballast train, could not be found and in consequence, Williams the Station Master was sacked!

The SUN 19th July, 1873:

> ACCIDENT AT UNION MILLS. A serious and alarming accident took place on Wednesday 16th by which a large number of persons (28) were slightly shaken and bruised but fortunately no lives were lost . . . 5.33 pm from Peel standing in Union Mills while tickets were being collected (N.B. Douglas is an Open station) when run into by SUTHERLAND with 12 ballast trucks which came round the curve and under the bridge at some 18 mph† . . . the signals it is alleged, having been moved

---

*WREXHAM. MOLD & CONNAH'S QUAY RAILWAY, page 47 etc. (J.I.C. Boyd) [Oakwood Press 1991]
†grossly exaggerated; it was more like 4 mph.

for repair (i.e. winch and chain, allowing signal to fall to clear) and no red flag or other signal having been sent along the line to prevent the occurrence. The driver of the ballast train had started from the ballast hole at St John's shortly after the passenger train had passed . . . reversed his engine and as the ticket collector had instructed the passenger train to move on as soon as the whistle of the other was heard, the shock of the collision was somewhat lessened. As the matter looked serious, it was agreed to run the train onto Douglas and obtain medical advice and assistance. Several of those on the train refused to enter it again, choosing rather to proceed by car. Mr Watson of the contractors, on the passenger engine, was thrown from it.

Hereafter, the General Purposes Committee 'lived in dread of learning of the next catastrophe owing to the state of the fencing, and declined to be answerable'; Mackenzie, culprit or otherwise, may have been made a scapegoat for the affair. Col Rich made a Report, which the SUN of 16th August, 1873 quoted:

. . . when semaphore was out of order, the signals were so arranged that 'alright' would be shown – a most stupid, dangerous arrangement which he pointed out to His Excellency the Lt Governor at once as a matter calling for amendment. Col Rich recommended that distant signals, catch points for sidings and interlocking should be installed 'at all other stations of the Line'.

Rich's Report* itself adds usefully to our knowledge of the state of things at this early stage, and may be summarized:

1. The man who took the weights off the signal received his instruction at 11 am whilst the accident took place at 5 pm. The man was employed 'moving the wheels'.

2. The passenger train left Peel at 5 pm comprising engine (bunker first), composite coach with brakesman, nine passenger carriages, and a guard's van. Attached to the rear was an open wagon carrying permanent way men who had been working on the track. It arrived 10 minutes late at Union Mills and was detained whilst tickets were collected. Meanwhile the Up signal behind the train remained at 'All Clear'.
[Rule 28 (IOMR Rule) required that a man with hand signals must be on duty at a signal if it is out of order and because this was not done, the passenger train was unprotected.]

3. The whistle of the ballast train was heard at the station just as ticket collecting ended so its guard gave the passenger train driver the signal to start and the Station Master rushed towards the ballast train in a vain attempt to stop it; it hit the wagon at the end of the passenger train at about 3 mph.

4. The ballast train comprised 12–14 wagons loaded with ballast. Its driver had seen the smoke rising from the train standing in the station just as he reached 'the Up Distant signal'. He closed his regulator, reversed the engine, put on steam again and whistled for the platelayers to put down the wagon brakes; meanwhile the fireman applied the engine handbrake, but the distance was too short to have effect. Though no vehicles were thrown off the rails and the stock was not damaged, about 28 passengers complained of injury.

5. Watson, riding on the engine of the *passenger* train, was thrown off.

The occasion caused widespread rumour and alarm; doctors were sent for and Mackenzie summoned. George Sheward was telegraphed to come to the Island without delay. The claims for compensation, valid or otherwise,

*Report by courtesy of Miss A. Harrison.

dragged on for years and made inroads into the Company's finances: ultimately Mackenzie lost his job.† The General Purposes Committee visited the site and found that the Station Master had allowed the signal to remain at 'Clear' after the passenger train had passed it. This event, and others like it, could be put down to inexperienced employees working in a strange environment: unlike railways on the mainland, the railway was an unfamiliar part of daily life to most Islanders. The ballast train driver had no experience of single line working save for a time when he was in France where the system was by telegraph. Other employees came from a near- or non-railway background. Stoppages to trains became frequent, mostly due to inadequate fencing and livestock on the track; compensation was usually arranged locally but costs mounted, and the Board gratefully accepted a loan of £3,000 from one of their number, J.T. Clucas, for three months. Expense was ever in the minds of management and after a number of cases of vandalism, men were placed at vantage points without success. In due course they were discharged. They had been lodged at Company expense and were paid £1 10s. 0d. each.

Farmers and landowners on the Peel Line now made concerted complaints about post and wire fences and some were given materials to improve their section; it was agreed to erect improved fencing on the Port Erin Line. Further relief came when Dr Wood, who had attended the injured at Union Mills, confirmed that no one had been seriously injured.

Mr Quayle's cow was killed by a train at Ballaquayle, Patrick: he received £14 compensation against a claim of £14 10s. 0d. and was allowed to keep the carcase. Late in autumn the 6 pm ex-Peel train (in darkness) rushed through the gate at Bell's Crossing, Ballacraine, which had been left open and seven carriages had their panels smashed. It was the Company's policy to let off many fringe activities rather than employing persons themselves and this policy extended into new buildings, rolling stock painting, etc. Maintenance of rolling stock, track and signalling was always carried out by employees.

Watson & Smith wished to put up buildings for their own purposes at Douglas but the site envisaged on the north side of the premises, was sold. The facility for boys to sell papers on the station there was granted and the extra police employed for the opening were paid £8 1s. 0d. Consideration was given to lighting Peel and Union Mills stations by gas and the St. John's Brick & Tile Co. asked for a siding there – which appeared in due course.

An outcome of Rich's Accident Report was to underline the contractor's responsibility to maintain the track for six months after approval, and to sow the embankments with grass seed (the latter had not been done). An attempt to make the Company pay for the services of the Fusiliers Band and 'Detective Police' from the mainland used on 1st July was resisted. On 4th August, a contractor's ballasting 'lurry' left the line at Kirk Braddan and held up the 4.45 pm train from Douglas. It was found cheaper to land locomotive coal at Peel and this was first done in the same month.

These and other apparently parochial matters were the problems of a new undertaking.

†but not until other mishaps had followed.

The Racecourse Platform was in the news in October – Watson & Smith wanted £166 8s. 0d. for building it when £71 10s. 0d. had been agreed. It was left to Gelling & Kaye to move the ticket offices from Douglas to the Platform on race days, but what happened at Douglas in consequence is not clear; the same firm also began supplying replacement wooden 'break blocks'.

Economies now edged-in; passenger traffic was falling away and other traffic had not yet developed so to reduce expenses six employees at Douglas were dismissed, and one at Peel. A brighter light on the non-passenger business shone when the IOMM Co Ltd. asked for the rate from Douglas to Foxdale, for coal and lead ore. [Vignoles had recommended a tramway to serve Foxdale and possibly a continuation to Ballalonney on the Castletown Line, but thought a wire ropeway would be cheaper.] The Mining Co. was asked to make a depot at St John's instead of Douglas. Continuing the search for economy, it was agreed that a second driver was unnecessary in the winter and a Foreman/Engine Driver could be appointed to oversee the repair work.

A Mail Contract @ £80 per annum was now obtained: this put special problems at the feet of the Railway. When the steamer was late, how long should the train be held? The final arrangement was that the 7.30 pm ex-Douglas for Peel should be detained up to half an hour; this followed a trial period when the train would be held 'if the Mail Packet is in sight', an arrangement open to all kinds of abuse.

A nice little piece of business came about when the carcases of three pigs, killed on the line at Union Mills, were sold for 2s. 6d., and the claim was reduced thereby. Evidence of signalling development is seen in an account from Thomas Radcliffe for supplying Train Staffs for £4 6s. 0d. The now-familiar matter of a Douglas Harbour Tramway arose again and was deferred, the Board reckoning the line should be under the control of the Harbour Commissioners. Watson & Smith claimed further expenses on the Opening Day, the arrangements for which appear to have been especially lavish; they had altered the Peel Drill Shed, paying for Police and Band and put up the decorations.

Problems now loomed over the private level crossings where the arrangement was that users should open and close the gates themselves; landowners now claimed compensation for doing this work and, faced with what appeared to be a perpetual problem, the General Purposes Committee agreed that 'a small cottage', which would be rent free, be put up at each 'and a person appointed who could labour on the line'. Thus, cottages were now erected where appropriate on the Peel Line, whilst the Port Erin Line had them from time of opening.

Out on the Port Erin Line, Watson & Smith were having an unhappy time with the earthworks: their workmen were said to be idle and had returned to the autumn fishing. Now that MacKenzie had gone, there was no supervision and Greenbank was called in to supervise temporarily: only 350 men were now employed on the scheme and it was falling behind schedule. Watson asked for more money in view of rising costs. There was a proposal to move their equipment to a Ramsey Line if the Government would agree to advance the necessary capital at a low rate of interest but the Government was not inclined to listen. There were dreams of extending the Port Erin Line down to the troublesome new breakwater ('the new landing stage') but how the difference in levels could be overcome is not made clear. Ramsey folk, foreseeing the end of railway building with the completion of the Port Erin Line, pressed for a horse-bus to link their town with trains at Peel.

The Highways Board complained that Watson & Smith had made the road overbridges at Oakhill and Kirk Braddan too narrow. Watson & Smith excused delay by saying the heaviest works 'were remote from the working population'. But by December, the contractors had 420 men working on the South Line. Shortly afterwards, they came out on strike. It was decided that station buildings on that Line, with the exception of Castletown and Port Erin, be 'much in the same style of that constructed at Union Mills . . .'

Although his Report is missing, Rich's requirements of 28th June previously come through at this late time; they included:–

> Completion of unfinished work on the Peel Line including ballasting.
>
> Signals at Douglas, Crosby, St John's and Peel to be moved further away from the nearest pointwork and locking with the points. In this matter he was anxious to avoid undue expense and recommended the Distant Signals at Douglas, Peel (and Port Erin when installed) be moved away from the stations, and 'Station Signals' locked with facing points.
>
> Fang bolts in addition to ordinary dog spikes be used. (Vignoles disagreed with this on the score of being unnecessary and expensive and compromised by adding them to the outside of curves only).

It was now the turn of Rixon (London Board Solicitor) to make recommendations (November); based on the Company's contract with men at Douglas and Peel (the former being provided with a Company horse and cart) to carry luggage, parcels etc. to and from the station, he again raised the matter of Ramsey which might be served by 'a one-horse car to carry four passengers and the driver'. The first horse provided for Douglas 'would not draw in harness' and one had to be hired instead: costing £30, it was sold for £20. Advertising now reached the mainland and IOMR posters would now appear on LNWR stations; Rixon lay behind this. He also added his views on the Port Erin extension, saying that a line to Ramsey was more important, the equipment would be there when the South Line was complete and it only needed someone to persuade the Insular Government to advance the capital.

The existing telegraph system on the Peel Line should be taken over by the Government it was insisted, and the poles and apparatus for the Port Erin Line should be installed at Government expense, it was claimed. And the Government was moved so to do. Peel now received gas lighting.

The employees who took part in early and critical train tests were again in trouble; Guard Hogg (*as noted*) had been dismissed for drinking and now W.D. Wilson, engine driver, had been discharged – reasons not given.

The year ended on an upbeat note:

> The longest train yet to run left Peel 26th December, 1873 at 10.30 pm. It had two locomotives and twenty-eight carriages, and was a Special for those attending the Manse Readings at Peel for the benefit of the poor of that town.

Arrangements were made for more locomotives and carriages from Beyer, Peacock and Metropolitan respectively and a new horse cart for Douglas had to be bought 'rather than the old one break down in the street'. A contract with the IOMM Co. @ 4s. 6d. per ton for ore was agreed and Vignoles was to 'put up any kind of shed at St John's which might accommodate the traffic' – it could be that the Mining Co. considered this to be somewhat cavalier treatment with consequences yet to come.

Watson & Smith discovered they were owed for laying a 'Holland Cover' on the floor of the Drill Shed for 1st July, but the Board would not entertain recompense. So ended 1873, a year of anticipation, celebration, anxiety and problems. For the Isle of Man in general and the railway promoters in particular, there had never been a year like it and there has probably been none ever since.

Rich's comments were set down on 28th June, the date his Inspection finished; they included:

1. The railway was 'incomplete in many ways'.
2. The ruling grade was 1 in 78 and the sharpest curve 10 chains radius. It was desirable to reduce the grade to 1 in 260 at Union Mills and St John's stations.
3. Stations were unfinished and would need clocks.
4. Gatekeepers' lodges were too small for them to be lived-in. Level crossing gates needed stops to prevent them blowing about, and signalling. Gates at 4 miles 13 chains were too narrow for the road (i.e. at Close Mooar). Check rails had to be fitted at all level crossings.
5. Sleepers were of half-round section, 6 ft × 9 in. × 4½ in.; there were nine under a 21 ft rail which was flatbottomed, 45 lbs per yard. Ballast was of stone, sand or gravel, 'deficient in quality and quantity, and needs packing'. Sleeper ends needed boxing-up with ballast, and rails 'should be bent to suit curves'.*
Each rail needed three fang-bolts per length – i.e. at ends and in the middle: existing dogspikes would soon work loose so the line 'should be worked at moderate speed'.
6. Fencing was mostly galvanised wire on wooden posts, 9 ft apart: it was incomplete and had numerous openings.
7. Supporting brackets for the telegraph wires had been fixed within the arches of the three overbridges; they would foul a carriage door if opened and were to be moved.
8. Old retaining walls at Braddan and Union Mills were collapsing under the weight of the additional road filling which had been placed on top of them. They had to be buttressed.
9. There were eight bridges or cattle creeps in wrought iron under the lines: they deflected slightly when loaded. Their masonry was too near the girders and being shaken by trains; the feet of piers would need protecting from floods: their wooden platforms were a fire hazard. Some had dangerous openings and all must be 12 ft wide minimally.
10. There were 'sidings' at Douglas, Crosby, St John's and Peel, but none at Union Mills. The distance between running line and siding was 7 ft.
11. Signals: these 'flew to clear when the lever was released'. They must be arranged conversely. The east signal at Quarter Bridge was obscured by boscage.

---

*Presumably many curves were 'dog-legged'.

'Distance' signals at Union Mills were too near the station (in the United Kingdom they are at least 650 yards from the station): 'they will answer as presently only if no siding is put in there'. The signal levers should be brought together at once.

Signals at Douglas, Crosby, St John's and Peel must be moved 250 yards from the nearest points to be seen by a driver 550 yards away, and points on the running line must be locked with the signals.

12. At Douglas a pair of points must be removed, and buffer stops placed at the end of the Peel arrival line 'to prevent the engine over-running the station and falling into the water'.*
13. It was 'desirable' to have turntables at the termini.
14. Traffic must be worked on the Train Staff system.

1874

It was not until early in 1874 that some peace began to settle over the battle between landowners/occupiers and the railway concerning the Peel Line fencing. The General Purposes Committee, which had taken up the matter with Vignoles to investigate, found he backed the contractor whom everyone else blamed. This put the Committee in a pickle. It claimed that Watson & Smith's fencing out of Douglas was 'fair' but from there and through the Ballahutchin Estate, the five-wire fence with posts at 9 ft intervals had in places become three-wire and these were held up by stones; sheep could easily come through it while horses grazed along the line and jumped the fence with ease. Complaints included:

> ... my sheep were on the Railway having got through the fence ... the driver of one train had to hold up while someone on the train drove the sheep away – they got through the wires again and into a newly-thinned turnip field ... at the same time a fat cow jumped over the wire fence and got into a corn field. Only let the old women and nervous old gentlemen get to know that cattle and sheep are constantly on the line and I will warrant that there are not many passengers.

Ultimately, the growth of thorn hedges diminished the problem.

A curious scheme comes to light in a letter from William Lewis to G.W. Dumbell on 6th January, 1874. This proposed a railway which would leave the Douglas–Peel Line, carry on northwards up the valley of the Glas to below Glenville and then northeast towards Hillberry, so following down the Groudle river to Port Groudle. The object of this scheme is not clear unless there were personal reasons for the destination. The idea had no consequences.

Early in January arrangements were made with Lumsden, a carrier, to cart IOMM Co goods between Foxdale and St John's.

In typical fashion, Henry Loch the Governor, using the powers given to him, called on the Company to replace the level crossing at Quarter Bridge with an overbridge on his terms: the Governor was given a suitable reply and the crossing remained to the end.

---

*The remains of 'The Lake'.

The year started off with New Year's Day Specials for sports at Strang Racecourse and a Temperance Tea Festival in Douglas, with another running for the Oddfellows' Ball on 5th January. There had been a new timetable published each month but January marked the end of this practice and they now appeared weekly in the newspapers.

Teetotal spies made complaint to the papers on 8th January concerning a 'Hush Shop' being run at Peel station where spirits were being resold by the glass when only a wholesale licence was held. Some customers became so drunk that they could not perform their employment e.g. the man in charge of the local Public Weighing Machine. Lights were not being extinguished until 11 pm and the correspondent was sure railway officials would fall under the influence of the 'Demon Drink' and risk the safety of the public. It seemed that the name 'Peel' was synonymous with 'drink'.

The Mail Contract to commence 22nd January, required the railway timetable to be altered to allow mails from Peel to reach the steamer at Douglas. Flexibility up to 30 minutes was allowed for Douglas sailings as the harbour there was tidal and ship arrival times varied.

The new railway was bringing Island events within the reach of many; trains were now used to carry the public to places for the laying of foundation stones, grand concerts etc. with ill-effect on train timekeeping. Speculative building at Crosby was advertised, emphasising that houses were near the new railway.

On 10th January, Robert Waid suffered a broken leg when the embankment fell on him at Ballaquaggin (sic); (there was a similar accident two weeks later). Oakhill and Ballakelly cuttings were not complete by June so 200 men were imported and paid 4s. 0d. a day, which was considered very liberal.

The General Purposes Committee, now flexing its muscles somewhat and without knowledge of London, ordered ten Gold Passes for a sum of £35 10s. 0d. Rixon, who had recommended Frederick Henry Trevithick for the post of Superintendent of the Line, said 'but he was not to be responsible for the track until it had been repaired after recent flooding'. Both the Douglas and Peel ends of the line were wont to suffer from swollen river water, being also affected by tidal conditions.

The SUN (10th January, 1874) reported that:

> On 8th January another serious accident occurred at Glenfaba on the IOMR due to a heavy fall of rain which has taken place this week ... the engine driver on coming around the curve and seeing, although it was hardly daylight by this hour of the morning, that the permanent way had been washed away by the swollen river, strenuously attempted to avoid dangerous ground ... the engine was reversed and full steam put on to avoid an accident ... on reaching part of the bank which was unsupported, the engine toppled over and fell into the river: one engine man was rescued after holding onto the engine for ten minutes, by a man who attempted to warn the crew of the danger ... the other was washed some distance before recovering his foothold ... only one passenger was in the train and was in the last carriage and escaped ... one or two carriages were overturned ... the engine still lies in the river, three feet under the water.*

---

*Train was 7.50 am from Peel, Thursday 8th January. DERBY plus four carriages, Driver Steele and Fireman Smith. H. Greenbank – Engineer. (The TIMES, 10th January, 1874.)

(At a subsequent date the railway was realigned 20 ft from its original centre line.)

Trevithick† took up duty on Monday 26th January and lost no time in making his presence known. He wanted coal stores at Douglas and Peel and the erection and equipping of a workshop at Douglas, 'at present the railway is entirely without'. He also suggested a bookstall for Douglas station. On signalling he disagreed with his predecessors as to signals.‡ Distant Signals were essential but 'main or home signals' not so; signal arms should never 'be lowered entirely as this makes them look like telegraph posts, instead, the arms should be left in the position usually understood to imply caution'. (This confirms the original signals were used in the-then customary three-position system i.e. horizontal for danger, down 45° for caution and fully vertical for clear, the arm falling into a slot in the post.) There were at that time no signal lamps and Trevithick deplored the necessity for staff to walk to a signal at night to check its indication in the dark.

He wanted revolving lamps placed on signals and the winches which operated the signals brought together into the station instead of being near the signal. He disliked the proposed junction of Peel and Port Erin Lines outside Douglas; instead they were to be carried into Douglas station as two separate Up and Down single lines from the position where both came together on level ground. Other deviations recommended were:

> Peel – to move the station in anticipation of the Ramsey Line being built (this was not carried out).
> Castletown – to move the station nearer town.
> Ballacraine – to improve alignment.
> Ballasalla – ditto.
> Nunnery – to meet Major Taubman's wishes.
> Ballaquiggin – to avoid excessive compensation for land taken.

A contract* was entered into in 1885 with Messrs Creggan for conveyance of lime from the long-established Billown quarries near Ballasalla; 'Wharves and sidings' were put in at the station, and from 1890 the facility was advertised in the public timetable. [Later, a branch was considered to serve this quarry.]

By February the oil-lighted Douglas, like Peel before it, became gas-lit. Both stations were deprived of train services for three days in the same month, when floods severed the line between St John's and Peel and road carriages were substituted. Cash became as scarce as fine days in that wet winter and Watson & Smith agreed to be paid in Lloyd's Bonds, to be exchanged for Debentures as soon as the Company was able to arrange it, the Bonds to be held to the order of John Pender MP for £7,222 (later increased to £12,076). In mid-March, £40,000 in Mortgage Debentures were authorised to take the heat out of the financial difficulties.

---

†Born in 1843, he was a son of Frederick Henry Trevithick and a nephew of Francis Trevithick, Locomotive Superintendent of the LNWR: he had been a pupil at The Hayle Foundry founded by his grandfather, John Harvey. He entered the Crewe Drawing Office in 1862 and later became Manager of the Danish Railways until they became state-owned in 1868; later he went to the Central Pacific Railroad, California. His time on the IOMR was short for he succeeded W. Barton Wright as Locomotive Superintendent of the Madras Railway. Trevithick died young, in Exeter, in 1893.

‡? a reference to disc signals.

*not seen.

The Postmaster General agreed to take over the telegraphs and a publicity drive with placards had its expenses shared with the Steam Packet Co., with whom then and later there was always cordial interplay.

In March Vignoles warned the Board that a shortage of labour was looming and that the date for finishing the Port Erin Line (1st July) was in jeopardy.

The desire of the London directors to have some independent account of the state of the 'solidarity of the works' (as the Minute has it) had resulted in the afore-mentioned visit of Sir Charles Hutton Gregory to inspect the completed Peel route and the unfinished South Line works; he was, at one time, President of the Institution of Civil Engineers with whom he had been associated since 1838. [Born in Woolwich on 14th October, 1817, son of an illustrious father, he wished to become a sculptor. However, he was apprenticed to Thomas Bramah to become a Millwright and Engineer. He then became assistant to Robert Stephenson on the Manchester & Birmingham Railway. His later appointments were numerous and far-ranging and around the time of his visit to the IOM, he was Consulting Engineer to the Government of Trinidad Railways and the Cape Government Railways. He frequently advised on decisions of railway gauge and acted as an arbitrator. He died on 10th January, 1898.] He was also to recommend an exact site for Castletown station which, by bringing the line southwards in a wide sweep, could touch the north fringe of the town instead of being perhaps a mile from it. In due season this course was thus amended and the route became longer. Gregory was paid £136 10s. 0d.

Gregory too, sensed that all was not well with the contractor's labour force and said 'They show want of energy'. He stipulated that four timber trucks were ordered and two new locomotives; the latter became LOCH and MONA. Extra land would be needed at Douglas for improved facilities, and Taubman (whose land it was) agreed to sell.

The Press reported the arrivals of the new locomotives and carriages which all went into the Peel Line requirements; the engines were 'giving great satisfaction'. Pocket watches were now provided for gate-keepers.

By a new timetable from 1st April, trains crossed each other (at Crosby) for the first time.

An extra £2,000 was paid to the contractors to improve the constructional position for, if the line was not open by the 1st July, the summer traffic would be lost; the General Purposes Committee passed this suggestion to the London directors for approval, which was given. By this time Adams was also accepting payment by Debentures.

In April the inhabitants of Greeba and Quine's Hill asked for stations in their respective districts, and the matter was left open. Cash now allowed the contractors to be given Preference Shares in lieu of the Lloyd's Bonds. The Company received an unexpected £100 from J.F. Crellin the land-owner, for the erection of a cottage and provision of a person to operate the crossing gate at Malew. Crellin insisted that the gates be left closed across the railway, but this could not be countenanced. Further good news included that the erection of telegraph poles along the Port Erin Line would be done by the Postmaster General and not the Company: the Mining Co. signed another contract for two years for the carriage of coal @ 1s. 3d. per ton.

The paper of 2nd May had 'A number of handsome carriages were brought by the DOUGLAS from Liverpool'. When Peel refreshment room opened in May, there were complaints that no strong drink was available on Sundays.

An example of the recklessness of young men employed was instanced by an accident to four young Douglas lads working three miles from Castletown on 18th June. They were engaged in taking 'jumpers' to and from the blacksmith's to be sharpened, and carrying gunpowder for blasting purposes. One of them had rested the red-hot implement on the side of a cask of gunpowder whereupon it fell into the cask; the explosion threw the four into the air. One of them died later in hospital. The Head Constable had not advised the Governor on the day of the accident as he was fearful that the Governor would not have approved the usage of the telegraph in the late evening in such cases.*

By June, eleven miles of the Port Erin system was laid with track. Vignoles' forecast had proved correct and Manx labour, dissatisfied with pay, returned to summer fishing, so Welsh and Irish labour was imported. Some men from the Island were induced to return by the lure of extra pay. Masonry work was ready and earthworks nearly complete and permanent way materials were on the Island but not all were laid. However, gates and fencing were done.

At the Annual General Meeting in Athol Street on 12th June, 1874, a dividend on Ordinary Shares at 2% was declared. Returns included:

Passengers carried	(ten months)	193,425
Train miles	"	31,054
Gross receipts	"	£6,405 8s. 5d.

The season had been short and very wet.

At Douglas there were four facing points in the main lines and the signalman had to move from one to another and also to the relevant signal (one existing and two authorised): Trevithick was allowed to connect all by rods and levers 'to one convenient spot'.

There was a special service for Tynwald Day (5th July) but the railway could not cope as inevitably everyone wanted to leave Douglas at the same time:

> three/four engines were in use ... 25 carriages in a train ... 13–16 persons per compartment ... suffocating ... from Douglas at 11.10 am ... engine hardly exceeded 6 mph and ran out of water before Crosby ... the ceremony was over when it reached St John's.

Some newspaper reports said 'the line leaving Castletown is on embankment until near Ballanorris where there is a stopping place with accommodation for the populous district of thereabouts including Ballabeg'. (Actually, there was no formal stopping place for some years, and then it was Ballabeg by name.)

The Port Erin Line was a far tougher proposition than the line to Peel: between Douglas and Ballasalla the route lay across the lie of the land and heavy earthworks were required. From thence the track was almost level, right into Port Erin. An experimental train ran on 25th July and made the

*Manx Museum: G0/29/83.

return journey in 40 minutes. On 30th July, Col Rich made a preliminary inspection which sufficed enough to gain his permission to open the line the next day.

Saturday 1st August saw the South Line open for public traffic. Though sixteen trains each way were provided, 'traffic was beyond anything that had been anticipated' with trains 'crowded to excess' to the extent that people were left behind at stations. Despite this new emphasis, traffic on the Peel Line was maintained, though it had had to be curtailed to release stock for the new line. The 56 coaches available for business were divided into four trains, two for each route; Trevithick urged the Board to order another train and locomotive for the Port Erin Line. On the opening day, two new engines for that line had arrived. The TIMES of 1st August pointed out that it had been intended to open the line on the previous Wednesday but owing to Col Rich's heavy diary, this could not be done until the Friday when at 10 am the train left accompanied by Vignoles, Adams, Greenbank and Trevithick. The paper gave a long, tedious description of the new route, hardly omitting any culvert.

August found the railway serving the Peel Regatta and the Metropolitan Regatta at Castletown: for the latter, the first two and last two trains of the day ran the full length of the South Line – the remainder worked into Castletown from Port Erin and Douglas respectively; 5,582 passengers were carried, the takings being £139 19s. 11d. The weather was poor. Race Days took place on 13th and 14th August and a train ran every twenty minutes to Peel and back. On 8th September the 'Isle of Man Derby'* was held at Peel for which a special was run, as was one for the Douglas Pantomime the same evening. The islanders were experiencing a great widening of their existences.

The additional system was not easy to work having crossing loops only at Ballasalla and Castletown: one at Santon to increase capacity was essential; one at Port Soderic (sic) was highly desirable to cope with the Sunday evening traffic from Douglas. Colby needed a loop as when special or extra trains were run, the existing timetable had to be suspended for the lack of it. On the Peel Line the pressure of business at the Racecourse Platform made a loop at Union Mills essential to avoid sending trains out from Douglas with an engine at each end. Peel refreshment room was so successful that one was to be built at Port Erin too, 'in similar style'.

Whilst it would seem from the foregoing that Watson & Smith had fulfilled their contract, the opening on 1st August (a month later than envisaged) disguised some last-minute problems. In the first week of July, Watson claimed he was not being paid promptly enough and that if he could not therefore pay his men, they would walk off the job; he would need £150 at once to meet that obligation. The General Purposes Committee was alarmed and advanced him the money, at the same time wiring Rixon to come to the Island. Two days later Rixon gave authority for £1,000 to be paid to Watson on account of work done whilst the remainder of the unfinished assignment was to be done by direct labour of the Railway Company. Within ten days Greenbank was appealing for £1,500 to pay the men sufficiently to complete

---

*first ran at Derbyhaven c.1630.

the works; this also was advanced and so it was not surprising that the actual opening, in contrast to the razmattaz at the opening of the Peel Line, went off without ceremony.

In mid-August, the Postmaster General agreed to pay £100 annually for conveyance of mails on the Port Erin Line.

Now and again the postponed St John's–Ramsey Line was considered by the London meeting, and it was explained to them that the mineral and goods traffic was as yet undeveloped. The General Purposes Committee was instructed to find ways and means of attracting fresh capital for the Ramsey project.

On 1st July, the Hon F.A. Stanley, a director, had resigned in order to take up a Government post and Lord Skelmersdale* took his place. At the Board Meeting of that day it was agreed to tool the Douglas Workshops, find a site there for a Carriage Shed, and build a siding and wharf at Colby. Due to 'Government men . . . moving wires laid down for crossing gate signals', and the telegraph not working properly, communications had gone adrift.

The Company's timetable appearing each week in the TIMES, now included the Port Erin Line; it was the only evidence that the system was now more than double the length of the Douglas–Peel section. Although not apparent then, the IOMR was to build no more railways: the existing system had cost £9,875 per mile, largely due to its substantial nature and the high cost of labour and materials at the time. Consolidation followed. Though it was intended that goods sheds should be built for Port St Mary and Port Erin, the South Line was opened without any at all. Col Rich did not actually pass the Port Erin Line for public traffic before 31st August when the line had actually been open for a month. The whole island knew of the progress and on 2nd August a train of twenty-one carriages travelled the line. Many passengers were left behind, such was the shortage of carriages. A new venture was the provision of through carriages from Port Erin to Peel and back at 9.38 am and 3.38 pm (from Port Erin) and 10.11 am and 4.05 pm (from Peel), running every day except Sundays. Shortage of carriages limited the extension of the timetable, and a Prospectus was issued to secure £22,000 by Preference Shares to meet that need.

Once the Port Erin Line was operational, Trevithick came back with additional 'wants'; goods sheds must be built at Ballasalla, Castletown and Port St Mary; urinals were needed at each and every South Line station (what provision did people make for themselves until that time, one asks?!); 'there must be a 'sunk siding' at Douglas and a weighbridge at St John's'; Ballasalla needed (and duly received) a raised wharf 'for tipping lime' and the cattle pen there was already too small; Douglas Workshops required enlarging already and finally, he needed one more engine and eighteen more carriages for the 1875 season.

During the year, rumblings of discontent were heard from Ramsey; there had been a meeting in the Courthouse on 31st March 'to secure extension of railway communication', stressing that when the Port Erin Line was finished, the equipment to build to Ramsey would be available. The meeting was not well-attended but on 30th April a deputation waited on the

---

*Lord Skelmersdale. (Bootle-Wilbraham) (1837–1898). In 1874 Provincial Grand Master for Lancashire: a prominent figure in Free-masonry. Captain of the Yeoman of the Guard and Lord Chamberlain. Became Earl of Lathom 1880.

Governor to propose a guarantee from the Island Government to secure interest on money borrowed for the construction of such a line. The newspapers referred to such moves as a 'sine qua non to all those who are not dawdlers and drivellers and can only see to the end of their noses ... the line was being pressed for because of the mining companies'.

As winter approached, the timetable was arranged to be worked by two engines on the Port Erin and one on the Peel Line; owing to poor timekeeping, late trains had to be run in November. These were called 'Goods Trains' in the timetable and presumably the Company allowed passengers thereon whilst taking no responsibility for timekeeping ... Specials were run at Hollantide* and Christmas.

With the weather deteriorating, complaints flowed in – there was a lack of carriages on Port Erin trains; the refreshment rooms had closed for the winter; waiting rooms had no fires; there were no quick connections between Port Erin and Peel trains at Douglas; if tides required the departing steamer to leave early, morning trains did not arrive in Douglas to catch it; there were passengers with 3rd class tickets using 1st class compartments ... and so on.

When two carriages were derailed at Peel, they had to be left behind. On 21st October, a gale blew the goods shed there into the road but luckily it was 6.30 am and no one was about. The same wind blew the crossing gates off their hinges and knocked over the gateman. In September, a milepost was placed by vandals across the rails on the South Line.

On Sunday 2nd November, the 6.30 pm from Douglas ran over Lewis Corkhill, a blacksmith, who was lying in the track between Ballasalla and Castletown; he had been drinking heavily and had come by the 5.15 pm from Port Erin and started to walk back down the track to Castletown.

The customary winter flooding stopped all trains on the Ballalonney embankment on the 8th December and made the bridge so precarious that it had to be shored up with timber. Trains worked either side of the spot and no through workings passed for three days.

The year of 1874 was one of extreme weather.

The eleven Reports from Vignoles or Trevithick during 1874 give illuminating insight into the first months of operating the Peel Line and the opening of the Castletown Line which, in its turn, brought fresh troubles.

Vignoles (15th January) stressed the extent of the flood damage to the civil engineering around Douglas when the river left its banks half a mile above the town: by and large, it stood the test well. Floods were due to a considerable fall of snow on 7th January; a sudden thaw meant that the rivers could not take the immediate volume of water. The river at Quarter Bridge was then – and was to be – a weak spot. It was otherwise at the Peel end where, at Glenfaba, the river had carried away the retaining wall, resulting in the train falling into the river where the track was unsupported and Driver Steele was injured. Carriages were lifted out the same day but the engine needed two days' work; meanwhile omnibuses carried passengers westwards from St John's. The carriages were manhandled down to Peel on their own wheels and in due course, the engine also. A temporary track with sharp curves enabled services to resume; a permanent diversion was to be put in hand immediately.

---

*Hollantide (Bank Holiday in November) originally the Fair Day when farm labourers were hired for the following year.

Plate 1: A posed photograph of the unfinished Douglas terminus in early 1873 with staff in their new uniforms. Half-round sleepers are prominent and a pile on one line seems to be serving as a 'buffer stop'; the nearer line ends in a single sleeper.
Manx Museum

Plate 2: Several years later there are many additions; bookstall on left, palings and fencing, buffer stops (the nearer with a hefty pile of earth and stone behind it) and lamps bracketted to the building. *Collection B.E. Crompton*

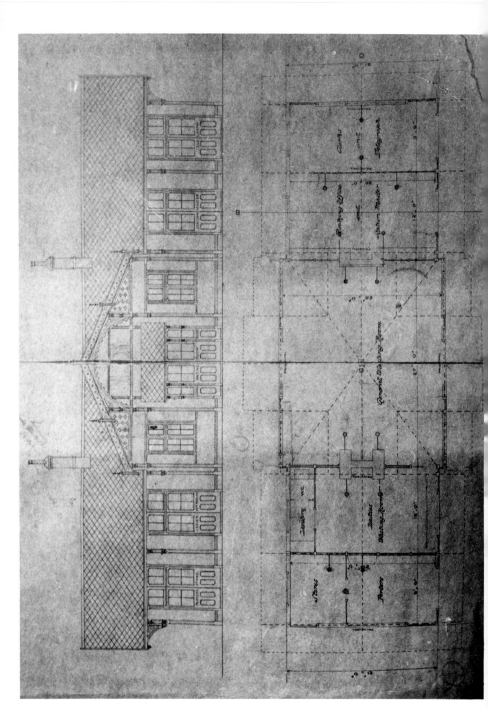

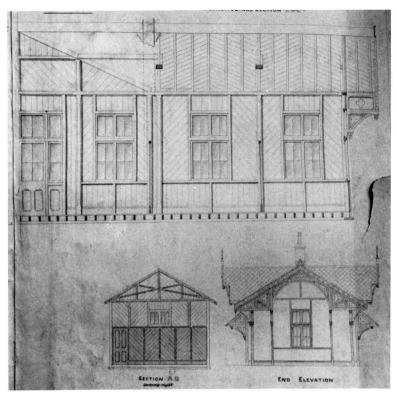

Plate 4:

Plate 5:

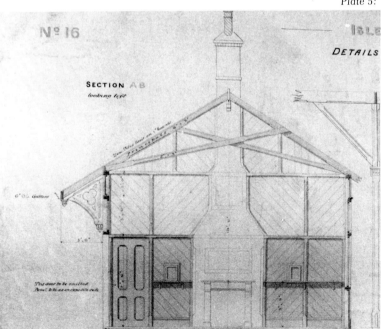

Plate 7: The 'Second Class' station at Peel can be discerned beyond the decks of Peel-registered 'Manx Nickies' laid up until the fishing season begins.
Collection J.I.C. Boyd

Plate 8: A late-1890s view of Peel, with engine No. 8 attached to a train of close-coupled four-wheeled stock (the last vehicle however, is a bogie coach). Illumination by courtesy of the adjacent gas works.
Collection J.D. Darby

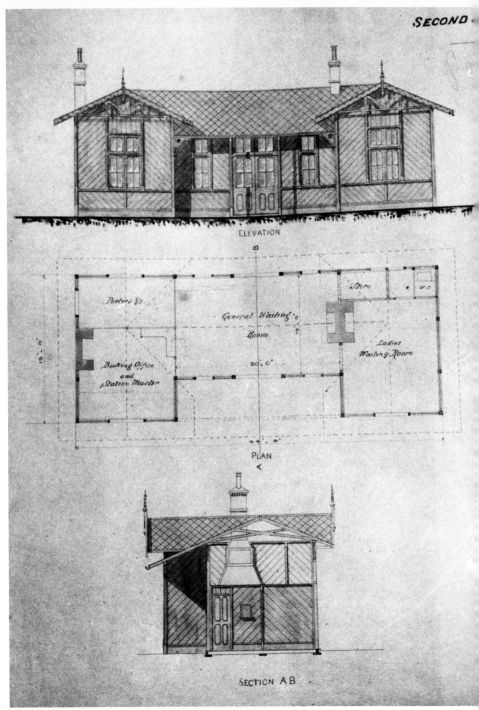

Plate 9: 'Second Class' station drawing, with diagonal boarding and zinc tiles. Peel is believed to have been the only station constructed to this drawing.   *I.O.M. Railway*

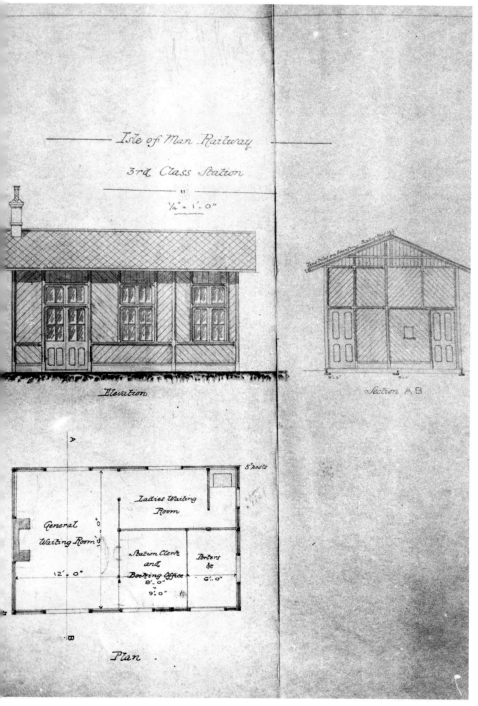

Plate 10: 'Third Class' station drawing. Crosby and St John's stations were built to this design, but it was not to be found on the South Line. *I.O.M. Railway*

Plate 11: St John's on Tynwald Day, 1932, showing temporary rope barriers to prevent passengers crossing the line except by the footbridge, and the 'Third Class' station building. The engine is No. 16, making one of its rare visits off the South Line. *C.E. Box*

Plate 12: South Line stations did not conform to the recommended classifications as did all those on the Peel Line; a notable South Line exception was Castletown, a substantial structure in local stone, with a verandah added in 1902. Note the traffic in milk in churns. April 1950. *J.D. Darby*

Plate 13: Port Erin before 1902, with engine No. 5 running chimney-first back to Douglas. Raised platforms and the new station building have yet to appear. The guard's composite bogie coach next to the engine is No. 19, the first to have double luggage doors; much of the rear of the train is of close-coupled, four-wheeled stock. *Collection J.I.C. Boyd*

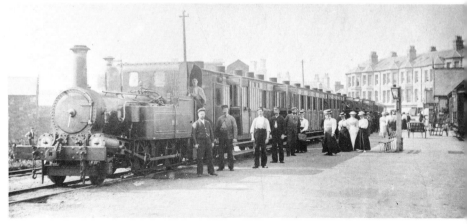

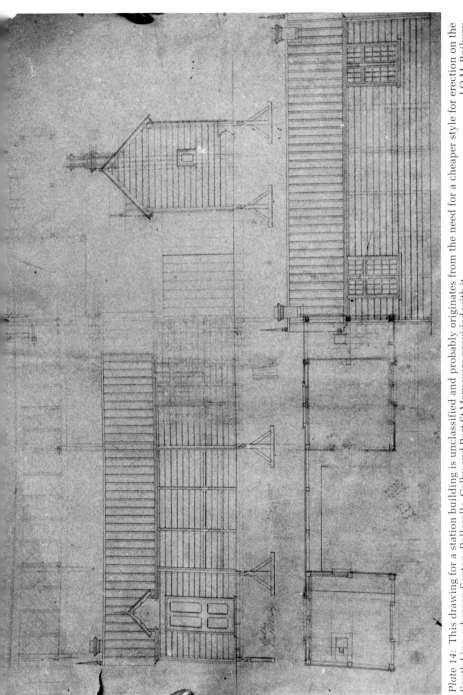

Plate 14: This drawing for a station building is unclassified and probably originates from the need for a cheaper style for erection on the South Line, whereon Santon, Ballasalla, Colby and Port St Mary were provided with it.
I.O.M. Railway

Plate 15: For many years Santon enjoyed the somewhat ghostly ima[ge of] a place which the Company rejects from time to time, accepts its re[turn] and it re-appears in the timetable. 'E' van body store shed and the ma[in] siding hoarding appear as dilapid[ated] as the station. April 1966.

J.I.C. B[oyd]

Plate 16: Colby in 1952, loo[king] towards Douglas, still retains its 1[890] station, with an 'E' van body pres[sed] into further life as a goods shed. Sta[tion] and nameboard were painted yel[low] with salmon-pink panelling [and] lettering. The roof was red oxide.

J.D. D[–]

Plate 17: Port St Mary before the t[urn] of the century would have long pro[ved] too small for its summer traffic; th[ere] does not even seem to be a space [to] hang the mainland railwa[y] advertisement boards! The corruga[ted] iron roof with its sun-blind effec[t is] most bizarre on this very conservat[ive] undertaking. [The image over the r[oof] of the booking office (*far left*) is n[ot a] disc signal but a blemish on [the] photograph.] *Collection J.I.C. B[oyd]*

Plate 18: Back at Douglas, this record of the opening day, 1st July, 1873, shows SUTHERLAND at the head of a train of four-wheeled carriages (painted in differing colours to denote class) with an open wagon in the centre to carry the Royal Bengal Fusiliers' Band; the Ducal Saloon is next to it. The engine sports the banner 'Douglas & Peel United' and its cab rear sheet has been removed, perhaps for ventilation.

Collection C.J. Jowett

Plate 19: A Port Erin train leaves Castletown (just visible on the right) to cross the Silver Burn. The engine is No. 7 with mixed bogie and four-wheeled stock; note how the roof-top lamps are offset on the short coaches. *Collection A. Lamberton*

Plate 20: The new Douglas signal box by Dutton & Co. Ltd. of Worcester has just been completed but the business of erecting the new carriage shed beyond is still in hand. The signal arms have centre-line spectacles and a white disc on the face of the arm. The counterweights are on the crossbar and as yet there is no means of climbing up to replenish the lamp reservoirs. The ganger at the foot of the staircase carries a rail-gauge and is dressed in heavy corduroy jacket and trousers. 1892.

Collection B.E. Crompton

Plate 21: Douglas goods yard from the sunken siding. Engine No. 2 on shunting duties, hauling open wagon M2 and roofless cattle wagons K6, K3 and K1. Note the load of hay cut from the lineside. Early 20th century.

F. Moore

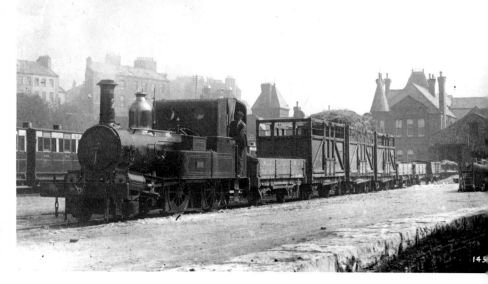

Plate 22: Special train at Douglas during the 'gas-lit' period. Raised platforms are in place but canopies are not erected; this suggests a date about 1904. It must have been an important occasion for uniform trains like this were uncommon. The Station Master holds the Single Line Staff, the first carriage is full of well-dressed ladies and G.H. Wood is in attendance. *Manx Museum*

Plate 23: Douglas about 1908, seen from an office window. A train from the South Line has just arrived and the engine has lost no time in running round. The dress of the passengers, the amount of hand luggage and the group around the luggage van suggests the holiday is ending and this train connects with the afternoon steamer departures. The two vehicles on the extreme right are ex-MNR stock, one a four-wheeled brake van and the other the through Ramsey–Douglas coach.
Collection J.I.C. Boyd

Plate 25: The railway side of Douglas station, possibly on the same occasion as the previous view. The stacked wicker baskets were used for coaling locomotives and are still labelled . . . on their way to the stores? The brush, together with the mop and bucket standing by the lineside notice, and the second brush leaning against the recently-built 'Gents' suggest a recent clean-up before the photograph. Four bolster wagons stand on the right.

Collection B.E. Crompton

Plate 26: Another memorable day – but for reasons unknown. No. 7 stands at the Peel platform, brake van No. F4 behind and bogie F6

Trevithick (9th February) confirmed he took over as General Superintendent on 26th January but Greenbank was to remain in charge of the permanent way until the above-mentioned flood damage had been repaired . . . 'I have been met by a very courteous and friendly spirit by the gentlemen and employees of the railway . . .' He found working arrangements could be improved and discipline among employees 'somewhat lax'. The mail contract meant changes to the timetable and anomalies existed in fares about which the public grumbled. The forty level crossings (nine having watchmen)

> . . . are a great source of uneasiness to me . . . an accident will happen sooner or later . . . these watchmen are of the most ignorant class and cannot be expected to exercise extraordinary vigilence . . . the watchmen should live at his post – instead of a hut big enough only to stand up and sit down, he should have a habitable hut. These men should also know train times, be provided with a timepiece . . . and be unmistakably warned . . . by an electric bell.

Two boxes already had clocks and four needed stoves and chimney.

Some Station Masters were living two or three miles from their stations: they had to be paid overtime when an extra train was due and in an emergency they might also be away from home. Residential accommodation was therefore essential.

The coal stocks lay unprotected and no check could be made of that used on trains . . . or stolen. Wooden enclosures at Douglas and Peel would prevent this.

Trevithick confirms there was at first no workshop, no tools and nowhere in the Island where repairs could be done:

> the existing engine and carriage shed is small for the purpose of a place of shelter for the engines and carriages for which it was designed, and inadequate to the requirements of a workshop . . . I recommend two buildings be erected opposite it on the other side of the main line.

(He then lists suitable machinery.)

> Douglas and Peel stations have a neglected and desolate appearance and need a little macadam, some fencing and ballast to give a more inhabited appearance. A bookstall would be both ornamental and profitable.

Union Mills was plagued by 'a crowd of idlers' and 30 ft of fence was needed to hold them back and prevent the ticket collectors being 'incommoded'. The urinal at Crosby was against the waiting room wall and could not be used; wooden buildings at stations were shrinking, and gaps in the planks needed filling with putty.

Trevithick had no good word for the telegraph instruments; they were complicated and delicate in construction and needed frequent adjustment . . . 'constantly out of order and quite unreliable'; Government offices had declined to install the pattern for the same reason. [They were of 'ABC' type and did not require operators to know Morse (or) Code to use them: Single Needle instruments (for Morse) were used by the Post Office and were simpler to maintain.]

The Distant Signals (two at every station) were too short and could not be distinguished from telegraph poles when the arms were fully down; they were the 3-position type with the arm falling into a slot in the post for 'Clear'. Trevithick intended never to allow the arms to fall lower than the 45° (Caution) position to avoid this confusion. The signals gave no light indication save red for danger and, if the lamp was modified to revolve bodily, it would show the signal position at night without the staff having to walk down the line to see the face of the fitting; the signal winches needed bringing together in the centre of the station. Points should be bolted and padlocked.

Trevithick was pleased with the locomotives '. . . as was to be expected from the makers of the reputation of Messrs. Beyer, Peacock'; there his praise ended. He found

> the carriages are not elegant or sumptuous in their appointments. Neither are they calculated to insure a maximum of comfort to the passengers; the springs are exceedingly hard and jerky in their action and the couplings will not admit . . . of being brought together close enough to check their mutual oscillation . . . but they are strong and substantially built . . .

Meanwhile J.T. Clucas was writing direct to Pender and causing trouble which Vignoles had to counter in a Report dated 11th February: it took the familiar pattern of a director concerning himself with matters on which he could have been informed before writing to London. Taubman had also been complaining. Matters were left to Rixon to take up with Vignoles whose comments include:

a. Slopes had not been soiled when the line was finished because the winter rains would have washed it off.
b. Crossing gates had not been made in oak but were of good quality larch, not in deal as suggested by Clucas.
c. Extra culverts would be needed at Pulrose Crossing and near the existing culvert at the engine shed to anticipate another flood.
d. The Douglas River diversion had been a direct advantage to the Railway, avoiding the expense of two iron girder river bridges; the bed of the old river was being filled by earth from Oakhill Cutting.
e. Clucas complained about abutment stonework and was told there were no large stones in the vicinity of bridge works and it would have been unreasonable for the contractors to be expected to cart them from beyond Castletown (Scarlett Quarry) or Peel, being the nearest points to procure large blocks.
f. When the carriage doors were open, they fouled Kirk Braddan and Union Mills road bridges, yet Col Rich had made no observation on inspection.
g. Vignoles defended the security of the line where it passed through The Congery, the section passing between sandhills beyond St John's. The flood had not injured this length.
h. At Creggans, the contractors had made an alteration to the line as originally set out, known as the 'Balla Salla Deviation', in order to save a cutting. The land for the original route had not been bought therefore there was no loss, and the contractor's benefit would also be that of the Company.
i. Taubman complained about 'fangbolts starting in hot weather'; he may have meant spikes.
j. Dependence on the telegraph was hapless – 'none of the employees understand it. A competent clerk used to manage the instruments but he had been dismissed at the end of the summer season, against Mackenzie's wishes'.

The nub of Vignoles' comment comes '... there has been a feeling throughout the construction ... on the part of the General Purposes Committee that the contractors were being unduly favoured at the Company's expense ... in many instances the contractor has done more than he could fairly have been called upon to perform'. In a Lump Sum Contract (it was explained) there must be 'give and take'. At St John's and Ballacraine the line was altered to give long straight runs to the advantage of the Company: to meet Taubman's objection to taking the line through his Estate, a cutting in rock was agreed upon by Watson & Smith.

Vignoles was slighted by the overall suggestion of a want of confidence in his ability, and was willing to accede to the Duke's suggestion 'that an Engineer of undoubted experience and standing should ... examine and report on all matters'. Sir C.H. Gregory was the man chosen ... and Vignoles 'fearlessly left the whole question in his hands'.

[Trevithick's Report of 14th February concerns a contract with the Foxdale Mining Co., and its worthiness: that of 21st March, a proposed Agreement with the Postmaster General as to telegraphs; a February item came from Taubman suggesting some 1st class carriages should have coupé-ends. (These are further discussed in Volume III.)]

On 1st June, Vignoles reported with the AGM in mind; the contractor had completed his six-month maintenance of the track since the Peel Line opening. As yet the habit of shopkeepers to continue to use local road transport, had not been interrupted. High praise was due to Watson & Smith for their progress on the South Line; Welsh, Irish and further internal labour had been necessary and now all track materials were on the Island: 11 miles had been laid and ballasted.

By Trevithick's Report of 20th August, 16 trains were running daily between Douglas and Port Erin ...

> not only filled, but crowded to excess ... beyond anything anticipated ... we have been quite outmatched ... large numbers of people left behind every day ... those who succeeded in obtaining seats complained of excessive overcrowding ... every day of the week every carriage is being dragged to and fro full of people ... it has been a regular thing to shut down the ticket wickets in the faces of a crowd of disappointed people ... passengers who got away could not get back ... it has been quite distressing.

Trevithick considered it might help if fares were raised at high season. 'Luckily the goods traffic is slack' in that season. The contract entered into with the Foxdale mines last April still required the sunken siding at Douglas and weighbridge at St John's. Such was the shortage of rails that it had become a choice of laying the sunken siding or putting in the much-needed loop at Santon: in the event, neither had been done and not a ton of Foxdale goods had been carrried in consequence. There being no goods shed '... goods are stacked in waiting rooms and well-dressed people protest at having to seek rest or shelter among piles of ham or sacks of flour'.

With no loop at Union Mills, Racecourse trains ran with an engine each end so as to return speedily to Douglas. (This method was frequently used in later years.)

1875

Early in the year the shortage of sidings was considered; the term 'through siding', meaning a loop, was currently in vogue, whilst 'blind' siding meant just that. It was agreed that loops should be made at Santon and Union Mills, and additional sidings at Colby and Port Soderick.* Five additional sidings were required at Douglas. As to signals, these were added at 'Closemoor', Ballagawne and Crogga crossings (those at the 'first two need only be of very simple construction') but at Crogga, Col Rich required a distant signal either side. Trevithick enquired as to Crogga and found it was seldom used: the landowner was already in dispute with the Company over the manning of the crossing but he was offered a cash sum, in consideration of which the gates would be left closed to the road in their normal position, and this would save the Company the wages of a 'watchman'. Two new ballast pits were to be provided, one at St John's and the other at School Hill on the South Line, in the deep cutting there. Existing sidings on the South Line were at Port Soderick, Santon, Ballasalla (for lime wharf), Castletown (lime wharf to be provided), Colby (?) and Port Erin. There were now 125 persons in employment, being 66 in the Traffic Department, 23 in the Locomotive Department, 32 on the Permanent Way and 4 in the Office. All the initial 52 four-wheeled carriages had been delivered, and their shortcomings were becoming obvious.

To encourage private house-building at Port Erin and Peel, the Company offered a Free Pass for ten years to new house owners, once twelve houses had been built. Against a background whereby there were more potential passengers than the Company could carry, this was a strange step. On Tynwald Day, passengers were carried 'in cattle trucks' and a boy was knocked out of one by the bough of a tree near Union Mills.

Money troubles persisted. Watson & Smith claimed £9,211 4s. 9d. still outstanding and issued a writ against the Company; in reply the London directors gave personal guarantees to bills paid by the General Purposes Committee in Douglas and authorised by London. It was now necessary to raise further capital to pay for land already taken, and the rails required for the loops and sidings just authorised.

A gentleman had adopted an appropriate name and had erected 'a refreshment room in connection with the Railway' at Castletown; he was 'Charles Ready Duck'. The dangerous habit of carrying gunpowder in the vans of passenger trains was stopped and perhaps with equal caution almost the whole of Watson & Smith's pointwork was condemned and, within a very limited time, new trackwork was built at Douglas from new materials, ready for the summer peak traffic.

In July, a train descending into Castletown ran into gates at Ballawoods as they were being opened by the woman gatekeeper, who was killed. The report stated 'Need for continuous brakes as it was 200 yards from gates when brakes were applied . . . this was the second accident there.' Gates were now recommended to be kept closed against roads.

---

*There was then no loop between Douglas and Ballasalla.

During August, Metropolitan delivered the last two passenger brake vans and the General Purposes Committee bought a supply of rails from Samuel Witham & Co with the sanction of the London contingent: Witham was paid by Bill at Six Months because the take-up of Preference Shares had not been wholly successful. Brown, Marshalls (carriages) and Beyer, Peacock (locomotives) had both received considerable sums for stock supplied and in September, the Duke of Sutherland called a meeting to consider the financial position of the Company after being informed that the subscribed capital of the Company was now exhausted. Brown, Marshalls politely reminded that they were owed a further £2,500 for carriages, and Trevithick submitted an estimate for a small station proposed for Ballabeg. He was prudent enough to add that a 'small building' was needed to house locomotives to separate them from the carriages and workshops at Douglas. About this time, James Brown & Son were permitted to build and man a bookstall at Douglas, and to save materials, the cattle pen at Ballasalla would be built out of old fencing.

If anything, October's cash position was worse. Brown, Marshalls were still shouting for payment, and the gist of letters from the Secretary to the Duke, Pender and Sheward was, 'Help'; London obliged by allowing payment by Bills. In a nasty accident at Ballasalla level crossing, Crellin the gatekeeper was killed by a passing train; gatekeepers and crossings continued to appear in this wise down the years. Evidence of that time reveals that certain gates were normally positioned to close against the railway but that others were under consideration for closure against the road; these were Pulrose, Cooilingle, Rhenny, Ballacurry, Ballawoods, Ballahick, Mill Road, Kentraugh and Colby (2 gates).

Money – or lack of it – again; this time Beyer, Peacock wanted £1,720 0s. 0d. and had added 5% for late payment. They appealed to Sheward and the account was met . . . less the 5%! To reduce costs, an investigation over employee levels was begun, and materials sent to landowners still embittered over inadequate fencing.

On 27th October, Police Inspector William Boyd reported to the Head Constable (Captain Monro) that Trevithick had been informed that after the 2.10 pm Castletown train left Douglas, two men had found stones on the track at the Nunnery Crossing. The same afternoon a workman found two pieces of wood driven into the timbers of the Crossing; he removed them. This length of line was frequently the scene of attempts to derail trains, more perhaps out of a sense of boredom or adventure, rather than one of spite.*

An interesting sidelight on Douglas station since the opening of both Lines was that the General Purposes Committee thereafter referred to it as comprising two stations, not one.

The telegraph instruments (the property of the Postmaster General) at this date were:

Peel Line – 'ABC Type'
Port Erin Line – 'Single Needle'

*Manx Museum: GO 29/214.

the former being more simple but slower, and the latter requiring a knowledge of the Morse Code. The latter was more efficient and the Company was pressing the Postmaster General to replace the Peel Line equipment with Single Needle Type.

Under the arrangements with the Postmaster General, the clerks operating the telegraph at railway stations were paid by him and the amount charged to the Railway; an additional charge on the Railway would arise if trains were suspended and the Postmaster General had to use substitute conveyances to carry mails – this occurred during times of flood, for instance.

So to the year's end. Trevithick gave notice of his resignation. 'He leaves in December to take up an appointment on Mexican Railways' said the SUN, which was incorrect. Before leaving Trevithick recommended that the posts of Secretary and Manager should be combined and a person found to superintend the working and repairs of rolling stock and maintenance of permanent way. Traffic matters could be in the hands of the Secretary. The General Purposes Committee accepted this suggestion from the date of Trevithick's departure (31st December) for India.

The matter of level crossings recurred; it was emphasised that the list previously considered were those over private roads and therefore it was not necessary to apply to the Governor for the gates to be closed against the road in the normal position; such would now be;

Pulrose, Cooilingle, Rhenny, 'Bell's', Crogga, Mill Road and Colby (2 gates); of the foregoing all but Pulrose, Crogga and Colby were to have added turnstiles for the use of pedestrians. At the following, the Company was compelled to keep the gates closed against the railway and with a person in charge:

Ballalonna, Ballastrang and Ballahick.

Another attempt was made in November to derail the train at the Nunnery by placing stones, timber etc. on the line ... the Company offered £20 reward for the apprehension of the perpetrator.

And what of a railway to Ramsey? Despite the lukewarm attitude of local people, a deputation had called on the Governor on 30th April, 1874, seeking a guarantee from the Island Government which would secure interest on any money borrowed for the construction of the line. Meanwhile on 21st April, 1875, the Governor Loch, wellknown for his backing for public enterprise and ultimate recipient of most Island complaints, had approached the IOMR Co on the subject; among other things, he seemed especially irritated by the monopoly which the road hauliers possessed. He told the Company that he would recommend the Legislature to promote a Government Guarantee on capital needed for a Ramsey Line in exchange for a lien (or mortgage) on ALL the company's property or, failing such a lien, on a part of the capital required.

The IOMR Co's directors Sutherland and Sheward did not look favourably on this – they feared that the Governor was putting public utility before commercial viability and that such a Line would forever be a millstone around the neck of the IOMR's present system. The Railway Company's reply was based on the findings of these two directors, firstly; that the Government should build the Ramsey Line, or secondly; that the Government should take over the IOMR Co on terms satisfactory to that Company.

Publicly, there was now an awesome silence as the idea developed into a feud as to what route a Ramsey railway should take. Some favoured the accepted plan of a line starting from St John's but other voices shouted 'Rubbish' and proclaimed that Glen Helen provided a natural and better-graded outlet to the north.

The annual supper of the IOMR employees took place in the engine shed on 29th December and was attended by approximately 200 men, making the Railway the largest employer in the Island. The room was 'well-lighted by a number of carriage and station lamps' and Trevithick was given a gold Albert, locket and pencil-case to remind him of the Island on the far-off Madras Railway. At 3 am special trains left for all stations.

During the year, the Glen Helen Estate was purchased by a company intent on developing 'a place for recreation' and the press reported 'a small station being erected at Ballacraine, the nearest point on the IOMR to the waterfall'; new traffic was expected from St John's Brick & Tile Works.* Final settlement for the Union Mills collision (16th July, 1873) was made; twenty persons received compensation and, together with medical and other expenses, the hardpressed-for-cash Company had paid out over £1,565 when the account closed in 1877.

As 1875 marked the end of the all-too-brief Trevithick period on the IOMR, it is helpful to review his influence on the infant railway. He was undoubtedly the man for the time and his Reports show his grasp of railway management, of the IOMR's shortcomings, his clear ideas of what was needed and demonstrate the unfinished state of the line when he was appointed. Never in the future would the Company enjoy the benefits of such resident expertise.

He quickly grasped the limitations which impeded the growth of goods traffic; such cart-roads as fed certain stations needed to be metalled as they were presently quagmires; the absence of any covered site at stations on the South Line meant farmers had to leave goods outside in all weathers and were threatening to return to road carriers. Passengers had no shelter at certain stations and six places had no urinals; Peel station boasted a cast-iron urinal and Port St Mary, Colby, Ballasalla, Santon, Port Soderick and Union Mills could enjoy the same feature for a total of £289.

Rain-sodden passengers embarking at Port Soderick (having been driven from the beach by a downpour), were forced to wait in the open. The Station Master, provided with a wooden 'Sentry Box' 'with hardly room to turn round in', would find himself penned in by a crush of angry passengers trying to find shelter; it was unacceptable in these circumstances that cash, tickets and documents were all open to view. Trevithick's answer was to bring the 'Box' from Santon and site it behind the existing one, joining the two together with a wooden roof and thus making a simple shelter.

The 8½ miles between Douglas and Ballasalla were a plain single line at the time and Trevithick's solution to the operating problems of a loop at Santon and a siding at Port Soderick should not be envisaged in a mainland context: such a loop would normally hold wagons for the convenience of farmers and be used to pass trains only on certain gala (sic) trains in

---

*These premises were shown on the promotional map of the IOMR as being on the north side of the line between St John's and Peel, a short distance from St John's.

summer, Castletown Regatta Day being the foremost. The siding at Port Soderick would enable the engine of a working from Douglas to 'abandon' 'Port Soderick Only' (and therefore empty) carriages in the siding and continue all the way to Port Erin, re-attaching them on return. (One wonders why it could not do so at Ballasalla loop and by what means the engine worked round the stock at Port Soderick where there was no complete loop – perhaps some primitive pole or rope methods were used?)

The proposed siding at Colby and loop at Union Mills would be used in the foregoing way, the latter essential for Race Days and Tynwald Day. Until all stations had goods sheds, wagons must be used as temporary storage in sidings – in this way the problem could be met, but temporarily until the patience of farmers ran out. Such sidings would also enable ballast and maintenance trains to move out of the way of passenger traffic; this facility was imperative as ballasting was far from complete.

Trevithick's conception of goods sheds for the South Line was one of an area 15 ft square with an external platform ramped at one end: Castletown would have to be larger and together with Port St Mary, would have a crane. He dismissed the idea of any more sheds being built in timber as rubble-masonry was not much more costly and was longer lasting.

Trevithick looked upon the whole of the Douglas station layout as but an interim measure, recognising that when the Ramsey Line was built the whole place would need re-organising and, with this in mind, his recommendations were for improvements of a short-term life. Current provision for sheltering carriages was a new shed (almost complete) and another idea was to board in the sides of Watson & Smith's shed where a further fifteen might be stored; with ingenuity this shed could be extended to cover another six. There was a Carriage Shed at Peel* holding five vehicles, and as there was always stock under repair in the Workshop, perhaps one third of the carriages could be covered. He needed rails to lay on the unoccupied side of Douglas' Peel platform, and for the whole of the near-ready Carriage Shed (a timber building with a felt-covered roof) which was awaiting track before it could be used.

And what of Santon now its 'Sentry Box' had been stolen for Port Soderick? Trevithick took an optimistic view, considering 'it was as good as Colby'; he further suggested an enginemen's and guards' room at Peel, alike to that he had just put up at Douglas. At the time, these men might have to wait 1–2 hours for the next working, and so made their way to the nearest public house where they were expected to 'pay their way' for shelter. At Douglas station there were two existing 'Booking Traps', insufficient on busy days and another booking office could be made from part of the present 1st class waiting room (as this class of passenger was not as numerous as anticipated, this would hardly inconvenience them).

The matter of extra signals was linked to the whole question of level crossings; Trevithick's overseas experience tempted him to abandon as many as he could, keeping gates closed against the road and putting cattle guards in the roadway to prevent animals getting onto the track – lambs

---

*an existing non-railway building, suitably re-constructed.

could penetrate gates. For £5 each, Closemooar and Ballagawne could be simply signalled, but the BoT wanted distant signals at Crogga and Trevithick hoped the landowner there would agree (for a cash consideration) to leave the gates closed; the watchman there was being paid 10s. 0d. a week by the Company. Level crossings 'cost £510 per annum for watchmen who are absolutely useless to us'.

Douglas Workshops were in full swing (sic) and had been fitted out with a 4 ft wheel-lathe (£305), a 8½ in. screw-cutting lathe (£70), a 10-stroke shaping machine (£70), a cylinder boring machine which would do its work without removing cylinders from the locomotive (£33) and a 10 hp semi-portable steam engine (£245) as its principal weapons. The foremost of these was at the beginning of a hard life for, despite the excellent workmanship of the Beyer engines, the South Line curves were grinding the flanges off the wheels. Engine springs were too weak and frequently broke (or was it the rough state of the unballasted track? JICB). The engines did not run the mileage he expected of them between repairs and this he blamed on the 'sharp dust on some parts of the road during dry weather cutting away rubbing surfaces; new tyres will be needed on at least four engines during the next twelve months'.

Under instruction to obtain quotations for new carriages 'delivered by 1st June, 1875 on rail at Douglas' the following quotations were received:

	1[1]	2[2]	3[3]
4 Carriages with brakes	£2,200	£2,200	£2,080
2 Carriages without brakes	£1,100	£1,040	£1,058

Of these, Trevithick preferred Brown, Marshalls & Co Ltd as 'they turn out truly good work ... and are well acquainted with the class of work we require'. Of Metropolitan he said 'the class of work already supplied is not of a kind which commends itself as desirable to perpetuate'. He felt Ashbury had not the experience of Brown, Marshalls; they had been dilatory in submitting tenders and also 'saddle us with extras for carriage'. Metropolitan had offered to make two more brake vans at the same price as their two last (£362 each), and they were duly ordered.

Another Beyer locomotive with a spare set of wheels was ordered, £1,580 + £140 ex Works.

Turning now to other matters which commanded Trevithick's attention: in the eleven months from May 1874 to April 1875, the South Line (always referred to as 'The Castletown Line') had earned very little but had cost a great deal ... 'it is a heavy drag'. He appreciated that not only was passenger traffic the backbone of the business but that it was mainly composed of pleasure-seekers (sic). His most far-seeing comment was; 'Receipts may be predicted by the rise and fall of the Barometer'.

The South Line traffic was dominated by the demand for lime (carried from Ballasalla to Douglas); such was the weight of tonnage that Douglas

---

[1]Brown, Marshalls & Co. Ltd., Britannia Railway Carriage & Wagon Works, Saltley, Birmingham. Founded as the Britannia Railway Carriage & Wagon Works in 1842.
[2]Ashbury Railway Carriage & Iron Co. Ltd., incorporated 1862 to purchase old-established business of John Ashbury in Openshaw, Manchester.
[3]Metropolitan Railway Carriage & Wagon Co. Ltd., Saltley Works, Birmingham. Founded to take over the business of Joseph Wright & Sons.

yard was blocked by carts hauling it away, 'much to the annoyance of passengers standing about in midst of the horrible dust ... our appliances for handling are of the meagrest ... improvement and more trucks are imperative'.

The South Line produced the heaviest cattle traffic, almost all loaded at Ballsalla (sic); here, the lime wharf was the only place of loading but it was small and dangerous for cattle, hence the need of a pen as otherwise farmers would send their beasts by road again. A lime wharf was needed at Castletown which would be used almost entirely by The Scarlett Lime Co.: such a wharf could be made alongside the present siding but far enough from the station building to obviate dust nuisance. It was believed that the necessary stone and lime for construction would be supplied free of charge by that Company.

On the Peel Line, the heaviest traffic was to and from the Foxdale Mines, and St John's was the interchange point between rail and road.

Passenger takings (May 1875) were (in order of importance): Douglas, Peel, Castletown, Port Erin and St John's whereas Santon and Port Soderick produced the lowest figures. Trevithick wrote, 'The Castletown Line has spoiled the Peel Line and drawn off Peel traffic and burdened the Company with a heavy capital investment in a less productive district'. (That was certainly true of the time, and it would take years before the position was reversed.) Asked about priorities, the General Purposes Committee was warned against developing a station at Ballabeg despite local pressure for one: there was serious need for the improvements at other stations which he had already listed and Ballabeg was a 'nonsense' until these were carried out.

The Board's constant aim was to reduce overheads and Trevithick was obliged to suggest ways of economy. During the winter 1874–5, he found that five trains each way daily on each route was more than ample for the business offering; the early morning trains from both provincial termini seldom contained any passengers but could not be taken off because of the mail contract. Such trains returned from Douglas about 10 am as this was a satisfactory time to suit passengers. The mail business was worth £180 per annum but there was scope for savings if the mail trains did not run on the days when the Mail Packet did not sail.

Until April 1875, there was still nothing but an old sleeper or two, dropped casually over the end of the metals, to prevent a train from dashing off the end of the railway at Douglas. With permission to put up three timber buffer-stops, Trevithick daringly doubled this number and quoted public safety as his reason; he was closely watched as regards expenditure. The draft Reports he prepared display by their marginal notes in pencil, the additional features Trevithick dreamed about but would hardly be countenanced ... thus, a new engine shed for Douglas appears. He did succeed in bringing gas lighting to the station as well as a bookstall. He complains that the fencing continues to give trouble and he was seeking prices for quickset hedges. Apparently all the carriages fitted with brakes were defective and would need £400 spent on repairs and re-painting.

Before Trevithick left for pastures new, he was obliged to present a paper on the 'Reduction of Winter working expenses when traffic is slack'. In the summary he offered:
1. Closing of the entire railway for the winter months.
2. Dispensing with men essential in summer but surplus in winter.
3. Reducing the wages of the winter employees.
4. To run two trains daily in winter and dispense with everyone not concerned with that exercise.
5. Removing the watchmen at certain level crossings.

He countered these suggestions by pointing out that if the men were laid off in winter they would probably not return when wanted; 'good men will not come for 2–3 months in the year and to employ temporary hands will only breed discontent among the regulars, especially if to attract temporary men, they are paid more'. He emphasised how he had worked alongside and talked to the men every day to create loyalty and an *esprit de corps* among them. To work with a skeleton staff, he demonstrated, would leave the railway prey to illness and epidemic; lower wages would hardly meet the situation as they were already lower than in England and mainland work always held certain attractions, enticing men to leave the Island. With each Report, Trevithick listed his employees, their pay and the staffing levels of stations.

Finally, he left with a plea for more goods stock explaining that the Foxdale traffic needed nine open wagons 'all the time' as did the lime traffic, leaving only two, which they tried to make available in a fair way. So short of wagons were they that 2nd class carriages were pressed into carrying dry and light materials such as hay, hemp (for ropemaking), cork, casks and the like. Such goods were also conveyed in the roofless cattle trucks when available. Six low-sided opens for ballast were imperative, two covered vans (with brake compartment if required), and more cattle and open wagons were essential.

Passenger traffic was better this year due to the Manx fishing fleet working in the Douglas neighbourhood for cod; most of the men resided in Port Erin and Port St Mary and used the train to and from Douglas. The following year these travellers were denied to the railway for they had rigged for mackerel and were off to Kinsale. Such passengers would occupy 2nd class carriages, then 71 per cent of the total stock. In an attempt to encourage more than the-then average 7 per cent using the 1st class compartments, 2nd class fares were raised somewhat and a few 1st class reduced: in consequence $7\frac{1}{2}$–8 per cent using 1st class became the familiar pattern for many years to come.

The Island being surrounded by seas and buffetted by weather, everything made of timber from signal posts, station buildings to rolling stock, soon began to show need of maintenance and paint. Of the 64 carriages, there was cover for but 21 and more was urgently needed to save future expense. Extra money would be needed for signals at Ballabeg, a lime wharf at Castletown, while many stations had no urinals ... worse, the newly-planted thorn hedges offered little privacy. Lime, which was used by farmers and building traders, could not be accommodated in the quantities offering and more open wagons were needed to carry it.

During the year, G.H. Wood, concerned that receipts were not rising as he hoped, visited Douglas traders to encourage them to advertise on the backs of railway tickets. Mr Greensill (a retail chemist) accepted the idea and took up the exclusive right for 12 months @ £35; this was sufficient to pay for the Company's ticket supply for that period. The arrangement was continued. Wood also offered advertising in 2nd class compartments.

1876

At Ballabeg, the intention to improve the 'station' was turned into fact when Mr Flaxney Stowell of Castletown was instructed to proceed with the building (including office fittings) for a sum of £40. (We have little evidence of the appearance of this building for the one in use between the wars was a replacement.) The signals, gates and fencing were put up by the Railway at a cost of £44 9s. 0d.

A good example of placing work to local contract occurred in February when Robert Gelling repainted and varnished twelve carriages for £59 12s. 7d.; clearly not single-handed. Some railways of this period forbade smoking on their premises and also in the trains. IOMR policy (if any) up to this time is unknown, but whilst Gelling was painting, 'Smoking Panes' were inserted in some compartment windows, these having been ordered by Trevithick before his departure.

Next month, Henry Barlow, Chief Constable, charged William Boyde, Station Master at Union Mills, with reselling used tickets and accounting for them only once. Over at Castletown the new road past the station was in building; a section of contractor's line was put in for the purpose. In April there was trouble at St John's where Station Master J. Grimmett was discharged because £26 11s. 3d. could not be accounted-for, and the amount was written off.

In mid-March, at Colby, a luggage van was blown away; it had been detached only a few seconds before wind set it in motion towards Castletown; it ran at great speed through Castletown and was stopped by the incline opposite the Creggan.

G.H. Wood, appointed Secretary/Manager since Trevithick's departure, was to be paid £25 a month whereas Frank Buckett, Station Master at Douglas was to have £10 16s. 8d. a month. Ballacraine station was 'to be made out of a Gatekeeper's Hut' and have a platform 'for the purpose of setting down passengers for Glen Helen during the summer months'. It was to be called 'Glen Helen'. Signals and fencing cost the Railway £47 4s. 10d. as £1 14s. 1d. had been saved by omitting urinals. An additional signal was put up at 'Close Moar'. In May, Henry R. Hunt was appointed Locomotive Superintendent.

The Scarlett Co. who operated the lime kilns at Scarlett were given leave to put up a loading wharf at Castletown; it was built for them by James Kissack who charged £20. Castletown station building was at length ready on 1st June and was built by Stowell's of the town.

The Railway was ever anxious to work in conjunction with steamship lines which proposed to serve the Island and in June the Barrow Steam Ship Co. offered to run a ship/rail excursion. The steamer would sail from Belfast to Douglas via Port Erin; on the Irish side there would be a special Belfast & County Down Railway working to serve the steamer. It was a very wet season and Station Masters and porters were all given waterproof coats and leggings . . . such clothing purchases became a regular feature.

Henry Hunt was given a rise in salary from £12 10s. 0d. to £16 13s. 4d., and the gas installation at Douglas was extended into the Workshops.

Agreement was finally concluded as to responsibility for the Union Mills collision (July 1873), the cost to be shared equally between the contractors and the Railway Company, an extra £3,000 to be paid out to the contractors to cover expenses of a hidden nature; this was done by issue of Preference Shares.

Taubman, who had not attended a London Board Meeting for 13 months, was warned that under the Constitution of the Company, he might lose his seat. At that same Meeting, Rixon, who had acted for the London Board since the beginning, was hereafter officially dubbed 'Honorary Secretary to the London Board'; this was to overcome the problem of there being already a Secretary to the Company.

The Glen Helen Estate & Hotel Co. Ltd., owned by Mr Marsden of Liverpool, was anxious to have Ballacraine established: the stopping place was short-lived however. It opened on 3rd June, 1876 and closed on 1st October following. It opened on the 1st June, 1877 and in the summer of 1878, but was not reopened in 1879. St John's was renamed ST JOHN'S & GLEN HELEN but the new title did not survive for long either. Marsden provided horse-buses to and from Ballacraine; 'Fare 3d. Admission to the Glen 3d., additionally'. For the IOMR the matter rested there, but the appearance of a 'proposed railway' to the Rheneas waterfall on some contemporary maps shows that Marsden did not allow the matter to rest . . . but more of this later.

In September, a keen-eyed member of the public drew attention to the timetable which showed a train left St John's for Peel at 12.14 pm whilst a Douglas-bound train left Peel at 12.15 pm. The correspondent referred to the number of accidents which had marred the opening years;

> many of the railway staff are young and it is miraculous how the public have escaped accidents; it is only by the zeal and caution of those who know their duty which has avoided trouble.

Over-full trains due to lack of stock were common and the situation reached a peak when an angry mob of disappointed ticket holders stormed the Douglas ticket office and demanded its money back; they forced entry and the clerk locked himself into an adjoining office to escape. The day of Castletown Regatta was instanced: the train stood in Douglas station and

> was uncomfortably filled long before departure time was reached . . . it required two engines to drag each train along, some trains consisting of as many as 30 carriages . . . the number of passengers carried that day was 8,799.

The correspondent who sampled this event was obviously a sailing enthusiast for he was back for more of the same when the Port Erin Regatta took place; in possession of a 1st class ticket, he travelled 'in a miserable dark fish van with 36 standing; 3 women fainted'.

Shortage of carriages was not alleviated for many years to come. This year the first bogie carriages came from Brown, Marshalls of Birmingham and more goods stock arrived. Accidents continued and when Mrs Crellin a gatekeeper was killed, the Company paid out £16 1s. 2d. in legal and medical fees.

The need for ample stock to carry the business is reflected in the Returns for June 1876:–

- 6 locomotives:
- 12 1st class, 4 composite 1st/2nd class + 42 2nd class + 6 passenger brakevans = 64 coaching vehicles:
- 20 goods wagons, 4 covered wagons, 2 cattle trucks, 4 timber wagons = 30 goods vehicles.*

Affairs affecting a Ramsey line were such that in February surveyors were working on the rival routes, Ramsey and Kirk Michael, and the other via Laxey. A Court of Tynwald, formed for the purpose of advising on the matter, met in March to consider the best means of progress, both as to route and a source of finance. That Committee considered that a line from St John's via Kirk Michael to Ramsey would be better than one via Glen Helen, but that either of these would be better than one via Laxey. This decision (though at this stage interim) kept up the disappointed Ramsey faction's spirits – despite the IOMR's AGM reaffirmation not to proceed; the Committee reported again in October, recommending certain financial methods and reminding us that no less than three courses on the western side of the Island had had to be considered. These were:

1. St John's via Lhergydoo surveyed by Vignoles. Estimated cost £81,117.
2. From a point preceding St John's via Glen Helen and Kirk Michael, surveyed by Wm. Lewis. Estimated cost of £88,976.
3. From Greeba via Glen Helen, Little London and to Ballaugh, (Kirk Michael was not served): another survey by Wm. Lewis. Estimated cost £74,041.**

The first (chosen) coastal route was supported by a Robert Scott,† described as a Civil Engineer and something of a mystery figure in this period and the formation of the later Manx Northern Railway. The steps leading to the Committee's conclusion of the problem are explained shortly but for the moment the ultimate decision of the Tynwald Committee (7th

---

*Annual Report June 1876.

**This second Lewis scheme came before Tynwald again in November, appearing to be promoted by the Estate & Hotel Company. There was to be a junction at Greeba, a station at Glen Helen pleasure grounds and the course would join that of Vignoles [1. above] at a point 6 m 6 fur from Ramsey, (i.e. near Ballaugh). The summit would have a short tunnel of 550 yds: the maximum gradient was to be 1 in 63.

†ROBERT SCOTT. Merchant and spinning manufacturer of 56 Mosley Street, Manchester. Born 1822 at Abbey Holm, Cumberland, son of a farmer, he went to Manchester to make his fortune in the cotton industry. Married at St Luke's, Cheetham Hill, then described as 'Salesman'. Built 'Denzell', Bowdon, Cheshire in 1874 at a cost of £18,000 after making a fortune; living there 1881 with nine servants. His wife was from St Marago, Cornwall, and twelve years his senior. Had a second residence at Ramsey, 'Dunluce', but it is doubtful if he was in fact, a Civil Engineer.

November) was for Vignoles' survey. [Even up to modern times some maps have continued to show by dotted line, the proposed course via Glen Helen.] The Committee added that 'supposing the state of the Insular Revenue to justify the amount of Guarantee . . . a Guarantee may be granted'. The IOMR Board was suspicious of Loch whom they saw as backing a Ramsey Line without regard to adequate financial rewards. When Spencer Walpole became Governor in 1882, he brought the same financial strictures to Island developments as were valued by the IOMR Board, giving more consideration to returns on expenditure; the cause of a Ramsey Line was less well served when Loch left.

Loch had already considered the IOMR's earlier reply and had put two suggestions before the Tynwald Committee:

1. That the IOMR should be taken over by the Government who would then be responsible for the Ramsey Line (or)
2. That should a company come forward to build the Line, it be guaranteed a net (limited) revenue should profits fall short of that sum.

In either case, funding would come from Insular taxation.

The Committee had issued its first Report on 20th June, but its deliberations had been clouded by further recommendations and a clear indication that the IOMR would set a high price upon its own head following a successful 1876 season. When the Governor amended his thoughts somewhat, the Committee produced a second Report on 31st October, 1876. This recommended a guarantee of limited duration, subject to the line being worked to the satisfaction of the Government and to its audit but if the profits exceeded the set limit then half of them would be set aside to pay for earlier loans.

During that same June, the IOMR announced again that it would not support any Ramsey plan 'because of taking people away from lines already open'. Meanwhile the Tynwald Committee was hoping that private enterprise would relieve the position and make it unnecessary for it to intervene; now there was the ridiculous spectacle of surveyors being employed on no less than three west coast routes, and one on the east 'to inform a company already being formed in London'.

The Committee now rejected the eastern route and supported one starting from St John's and reaching Kirk Michael via St Germain's; it would gain Ramsey via Ballaugh. This was despite it being put about that no other line than that via Laxey was likely, 'unless a guaranteed loan could be obtained from the Insular Revenue'. The Committee also had before them a branch from this Ramsey project; it would have left at Ballaugh, run northwards to serve Andreas through Jurby, so tapping the richest part of the Island from a farming point of view. The Committee's choice (via Kirk Michael) prevailed with Tynwald, who on 7th November, 1876, and backed by a statement from Loch that a guarantee was affordable, recommended a guarantee not exceeding £300,000. The Manx Treasury met this recommendation in February 1877 and no time was lost, for on 17th March (St Patrick, so much associated with the Island, would have been pleased) a Memorandum of Association to form a Manx Northern Railway Co. Ltd. appeared. Amongst the articles was one which stated that the Registered Office should be in

Douglas, but the eventual Act of Tynwald 27th March, 1878 stated that it might be anywhere in the Island. As if to emphasise the provincial origins of the Company, the office was in fact in Ramsey but moved almost immediately to Douglas; Ramsey had redressed the situation and was no longer snubbed.

The tale has now run ahead of 1876 and will be continued in 1877: events in the north must now be left to gestate, and attention turned to other matters. For instance, further examination of the Glen Helen route is worthwhile: it was considered that a 'temporary station' on the IOMR at Ballacraine would allow road omnibuses to serve the Glen but should the Ramsey Line be tempted to pass up the Glen, this would serve the Glen Helen Estate & Hotel Co. Ltd. admirably. [It was this Company who had employed William Lewis ('an engineer who has had great experience in laying down narrow gauge railways') to survey the Plans which were laid before the Tynwald Court.] Summarily, his Route Report stated:

> Insular Railway: extension to Ramsey via Glen Helen and Kirk Michael. Junction to be at Greeba station of the Douglas–Peel railway with a station at Glen Helen for the Pleasure Grounds, later joining Vignoles' survey of line to Ramsey at 6 miles 6 furlongs 2 chains from Ramsey. By this route Douglas–Ramsey would be 33.7/8th miles: the new line would be 17 miles 5 furlongs 4½ chains excluding any of the Vignoles route. Summit at Rheneas (11½ miles from Douglas) where there would be a short tunnel (550 yds). Minimum curve is 600 yds radius. Climb to summit at 1/70 and 1/65 to tunnel. Summit Level for 400 ft. Descent at 1/290, 1/63 and 1/115 to junction near Ballaugh. Estimated total cost £74,041.

Back on the IOMR computations were prepared for:

> a) 'Probable results of Insular Government acquiring Railway and extension to Ramsey.'
> b) 'Probable results of not acquiring by Insular Government but extending to Ramsey under Government guarantee.'

the former showing a credit balance of £5,278 14s. 3d. and the latter of £2,897 14s. 3d.*

The Manager's desk had seen its share of the year's difficulties and events: although passenger traffic was to prove exceptionally good, in a series of years growth would not come up to expectations. Goods and mineral tonnages grew steadily; they were, in order of importance, flour, grain, iron and timber, coal and lime.

Adams, the Advocate, had agreed to meet the cost of certain expenses but had failed to do so and now contested in the Courts; the Silver Light Co., which had supplied electrical fittings, was suing over payment. Over in the Locomotive Department, costs were rising due to heavy wear on flanges of the driving wheels on engines on the South Line 'where the curves are sharp'. Long before the tyres were wearing down, the treads had to be machined on the wheel lathe in order to restore the profile of the worn flanges. Hunt's answer to this problem was to recommend the installation of turntables at Douglas, Peel and Port Erin so that engines always run chimney-first, as it was in the bunker-first direction that most wear was taking place.

---

*Manx Museum: GO 23/43 and GO 23/44.

Rixon offered to contact C.&W. Walker & Co. of Donnington who had a turntable in their works, but Walker's table had been cast in one piece and they considered such a table would cost £63 and would be impracticable for the IOMR. After consideration, it was concluded that a table at Douglas would be sufficient and the matter rested there for the moment.

Clearly improvements had been made to some fencing as there was a 'slight decrease in the amount paid for sheep killed on the line'. The Peel Line was affected by heavy rains and had sunk in places; re-ballasting was done by contract and new culverts put in, all worsening the cash position.

To meet the need for more non-passenger stock, enquiries were sent out and quotations received as follows:

Vehicles	1	2	3	4	
6 Open Wagons	£67	£65	£58	£66 15s. 0d.	each
2 Covered Vans	£88	£86	£73 10s. 0d.	£89	
2 Cattle Trucks	£79	£77	£72 7s. 6d.	£80	
4 Lowside Ballast Wagons	£67	*	£57 17s. 6d.	£65 15s. 0d.	

*not quoted.

1. Craven Bros. Ltd., Sheffield.*
2. Metropolitan Railway Carriage & Wagon Co. Ltd., Birmingham.
3. Ashbury Railway Carriage & Iron Co. Ltd., Manchester.
4. Brown, Marshalls & Co. Ltd., Birmingham.

The goods stock supplied by Metropolitan in the past was considered to be satisfactory 'except for the springs': of the six bogie carriages from Brown, Marshalls two years before, 'nothing could give more satisfaction and Mr Trevithick had great confidence in their work'. However, Ashbury ultimately secured the order, but the matter was to arise again in 1877 before this took place.

Word had reached Vignoles in London that:

> on several occasions trains have gone to Castletown composed of 18 Carriages and 3 Break Vans, drawn I presume, by one Locomotive, but I am anxious to know if I am right in presuming that these carriages were full of passengers ... and at what speed they went up the 1 in 65 gradient at Oak Hill.

Would that we knew the reply! The same enquiry reveals that the official IOMR photographs taken at the opening were by a Mr Dean.

1877

This was an important year for the Railway Company (and any future railway undertaking which might be set up in the Island); the Bill for The Railway Regulation Act was published (it became law in the following year). This permitted, among other things, an increase in tolls for the carriage of goods and a charge which might be made for the demurrage of wagons.

---

*CRAVEN BROS. Established 1867 in Darnall, Leeds, producing everything for railway rolling stock except wheels which they added to their products in 1871. Became Cravens Ltd. in 1891 and Cravens Railway Carriage & Wagon Co. Ltd. in 1919. Added tramcar building early in the 20th century and railway carriage manufacture ceased in 1969. (The history of the firm after World War II is omitted from this summary.)

THE MANX NORTHERN RAILWAY COMPANY, LIMITED.

The Company is registered under the Isle of Man Companies Act, 1865, which limits the liability of the Shareholders to the amount of their Shares.

CAPITAL: £90,000, IN 18,000 SHARES OF £5 EACH.

Deposit, 10s. per Share on Application, and 10s. on Allotment. Future Calls to be made by the Directors as required, but not to exceed £1 each, and at intervals of not less than two months.

Directors:

J. T. CLUCAS, Esq., Thornhill, Member of the House of Keys, and Treasurer of the Isle of Man, *Chairman.*
W. B. CHRISTIAN, Esq., Milntown, Member of the House of Keys.
E. C. FARRANT, Esq., Ballakillingan, Member of the House of Keys.
J. C. LaMOTHE, Esq., Ramsey, Member of the House of Keys.
EVAN GELL, Esq., Whitehouse, Justice of the Peace.
M. T. QUAYLE, Esq., Castletown, Member of the House of Keys.
C. H. E. COWLE, Esq., Ballagaue, Member of the Isle of Man Highway Board.

Engineer:

W. H. THOMAS, Esq., C.E., 15, Parliament-street, Westminster, London, S.E.

Standing Counsel:

SIR JAMES GELL, Castletown, Her Majesty's Attorney-General, Isle of Man.

Solicitor:

JOHN FREDERICK GILL, Esq., Advocate, Castletown, Isle of Man.

ENGINEER'S REPORT.

15, Parliament-street, Westminster, London, S.W.,
30th May, 1877.

To the Directors of the Manx Northern Railway Company, Limited.

Gentlemen,
          Having been over the route of the proposed Railway from Saint Johns to Ramsey, and determined the position of the Line, I now beg to report on the same.

    The Railway will commence by a junction with the existing Line from Douglas to Peel, on the western side of, and immediately adjoining, the Station at Saint Johns, Ballacraine.

    The exact point of junction must be a matter of negotiation with the other Company; but I recommend that, if possible, it should be on the west side of the first stream bridge, where the Line is single; but, the points of the loop road being situated immediately on the east side of the said bridge, the whole of the existing Station accommodation would be available. Trains coming from Ramsey would work over the same line of Rails as those from Peel, and any additional sidings necessary might be laid in on the south side of those now existing, so as not in any way to interfere with the buildings.

    If the point I have indicated for the junction can be adopted, a bridge over the stream will be saved, and the points will be within such a distance as to be under the control of the Station.

    From the junction, the Line will run parallel to and on the north side of the existing Railway till it approaches the bridge on the main river, where it will turn to the northward by a curve of 2 furlongs radius, and, rising with an easy gradient, will pass over the main road from Peel to Douglas by a bridge.

    Thence running up a small valley and through land of comparatively small value, it will pass under the road near Poor Town (which will require to be raised a few feet), on the east of Ballalough; and, traversing some marsh land, will join the Line originally proposed by Mr Vignoles at a point about a quarter of a mile to the north of Ballakilworry. From the last-named point to near Glen-beg I should practically adopt Mr Vignoles' Line, only deviating from it to improve the radii of the curves. Thence, however, I consider that the Line may be very much improved and materially shortened by passing under the main road near Ballacregga, over Glenwyllin, to the west of Kirk Michael Church and immediately behind the vicarage, crossing the meadows at the back of Bishop's Court, and the road to Orrisdale (which will be passed on the level), and the private road leading to Broughjairg-beg, keeping on the west side of Ballaugh, till at the point near Squeen Lodge the Line will again become identical with that of Mr Vignoles.

    By this deviation the Railway will be shortened to the extent of 3 furlongs; the gradient of 1 in 90 will be avoided; a most convenient site for a Station for Kirk Michael, on a level grade and on the surface of the ground, will be secured; and the expensive crossing of the road in the middle of the village, and consequent damage to house property will be avoided.

    I have compared the quantities of earthwork on the proposed Line with those of Mr Vignoles' Line, between the same points, and find that a slight saving will be effected in this item.

    The crossing of Glenwyllin, which at first sight appeared formidable, will be by an embankment only 55 feet in height at the deepest part of the glen, and there is no engineering difficulty to be encountered at any point.

    The cuttings between Ballacregga and Bishop's Court, although somewhat heavy, will be through a material available and suitable for ballast, and, being about the centre of the Line, I look to this as the situation of the main ballast field. The depth at which the Railway will be formed is also such as to be most favourable for obtaining any quantity of ballast which may be required by widening the cutting.

    From Squeen Lodge to Ramsey the surface of the ground is so nearly level that the location of the Line is determined mainly by the description of property to be traversed or avoided, and it will be nearly identical with the Line originally proposed, terminating at Ramsey at a point most suitable for a Station, and equally convenient for North and South Ramsey.

2

The Station which would best serve the district would be at Peel Town (for Peel), Kirk Michael, Ballaugh, and Sulby Bridge; and for these third-class arrangements would be ample, consisting of booking-office and waiting-room, small goods-shed, and a loop line and goods siding, similar in fact to the arrangements on the existing Line.

At Ramsey, there should be, in addition to the loop line for shunting, a blind siding for spare coaches, and two lines for goods, the whole of which will be situated on the north of the running Line; and the Goods Depôt would be approached either from the road or the river bank, should it be deemed desirable to obtain water frontage.

The buildings necessary would be booking-office and waiting-room, goods-shed, engine stable, and tank, and, if possible, shed or roof over the carriage siding.

Considering the comparatively small number of trains which will run daily, I recommend that, with the exception of the most important road, level crossings should be adopted where practicable; but I advise that in every instance of a public crossing a small cottage of three rooms be erected.

Although this will involve additional outlay in the first instance, I believe it will be found cheaper in the long run than having mere cabins, as a platelayer will reside in each cottage, and his wife would attend to the gate, thus saving the wages of a gatekeeper.

I have carefully considered the question as to the necessity for platforms, and looking at the method of working adopted on the existing Line, I think that they may be dispensed with at the intermediate Stations without incurring danger or any great inconvenience to passengers, and a considerable outlay will be saved. At the Terminus, however, I recommend that a platform be provided.

The Permanent Way I recommend for adoption would be steel rails, 56lbs. to the yard; rectangular sleepers, 7ft. + 9in. + 4½in.; the rail to be fastened to each sleeper by 2 fang bolts; joints to be fished with fish plates, weighing 16lbs. the pair.

This will make a good strong road on which a speed of 25 to 30 miles an hour may well be maintained. The curves throughout the line are exceptionally good, the sharpest radius being 2 furlongs, and no case of reverse curves occurring on the Line. The steepest gradient will be 1 in 100.

FENCING.—Wire fencing, with six wires and wooden posts, and pink posts will, I believe, be cheaper than posts and rails. If a quick be planted, it will involve the purchase of additional land, to the extent of about 1 acre per mile; and, until it is grown, a fence of either wire or wood will be required. The Company might purchase the wire and staples themselves, only paying the Contractor for posts and fixing, and thus effect a saving.

ESTIMATE.—Until the plans and sections are complete, I cannot pretend to give a detailed estimate.

Line and Works	£67,000
Land	15,000
Contingencies	8,000
	£90,000

I am, Gentlemen,

Your obedient servant,

(Signed) W. H. THOMAS, M. Inst., C.E.

Outside statutory matters, it was to be the year when steel rails were introduced and these gradually replaced the initial iron ones. Rails were now shipped into Douglas by the Laxey Steamship Co. at 6s. 0d. per ton carriage. Hunt was dissatisfied with the 'peculiar construction of couplings, axleguards and axleboxes on our carriages and wagons' and recommended the Board not to order these again: laminated springs should be fitted to any new stock. There were difficulties with the letting of the Peel refreshment room, the contract for which was changing hands frequently; the Station Master there was reported to have taken a public house and was given notice to leave the service of the Railway Company.

The outcome of Hunt's observation was a re-consideration in April for supply of the extra 14 vehicles being six open box wagons, two covered goods wagons, two cattle wagons and four low-side ballast wagons. The following fresh tenders were received:

Arnold & Garside	£971 0s.
Brown, Marshalls	£935 10s.
Metropolitan	£897 10s.
Ashbury	£829 5s.

Hunt was sent to Manchester to finalise with Ashbury and his visiting expenses were £3 2s. 0d.

The matter of a Douglas Quay Tramway was raised again, and Greenbank was instructed to prepare a costing.

In August the MNR promoters were invited to meet the IOMR Board to discuss united opposition to the Railway Regulations Bill then before Tynwald.

Trouble was experienced on the South Line where rails were lifting from the sleepers and fang bolts were now substituted in places. It is not clear when the use of half-round sleepers was discontinued but it may have been when 30 tons of steel rails (28 ft long and 56 lb/yd) were delivered by Phillips & Nephew @ £7 5s. 0d. per ton, and an offer by Burt, Boulton & Haywood (of London) to supply a minimum 2,000 sleepers @ 2s. 7½d. each was taken. In Hunt's Report for 16th February, comes a reference to a decision by the Board to install a turntable at Douglas but that he (Hunt) had recommended (in November the previous year) that there should be turntables at Douglas, Peel and Port Erin. This is underlined by a pencilled note, 'but never ordered'.

Let us now return to MNR affairs; the initiative for the building of a Ramsey Line had come mainly from the north; objectives in the Memorandum were 'The construction, maintenance and working of a Railway or Railways between the Parish of German and the town of Ramsey, and elsewhere in this Island'.

Subscribers had first met in Douglas on 29th March, J.T. Clucas, MHK of Thornhill becoming Chairman; a financial guarantee was given by the Lords' Commissioners of Her Majesty's Treasury at the request of the Tynwald Court. Its principle was that if in any year during a limited number of years, one moiety of the gross earnings should be under £3,000, the deficiency would be made good out of the Insular revenue. A condition of guarantee was that gross annual income would exceed £6,000.

Little more now existed towards the MNR other than the formation of a limited liability company under the Isle of Man Company's Act (1865) and nothing specific had been agreed as to its construction. Enquiries now began to find a suitable person to do this, to take overall charge during building and, if required, design and supply rolling stock. (This was a frequent arrangement of those times, especially among the smaller Irish railways.) Henry Greenbank of the IOMR was approached and quoted £250 per mile, beyond the MNR reach. The services of William Henry Thomas, MICE, MIME (1834–1901) of 15 Parliament Street, London, were secured on condition he charged no more than £3,000 per annum. He was engaged from 8th May, 1877, and was originally co-Engineer with H.R. Woolbert on the Cornwall Minerals Railway (incorporated in 1873).*

Extracts from the Report of the Committee of the Tynwald Court† 'to enquire whether the MNR Co. (Ltd.) had complied with Standing Orders', meeting in Douglas on 25th July, 1877, reveal that:

MNR. Engineer William Henry Thomas' estimate was £88,320 for 16 miles 3 furlongs 85 chains of railway; the Company capital was £90,000 in 18,000 shares of £5 each.

Present conveyances. Common coaches take 3½ hours between Douglas and Ramsey and potential passengers are frequently left behind.‡ Sixty five vehicles each weekday leave Douglas in a season of thirteen weeks, carrying an average of eight persons. Railway 3rd class passengers' fare would be 2s. 9d. return St John's–Ramsey. A smaller number of visitors arrives by steamer at Ramsey and goes to Douglas: a coach driver takes £1 a day average fare and £2 a day in summer between Douglas and Ramsey.

Goods traffic. It is calculated that, based on current road traffic figures, 8,000 tons lime, 1,000 tons bricks and tiles, 2,600 tons turnips, potatoes, hay etc., 5,200 tons coal, iron, manure, plus drapery, fish, livestock, parcels, mails etc. would be carried per annum. In 1875, 16,000 tons of lime from the Ballasalla district went north by cart. Lime shipments out of Castletown might wait a month for a favourable wind to ship from there to a port in the north. About 1,400 tons of grain were carried into Ramsey each year, mainly for shipment to Whitehaven;# very little grain was shipped from any other Manx port. Carriage of 400 tons of hay and straw annually could be expected, plus that of Ramsey town's manure. Coal imports into Ramsey could be distributed inland by railway at about 100 tons per annum, mainly to Peel which was inconveniently situated for accepting Cumbrian coal+ by sea when long periods of adverse weather obtained.

Vegetables mainly went to Douglas market, as did livestock. Flour Mills in Laxey, Ramsey, Kirk Michael, Ballaugh sent considerable tonnages by road: there was a Starch Mill (Sulby Glen Starch Mills Co.) which consumed huge

---

*W.H. Thomas (1834–1901) Civil Engineer.
 A pupil of John Fowler, his first engagement was at the age of 19 on surveys for the St Petersburg–Peterhof system. He became Engineer of the Cornwall Minerals Railway (incorporated 21st July, 1873), three years after starting on his own account, spending four years laying out and building that line. Later with Barry and Brunel.
†Copy in Tower Collection.
‡In places, due to the steep road, passengers had to get out and walk 1½ miles in all.
#One Ramsey merchant 'shipped 25,000 bolls of wheat per annum to one firm in Whitehaven'.
+The principal coalfield for Island supplies.

quantities of potatoes and rice, the latter being shipped into Ramsey. All the foregoing would underline the need for a railway on Ramsey quays, 'we shall also make a tramway to the Pier at Ramsey'. Oddly, Douglas-bound road traffic from the north had not been calculated 'as it all travels by night'.

On a second issue, the Committee was empowered to ascertain that the line of route was to the advantage of the Island generally such as to justify a Government guarantee. A second course was being considered between Ballaugh and Ramsey and this would take the line on a more northward path, involve an additional 1½ miles between these two places and require another five minutes running time on a journey. It would also take the railway further from the Mills at Sulby etc. and Lezayre, and visitors to Sulby Glen would have to walk a mile further before entering the Glen which was not at its most attractive in its lower portions anyway. The two routes diverged a quarter of a mile west of Ballaugh and the one preferred (via Sulby village) 'was proposed by Mr. Scott'. The 'opposing line' (sic) was described as The Jurby Line but did not in fact, serve that village, but passed nearby Sandygate. The Jurby Line would involve eleven level crossings and the preferred route only seven; the Jurby Line also had sharper curves.

The MNR acknowledged that it would depend 'on the three month's traffic', especially to Sulby Glen; a station at Sandygate (on the alternative route) would not serve Sulby Glen.

G.H. Wood of the IOMR was asked what the cost of working the MNR would be, using a single locomotive and answered, '5d. per mile, if drawing a train'. He said the IOMR ran five trains daily each way in winter and eight in summer and his calculations were based on the same intervals. That sum would not allow for wear and tear. He looked upon every level crossing as a hazard and they were to be avoided where possible, especially as each cost about £34 a year to keep manned. Wood also stressed the intensive competition from 'cars', and thought the estimated number of people travelling to Ramsey 'is rather over-stated'. He did not think a Ramsey Line would produce the same income per mile as the IOMR.

In a backhand way Thomas criticised IOMR track, commenting on its half-round sleepers, light rails, and poor fencing. The MNR 'would not require as much spent on upkeep as the present line'. Thomas said the 'tires' on the present railway were cut away in two or three years – 'it would not occur on a line with better curves'.

At this period the Manx fishing fleet was based on Peel, but many of the fishermen lived in the north of the Island and it was their habit to return home at weekends, almost one third of them leaving Peel for northern destinations on a Saturday night and returning on a Monday morning. Proposers said this was a basic reason for having the MNR station actually in Peel, but Thomas said it could only be near the cemetery and then make a junction with the IOMR near there; the fall into Peel would be very steep. The original plan was to have a near-level line into Peel but that would have ended on the high ground above the town. Should the MNR propose to have a station in Peel, there would be formal objection from the IOMR. The MNR had been warned over this.

Cattle were walked to Douglas for shipment, a distance of 16 to 17 miles, and were the worse for it on arrival. There would be a bigger trade in mackerel (packed in boxes) if fish could be sent to Douglas by train. Three cartloads of shellfish went into Douglas weekly, and the same came in codfish for loading on the outward bound steamer. Wood confirmed a good traffic in fish on the IOMR into Douglas, mainly from Peel and Port St Mary. He agreed that quayside tramways 'at either end' would greatly enhance the traffic (presumably meaning Peel and Douglas?).

Tourist traffic to Sulby Glen would continue to be handled mainly by cars, said one witness, as the pretty part of the Glen was a mile away from the station. As Lezayre appears today (1992), with its derelict station building and bare expanse of fields surrounding, it is hard to believe 'there are three corn mills as well as cloth manufactories in Lezayre which are assuming large proportions'. Farmers in the district through which the railway would pass would welcome it as it put them on equal footing with farmers nearer Douglas, but they hoped the line would cut through a neighbour's land rather than their own!

The Committee reported on 14th August: the population of the north was given as 12,647 but it was stressed that a farming community does not travel about, save on Market, Fair Days etc. The Committee had to decide if the gross traffic would exceed £6,000 per annum and bear in mind (as previously mentioned) that if 'in any year one moiety (50%) of the gross earnings of the line be under £3,000, the deficiency be made good out of Insular Revenue'. It was the Committee's opinion that, in all probability, no deficiency would have to be made good out of the Insular Revenue, the traffic being estimated at £10–12,000 per annum: they backed the proposed Ballaugh to Ramsey route by way of Sulby.

On the 8th June the newspapers published a copy of the Prospectus, showing the directors as: John Thomas Clucas, Rev. William Bell Christian, Edward Curphey Farrant, John Corlett La Mothe, Evan Gell, Mylrea Tellet Quayle and Charles Hamilton Edmonds Cowle.

Information was that the Company was being:

> Formed for the construction of a railway from St. John's to Ramsey and elsewhere in the Island. Also intending to make tramways to connect Ramsey with Ramsey Quay, and the parishes of Andreas and Jurby where practicable ... length 16½ miles ... passengers to travel by through trains between Ramsey and Douglas ... Sharpest radius of curve 2 furlongs, maximum gradient 1 in 100, with steel rails of 56 lb/yd. The directors are to make satisfactory arrangements to have the line worked by the IOMR or provide their own rolling stock, as they consider most advantageous.

Capital was £90,000 in £5 shares with borrowing powers up to £45,000. On the day of Thomas' appointment, Henry Washington was made Secretary: after a brief stay at 2 Upper Church Street, Douglas, the Registered Office was moved to 19 Athol Street.

In the late summer, the SUN reported that though on 14th August, 1877 the Tynwald Court had suggested a longer route (by 1½ miles) via Jurby to Ramsey at an enhanced cost of £8,000, the Tynwald Committee had rejected it and adhered to its own proposition. The same paper also noted that on 6th November, 1877 the Legislature finally approved the Bill.

A revised Prospectus inviting applications for shares was sent out in December, based on Thomas' estimate of a cost of £88,320. Two Tynwald Committees had meanwhile investigated Company affairs and especially the potential for business: G.H. Wood (the IOMR Secretary) wanted estimates for traffic reduced but nevertheless this did not put the Government Guarantee at risk.

At length the Manx Government gave an undertaking to pay a minimum dividend of 4 per cent for the first twenty five years on £25,000 of the £50,000 5 per cent Preference Share capital: Government shares were marked 'B'. The £25,000 unguaranteed 'A' 5 per cent ranked equally for dividend. To look after their interests, the Government appointed none other than the BoT Inspector, Col F.H. Rich, as Government Director.*

A scheme to extend the Railway 'at or near the harbour at Ramsey' was acceptable to the Legislative Council, who on 23rd November passed the Bill with a suitable extension clause; other potential destinations were not authorised. It had been an eventful natal year.

In November of 1877 tenders were invited for construction of the line and four were submitted:

J. Oliver	for £40,865 to complete by 1st July, 1879.
J. & W. Grainger	for £44,000 to complete in 16 months.
H. McKeone	for £49,628 to complete by 31st July, 1879.
A.H. McNair	for £52,300.

Only the first two were considered and neither was favourable. However, Grainger offered to take up £5,000 shares and to finish the work by 1st June, 1879. In mid-February 1878, the firm of J.&W. Grainger & Co. of Perth and Glasgow was formally contracted at a directors' meeting in London with work to commence on 1st March – in the event, Grainger only just failed to meet his completion date.† The meeting announced that the cutting of the first sod would be a subdued affair, to take place on 1st March, 1878 in a field owned by Rev. Christian, a site later to be occupied by Ramsey terminus on the Lezayre Road; it was adjacent to the Sulby River and partly in a former timber yard. The SUN followed affairs with close interest, noting the arrival of W.H. Thomas 'together with some big shire horses' and that work would commence 'close to Peel' particularly monitored by Thomas. The initial equipment was landed at Peel early in March and the paper for the following week announced the arrival in Douglas of 'some 200 navvies . . . with their wives and families to the third generation'. By the next month, work had also started at the Ramsey end and there were widespread fears about the behaviour of the navvies, some of whom rioted almost at once after being dismissed.

To complete the year's events, some extracts from Thomas's preliminary Report to the MNR directors dated 30th May are of interest:

a) The Railway to commence on the western side of and immediately adjoining St John's, Ballacraine . . . the exact point to be negotiated with the IOMR . . . if

---
*There are many MNR matters among the Government Office Papers in the Manx Museum.
†Partners: John and Allan Grainger.

possible on the west side of the first stream bridge, but the points of the loop road to be immediately on the east side of the bridge . . . by this means the whole of the existing station accommodation would be available . . . train from Ramsey would work over the same line as those from Peel . . . sidings could be laid on the south side so as not to interfere with the buildings . . . by so doing, one more bridge over the stream would be saved and points would be within the station area.
b) Glen Wyllin to be crossed by an embankment 55 ft high.*
c) Stations are suggested at:
   Poor Town (for Peel)†
   Kirk Michael
   Ballaugh
   Sulby Bridge
and the above would be 'Third Class stations' i.e. with booking office, waiting room, small goods shed and siding, loop line. (This confirms Peel Road (alias Poortown), Sulby Glen and Lezayre were not part of the original conception, hence the slightly different form of buildings at these places.)
d) Ramsey to have booking office, waiting room, goods shed, 'engine stable and tank and if possible a shed or roof over the carriage siding'. Also suggested, 'in addition to the loop, a blind siding for spare coaches and two lines for goods . . . the whole situation on the north side of the running line. A goods depot approached from either river bank or road bridge should it be deemed desirable to obtain water frontage.'
e) Working arrangements with the IOMR were envisaged from the start e.g. 'advantageous to arrange . . . with existing company for rolling stock'. (As under this conception the MNR would possess no rolling stock of its own, no workshops were at first provided at Ramsey, 'though land would be available if required'.)
f) Save over important roads, the line would cross roads on the level: at these 'small three-room cottages at public crossings would be cheaper than cabins – cottages would be occupied by a platelayer and his wife could attend to the gates, so saving the cost of a gatekeeper'.
g) Platforms would only be needed at Ramsey.
h) Track materials recommended: 56 lb steel rails on rectangular section sleepers 9 ft × 7 in. × 4½ in. to be fastened to each sleeper by two fang bolts. Fishplates to be 16 lb per pair.

Although not every recommendation was followed, by and large Thomas's ideas were carried through.

Back now to IOMR affairs; during 1877, the Company was asked to install a siding at Union Mills and the Highway Board made an approach road to the station in consequence.# In August, Special Trains were advertised 'as required on Bank Holidays' in connection with Athletic Sports held at the Racecourse. 'Party Rates allowed: not less than six 1st class or twenty 2nd class passengers to travel at single rates for the return journey.'

---

*No reference to crossing Glen Mooar.
†In the event, this was St Germain's.
#The mills here had been operated by William Kelly from the first decade of the nineteenth century. During that period woollen broadcloth was manufactured there; 'customers may bring own wool (blankets etc.) or a cart may come round to collect it' (1811). Some sheep's wool would have been picked from hedges etc. by children who would be paid a small sum for taking it to the mill. In 1827 the premises were offered for sale, then described as a 'Water Corn Mill and a Spinning, Carding & Woollen Factory etc., property of Wm Kelly of Snugborough'. Destroyed by fire in 1828, it re-emerged solely as a woollen mill.

The Company disclosed delays to mixed trains in 1876 and the 1877 timetable now marked certain trains with an asterisk, pointing out that they would be liable to delay if they 'picked up goods waggons on the road'. At the year's end, a new connecting road in Castletown was opened which linked the station, The Green and the Malew Road.

Passenger traffic in 1877 brought in £16,236; 509,422 persons had travelled against 535,750 in 1876. A net profit after payment of interest was £8,653; 5 per cent dividend was paid on the Preference Shares and 4½ per cent on Ordinary Shares.

Means of raising the income from goods traffic were considered but the rates were clearly too low and the constitution prevented general increases. For instance, it was possible to carry hay and straw up to 18 cwt in one wagon but the rate was limited to 4d. per ton per mile and if legal, the Company intended to impose terminal charges on this and other traffic.

The Rule Book was proved to be incorrect as some workings were contrary to its contents and certain regulations did not apply on the IOMR anyway. A fresh book would be needed. Further expense would be faced as many sleepers and fencing posts were already rotten after a life of only five years.

There was £5,000 in Preference Shares held as fully paid-up and due to Watson & Smith once various outstanding matters had been settled; until these had formally passed into their hands, the Company could not make application to the High Bailiff for a fresh issue of Debentures. New money was vital and Watson & Smith was still owing £519 3s. 1d. as their share of costs for the Union Mills collision of July 1873.

The summer proved to be a poor year for the whole Island; 'Cars and road conveyances' were competing with the railway and accepting any fare rather than miss custom; figures of 2s. 0d. return for Douglas to Port Erin were rumoured. Trade in England was bad and Manx weather was dreadful; worse, there was a 'visitation of Small Pox' in Douglas which lasted into the following year. In the bad summer, the farmers did not need so much lime and the Peel merchants had banded together and chartered a steamer direct from there to Liverpool; IOMR + IOMSPC rates for their traffic amounted to 12s. 0d. ton and this new competitor was 4s. 0d. a ton cheaper. As if this was not enough, an accident to the mines' machinery at Foxdale suspended all traffic (collected and delivered at St John's and carried by road for the remainder) and on 6th August a collision at the Racecourse Platform injured two people and was to cost the IOMR £65 compensation.

Looking back over the year, it was shown that coal and lime were the heaviest traffics and that the Peel Line continued to be more profitable than the South with a 33⅓ per cent better return thereon. Fencing, though quick-thorns were now replacing it rapidly, still allowed lambs to penetrate it and considerable sums were paid in compensation. Cattle handling arrangements at Ballasalla were hindered for the want of a cattle pen there.

A worrying feature of the increasing goods traffic was the lack of covered accommodation for it. The main goods shed and warehouse at Douglas was too small and though there was additional shelter there, goods awaiting wagons or collection had to stand out in the rain – and there had been plenty of that. A trial purchase of a dozen wagon sheets was made to cover items left in the open, and further like purchases were to follow. Port St Mary and Castletown in the provinces were worst hit, having stations some way from the town and owning no buildings to warehouse goods. Although the following year plans were prepared for goods sheds at these places (buildings @ £381 each and the Ballasalla cattle pen @ £20), they were put into the 'Pending Tray' . . .

1878

By the Manx Northern Railway Act of 1st January, a junction with the IOMR at St John's was authorised. For the first time, the IOMR was not to be isolated or have the monopoly of the Island railway business. In consequence, attention was given to Trevithick's ideas (which had lain dormant) to increase accommodation at Douglas. However, the Company offices, up until now in rented premises, were to be allocated a station building. Although there was refreshment accommodation at Douglas, it was very basic and it could be moved to Port Soderick where business was increasing, if land could be obtained there. Goods sheds were still needed at Port St Mary and Castletown and a new cattle pen at Ballasalla. Such intentions were hastened by the approach of the MNR.* The first steel rails were laid on the Peel Line, at 'the Douglas end' and from 1st July, 2nd class became 3rd class (it was strange that the MNR did not follow suit but provided three classes from the outset in 1879).

A hint of basic changes to come in administration began when Lord Skelmersdale, a London-based director, resigned in December, to be replaced by Major-General James Beadle of South Kensington. This was not all as in the same month the Duke of Sutherland did the same thing. The 'power behind the throne' was greatly diminished and it may be asked if it was to be deprivation for the Railway Company or advantage? Certainly in terms of frequent 'interference' (as some saw it) by Governor Loch on the Manx railway scene, the General Purposes Committee had often called upon the Duke to intercede with his influential potential.

The matter of working the MNR came to the fore again, and consideration was given to the costs of extra stock required for working the Ramsey Line.

The failure of the IOMR to prosecute a railway to Ramsey and the subsequent effect, promotion and construction of a MANX NORTHERN RAILWAY has already been imparted. The issue now returned to the IOMR in the form of discussions as to terms on which it might operate the new line. By May the IOMR had set out its terms:

1. If not required to provide capital.
2. If Plans and Sections were agreed upon.
3. If completion was satisfactory to an Engineer appointed by the Governor.
4. If not more trains than would be economically desirable were run.
5. If certain financial help was forthcoming.

The effect of the Railway Regulation Act (now law) resulted in a Rule Book being prepared, Trespass Notices being displayed, and a List of Tolls

*Manx Museum: Drawing R/233 of 10. 1878 re accommodation at St John's.

THE
Manx Northern Railway Company,
LIMITED.

SECRETARY'S OFFICE, 61, ATHOL-STREET,

Douglas, 16/10/1878

Sir,

I am instructed to inform you that the Directors of this Company, at a Meeting held on the 12th day of October 1878, made a further Call of One Pound per Share upon the Shares in this Company, payable at this Office ~~on the expiration of twenty one days from this date~~.

There are now standing in your name Ten Shares in the Company, the present Call in respect of which amounts to £10, and I will be glad if you will pay the same at this Office within the time above stated.

I am,

Your obedient Servant,

Henry Washington

Secretary.

Amount of Calls previously due by you £ ——
Amount of present Call ...   ...   £ 10
£ 10

W. Creer Esq.
Ballavarr
15b

Instruction to Shareholder to pay his call due on MNR Share Offer.

exhibited at every station. A survey revealed that 1,205 of the boundary fence posts were broken.

Let us turn for a moment to MNR matters; the IOMR calculated that to work the Ramsey Line the operator would have to provide two locomotives, eighteen 'long bogie carriages', two 'guard' vans, four covered goods wagons, twenty open box wagons and two cattle wagons. Early in the year Rixon had parley with the MNR Board; this followed consideration by the General Purposes Committee which had informed London that

> ... working the MNR, it was not advisable if less than six trains are run each day in summer (a period of 105 days) and three during the remainder of the year ... IOMR terms would be a cost of £4,500 per annum or @ 50% of gross receipts if such exceed £9,000 per annum ... would also require a Renewal Fund to cover track and rolling stock of £2,483 7s. 6d. per annum.

An envisaged agreement would last for 5 or 7 years.

Rixon's offer, no doubt the judgement of the IOMR London Board, was to work the MNR for 50 per cent gross receipts provided the MNR found £10,000 for stock etc. The IOMR was now looking for a perpetual arrangement.

So the matter rested pro tem. The IOMR was uneasy; it had made 'repeated applications' to the MNR to be shown the proposed Agreement between the MNR and the Government regarding the guarantee on certain MNR shares. Whilst the Agreement was not yet signed, nonetheless until the IOMR was made aware of its contents, it would take no further part in negotiations.

Whilst it would be easy to dwell on events and become wearisome at this stage of deliberations, it is sufficient to say arrangements were made at length, whereby the IOMR would work the MNR from 23rd September, 1879, (locomotives, rolling stock, repairs and all running and traffic expenses to be met by the IOMR) at a charge of 1s. 6d. per mile. The MNR was to maintain permanent way, civil works and levy passenger fares and freight charges. It would provide its own rolling stock and wagons would be interchanged on through freight facilities. Through passenger bookings would be delayed until December 1879, and through coaches until 1884. (The through working of locomotives was in the event, uncommon.)

In its 20th April, 1878 issue, the SUN told of the arrival of the Laxey-registered steamer RELIANCE with 250 tons of MNR rails on 12th April at Ramsey Harbour, evidence at last to the townsfolk of substantive progress. Materials of many varieties then followed, as did the invoices against them, and it was soon clear that steps would have to be taken to meet costs. To this end, an Extraordinary Meeting was held in Ramsey on 27th July, 1878 (the Registered Office, though recently moved to 61 Athol Street, was still in Douglas) to create £35,000 5 per cent Preference Shares, priority of purchase being given to Ordinary Shareholders, one for one.

In view of the work involved on the St John's to Kirk Michael section, Grainger's took it upon themselves to build this, the hardest part of the route – they did, in fact, construct the line as far as Ballaugh (the next station beyond Kirk Michael) leaving the relatively flat and easy section from thence to Ramsey to sub-contractors Brebner & Fleming of Edinburgh.* All the wooden buildings at the Ramsey terminal were built by Boyde Bros. who were local builders in the town. Malcolm Grant-Dalton was appointed Resident Engineer, whose work was to supervise all construction.

There seems to be no evidence that work had in fact, started near the St John's end of the line but rather the convenience of materials arriving by sea would make Ramsey a more practicable starting point. By August 1878, the newspaper could report:

> The contractors are prosecuting their work with great energy all along the line, and over 1½ miles are laid out of Ramsey.

Of course, this was Brebner & Fleming's section and the going was fairly easy; Grainger's began their section in March, probably at several places.

The Minutes reveal that the position of stations had been considered by the Board in the previous June (1877), it being September following before contracts were completed:

> Ramsey – 'near Watson's house on the Loughan-y-eigh Road' (or Lezayre Road)
> Sulby
> Ballaugh
> Kirk Michael
> Lhergydhoo (later St Germain's)
> St John's

In addition there might be need for a station between Kirk Michael and St Germain's, and a siding at 'Orry's Dale'; when the service began, there were stations at both Sulby Bridge and Sulby Glen.

Ramsey station apart, Grainger's tender for the remaining stations was accepted and it appeared this was on the basis that the Board wished all remaining building construction to be in the hands of one builder. 'Gate Lodges' were also erected at level crossings.

The only source of information as to progress of construction comes from the newspapers and, as usual, they concentrated on the sensational. In a small community with strong dissenting and temperance views, the arrival among them of a minority of intemperate hard-living navvies 'from across', was a source of anxiety. When dissatisfied with their lot, or simply drunk, some navvies were violent. The Bishop was threatened with a knife and the Bishop's wife hit on the head by a flying stone from one of them, during a road journey to Bishop's Court. Certain factions would strike and in some ways it was a miracle that Grainger kept the work mainly on schedule. BRADSHAW'S MANUAL excused delay: 'the severe winter weather having greatly interfered with the progress of the work'.

Boyde Bros. who had agreed to build the wooden station buildings at Ramsey for £912, had produced the lowest of three tenders for the job and in December they obtained another order to build the corrugated iron Carriage Shed there for £360.

To close MNR matters for the year; in December Thomas set out to obtain tenders for locomotives and rolling stock, and Grainger's request for the loan of an IOMR locomotive and wagons to ballast the track, was refused.

---

*a partnership formed 1876.

Returning again to the IOMR; what the newspapers described as a 'valuable limestone quarry at Turkeyland near Castletown' worked by Jefferson & Moore, had been opened on the Ronaldsway Estate, and in the autumn a tramway was proposed to link it with Castletown station.* With a length of approximately half a mile it had already been surveyed and set out by 'Mr D. Cregeen CE who assisted surveying the MNR'. There would be an embankment 13 ft high at maximum, a deepest cutting of 10 ft 6 in. and a mean rise of 1 in 66 from the limekiln mouth to a junction with the IOMR

> near the gatekeeper's cottage on the road to Ballawoods ... work is now in progress ... a formidable staff of workmen engaged ... when complete the lime will be loaded into trucks at the kilnmouth ... conveyed direct to a siding at a point about a mile nearer to Douglas than Ballasalla station ...†

Accidents due to the movement of level crossing gates by high winds – a feature of the Island – were regular. In November, the 2.10 pm train to Port Erin was passing Ballasalla when one of the crossing gates blew open against the train and hit the brake van at the rear. The force of the impact 'separated it from the other carriages which continued to Castletown without it'.

Now let us turn to some snippets from the newspapers during the year: during June, a steamer landed railway plant at Peel, presumably for the MNR? The next month 'Mr Raby, at the Sale Rooms, Douglas ... Auction of Ground Rents and IOMR Shares ... a promising investment; the difficulty heretofore has been to secure so large a number at one time ...'‡ On 20th July, Mrs Loch held a Garden Party ... 'special train will be run for the convenience of persons invited' ... free of smuts and soot, it is to be hoped. The same day the TIMES had: 'Warning to Railway Travellers', when a man was charged with boarding a moving train on Tynwald Day (5th July) [fined 40s. 0d. or one month in prison.] The accused's excuse was that he intended to catch the last train but 'was just in time to be too late'. He had been dragged along by the train and rescued by the Douglas Station Master.

During August there were frequent and detailed newspaper accounts of MNR arrangements to raise money by Mortgage Bonds and Borrowing Powers, Preference Shares etc. High praise was accorded to the IOMR

> The management of this Company spare nothing in their efforts to meet the accommodation of the public ... next week special trains on two days leaving Douglas for the Race Course platform every 25 minutes from 1 o'clock in connection with the great athletic festival that day ... (on Thursday) ... for persons desirous of attending the Agricultural Show at Castletown ... trains every 20 minutes'.#

The tenants growing crops along the course of the intended MNR might be satisfied to read that the MNR had engaged 'practical men to value those crops on behalf of the Company'. There were the usual merrymakers, drunk and disorderly on stations and trains on a Saturday night and travelling

---

*a wire ropeway to Derbyhaven was also considered.

†In view of the eventual failure of this unfinished work (for some of it survives), it is unclear why it was prosecuted when apparently there had been no formal agreement with the IOMR for a point of junction. It can only be conjectured that the operators may have proceeded on a 'nod and wink basis' from someone of authority, only to be misled. (See also 1883 and 1886.)

‡Prices fetched £4 18s. 0d.–£5 1s. 0d. per IOMR Share.

#In 1991 there were but 36 trains to Castletown *in a week* in high season.

without tickets; men and women were involved (fines were 2s. 6d. to 5s. 0d., with costs). Finally, the paper suggests the IOMR was not all that generous in the provision of cleaning materials, for William Crellin, engine cleaner at Peel, was committed for trial for stealing cloth, the property of Mr Philip of Peel.

The traditionally damp climate of the Island continued to affect sleepers and three-quarters of a mile needed replacing each year whilst old ones went into improvement of fencing.

By the end of the year another attack was being made on rotting sleepers, and by early 1879 almost another mile had to be replaced.

The season once more was a poor one and the Board blamed poor economic conditions in England for dissuading 'that class of person who visits the Island', whilst the more wealthy had been lured away by the sophistication of the Paris Exhibition.

The IOMR Board continued to adjust their expenditure to the goal of dividend and satisfying the Ordinary Shareholder; prudence was allied to future thinking and the spectre of increased expenditure to come on maintaining what they possessed against the ravages of weather and the unexpected pace of wear and tear. Wood counselled expansion whilst at the same time warning of 'keeping our powder dry'. In November, he reminded that Greenbank had prepared plans to extend Douglas station along the lines recommended by Trevithick; recently more land had been bought from Taubman (Nunnery Estate) but had not been put to use. In Trevithick's time, there seemed no immediate threat of a line to Ramsey but now, though in the hands of others, that line would bring more traffic in and out of Douglas, and provision had to be made with increased accommodation. A large piece of land was owned 'opposite the public street, and the present offices are a considerable distance from the station'; the General Purposes Committee thought that Company offices should be built on it, together with a refreshment room whose rent would offset many on-going expenses.

Wood put the plan for the foregoing before the Board, together with a second one, prepared by Thomas of the MNR, showing the proposed MNR/IOMR junction at St John's; Wood cautioned by reminding his employers that on Tynwald Day, as many as three trains stood in St John's station simultaneously.

Abbreviated List* of Tolls
(authorised by the IOMR Act of 1872 and Railway Regulation Act 1878).

Passengers – 1st class 3d. per mile – for a distance not exceeding one mile,4d.
              2nd class 2d.   ditto   ditto   3d.
              3rd class 1d.   ditto   ditto   2d.
              [Children under 12, half-fare: under 3, free.]

Luggage Limits – 1st class   120 lbs
                  2nd class   100 lbs
                  3rd class   60 lbs
[Excess Luggage – 1s. 0d. per cwt, minimum 3d.]

*There is a copy of the full List in Tower Collection.

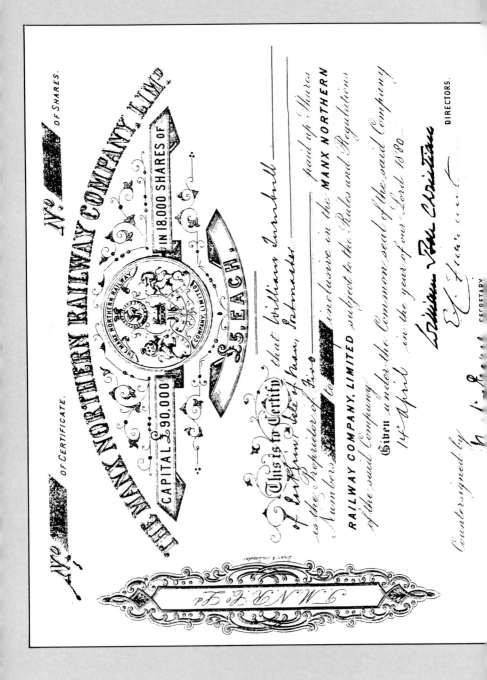

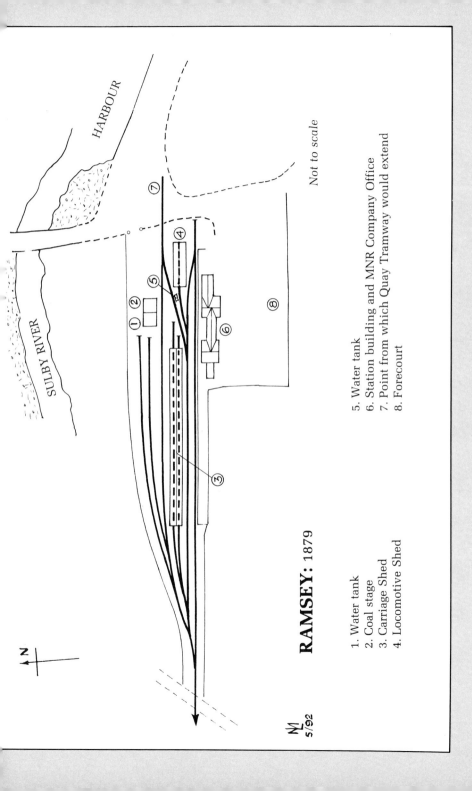

Soldiers, sailors, police etc. on duty in uniform:
  Commissioned Officers   1st class   2d. per mile
  Soldiers, sailors etc.   3rd class   1d. per mile
Widows of soldiers, sailors, children above 12, 'entitled to be sent to their destination at public expense . . . entitled to being in covered carriages which shall be provided with seats with sufficient space for reasonable accommodation of the Persons conveyed, and which shall be protected against the weather.'

(Here follows list of other charges; among them . . .):

Horse, Mule, Ass, Ox, Cow, Bull etc.		5d. per mile
Horse in covered Horse Box		8d. ditto
Calf, Sheep, Pig, Lamb, Hog etc.		2½d. ditto
Dung, Compost, Manure, Lime, Limestone	per ton mile	2d.
Coal, Coke, Culm, Building-stones, Sand, Ironstone, Bricks, Slates etc.	ditto	4d.
Sugar, Grain, Corn, Flour, Timber, Bar-iron, Castings, Chains etc.	ditto	5d.
Fish, Cotton, Earthenware etc.	ditto	6d.
Hay, Straw, Cork, Wood Baskets (goods of bulky description if not exceeding 500 lbs in weight):	minimum charge may be as for 1 ton for each 500 lb	

[Parcels were limited to 500 lb weight and charged on a sliding scale: 'over this weight the Company may demand any sum they think fit'.]

1879

Moving on to 1879, a break with the origins of the Company came when the Duke of Sutherland stated (as already mentioned) that he did not wish to offer himself for re-election to the Board on 8th March. (He had notified in December 1878).

It was announced at the end of March, that the existing iron rails were to be replaced by steel, and sleepers of 'better quality' would go under them. (Presumably this meant that rectangular-section sleepers would replace the existing half-round section.) The summer proved to be one of the 'typically English' variety; in August flooding at Douglas station was especially severe and trains could not use the terminus. An incoming train from Peel was stopped by rising waters near St John's, and a train was despatched from Douglas (despite the floods, it seems) to rescue stranded passengers; however, it became stuck at Quarter Bridge 'where the embankment and Signalman's House behind had been carried away by the waters'. Crosby station was an island, surrounded by water.

Some trucks on a Down train were derailed near St John's and were detached to allow the passenger portion to continue. Later, the offending trucks, re-railed, were 'propelled to Douglas in front of the next train'. [An expedient which certainly would not have been permitted on mainland Britain.]

The year began badly for the Station Master (Hodgkinson) at Castletown who was dismissed for cash shortages and a 'general post' followed, the Port St Mary man going to Castletown, Santon's to Port St Mary and Ballasalla's to Santon. Was Santon considered to be a more important traffic point than Ballasalla?

Though work on the MNR was progressing, it was far from ready and its Board was showing the stuff of independence, refusing at this date to accept an offer from the IOMR to work its traffic for 1s. 6d., per train mile. The IOMR countered by saying they never made such an offer and they 'had not heard of it'. During April the IOMR reminded the Ramsey faction that no arrangement had yet been made for a junction 'at or near St John's', nor for the proposed girder bridge over the river there, 'This must be done before our busy season commences'. There followed one of those typical interchanges between London Board, the General Purposes Committee and another party. Rixon (for London) told the Committee to keep out of MNR negotiations. The Committee told London it was they who would have to make arrangements with the MNR Board 'to avoid complications and the settlement of details'. It seems Rixon was negotiating directly with the MNR Engineer, Thomas, at the London premises.* Douglas had its way and settled with the MNR on 31st May; conditions for a financial agreement included:

1. That the IOMR made financial arrangements with the Isle of Man Banking Co. Ltd., who had placed MNR Debentures for them.
2. That the IOMR's Receipts and Expenditure Account for working the Ramsey Line would be kept separately at the IOM Banking Co. Ltd.

The IOMR agreed to open such an account.

Next it was the Governor's turn to interfere; he insisted that the two Railways' timetables should be published as one and that IOMR times should not be altered without reference to the MNR Board. This incensed the IOMR Board as the MNR was certainly not going to be placed in a position where it could control train times on Peel and Port Erin Lines. Nor was the Governor to be allowed to interfere when, as was the practice, the ordinary timetable was suspended for a day such as on Gala Days etc.

Now it was July; Grainger (contractor for the MNR) wanted to move the IOMR St John's station building 'to the other side of the line'; we may imagine the uproar at this. And then the order came, 'The station is not to be further interfered with.'

There followed a row over through bookings which the Governor insisted should be available within three months of opening the MNR. Neither Company would comply, the IOMR especially not wanting to add to its stock of tickets whilst the contemplated arrangement was only for one year. The Douglas directors sent a stiff note to London underlining their objection to the Governor 'having power over the line' but adding that they were willing to comply if the London directors overruled them. 'Through booking was never contemplated', it was told. Which seems rather shortsighted.

One limitation on the Peel Line was obviated when the Postmaster General agreed to install Single Needle instruments and remove the 'Alphabetical ones presently in use'. It was a single bright light in what was becoming a gloomy year for the IOMR and in the middle of August, word reached Douglas that the MNR *was* interfering at St John's, altering the place and had had 'a van and engine off the road'. Douglas sent a telegram to Greenbank urging him to come over immediately and make a report. The

---

*Watson & Smith's office also occupied Rixon's building!

MNR's view of this was that they had made alterations as per a Working Agreement, this having been executed on 6th May previously.

Leaving MNR affairs for the moment; back in Douglas, Gelling & Kaye had the building of an extension to the Carriage Shed well in hand, and at St John's a new siding was being laid. The MNR station there was incomplete. The oft-poor August weather had brought heavy rain and a second flooding caused the cessation of trains for two days on the Peel Line, which was washed away. In that same week, both Companies did a 'U-turn' and agreed to issue through tickets and from this time the Minute Book makes monthly reference to MNR traffic; the entry for October 1879 reads:

Receipts	£713 16s. 7d.
Due to IOMR	£410 2s. 6d.
Due to MNR	£303 14s. 1d.

It may be noted that G.H. Wood was in receipt of £29 3s. 4d. a month; he may be said to be the focal figure of *both* undertakings at this juncture.

It was reported at the MNR, AGM on 27th February, 1879, that three-quarters of the line had been built and confidence to complete the job by the end of June was expressed. This proved optimistic; even though revised dates of an opening on 15th July were soon put about, it was not until 17th July that Col Rich (described as 'the Government Surveyor') inspected the work and finding it wanting, returned again on 29th July. Even then, he listed further requirements. Bravely, the Board and a few others made a trial trip on 1st August . . . so far, so good. But the narrative has run ahead somewhat and return must be made to earlier matters.

Finance was a recurring MNR problem, but its detail and the resort to Government borrowing made for frustration all round, and it is probably wiser to do no more than hint at everyday difficulties than return to them repeatedly.* Sufficient to say that the Company relied entirely on the Government guarantee and fought the setbacks on the construction front with such vigour as was left to it, when battles with the Governor, the Keys and the Treasury engaged so much time. All along, the Board was confident that if the IOMR could earn an average of £740 per mile, then a similar target of £600 was within MNR reach. The accounts for 1878 showed that £32,952 had come in whilst expenditure was £49,188, but by March, the outlook was healthier when further financial arrangements had been settled. On 14th October (in the year following) an Amending Act was passed by Tynwald to clear up the details.

Anticipating the coming of the MNR, the SUN had said in February that the Ramsey coach driver would receive a testimonial as his coach would be withdrawn when the line opened. The SUN's energetic reporter then spent some time describing the several bridges on the line, the RELIANCE arriving in late March with more iron girders: he noted on 9th April that the 'new girders for the Michael Bridge are lying on Ramsey Quay'. It was May before the last girders were off the Steam Packet Co.'s MONA'S ISLE. Continuing, 'Ramsey station is nearly complete; it is a neat but not large wooden structure'. Boyde Bros. now added an engine shed in corrugated iron to the Ramsey site, receiving £289 for the work. The same edition of the SUN remarked on the good fortune of the contractor who was able to recruit extra

---

*A copy of the Indenture between the Governor and MNR re Government Guarantee (29 Nov 1879) is in Tower Collection.

labour at the eleventh hour from Laxey miners, who were on strike.
It was convenient to hold MNR Board Meetings at Thornhill, the residence of J.T. Clucas, the Chairman (after whose house a MNR locomotive was named). In early June 1879, Alex Mitchell of Ramsey (soon to become its first Station Master) sent the directors a letter 'What of the general holiday to which the people of the town had been pledged? We trust the line will be opened, if not in the presence of royalty at one time anticipated . . . at least with a . . . public celebration.'

The matter of how the line was to be worked was still an open question in early March and now the MNR offered the IOMR 1s. 5d. per train mile. The IOMR wanted 1s. 6d. at least but eased the pressure when the MNR threatened to work it themselves. Final agreement at this higher figure was on 14th July although the SUN had reported it a fortnight earlier. Rather than the IOMR should work the line with its own stock, the MNR agreed to provide it (complete) by 15th July and if failing to do this, would give the IOMR up to £5 per day additionally until the Inspector was satisfied and the line opened in due course. The terms were for twelve months, thereafter at one month's notice on either side: the rate was indeed 1s. 6d. per train mile, with a minimum payment of £3,587. Final arrangements were concluded on 18th September; the IOMR was to work the Railway from 23rd September, opening was further delayed to this date when Col Rich came a third time and found matters still wanting on 10th September.

Arrangements were also made for the use of each Company's stock working over the other's rails:

    Locomotives   6d. per mile
    Carriages (1st class)   1d. per mile
    Carriages (composite)   ¾d. per mile
    Remaining stock   ½d. per mile
    ['Double carriages' (i.e. IOMR bogie or MNR six-wheel) were charged at double rates.]

The Engineer's enquiries about rolling stock resulted in five tenders for locomotives being submitted before a Board Meeting in January 1879. The Avonside Engine Co.,* Avon Street, Bristol, quoted for two locomotives @ £1137 each. In competition, Sharp, Stewart & Co. Ltd.†, Atlas Works, Manchester wanted £1100 each. In the event, the latter won the contract. The foregoing were the only tenders of the five to be given consideration.

As to other stock, The Swansea Wagon Co. Ltd.‡ received an order for four

---

*The Board may have suspected Avonside was in financial difficulties.
   Originally Henry Stothert & Co. incorporated 1837: became Stothert, Slaughter & Co. 1841: thence, Avonside Ironworks 1844: Slaughter, Gruning & Co. 1856: Avonside Engine Co. Ltd., 1864. Into voluntary liquidation 31st May, 1879, dissolved 1887. Meanwhile Edwin Walker formed new Company of same name. Avonside Engine Co., liquidated 1934: goodwill etc. to The Hunslet Engine Co. Ltd., Leeds.

†Thomas Sharp and Richard Roberts established 1828, of Atlas Works, Bridgewater Street, Manchester: became Sharp Bros., 1843: thence, Sharp, Stewart 1852: Sharp, Stewart & Co. Ltd., 1864. Moved to Glasgow (Clyde Locomotive Works) 1888. Amalgamated with Neilson, Reid & Co., Dubs & Co., February 1903 to form The North British Locomotive Co. Ltd.

‡Registered 1866 as Shackleton, Ford & Co. Ltd.; name changed February 1868 to Cheltenham & Swansea Railway Carriage & Wagon Co. Ltd. and again October 1922 to The Swansea Wagon Co. Ltd. Into voluntary liquidation December 1927. The MNR therefore, was actually supplied by the C&SRC & WCL though maker's plates on the vehicles read SWANSEA WAGON CO. LIMITED.
(Details of all rolling stock will be found in Vol. III.)

(later reduced to two) 'passenger brake vans', four 'covered vans' and three 'cattle wagons'. The passenger carriages were carried on six-wheels with flexible provision for curves and, in the Working Agreement with the IOMR were classified as 'double-size coaches' as opposed to 'ordinary-sized coaches' i.e. the four-wheeled stock of the IOMR. The wording of the Agreement stated 'in case double ones (long cars) are used, double the above charges will be made'.

In mid-July the Press announced that opening would take place on 29th July, 1879, but this proved premature. In fact, rolling stock had only been landed earlier that month, firstly carriages on the MONA and then the first locomotive from the CAMEL a few days later. Following Rich's second inspection the aforementioned private trip by directors and some friends took place on 1st August, the paper noting it involved 'a pilot engine and tender' and that some experience had been obtained in the person of Mr Frank Buckett, the IOMR's Traffic Inspector. Another month followed, during which some of Rich's requirements were followed up.

The TIMES had a nice entry about the IOMR's AGM of 5th July; there was a slightly sanctimonious air about the Chairman's 'throwaway',

> our desire has not been to make an undue profit out of the working of the Ramsey Line, nor do we wish to surrender any advantage which we are justly entitled to (hear, hear).

On 30th August the SUN noted that the MNR 'is about thoroughly completed' as Brebner & Fleming were advertising their 'stock of horses and miscellaneous materials for sale the following month'.

This news appeared in the same paper alongside:

> On 29th August, by special invitation, the directors, shareholders and their friends trundled from Ramsey to St John's in a train of six double coaches and a break van well filled. Leaving Ramsey at 9.15 am it called at Bishop's Court for the Bishop (who did not come) and arrived at St John's at 10.50 am. Douglas residents left there at 10.30 am to arrive at St John's at 11 am. The two trains then being joined, returned to Ramsey.*

At Ramsey the party inspected the Works and shed. A train,

> ... left Ramsey at 4.15 pm with eight double coaches and break van. A few miles out of Ramsey, owing to the weight of the train and stiffness of the new rolling stock, the engine was brought to a standstill, so half the carriages were taken on to Michael whence the engine returned and took the remainder to St Germain's. It returned to Michael, picked up the four carriages and took them to St Germain's, where upon all proceeded to St John's to arrive at 7.45 pm. Douglas passengers having alighted, shareholders and others entrained for the return to Ramsey. One engine being found insufficient to take the train over the highest portion of the line, G.H. Wood placed an IOMR's engine at the disposal of the MNR to assist the train to Michael ... In the hurry of the opening, no doubt, the directors seem to have omitted the usual courtesy of sending a ticket to this office.

Of course the extended time taken by the morning train from Ramsey was not entirely due to calling upon the Right Reverend, but speed was naturally low on the rough, unfinished track. It is helpful to remember that the MNR only possessed one engine at this date.

---

*[From St John's to Kirk Michael the IOMR provided an extra engine. J.I.C.B.]

The same reporter commented on the excellent goods and passenger accommodation at St Germain's (then nearest for Peel) 'built in red stone from a quarry near Peel'.* He was also alert enough to learn that ballast – save the river ballast used for the first three miles from Ramsey – 'came from a cutting through drift gravel at Michael'; he also added details on various features of the line.

At St John's, the line crossed the River Neb by two 30-foot wrought iron spans, then climbed at 1 in 132 to Peel Road which was crossed by a 50-foot wrought iron bridge. It then passed under Poortown Road (there was no Halt 'Peel Road' at that time) and reached St Germain's. It passed along the coast at Gob-y-Deigan (Devil's Mouth) and crossed the mouth of Glen Cam on an embankment 70 feet high. The nearby road formed a hairpin bend – and still does. Before the summit of Ballaquine (200 ft) it passed under this road by a 100-foot stone and wrought iron plate and girder bridge. Crossing Glen Mooar the rails were 75 feet above the river level and here was the first of several platelayers' cottages, which were so designed to convert them into small stations if traffic demanded. The viaduct over Glen Wyllin was 55 feet above river level and at the next station, Kirk Michael, a passing loop had (fortunately) been provided for the opening. The line approaching Kirk Michael provided the steepest bank on the MNR line, 1 in 100 for Ramsey-bound trains.

Before Ballaugh (the next station) a twin span bridge crossed the Dhoo River where a passing loop was in course of construction but had not then been completed. No mention is given of any further stations until Lezayre is reached, this was also called Garey. The bridge over the Sulby River which followed, had the longest span of any and at that time was a bow-string girder of 80-foot span whilst the next bridge, crossing the Auldyn, was 40-foot span of wrought iron. The Sulby bridge had been tested with four locomotives, so presumably at least two must have been borrowed from the IOMR for the occasion. Ramsey engine shed was designed 'to hold two engines' and there was an 'iron shed' for carriages to 'hold two trains'. The platform was (then) 100 yards long. The Harbour Tramway was not then begun but would be commenced later and be about ½ mile long.

There would be much relief on 1st September when the steamer DOUGLAS unloaded the second MNR engine at Ramsey. This possibly eased the situation when on 8th September another Special was run for the benefit of 450 National Schools' children between Ramsey and Ballaugh. The SUN's reporter was among them:

> ... marched to the station and were admitted in relays till seated ... in a field in front of Mr J. Brooke, H.K. residence, buns were served out and there were scrambles for nuts and apples. After thoroughly enjoying their day in the country, a few songs were sung by the children followed a hasty walk to Ballaugh station as rain began to fall; the procession in Ramsey was abandoned due to the heavy downpour. Tea and buns were provided in the Schoolroom and at 8 pm the children were dismissed ... teachers and friends had tea in the Girls' School ...

It is difficult for us to conceive the great wonder which that occasion would bring to all involved.

---

*Near the north end of the present promenade.

Within days the same procedure was twice more adopted, a train of eight coaches being required but the journey again confined to the level stretch of the system. Firstly, Dhoon children were taken to Sulby where tea, buns, jam and nuts featured again, and secondly, Presbyterian Church children went to Ballaugh.

Between 18th and 23rd September there was some haste to complete the work – a joint inspection by the Boards of the two Companies involved, brought to light various shortcomings as some stock would not pass over pointwork and certain sidings had not been laid correctly. An intensive training period for operating staff had been assisted by Henry Hunt, the IOMR Locomotive Superintendent, whose men would have to familiarise themselves with the terrain of a railway line quite different from the existing IOMR. Problems were now encountered with the 'Norwegian' type couplings specified by Thomas, which would not work engine-to-carriage nor satisfactorily with IOMR vehicles: the suggestion is that the 'choppers' were mis-shaped and of different height.

Only two days after the MNR opening, the MNR informed the IOMR that the couplings were still 'unsatisfactory' and asked for them to be further modified. Hunt agreed to do this as a transient arrangement only, (purely to enable MNR stock to couple to IOMR 'coaches and waggons until a permanent coupling can be procured') and was authorised to make this temporary work, 'but not more'. [The IOMR Board would not place Hunt in a position where he might take responsibility for complaint by the MNR]. In early October, the MNR arranged for Ashbury (Belle Vue, Manchester) to alter the couplings, Mr Ashbury having been over to make a personal inspection of the problem. He was sent a sample of the IOMR combined buffer/coupling for the purpose.

The MNR opened without ceremony on 23rd September and passenger business went off with reasonable *éclat* but other forms of traffic were postponed until 4th October. The IOMR had noted the poor condition of the MNR freight stock which Grainger had been using as contractor's vehicles(!) and promptly refused to permit it to run over their metals. So the six daily trains (each way) – though of such novelty that the local populace (according to the Press) continued to watch the trains go by at their local station – were not made up of mixed stock as anticipated. Correspondence between the MNR and the IOMR sought to allow the former traffic in such vehicles as might be patched up – it would seem that goods working gradually built up from about mid-October 1879, the weekly cattle market (Monday) in Ramsey being of especial attraction to the Company. By November, the MNR timetable required two locomotives on Saturdays.

Grainger was still about the place, and continuing to use MNR wagons. To prevent conflicting situations, Wood had prepared special Operating Rules* for the time up to and immediately following the completion period, yet in October, Grainger was not only ignoring them, but his men were leaving equipment on the running line to the danger of passing trains. Angry letters were exchanged between director J.C. LaMothe† of the MNR, and Wood, whilst Grainger pressed for payment of work which he claimed was

---

*See end of chapter for summary.
†a High Bailiff of Ramsey.

over and above that specified in the contract, at the same time slowing down his efforts to complete outstanding work as evidence of his displeasure. The Board took it out on Thomas, who does not come out of the affair in good light and was apparently unable to carry any weight with Grainger. The Highway Board decided it would be prudent to inspect all level crossings and Malcolm Grant-Dalton, Resident Engineer to the MNR, was given urgent instructions to fix lamps on all crossing gates.

Ramsey station, designed to contain the Head Office but as yet not ready to do so, was even then incomplete. Lighting had to be installed and a decision to extend the Carriage Shed was ineffectual as a delivery of corrugated iron sheeting had not arrived. The newspapers contained many complaints of the shortcomings of the first timetable, letters emphasising it was virtually impossible to visit Port Erin from Ramsey and return in the same day. From its timetables of 20th September, 1879, the IOMR commenced to include the MNR line in much the same way as the whole of the Island's railways' timetables were set out for almost the next century.

Any harmony between the two railway companies stemmed largely from personalities, of whom J.T. Clucas and G.H. Wood were the most prominent. John Thomas Clucas was not only Chairman of the Manx Northern but a member of the IOMR General Purposes Committee, the local body of shareholders who implemented the London Board's broad decisions at Island level. Clucas it was who had conceived the idea of forming a separate company to promote a railway from St John's to Ramsey, and thus attract capital from a fresh source; it was apparent to him that IOMR affairs still suffered from want of early finance and interest from this source was unlikely. If a new company could build the Ramsey line, the IOMR might work it. In part he was successful, for the fresh undertaking was formed and he himself drew up a plan whereby the line would be worked by the IOMR but, in the event, this arrangement only lasted fourteen months. In its early months, the MNR benefitted from the goodwill and enthusiasm of Wood (a Yorkshireman with an immense capacity for work) whose generosity towards the infant newcomer was shown by the loan of expertise and men who showed raw MNR employees the ways in which the job could be done . . . how fortunate was the MNR, remembering how uninformed were the IOMR employees when it commenced operations! Not that Wood's judgement was entirely based on goodwill, for he had that intelligence of a northerner to see what was good for the MNR might also benefit his own Company. However, this did not always bring financial rewards to equal degree and in writing to T.J. Hughes, Manager of the Festiniog Railway, on 20th February, 1883 concerning the working period IOMR/MNR, he said:

> The amount we received did not pay us apart from the benefit we got by Passengers having to travel about 9 miles over our line.

The MNR soon found it could not cope with the traffic with only two engines, one of which would often be out of service for repairs; a third engine was then added. The carriage stock was adequate for normal times but the IOMR loaned extra vehicles when required. At this time, St John's was of the nature of an end-on-terminus, a 'frontier station' where passengers (between Ramsey and Douglas) had to leave the terminating MNR train and enter the Peel–Douglas working of the IOMR; the MNR terminus was on the west side of the Foxdale road and to reach the IOMR station on its east side, passengers had a short walk – it was not simply a case of crossing a platform. There was, however, a track connection between the two systems linking the MNR running line and the IOMR station loop. A telegraph agreement with the Post Office was arranged and a line was ready for the opening. Whatever MNR signalling existed at St John's, there was no lever frame until weeks after the event . . . What did Col Rich (the Railway's Inspector) have to say about this?* Whilst perhaps confident about the design of Ramsey signalling, the MNR was not so certain about the interchange at St John's and sought the advice of the Signal Superintendent of the LNWR who sent a suggested arrangement on 18th July, 1879.† He described this as a 'minimum arrangement provided BoT inspection is not made. Something more complete would be needed if this is carried out'. Costs of £550 or £780 were quoted.

By and large, Thomas received a lot of stick from the Northern Board; he was blamed for the loss of the summer traffic and, there being indecision up to the last few days about a formal opening date, publicity for that event (apart from newspaper coverage) was minimal until the last minute. Correspondence exchanged at this time confirms that the Ramsey-based undertaking felt it had had more than its quiverful of problems. At least the Board could enjoy the relief of knowing that for the first year of operation, Grainger's would be required to maintain the line under their Supervisor, John Cameron.

If there was one subject which caused bitterness everywhere, it was the system employed to determine who was eligible for a Free Pass. In December, the MNR directors received them for travel over the IOMR between St John's and Douglas, but only so long as for the time the IOMR was working that Railway.# That same month found Gelling & Kaye extending the Douglas Carriage Shed and altering the river bridge at its end, to join the old river walls there: for this purpose, they had had to move the telegraph poles to the other side of the line.

In mid-December, at 9.26 pm on a dark Saturday night, there was a late 'Market Train' from Ramsey which terminated at Kirk Michael and ran back to Ramsey. That night the driver had detached his train and run forward to reverse round the train again. But he misjudged his position and ran back over the loop points which had not been changed. He hit his own train with considerable impact, breaking buffer beams on both engine and brake van. The driver, Cain, had been in the Company's service from the beginning, and his conduct was hitherto unblemished. He was reduced to being a fireman for three months and would be restored to driving then, if satisfactory; this was a typical imposition.

Early in December came the announcement,

> Passengers can book from any station to any station on the two lines, instead of booking to St John's and re-booking there.

---

*Col F.H. Rich was appointed 'Government Director' on the MNR Board wef 16th December under Section 36 of the Railway Regulation Act (1878).

†The plan is missing.

#The MNR had already given Passes to the IOMR.

The year was importantly marked by the introduction of a daily Mail Boat service; heretofore a Tuesday and Friday sailing operated for nine months of the year, with one daily sailing for three months in the summer. Daily sailings would now occur throughout the year; a financial dispute with the British Government was partly the cause of this improvement.

Return must now be made to Wood's Supplementary Rule Book issued on 9th September to cover the remaining period of construction of the MNR and the period of IOMR operation. This followed complaints about slackness among Grainger's men, the leaving of 'trollys' and tools on the running line by construction gangers, and anticipated further slackness of the same order when the line opened and Grainger continued his responsibility, not only for completing works yet unfinished, but also during his period of responsibility for maintaining the line. [Only extracts and not the full set of rules is quoted:]

NOTICE TO GANGERS ETC. ON RAMSEY LINE OF RAILWAY

3. Men must desist from work when a train is 400 yards from them.
5. The line to be inspected by platelayers every morning before 7 am in summer and 8 am in winter and in every evening before they leave off work.
9. After sunset and in foggy weather all engines . . . must show a white light on buffer plank.
10. After sunset and in foggy weather empty engines must carry a white light on the buffer plank and a red tail light.
11. Every train (after sunset etc.) must carry two red sidelights in the rear of the train;* a red board or flag by day, or an extra red tail light by night or in foggy weather must be hung on the back of the engine and/or train to undernote a special train is to follow.
22. No ballasting must be done in foggy weather.

Once more the summer season was a poor one for the Island; such visitors who came were short of money and did not travel much outside Douglas. Those who did were tempted off the railway by extremely low fares offered by the road car operators whose fares became so low that most were sensible enough to conclude that the bottom was too low for everyone. The Barrow Steam Ship Co. and the IOMSP Co. competed in a fare-cutting war whereby 'Round the Island' tours by steamer were offered at 2s. 0d. for Saloon and 1s. 0d. for Steerage class: the IOMSP Co. decided not to repeat the experiment.

Of the two railway systems, the MNR suffered most; expecting to be open for the summer traffic (however poor) they were denied it by a lax Engineer and contractor. What the guarded and careful Wood had in mind when he had reported to London way back in January, 'We have taken possession of the Ramsey Line', can only be surmised, for there were then many hurdles to jump.

---

*The tail light brackets were on the cornerposts of carriages and on the side, not the rear of the post.

Appendix to 1879

Summary of Working Agreement between Isle of Man Railway and Manx Northern Railway re-authorised junction at St John's under MNR Act 1878 Section 8 'at or near St John's'.*

1. IOMR property at St John's includes weigh bridge, water tank, goods shed & sidings.
2. MNR to carry out the work at own expense & IOMR to contribute £300 on completion, MNR to enter IOMR land for the purpose.
3. Existing IOMR passenger station, goods shed, weigh bridge & water tank to be dismantled and re-erected as plan No. 2, save for water tank. Tank to have steam pump and boiler separately housed or below tank, and have constant supply of water sufficient to satisfy IOMR Engineer Henry Greenbank.
4. Payment of £300 by IOMR to be within one month of Greenbank giving Certificate of Completion.
5. MNR to subscribe (at own cost) 'joint girder' for both Railways over brook on west side station.
6. Should MNR's Government Inspector find MNR line west of level crossing to be too close to IOMR, MNR to place further away and be restrained from using the new line until the work is complete.
7. Where MNR rises higher above IOMR, the former to sod slopes from point of rise to a point 25 yards west of bridge over River Neb.
8. MNR to have joint use of island platform but not interfere with IOMR traffic.
9. MNR to have joint use of northern half of footbridge in communication with island platform.
10. All signals, gates, junctions etc. to be under the exclusive control of the IOMR; expenses and maintenance of same, and of working signals together with half the cost of maintaining island platform to be repaid to IOMR quarterly.
11. IOMR reserve right to move junction eastwards at cost to IOMR.
12. All costs incurred in foregoing to be paid by MNR.

Summary of Schedule attached to foregoing Working Agreement.

1. Whole station area except platforms to be filled to level of existing IOMR platforms to be enclosed in 1 ft 6 in. thick concrete walling and to finish 6 in. above rail level.[a]
2. Existing passenger station, brick chimney, urinals, goods shed, weigh bridge and office to be dismantled and re-erected at positions as on Plan No. 2, with interior fittings replaced as directed: the station to be on masonry foundations.†
3. Gate hut at level crossing to be demolished and materials used for any purpose in this Specification.[b]
4. Buffer stops to be fitted to all sidings.
5. All IOMR permanent way materials found defective to be replaced by MNR: ballast to be 8 in. thick under sleepers: points and crossings to be of correct angle.[c]
6. Timber watertank containing 3,000 gallons to be 10 ft above rail level. Well to be provided and steam pump and boiler capable of lifting 1,500 gallons an hour; delivery from tank to track at either side in 4 inch hoses. A water supply from tank to serve urinals.[d]

*From a draft dated 1st August, 1879 in Tower Collection. (The above uses the vernacular of the original document.)

†(The plans referred to are missing from these documents: reference should be made to diagram of St John's 1879 which was prepared from official IOMR documents in Douglas in 1959. The present whereabouts of these plans is not known.)

7. Footbridge to be erected giving 12 ft clearance underside from rail, with three flights of steps, width 8 ft. To be made of timber if desired, but on masonry piers. Lamp room to be placed under south end with fireproof ceiling.[e]

8. Signalling: at west end, levers for Distant signals to be placed opposite points between footbridge and level crossing gates. At east end, the arrangement to be as recommended by Colonel Rich.[f]

9. Name boards to be erected stating ST JOHN'S CHANGE FOR DOUGLAS AND PEEL, and ST JOHN'S CHANGE FOR RAMSEY; to be maintained by IOMR for the first 12 months, and the cost charged quarterly to MNR.

Author's notes on above:

[a]This confirms that the two existing platform areas were at ground level.

[b]In the event, a signal cabin was built at MNR expense at the east end of the station. Only one point at the west end of the station was connected to the cabin.

[c]Note that it is not specified that defective material should be replaced by *new*!

[d]The pumphouse was situated below the tank which was mounted on a base.

[e]This gives a date for the construction of the footbridge, notable for being seldom used . . .!

[f]Information about Distant signals at the west end is lacking: if they existed, they have long disappeared.

1880

Towards the end of January, Wood reported to Pender concerning MNR working results from 23rd September to 31st December of the previous year. 'Very satisfactory', is his conclusion, but he recommends detailed accounts of the working should not be made known outside the Board Room . . . 'even to the local directors' as it had been arranged that the General Purposes Committee would be kept in the dark over MNR financial arrangements.

> I feel sure that if it were known to the directors of the Ramsey Company that we had made a direct profit out of working, we should not be able to continue the Working Arrangement on the same satisfactory basis after the expiration of the first year.

(This criterion was especially necessary in view of the common personalities to both Companies.)

It is helpful to look ahead to 6th November, 1880 when the said Arrangement came to an end and the MNR took over the responsibility. The question was then voiced by the IOMR: had the ending come about due to the IOMR experience of working the 1880 summer traffic? Or had the figures been 'leaked'? It was assumed that something of both had taken place.

By late February, the IOMR had reduced its running time Douglas to Ramsey from 1 hour 45 minutes to 1 hour 31 minutes almost all due to the upgrading of the track. First class return for the journey was 4s. 0d. and 3rd 2s. 6d. and Party Rates were reduced, a 'Party' being eight 1st class or twelve 3rd class passengers.

A new wall and siding were built at St John's, together with other alterations, but when the MNR sent the IOMR a bill for £900 as the latter's half-

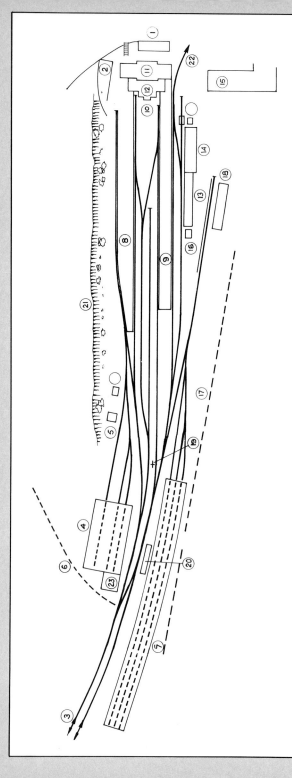

DOUGLAS: enlargement of 1873 arrangements by Greenbank in November 1880 to accommodate additional MNR business

1. Quiggin's premises
2. Stable
3. Main Lines
4. Locomotive Shed & Workshops
5. Guards' Room
6. River boundary
7. Carriage Shed
8. Peel Line platform
9. Port Erin Line platform
10. Bookstall
11. Station building
12. Concourse
13. Goods platform
14. Goods Shed
15. Quiggin's premises
16. Goods Office
17. Ropewalk's wall
18. Sunken Siding & platform
19. 'Signals' (sic)
20. Signal Frame
21. Boundary
22. Quay extension (proposed)
23. Office
24. Water Tank
25. Weighbridge

Plate 27: Union Mills in 1911, and looking towards Peel. The Down platform appears, as does the goods siding, on the left. The 'Sentry Box' (now replaced by a larger wooden building out of sight) is believed to have been the station's pioneer structure. *Collection B.E. Crompton*

Plate 28: A 1930s view of Union Mills, seen again in the Peel direction. Note the gardens developed by Station Master Hogg and how the trees have grown since the previous illustration. The station building and Peel road overbridge are behind the waiting passengers, and UNION MILLS is picked out in whitened stones on the grass banking. *Collection B.E. Crompton*

Plate 30: Tynwald Day, St John's 1932. The ceremonies are over and the niceties of using the footbridge are largely ignored . . . people swarm over the tracks. Also to be seen; the Manx flag flying bravely from the pole, four road motor buses lined up in the yard, four loaded coal wagons standing in the carriage shed siding. Extra ex-MNR and IOMR spare coaches stand at the goods platform on which the ex-WD Knockaloe goods store has been erected. A stack of lineside hay appears on the right. *C.E. Box*

Plate 31: Three-quarters of a mile from the start at Peel, a Douglas train enters the defile of the River Neb at Glenfaba; behind the engine is an 'E' van with duckets removed. The carriages of mixed MNR and IOMR origin, have been fitted with electric lighting. The stock is in the two-tone brown livery of the early 1920s. *F. Bareham*

Plate 33: Port Soderick, with a Port Erin-bound train at the Down platform. The new building on the right was put up in 1896, and the raised platform in the following year. September 1911.
Collection B.E. Crompton

Plate 34: Port Soderick itself was a microcosm of all that Manx holidaymakers expected. A small bay, promenade, swings, rowing boats,

Plate 35: It is a sweltering afternoon at Ballasalla in August 1947 and the young Boyd family wait patiently for a Port St Mary train. Painfully thin after wartime rationing, they expect great things of their host in regaining some weight! The Railway is undergoing great changes; Ballasalla had seen several wartime years of military traffic but by now it was a memory; a reliance on summer numbers was becoming the familiar pre-war pattern. *J.I.C. Boyd*

36: Compare this view of Port St Mary
n with the wooden shack it replaced; a
 grandiose affair is hard to imagine.
e was no more imposing railway build-
n the whole system and for design,
shone even Douglas itself. 1972.
J.I.C. Boyd

37: A quiet moment at Port Erin,
st 1947, a year when the Railway
pany had just spent hundreds of pounds
-upholstering carriages, painting stock,
es and stations and was examining
s to build larger locomotives; diesel and
ric propulsion was under consideration.
unavailability and postwar costs broke
ream. *J.I.C. Boyd*

Plate 39: This may be the second of two early-period pictures taken at Port Erin in the first years of the present century. Both photographs show engines running chimney-first into Douglas, being Nos. 5 and 8; these may have been the two shedded at Port Erin. The fact that the first vehicle is numbered F29 raises a problem without positive answer!   *F. Moore*

Plate 41: St John's from the footbridge in the mid-1930s, looking towards Douglas and the Foxdale Line overbridge in the distance, is depicted in a quiet moment before all three trains depart simultaneously. On the left the train with No. 9 and an ex-MNR six-wheel carriage in the middle, is bound for Ramsey. Centrally is a train from Ramsey to Douglas. It looks as if the arrival from Peel is holding up business. *C.E. Box*

Plate 42: On the same day as the above, this view looks towards Peel from St John's. The double single lines reach westward, that to Peel being the nearer, the ex-MNR line to Ramsey the farther. At top right is the rear of the Foxdale Line station ... and surely this is the late-running train arriving from Peel, for which we all have been waiting? (*see above*) *C.E. Box*

Plate 43: Although this scene at St Germain's was taken as recently as May 1951, it is unlikely it had ever looked much busier in the whole of its lifetime. It was a typical MNR building.
J.D. Darby

Plate 44: Looking up the Donkey Bank towards Gob-y-Deigan on the St Germain's–Kirk Michael section of the MNR. This was a most unstable portion of railway, laid close to the cliffs and requiring constant watch and expense to restore its level and alignment. The track here is chaired. April 1960.
J.I.C. Boyd

Plate 45: The Halt at Gob-y-Deigan was to serve picnickers from Ramsey.
Collection J.I.C. Boyd

Plate 46: Kirk Michael village, looking south, with the railway to the right. Near the top edge of the picture the Glen Wyllin viaduct can be discerned, and towards the lower, the smaller overbridge at Glen Ballyre.
Manx Technical Publications Ltd

Plate 47: In April 1960, Kirk Mic[hael] was deserted; the summer would b[ring] a different impression.   *J.I.C. B[oyd]*

Plate 48: Bishop's Court Halt (look[ing] towards Ramsey) the subject of sev[eral] problems with the Bishop. Orris[dale] No. 1 gates can just be seen in [the] distance; the signal here was linke[d to] the gates and not used in conjunct[ion] with the Halt. April 1950.   *J.D. D[arby]*

Plate 49: Trains pass [at] Ballaugh, the mixed o[ne] of coach and wagons is o[n] its way to St John's. Th[e] sidings in the foregroun[d] were so laid out in 1920[/]22. April 1960. *J.I.C. Boy[d]*

Plate 50: The old station at Sulby Glen, and the only one of its type on the MNR; it was intended to call it Sulby Siding when opened in 1880. In 1910 the building was deemed to be too near the running line and was razed to the ground in favour of a new one.

Manx Museum

Plate 51: Sulby Glen as rebuilt and appearing in August 1951. This was arguably the most modern looking station on the Island, but the shortish platform created difficulties during the Second World War. *J.I.C. Boyd*

52: Lezayre, looking towards ·y in May 1961. Tickets were from here until that month, gh it had ceased to be a Request n 1958 . . . it was simply a matter om you knew . . . and the train- ould oblige. *J.I.C. Boyd*

Plate 53: The end – or the beginning – of Ramsey Line. The main platform has ca vans in it, so it is probably a Monday, N day. So the St John's train leaves from bay platform. A second engine stands outs the carriage shed. 1931. C.E.

Plate 54: Ramsey, as seen from the buff The ornamental chimney tops, barge bo the workshop end (*extreme right*) and difference in the original engine shed v and its extension are of note. Beyond lengthy corrugated iron carriage shed, main line reaches out monotonously to west. Engines standing on the revers neck have created a solid apron of oil clinker on the ground. March 1962.

J.I.C. Bo

Plate 55: In the mid-1930s the Ramsey Harbour line saw feverish periods of activity when a coal boat arrived, followed by days of complete desertion. There is hardly a person about; the dredger is laid up, men lean disconsolately on a cart stopped in the middle of the road, and yarn. The swing bridge is closed against river traffic; the quayside warehouses are inactive. It is probably a Sunday! C.E. Box

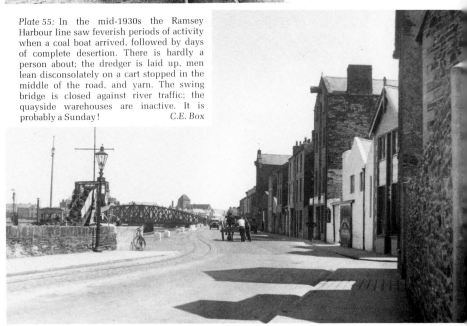

share of the business, there was trouble. The IOMR maintained the estimated and agreed cost was £600 and would pay only £300. By and large, relations were deteriorating anyway.*

Business between the IOMR and MNR was not very brisk; after the MNR asked and received the aforementioned fare reductions, Picnic Party tickets for 10 persons or more were introduced and single fares would apply. In June the IOMR only made 7s. 7d. from working the MNR over a fortnight.

There was mixed opinion within the MNR concerning the Arrangement and at an Extra-Ordinary Meeting on 18th October, shareholders who thought that they were victims of a bad bargain and feeble direction, refused to enter the meeting room and thus prevented the forming of a quorum. The directors were quite unprepared for this method of attack, but ultimately the opposition was defeated. On 16th October, the Press reported the collapse of IOMR/MNR negotiations and oddly, mention of the final day of IOMR operations did not reach the pages of the SUN until 26th February the next year.

And what was the IOMR view of things consequent upon working the MNR summer traffic? There were several factors which aggrieved and they would not, therefore, continue as now without changes: a more-acceptable scheme would be: (August)

1. The MNR to receive 55 per cent of gross earnings but 50 per cent of any sum exceeding £8,000 per annum.
2. The IOMR to maintain the MNR rolling stock.
3. The number of trains to be not less than last year.
4. The Agreement to run for 3, 7 or 10 years or six months' notice by either party at the 3rd or 7th year.

The IOMR maintained that traffic was far less than anticipated by the MNR promoters before the Tynwald and in consequence, the IOMR would not work it, save on a percentage they named themselves. Further, because of a dry season, track and masonry work had not been through a testing time. Lastly, the IOMR had expected the MNR to develop the traffic. Another IOMR proposal appeared in October but was rejected by the MNR who gave a calendar month's notice to terminate the current system on 5th October.

From 7th November through bookings would continue and IOMR staff would still work MNR stock within St John's station at a charge of £330 per annum. Joint timetables would be issued and the cost shared but Free Passes to MNR directors would be withdrawn.

The Steam Packet Co. asked the IOMR to support a special steamer which it would put on each evening to Liverpool for the carrying of fish for the early morning Fish Market on the mainland; the matter disappears for several months without answer, only to be resurrected as an enquiry from the Railway to the Steam Packet Co. (this in July) for a night steamer for that purpose. Agreement was reached on the basis of there being a minimum of 400 boxes (40 tons) each night. The two concerns then circulated both fishermen and fish buyers; the boat would leave Douglas each evening 8 pm – 1 am.

To promote extra holiday business, an imaginative scheme to take visitors to Peel and then by 'coaches over the mountain' to Port Erin, was devised in

---

*Manx Museum: St John's Plan (Daniel Cregeen) R/174; Douglas alterations (ditto) R/175.

April. Mr Thurston of Peel was prepared to furnish coaches @ £50 per season but the Railway would have to send the horses and men. The Company found this 'undesirable'.

A new IOMR locomotive was delivered from Beyer, Peacock at a cost of £1,230 (No. 7, TYNWALD). The Greeba community having once more asked for a station, was refused one.

A strange mishap occurred at Crosby on 15th May

> ... on reaching Crosby something in connection with the cylinders got out of order and the engine could not be started ... of the Down train. Delay was considerable as there were only two engines with steam up. The other, intended for the Castletown Line, came to the rescue.

Stations on the IOMR were now becoming a more frequent objective for thieves and Santon was robbed at the height of the July season when two men made off with £6.

The IOMR, AGM had minuted that, although the railway system was now complete

> the island will not receive the full benefit of it until the Port of Douglas is brought into communication with the principal terminus by an adequate thoroughfare to the New Pier, and a Tramway along the Quay. This rests entirely with the Government of the Island.

[It was the Railway's complaint that Boat Trains had to reach Douglas unnecessarily early in order to transfer passengers and luggage from station to steamer.] Legislation was to be sought.

New pointwork was purchased from Ransomes & Rapier Ltd., Ipswich[*] and a new siding was laid at Union Mills (and almost at once, it was agreed to convert this to a passing loop). The existing siding at Port Soderick was to become a passing loop, and a house built there for the Station Master at a cost not above £120.

The MNR was asked to share the cost of covering two platforms at St John's but after estimates were examined, the matter was shelved.[†]

With a view to wider publicity on the mainland, MNR and IOMR came together with the Steam Packet Co. and produced a joint Guide in December. There was an expensive incident at Colby where a field gate had been left open and the first train from Port Erin ran into a flock of sheep in the dark.

The IOMR year ended in progressive mood: Greenbank was to submit yet further Plans[#] for extensions at Douglas namely; goods office, booking office, parcels office, waiting room, refreshment room etc. (The plans were to lie on the table until October 1882 when they were rejected.)

We may now look at the year from the MNR point of view. On the 17th January, Col Rich inspected the route again and found an abutment of the road overbridge just north of Kirk Michael was unsound – the resultant alteration was an unusual curve buttress.

---

[*]RANSOMES & RAPIER, Waterside Works, Ipswich, was founded by J.A., R.J. and R.C. Rapier in 1869, initially for the manufacture of railway equipment but they diversified into cranes, excavators, water-control apparatus etc. Took over the railway and bridge business from Ransome, Sims & Head (later Ransome, Sims & Jefferies) so that the latter could concentrate on agricultural machinery etc. The Waterside Works closed 1987–8.

[†]Manx Museum: Greenbank's Plans for platform covers are undated.

[#]Manx Museum: Plans include a 'Grand Hotel' in stone and brick.

The slopes of cuttings and embankments were too steep and had not been grass-seeded; the track at Gob-y-Deigan was subsiding (a habit which continued thereafter). Some of the rails on curves were dog-legged and, on the viaducts, rails were not level. The St John's signalling (clearly the more expensive installation to meet an Inspection) was unsatisfactory and there was no diagram in the signal cabin. Most of this was put down to inadequate supervision during construction . . . and Thomas was blamed. Nonetheless, the Board was prepared for him to continue as Engineer but only at the cost of his 'travelling expenses'.

In an expansive mood, the MNR Board enquired of Ashbury for the supply of timber bolsters and of Beyer, Peacock, Black, Hawthorn† and Sharp, Stewart for another locomotive. Two bolsters were duly ordered, and Beyer obtained the locomotive order, it being considered they were the most reliable supplier, albeit they were the most expensive: that choice proved to be the correct one.

Still on the MNR, a lodge was erected at West Kella crossing and a 'Booking Office' at Lezayre,‡ both by Boyde Bros. each being built in stone. They were completed by November. Variations in the timetable according to season were no doubt recommended to follow the IOMR's own experience, whose interest was clearly one of profit by working the MNR. Running time over MNR metals, including all station stops, was a few minutes under the hour; summer fares St John's–Ramsey were 3s. 0d. and 2s. 2d. return for each class. Eight trains each way daily operated during high season July–August. Also in July, the MNR wanted 'to introduce through coaches when practicable' and sugared the request by asking if the IOMR would extend the Arrangement beyond November. For that period, the IOMR then relented and allowed 'two through coaches and a van on the first train to Douglas and the last out of it daily', the MNR's portion of the train to be without cost to the IOMR who, in the peak period, still needed all its stock available. Out of season, five trains each way sufficed over the Northern Line for its own purposes.

The delivery of MNR locomotive No. 3 THORNHILL brought to the fore the matter of Ramsey quays and the station; a plan to extend down the Ramsey quays from the terminus was not new,* but without that facility it had cost £9 to bring the engine from ship to station. John Cameron, (formerly overseer for Grainger and now the MNR's recently-appointed Permanent Way Inspector), was in charge of the trans-shipment; he was a man who could set about any job and was to become one of the MNR's principal assets. A suitable 1,050 yard long tramway had been the subject of a Tynwald Committee set up on 25th March, and Thomas had produced a Plan† showing the Extension as a continuation of the track through the Locomotive Shed, crossing Bowring Road, running along a road constructed for the purpose to join the West Quay, continuing along it and then, by a sharp

---

†Black, Hawthorn & Co., Gateshead. Founded by William Black and Thomas Hawthorn who took over from R. Coulthard & Co. in 1865. Built mainly industrial locomotives; ceased trading 1902. Goodwill etc. to R.&W. Hawthorn, Leslie & Co. Ltd., Newcastle on Tyne.

*The MNR applied for the Extension under Section 12 of the MNR Act of 1878.

‡In reality, a small and substantial station.

†Manx Museum: Ramsey Extension Plans were scrutinised in the IOMR's Company storeroom in 1969 but have not been traced by the Author subsequently.

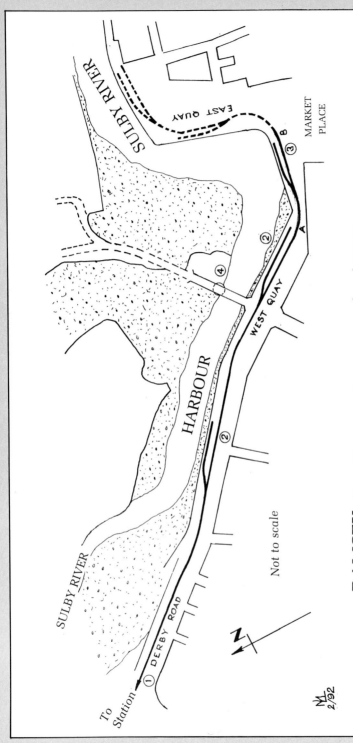

RAMSEY: Quay Tramway (Lease surrendered 1951)

1. Connection to station yard
2. Loading etc. sidings
3. Ultimate extent of Tramway
4. Swing Bridge

A. Station to point B lifted 1954–7
B. Beyond this point lifted 1925

curve, terminating on the East Quay. The Committee visited the site on 29th March and objected to the Plan, to the effect that Thomas produced another in April, this time the Extension leaving the station yard north of the Locomotive Shed. Certain roadway alterations of this first Plan were now obviated and the nasty curve to the East Quay was eased. Finding the scheme was agreeable, the Committee duly reported and while as yet awaiting approval of the Harbour Commissioners, Tynwald gave authorisation on 13th July.

The Clerk of Rolls said he was glad Ramsey was setting such a good example, and 'hoped it would be followed by another Company' (hear, hear). He did not think the IOMR would be 'fully developed until they followed the example of the other ports'. No sidings were shown at first but the amended Plan had 'side lines' as recommended by the Committee.

(To summarize the future of the Extension; construction began in summer 1882 but official permission to use the line did not come from the Harbour Commissioners until March 1883. The East Quay Line was never built. The easternmost section along the West Quay was lifted in 1925 and the whole of the remainder was covered by concrete in 1954–7.)

The Extension's most important era came after the MNR was connected to the Foxdale lead mines by the building of the Foxdale Railway; traffic in lead into a Ramsey store and shipment thereof, plus inwards coal traffic for mines and other users including the railway, was its staple purpose. When mining ceased before World War I, its business diminished almost solely to coal coming in off Ramsey Steamship Co. boats (frequently ex-Whitehaven). Secondary traffic included building materials and bagged feeding-stuffs. No special workings were required and the Ramsey-based engine would work the line between passenger turns. Following World War II, all railway coal came in through Ramsey for distribution to the various engine sheds and even Douglas was so served until closure of the Ramsey Line. From the rearmost siding at the station, the Extension continued by the gateway through the walled yard, crossed the road on the level and ran down the street alongside the quays; turnouts to the sidings were of street-tramway-type, single-blade fashion. Being the only railway-connected port on the Island's railway system, gave Ramsey a one-time importance which Douglas, Peel and Port Erin did not enjoy. (Coal shipments still arrive by sea.)

As the year closed on the MNR scene, Col Rich was back again to inspect: the MNR must have been among several railways which gave him sleepless nights. Gob-y-Deigan was still subsiding and Rich needed drains improving and walling to be made. St Germain's was to have improved living accommodation and Ramsey some new offices: at Cooilbane, a gate lodge was to be erected. The-then station building at Sulby Glen had been sited too near the rails and was moved back. Unlike the timber buildings on most of the IOMR section, such work would be done in stone from a small quarry working in Glen Cam.

Up to now the MNR Company possessed no workshop because important stock repairs had been done at Douglas; for £155 a workshop was now to be built at Ramsey. Herein, the Company's foreman-fitter Halstead (employed since November) might, in due course, have held sway. [He was a substitute for the man recommended for the job by Beyer, Peacock but who was deemed to be too expensive for the Company to take on.] Only paid £2 10s. 0d. per week and without premises, he once drove a ballast train through the unopened level crossing gate at 'Ballacrye', and his department was then put under the command of William Hughes, the Traffic Manager. Disgusted, Halstead left before 'his' workshop was finished.

Back on IOMR metals, special workings were run for fishermen from Peel for the Tynwald celebrations, night trains for the circus, school trips for literally hundreds of children, for Rechabite Meetings in Peel, Glen Helen Flower Show, Brass Band contests, Ramsey Agricultural Show, Peel Flower Show, 'Foxdale Pay Day', Peel Regatta and Races, and there were Specials for the Governor.

Wood's daily diary was a personal record reflecting his Yorkshire origins; what he wrote to the Board and what the diary contained was couched in quite different terms: some features of his Board Reports for the year touched on matters as yet unmentioned.* Firstly, the transfer of the £5,000 Preference Shares to Watson & Smith to terminate their relationship was now held up by a lawsuit between them and Mr Dumbell. Secondly, the net profit of working the MNR for 23rd September to 6th March this year had been £9,164 3s. 0d., a bright light in an otherwise bleak time. Wood was especially worried that passenger figures had shown an overall drop since the IOMR opened, though other traffics were doing better. He kept myriad statistics; one was:

> stations producing the greatest receipts – in order: Douglas, Peel, Castletown, St John's, Port St Mary, Ballasalla.

Excluding the Ramsey system, the employees were: Permanent Way, 37; Traffic, 66; Locomotive Department, 22; Head Office, 6; a total of 131 men with an average weekly pay packet of 19s. 8d.

Late in 1879 the IOMR purchased from Taubman, Quiggin's† old rope-walk and, during a severe frost period when road haulage was almost at a standstill, Wood employed outside carters to 'fill in the low ground there, at a low rate of pay'; this area formed part of 'The Lake' mentioned earlier. Beyond, the track gangs were lifting iron rails from the sharp curves of the South Line and putting down steel ones in their place.

Col Rich's notes after Inspection of MNR on the 9th December, 1880.#

Inspection of Works.
Weekly by Ganger. Monthly by Inspector with written reports. Gangers should be provided with flags and lamps.

---

*Manx Museum: MD15073. 1880–1, 1884–1905.

†'QUIGGINS': established 1821 by Robert Quiggin as ropemakers, but soon extended into timber and building materials importers and suppliers. In the 1850s, a son, Edward Todd Quiggin, joined the firm and took in a partner, John Joseph Taggart. When Edward died, Taggart bought the shares from his widow in 1899 and in due course his successors (the Dean family) became the owners – as pertains today. Ropemaking ceased in the 1950s but timber and building materials now form part of a wider business involving timber preservation and manufacture of roof trusses. The firm's address, Quiggin & Co. Ltd., Lake Timber Yard, is mindful of the historic feature of the site: the firm has always been a neighbour of the IOMR since the latter's formation.

#Original in Tower Collection.

Works.
Bridges at Peel Road should be marked and watched and contractor should be required to put this bridge in a permanently secure state. A drystone wall should be built at the toe of the breach on the east side of the Railway at Gob-y-Deigan. This will keep water table clear and assist in securing the breach. The surface of the side drains should be regulated and kept clear at both sides, all along the Railway.

The stream of water which crosses the public road at the north side of Gob-y-Deigan should be carried to the drain or culvert under the Railway by pitching the sides and bottom from the east side of the Railway culvert to the rock above, a distance of about 6 yds. This will prevent the soil washing into the Railway culvert and stopping it up, and secure the bank which is slipping.

The water should be prevented from lodging in the horizontal breaks on the brows, by cutting surface drains straight into the sea.

F.H. Rich

10th December, 1880.

P.S. Engine NORTHERN which drew the 3 pm train from Ramsey yesterday is dangerously unsteady and will do a great deal of harm to the permanent way.

*Précis of Wood's letter, dated 27th January, 1880, to Board of MNR re IOMR working of MNR.

... a brief report of working your Railway from 23rd September last (the date of its being opened to public traffic), to 31st December or end of your financial year ...

... three months over which we have had experience are about the worst three months in a year to test an undertaking which in all probability which derive most of its income in the summer months ... on IOMR receipts for years 1878 and 1879 during four months June–September were 59% (Peel Line) and 5% (Port Erin Line) of the total year ... earnings on MNR in (period of our working) averaged £6 8s. 5d. per mile per week (IOMR for same period was £7 10s. 11d. per mile per week) ... 27,192 tickets issued in 14 weeks: proportions 1st to 3rd class were 10% 1st and 90% 3rd (greater than the Peel and Port Erin Lines as to 1st class) ... through bookings came into force in December ...

[Wood's report shows the heaviest tonnages of goods traffic were (in order of weight): lime, bricks/tiles/cement, coal, potatoes/vegetables etc.) ... of these weights 732 tons were transferred from Peel to Ramsey Line and 330 tons in the opposite direction.]

... Complaints have reached me ... on apparent high rate charged for goods ... I should be happy to revise the whole of the rates ...

In anticipation of a heavy traffic during the coming summer I respectfully suggest ... purchasing an additional locomotive for your line is worthy of the consideration of your Board ...

*Précis of Wood's comments etc., dated 31st January, 1880, to John Pender MP (Chairman IOMR) re working MNR.

... submit Statement of Accounts for working Ramsey Line 23rd September–31st December, 1879, and brief report ...

*Original in Tower Collection.

... working has been very satisfactory and the accounts and this report deal fully ... I think the information they contain ought to have a limited circulation and should not be known outside the Board Room ... not shown this report or accounts ... to the local directors ... if it were known to the Ramsey directors ... we had made direct profit out of the working we should not be able to continue the agreement on the same satisfactory basis ... clear profit of £202 7s. 2d. for about 14 weeks ... and in the winter portion ... only run five trains a day each way ...

... MNR to pay all engineering and legal expenses under the agreement ... (£50 paid to Mr Rixon) ... account includes ... £17 being cost of repairs to the rolling stock rendered necessary through one of the Engine Drivers on 13th December running his engine into an empty train of carriages standing at Kirk Michael station ...

... run 15,043 train miles over Ramsey Line at average cost of 14.08d. per mile: we receive for working it 1s. 6d. per train mile ... 1,062 tons of goods over our Peel Line and about 627 tons over the Port Erin Line in consequence of the Ramsey Line ... 11¼% of MNR passengers travelled over some portions of our own lines.

*Col Rich's letter, dated 11th February, 1880, to J. Pearce (Secretary & Manager MNR)

The Abbey,
Whiteabbey,
BELFAST.

Dear Sir,

I am not aware of the builders of the engines on the Manx Northern or Isle of Man Railway.

Beyer, Peacock have built the most satisfactory engines for the Light Railways with which I am acquainted.

Sharp, Stewart are pretty nearly as good engine builders in my opinion Hawthorn of Newcastle has also built some that have not given satisfaction. I think a great deal depends on the specification on which the builders tender or make their price.

For instance, some that Hawthorn have built have cast iron wheels and Bessemer Steel tires which are not nearly so durable as Wt. Iron wheels with Crucible Steel tires. The class of iron used in the boilers also varies very much. My advice would be to ask for tenders from each of the three above named builders requesting them to specify the nature of the materials in the several parts of the locomotive that they propose to supply and then make a resolution from the three tenders. If this plan is not followed I would ask Beyer, Peacock for a price of their best class engine for narrow gauge rys. and request them to send in spcn. at the same time.

Yours truly,
F.H. Rich (Signed)

P.S. Address to me always at 5 New Street, Spring Gardens, London.

J. Pearce, Esq.,
MNR,
Ramsey.

*Original in Tower Collection.

Col Rich's letter to J. Pearce (Secretary & Manager MNR) re Permanent Way Men and re Sharp, Stewart etc.

> Board of Trade,
> Whitehall Gardens,
> S.W.
>
> 4th November, 1880
>
> My dear Mr Pearce,
> The men on Capital Account ought if possible to be kept distinct from the 'Regular' permanent way men. The latter service should not I think require more than 12 permanent men. The Manx Northern has no clipping of Hedges or mowing. It is well ballasted and the rail is well and permanently final. A man to each mile is the complement on ordinary Railways with Hedges to clip and dig and hay to Mow and hooke and the ordinary Guage requires more maintenance as the traffic is heavier. The drainage of the MNR is also fairly good and I certainly think Cameron should do with 12 permanent men. He might probably have to employ a few Extra Men after any extraordinary wet weather or on the sudden break up after a long severe frost. Bear in mind that these Inspectors always ask for all they can get.
> I think Sharp, Stewart are not behaving well in asking the Coy to pay for putting their defective engines to rights. You may tell them such is my opinion and if they offer to put them right at their own expense the Coy. might employ one of their men to examine the stock on taking it over from the IOM Coy. OR BETTER STILL they might ask the Loco. Engineer of the Belfast & Northern Cos. Railway to do it saying they would be happy to give him a fee of £10 10s. 0d. for his services in addition to his travelling expenses. I think his name is R. Malcolm. He would advise as to the engines.
> Thanks also for the newspaper. I congratulate Mr Clucas and the Directors on their Victory over J.W. Corotry & Co.†
>
> Yrs. truly,
>
> F.H. Rich (Signed)
>
> P.S. I recommend that Sharp, Stewart be told in reply to their letter that the Dirs. think such LATE BUILT engines should not require NEW SYSTEMS but should be fitted by the Makers with good and durable working gear at the Maker's expense.

1881

The added responsibility of operating the MNR had fallen mainly on the shoulders of three loyal IOMR employees, Messrs. Wood, Frank Buckett (formerly Douglas Station Master but now Traffic Superintendent), and Hunt, the Locomotive Superintendent. Each was given a bonus for his services and Wood, in addition, a testimonial. It must have been too much for Buckett for his heart failed and he died early in the year; the Company acknowledged its debt and paid his widow to assist the children's upbringing.

The extra trackwork, approved in 1880 for Union Mills and Port Soderick, had been delayed due to a shortage of labour, but work now began. The goods sheds intended for Castletown and Port St Mary remained deferred.

*Original in Tower Collection.
†No trace of this name elsewhere.

Anticipating increased summer traffic, Wood visited both Ashbury and Brown, Marshalls; six new carriages were ordered overall; the latter also made contract with the Railway Company to send men over to paint six existing bogie carriages. The men would paint only the 1st class for £12 9s. 6d. each, but when the quality of their work was noted, they might be retained to paint the 3rd class @ £12 5s. 0d. each.

Order for carriages of bogie type went to:

    Brown, Marshalls – four 2nd class carriages @ £500 each
    Ashbury –   two 2nd class carriages @ £425 each

and it is curious to see that despite the fact that 2nd class had been abolished since 1st July, 1878, the order was phrased as above. Complaints about the rough riding of the four-wheel carriages now brought letters to the newspapers and in February, it was decreed that laminated springs be fitted under the 1st class (but not under others) to replace the existing system (see Volume III).

Rail connection with the harbour at Douglas raised its head again in the Annual Traffic Report in February but this time, the proposal was for a line along the South Quay. A warehouse was also required at St John's. The rail link to the harbour fluctuated between this South Quay route and a line to the Landing Pier; of the latter it was said: 'there being no adequate access from the Landing Pier to Douglas station, the district served by your Railway and the Fisheries (the most important industry of the Island) have not yet enjoyed the full benefit of the railway system'. The Report deplored the failure of 'local arrangements' to bring fruit to the idea. Business on the Railway was never better, but more rolling stock, better stations and more passing loops were urgently needed. Rixon, now dubbed 'General Assistant to the London Board' was given £100 per annum for his services. At Peel, the tenant of the refreshment room forfeited his lease for 'irregularities'. A stopping place at Quarter Bridge (to be called Spring Valley) was considered desirable, but land was not available. A long association with the Ebbw Vale Steel & Iron Co. Ltd. began when 5 tons of fishplates were supplied in May and this was the first of many consignments.

The attitude of the Board towards charitable appeals and on-line events depended on geographical location; athletic sports, flower shows, regattas, church events etc. were always given financial support so long as they might bring business to the Railway but the Douglas Regatta, for instance, was ignored and functions on the MNR given but half a glance – they might bring some traffic. Tourist business fluctuated from year to year and places like Castletown, Port St Mary and Port Erin might cancel a Regatta if the previous season had been disappointing. The level of financial support (including that of the Railway) frequently allowed the event to be reinstated. The Hospital, (commonly known as 'Noble's')* could be sure of an annual donation and care was shown to note which members of the Railway Board were also involved in such institutions.

On 3rd August, 1881, a train from Port Erin to Douglas had been standing in the Santon loop, awaiting arrival of a train from Douglas which was

---

*Henry Bloom Noble (timber merchant) was the benefactor.

running nineteen minutes late: the Up train would require the Staff for authority to enter the section (Port Soderick loop was recently commissioned but apparently not officially in use) and this, of course, was being carried on the approaching train. For reasons unknown the Douglas-bound train left Santon without this authority and succeeded in reaching Port Soderick before the Down train had left Douglas! The Santon Station Master, driver and guard of the train were all dismissed; the case for these men is not stated, but they may have considered it was safe to proceed to Port Soderick even though it had yet to be opened as a Staff station.

The delivery of the carriages from Manchester and Birmingham took place in June, and August appears to be the first instance when such were delivered in 'knock-down' form. Men from both suppliers spent time in Douglas erecting and painting them, as well as repairing and repainting existing stock; housing these men would bring in a little extra business for local landladies. Brown, Marshalls' account was paid by a £2,000 Bill at three months.

Although the original orders for stock have not survived, the terms of supply were that it was to be delivered to Douglas station, erected (if necessary), tested in traffic and, when approved, paid for as quickly as Company finances permitted. With carriages, it had been customary to send complete bodies and frames separately (but probably on the same ship) but as first shown, bogie coaches sent over this year were assembled at the makers, dismantled again and shipped in parts. A foreman of the manufacturers would accompany them on the voyage and supervise unloading, re-erection etc. and correct any imperfections. It was also the manufacturers' responsibility to see that cartage from Douglas quay to station was carried out: thus in August 1881, Philip Sayle was paid £7 'for horsepower' for 'bringing two new carriages from steamer to station on behalf of Ashburys'.

It would be hard to find a concern which was more cost-conscious than the IOMR; using local labour (to avoid mainland involvement) was their constant policy. Wherever possible, work within the capacity of insular firms was preferred and a typical case was the instance of carriage upholstery. It might be inferred that suppliers would have furnished carriages completely but not so; whilst the makers' men were painting new stock, Douglas contractors were fitting cushions etc. in such compartments as merited them. Mainland painters on carriage stock might be found working alongside local men. Brown, Marshalls men were still on the job in April 1882 and there is reference to them being employed on similar work as early as June 1872.

In the late year, it was decreed that the road from Colby Bridge to Colby station was a private one and the Company must pay £2 a year in rent.

Improvements at Peel Harbour, begun during the year, involved the use of the contractors' railway equipment. The Minutes of the Isle of Man Harbour Committee read:

16th September: Suitable wagons are lying at St Germain's for the Peel Work @ £4 10s. 0d. each.

16th September:	Mr Walker (Engineer) produced a photograph of a locomotive engine which could be got for £300 and which would be required effectively to carry on the work at Peel.
7th January, 1882:	The Receiver General reported that the locomotive for the Peel Works has now arrived and is in use.

There is nothing further in the Minute Book until June 1885; meanwhile the locomotive had completed its work at Peel and was lying out of use on the quay at the west bank of the river estuary; in this position it was incorporated in a pen-and-ink sketch of 'Peel Castle and Harbor' (sic) in Harper's NEW MONTHLY MAGAZINE No. 448 for September 1887 page 519, in an article, 'Home Rule in the Isle of Man'.*, showing a small four-wheeled vertically-boilered machine. The matter then disappears until Minutes from the same source show:

20th June, 1885:	Mr Hugh Kennedy,† contractor for the Foxdale Railway, having made an offer of £120 for the locomotive at Peel as it stands on the ground, it was unanimously agreed to let him have it at this price on immediate payment.
	Also agreed Mr Kennedy should have the loan of 24 wagons from this date for the sum of £5 – he returning the wagons in no worse state of repair than they are now in.

(Return to this subject will be made during 1885.)

There was still an extensive area of low-lying ground in front of Douglas station, evidence of the marsh and lake which was formerly situate there; 'sooner or later work must be done there' i.e. the creation of new buildings, so the cutting beyond Port Soderick station was used as a 'quarry' to bring down material to fill the site.

Thorn fencing (as it was termed) had now been planted for 37¾ miles (or almost 19 miles of railway) and there were now three miles of steel rail in the Port Erin Line.

The quality of the four bogie carriages from Brown, Marshalls delighted the Engineer but of the other two suppliers he had no comment to make. The summer weather of 1881 was so poor that he regretted so little use had been made of them '. . . Many people never left Douglas.'

A more cheerful element was £3,961 3s. 7d. received for working the MNR for '1st January to 6th November (incl.) 1880' making an up-beat item

*Manx Museum: B192/1x.

†Hugh Kennedy & Son(s), Railway & Public Works Contractors, Partick & Glasgow; the Post Office Guide in 1854–5 notices 'Hugh Kennedy, Wright & Builder, Windsor Place, Partick', becoming '. . . Wright & Contractor, Merkland Street, Partick' by 1858–9. By 1876–7 the concern was styled 'Hugh Kennedy & Son, Builders and Railway Contractors, 14, Merkland Street . . .' They moved to 20 Merkland Street in 1889–90; ten years later they were styled 'Railway & Public Works Contractors' and as Hugh Kennedy & Sons. Thereafter they traded as Wm. Kennedy, Railway, Dock & Harbour Contractor, 40 Merkland Street. Trading ceased in 1930–1.

Hugh Kennedy had died in 1896, leaving an estate of £52,202. He was a Conservative, a one-time Provost of the Burgh of Partick, but refused nomination for Parliament.

At the time of its connections with the Isle of Man the firm was described as having 'old standing and extensive connections', an 'eminent house' established about 1845, and that in 1875 Hugh Kennedy was joined by his two sons. The firm carried out some large Scottish contracts including the Wemyss Bay Railway, Greenock & Ayrshire Railway, Craigendoran Railway & Pier, and No. 3 section of the Glasgow City & District Railway. They were also prominent in pier construction.

The foregoing underlines the strong influential standing of the Foxdale Railway contractor.

for the 1881 AGM; 1880 had been the best year yet for the IOMR. However, the high cost of level crossings was again before the Board as 13 sets of gates (with a keeper) was costing £351 each per annum, but at a total cost of £2,000, each could be given a small cottage wherein a keeper might live rent-free and operate the gates.

There are some nice snippets from Wood's diary:

> 7th February: a Special Train guaranteed by the hirers for £5, only produced 13s 6d.
>
> 14th April: late arrival of the Liverpool steamer meant trains left Douglas at 10.30 pm.
>
> 14th July: Special train for Douglas Regatta.
>
> 16th July: Special Train for Promenade Concert, Castletown.
>
> 18th July: Excursion from Sheffield.
>
> 28th July: Peel children were taken to St John's where a MNR Special took them to Bishop's Court. The fare (Return) was 8d., each (over IOMR, 3d. and MNR, 5d.).
>
> 29th July: Ramsey Regatta saw combined working IOMR/MNR; MNR engines working Specials St John's to Ramsey, and IOMR remainder of the system. The Douglas shunting engine was utilised to double-head between there and St John's.

And now to matters on the MNR.

The SUN made notice of the ending of the IOMR/MNR Agreement on the previous 6th November in its issue for 26th February, wherein the disappointing figures for through traffic were blamed on the IOMR's 'lack of access from the Landing Pier to Douglas station'. The MNR was anxious to justify its break with the IOMR and when twelve months of working its own line had passed, it announced 'The year's working had satisfied the directors as regards the wisdom and economy . . .' In Ramsey, though the Harbour line was not yet begun, low platforms were added and these would be the only ones on the system until Peel Road was built in 1883. A gate lodge was to appear at Cooilbane crossing and the occupation crossing at Lhergydoo was replaced by an overbridge. A Temperance Refreshment Room at Ramsey opened in early June but did not survive the season . . . nor did Martin Pearce, the MNR Secretary who had been in office since 1879 who resigned. William Hughes, the Ramsey Traffic Manager, took his place as Secretary and Manager. The Registered Office was now settled at Ramsey station.

Alteration of the layout at St John's took place, whereby the original MNR terminus and locomotive run-round was abandoned and a new connection made into the IOMR station, each Company having its own level crossing over the intervening roadway, thus allowing through coaches (one at a time) to be attached and detached between the two Company's trains there. Such vehicles carried roof boards 'Through coach to Douglas'.

Hughes had emphasised the need for workshop improvements and extra tools for Ramsey so James Callow was employed to build a workshop. Spare wheel sets, brake gear for wagons were ordered from Ashbury . . . it seems extraordinary that the railway had been allowed to operate without them. Until this date, the Carriage Shed had been a simple, open barn-like structure but now corrugated sheeting was to enclose it completely and doors would be added.

Cameron· instigated the auction of the grass cut from embankments and cuttings along the lineside.

An expensive direction from Col Rich required that two men must be employed at MNR stations where there was a passing loop. To obviate this, Cameron began alterations, firstly at St Germain's (June) where, by padlocking the points and bringing the signal levers into the station area, he could satisfy the Colonel and continue to employ but one man. Sulby Bridge, Sulby Glen and Lezayre were then similarly treated. Though the system met the problem, it only suited stations where an occasional use of the loop took place, so at busier Kirk Michael and Ballaugh, both point and signal levers were brought closer to the station. Whatever improvements were to be made, there was a near-accident at St Germain's on 14th July when a driver approaching but slowly, noticed the point blades were not sufficiently set. He jumped off the engine, ran ahead and closed the blades before his engine derailed.

The Mail Contract was obtained on 8th August, but not on the same advantageous terms as those for the IOMR.

We must remind ourselves of the importance of St Germain's at this time, being the nearest MNR station for Peel – it was still a basic structure but Waddell Bros.' tender for £110 to add living accommodation was accepted. Callow was having problems with the Ramsey Workshop; poor foundations caused the gable wall to crack and so the work began afresh.

There was now to be a watershed in the affairs of the MNR. J.R. Cowell (a director and Ramsey businessman) and Cameron together with Hughes, arrived in England on 25th October and made inspection of various minor railways in the north and Scotland so to improve their knowledge. They returned, and such was the force of their criticisms, that Cameron was to become Outdoor Inspector (virtually dictator of everything that comprised the operating side) and Hughes to be Secretary & Accountant. The latter's business did not extend outside his office door. Sweeping reductions were made in the number of employees: a policy of 'emulating several small Scotch railways to achieve economy' ensued.

The complex litigation between J. & W. Grainger (the contractors) and the Company, was finally settled on 30th November when they were paid £2,258 9s. 7d.

1882

For the sake of continuity, it is helpful to pursue MNR matters as we left them in 1881; the March 1882 MNR, AGM at Ramsey station was told the passenger figures for 1881 were 163,820, a disappointing total for which the IOMR was given much blame for lack of co-operation. Over £1,500 would be needed for the work at Ramsey station, Cooilbane crossing lodge and Lhergydoo bridge; there was £2,872 13s. 4d. outstanding on the Agreement 'for the Hire and Purchase' of carriages. All trains ran mixed (no separate passenger or goods trains) and their total mileage was 74,381. The auditor recommended the establishment of a fund for renewal of track and

1882   141

FORM OF APPLICATION FOR SHARES.

TO THE DIRECTORS OF THE

Douglas, Laxey, & Ramsey Railway Company, Ltd.

GENTLEMEN,

Having paid to your Bankers the sum of £ .... being a Deposit of Ten Shillings per Share on .... Shares of £5 each in the above Company, (a) .... hereby request you to allot (b) .... Preference Shares and (c) .... Ordinary Shares, and (d) .... agree to accept the same, or any less number that may be allotted to (e) ....

Name in full, ...

Address, ...

Profession or Business, ...

Date, ...

(f) .... desire and agree to pay up (g) .... Shares in full on allotment,

Signature, ...

BANKERS' RECEIPT.

Douglas, Laxey, and Ramsey Railway Company, Limited.

Received this .... day of .... 188...

of .... the sum of £ .... on account of THE DOUGLAS, LAXEY, AND RAMSEY RAILWAY COMPANY, Limited, being a Deposit of Ten Shillings per Share on .... Shares of £5 each of the Company.

FOR   STAMP.   BANKERS.

Left margin notes:

This Sheet, filled up, and with a Cheque for the amount payable on application, should be forwarded entire to the Bankers of the Company, at Manchester, London, or Douglas.

1) "I" or "we."
2) If you elect to take Preference Shares only, strike out the words "and Ordinary Shares."
3) Or "Preference Shares," if Ordinary Shares are taken.
4) "I" or "we."
5) "Me" or "us."

6) "I" or "we."
7) "My" or "our."

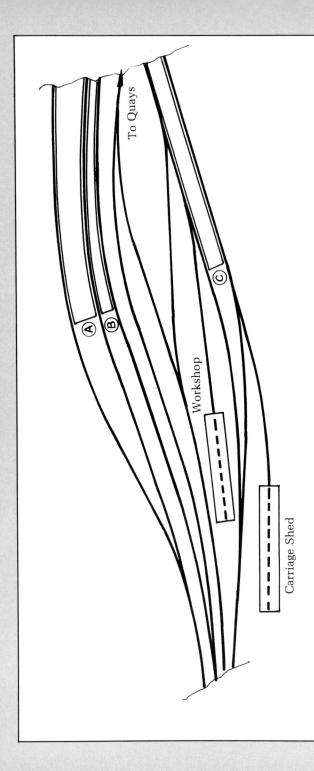

DOUGLAS: proposal to incorporate Laxey terminus (16 September 1882)

Source: Part of incomplete plan by H. Woodhouse 1882 to accommodate Laxey trains

A. South Line IOMR
B. Peel Line IOMR
C. Laxey Line

rolling stock, but the Board decided that at this stage the equipment was too new to require it.

On 1st March, a company was registered styling itself the Douglas, Laxey & Ramsey Railway Company Limited; of its eight subscribers, four lived in the Manchester area, one from Flintshire and three were Manx. The capital was to be £130,000 in £5 shares; Daniel Cregeen was Engineer. This creation had followed on a Prospectus of 18th February for 'The Isle of Man Tramways Ltd.' (Major J.S. Goldie-Taubman, Chairman) which purchased the Douglas Bay Tramway* on 21st March. Alarmed by these developments, the IOMR gave consideration to building a tramway from Douglas station to the Victoria Pier (not to be confused with any previous IOMR project to build a railway-linked Quay Tramway) and applied to the Town Commissioners so to do.

The thinking behind the DL&RR was succinctly put by the Clerk of Rolls who said promotion 'was due to the fault of the MNR being laid on a circuitous route, leaving Laxey out in the cold ... there was more traffic between Douglas and Laxey than between Douglas and Castletown'. Obviously the three Manx promoters, who were in fact, MNR directors, had shown no loyalty thereto and ultimately they became directors of the intruder. (It was a popularly-expressed opinion at the time that the MNR must take the blame for this development, being laid in the 'wrong place', 'not going into Peel' etc.)

The line was to make physical connection with the IOMR about ¾ mile outside Douglas station, share Douglas terminus with the IOMR, and branch off it northwards behind the town to link with towns in its title by one of the most hilly routes imaginable. From a junction at Quarter Bridge, there would be intermediate stations at Ballaquayle, Falcon Cliff, Summer Hill, Onchan, Ballameanagh, Glen Gawre and Laxey: between Douglas and Onchan the line would be virtually a suburban 'ring' system. As nothing further transpired during 1882–4, and the matter does not re-occur until August 1885 when new Articles of Association were drawn up, it is for the moment, a matter of MNR and IOMR reaction to the project which concerns us. There had been evidence of this railway for some time, it being impossible to disguise the activities of its surveyors. The SUN had noticed in October 1881 that due to objections by landowners, such were 're-aligning the DL&RR route on a lower and more circuitous course', and this of course was weeks before its public promotion. The MNR made formal petition against it being aware that any line along the east coast was a threat and the IOMR would ultimately consider building its own line to Laxey [... but this is looking ahead to March 1888 and it was to be killed by the relative failure of the Foxdale Railway scheme which has, as yet, not even come to our notice!]

Alerted by the scenario of having to share its Douglas station with an incomer, the IOMR Board discarded the Greenbank Plan of 1880 for

---

*This tramway was the second proposed for the route. The first concerned the horse-drawn Douglas Bay Tramway (opened 7th August, 1876) which wished to connect the 'new' (sic) station with Victoria Pier in 1878, without result. The horse tramway became the Isle of Man Tramways Company (Limited) – (Prospectus 18th February, 1882) with wide powers sought. Major J.S. Goldie-Taubman was a director ... one might also add, inevitably!

On 18th December, 1882 the IOMR itself made application to Douglas Town Commissioners for a tramway along that same route. Nothing eventuated.

(See also Pearson page 31 and S.R.N. No. 13 page 12.)

enlarging Douglas station,* for it had become obvious that passenger and goods facilities must each be developed on quite different sites. Existing platforms were too short and additional sidings were needed alongside each platform whereon to stand empty passenger stock. The existing Workshops and engine shed were wholly inadequate but any improvement carried out would have to be done 'without removal of the present station building'. The General Purposes Committee Minute on the subject was a good example of Douglas telling London of its ignorance of need. When the DL&RR took formal shape as a Bill before the Legislature, it was now entitled The Douglas & Laxey Railway Co. Ltd. and when an Act was obtained, this title was retained.† It was not only to share Douglas station, but envisaged the IOMR would work it. G.H. Wood was very enthusiastic about the idea and stressed that station improvements must bear in mind the proposed tramway along the quays.‡

Whilst Wood may have been excited by the prospect of adding to the IOMR's influence, the London directors gave notice in June to oppose a site on the IOMR near Pulrose where the new railway would cross over it; without informing the General Purposes Committee they engaged Henry Woodhouse, CE to advise them on the form of opposition to be taken, to recommend terms of working the DL&RR system, the form additional accommodation at Douglas should take and the precise re-design of the station. The General Purposes Committee (firmly behind Greenbank) persuaded him to amend his own Plans and both schemes went before the Board in July but, as aforementioned, the Laxey scheme was not prosecuted and the risk of another instance of Douglas v. London interests in conflict died down. When the time came to rebuild and enlarge Douglas it would not be due to the knocking of an incomer at its gates. The Laxey faction could claim a minor victory in that it was prepared to amend its course at Pulrose and accede to IOMR demands over joint use of Douglas station, 'on condition the IOMR does not oppose the Laxey Bill'.

The oft-deliberated cattle pen at Ballasalla, still deferred, was now to be built. William Lowe, Station Master at Douglas, was made Inspector to succeed Buckett at a salary of £10 16s. 8d. per month. Advertising was extended to cover the London & North Western, Lancashire & Yorkshire and Midland Railways, and the Cheshire Lines Committee; these railways covered the areas of northwest England most likely to curry traffic whilst the old saying persisted that no one south of Birmingham had heard of the Isle of Man, (and was commonly expressed even in 1970). Thomas Cook and Gaze & Son were given Ticket Agencies and they contributed towards Tourist Guides.

Sir Henry Loch's term of duty ended (1863 to 1882; he was knighted in 1880) and in spring 1882 he left the Island, and behind him, some mixed memories; he had done much for the improvement of Douglas, its shipping and the image of the Island, and more. However, he had pursued his responsibilities towards the two railway companies with what they considered to be unnecessary zeal. The IOMR carried out in its turn the customary formula in the circumstances both then and thereafter; they

---

*Manx Museum: R/4.
†This and other schemes may be found in Pearson (Appendix I).
‡Manx Museum: R/12 for Quay Tramway (August 1885).

returned the Governor's Gold Free Pass as a souvenir. To an incoming Governor they presented a new Gold Pass together with a letter reading:

> The Board will have great pleasure in placing a First Class compartment at the disposal of His Excellency whenever he wishes to travel . . . if accompanied by friends . . . they can arrange for the use of a Saloon Carriage . . .

Sufficient notice had to be given in either case. It was usual for a Governor to send a contribution to be distributed amongst the Saloon Carriage staff at the end of his term of office; thus the niceties were observed.

One of the through MNR carriages, travelling between St John's and Douglas, left the rails on 8th July at Union Mills 'due to its bad state of repair'. This was the opportunity for which the IOMR had been looking and thereafter MNR carriages were banned from IOMR metals.

We have to return to late 1881 to introduce the next subject – the connection of the Foxdale Mines to the existing railway system.

First evidence for this comes from a series of letters passing from Greenbank to Wood, the first on 30th December, 1881 after Wood sent Greenbank two items: the first a Book of Reference for 'The Foxdale Railway' and secondly an 'Estimate of the opposition line' (also described as 'the enemy's line'), as Greenbank dubs it. Greenbank replied on 2nd January and his absence of surprise suggests the matter was not new to them and further, it appears that at this stage, it was not shared by others. He makes reference to a 'St John's & Foxdale Railway' and although he is fond of creating his own titles in correspondence, this is probably the aforesaid 'enemy line'. He continues, 'I am anxious to know how (that Coy.) propose to construct the line with their capital of £8,000! and if Mr Clucas* will NOW guarantee the necessary capital himself'. Here, Greenbank expresses astonishment that the Estimate is not signed, 'A distinct breach of Standing Orders'.

The documents must have been prepared in late 1881, and showed that the SJ&FR intended to make junction at Ballaleece with the IOMR, a quarter mile west of St John's station. The IOMR intended to oppose the SJ&FR scheme on the grounds of breach of Standing Orders, and had until 26th January, 1882 to make petition. Greenbank left for Douglas early in January 'to get a correct copy of the Opposition Plans for myself'.

What about 'The Foxdale Railway' Book of Reference sent by Wood? Greenbank refers to it as a 'competitive scheme', and it must be assumed that it was therefore competing with the Clucas-linked SJ&FR. A survey must have been attempted or else there would be no Book of Reference: suffice to say, no further mention of it has yet come to light.†

It may be asked how far this news had circulated by October 1882, when it reached Wood from another source! Was Wood keeping it to a dialogue or was the IOMR Chairman informed? The IOMR Minutes make no reference, but Greenbank (whose next letter to Wood was not until 17th November) had certainly been toying with the idea of a *IOMR branch to Foxdale*, starting from St John's (preferred by Wood) or from Ballacurry (preferred by Greenbank).

---

*Chairman, MNR.

†Greenbank's letters, with their unofficial 'titles' are a little confusing, but there is no doubt that he literally means that there was an opposition line to that referred to in late 1881 as The Foxdale Railway, albeit no such concern had yet been registered.

Oddly, Greenbank's letter of 17th November was written the day after a MNR-backed Foxdale Railway was registered and in it he commends the idea of starting the IOMR Foxdale branch at Ballacurry, the highest point of the Peel Line, and so reduce the gradient of the climb into Foxdale to 1 in 65, as against The Foxdale Railway's 1 in 49. Greenbank was against starting the branch at St John's, which would not only create a gradient of 1 in 37 but was one on which 'your present engines ... would have difficulty'. He then asked Wood if he should go into a more precise question of levels?

Greenbank was working on a revised layout for Douglas throughout this time and submitted plans for this at the same time as Plans and Sections for what he called 'The Ballacurry & Foxdale Railway'. Estimates apart, these were in Wood's hands for Christmas 1882 and at the Rolls Office on 27th December. By then, Greenbank had assumed the IOMR would buy a special locomotive for the branch. It should be noted that The Foxdale Railway lodged its own Plans & Sections at the Rolls Office in December (1882), so Greenbank had wasted little time.*

In the previous October a trustworthy informant leaked the news to Wood that William Kitto, Manager of the Foxdale mines, had told him that 'he must not be surprised if a railway was built between St John's and Foxdale and if the IOMR lost the Foxdale mines' traffic'. (This traffic was the carriage of ore from St John's to Douglas, and the return traffic in coal, timber etc.; between St John's and the mines, horse carts were used.) Re-action of the General Purposes Committee to this disturbing information was to concentrate its thoughts on the North Quay Tramway again, this being the Achilles' Heel of the IOMR transport system. Mines traffic was bringing in £600 annually and it was not to be lost.

Without delay the Governor was informed of the weakness of the IOMR, compared with the MNR whose Ramsey Quay line was 'laid as far as West Street' by the end of September and would reach the east of the quay '... in a couple of weeks'. It passed its first train of inwards coal in December 1882 to the annoyance of the Harbour Commissioners who had not inspected the line. Inspection was made on 9th January following.

The Governor's backing was sought and Greenbank was instructed to prepare new plans for both North and South Quay lines; Greenbank favoured the North Quay as this would avoid a bridge over part of the Harbour, and a steep gradient. Rixon maintained a tramway was useless unless it gained the Victoria Pier.

With its trump card of a Harbour branch railway, the MNR was now courting the IOMMC by quoting a rate of 1s. 0d. ton less than the current IOMR rate – the existing Agreement between IOMMC and the IOMR would terminate in 1884. The lure of conveyance from St John's to Ramsey waterside was irresistible to the Mining Co. who were currently paying 1s. 0d. ton to convey from Douglas station yard to the ship's side: the IOMR countered with the promise of a North Quay Tramway and a store at St John's ... the latter was a bit hollow as such had been intended from the start of the Agreement but had never been built.

Building on the IOMR's unease, the IOMMC increased the pressure by emphasising they would require a railway between the mines and St John's

---

*Manx Museum: R/2 (Foxdale Railway); R/163, R/183 and R/184 (IOMR branch).

so, moving very quickly for the IOMR, Pender had agreed that Greenbank survey for a branch line into Foxdale. A route 2¼ miles long between Ballacurry, on the Douglas side of St John's, to Foxdale, with an up grade of 1 in 52 was preferred – had connection been made at St John's the inclination would have steepened to 1 in 40. £550 was reserved for expenses incurred in the promotion but later used to buy steel rails.

The IOMR was also involved in the carriage of sand @ 5s. 3d. a wagon from St John's Sand & Gravel Co.'s siding to a dump at Douglas yard.* This was a useful way of employing wagons which had gone to St John's on mine traffic and would otherwise return empty to Douglas. At £220 per annum it was not very profitable but its retention was vital, and knowing this, the MNR offered a similar sand service to Ramsey at 3s. 0d. less per ton than the IOMR rate to Douglas. Development in this regard was placed in temporary limbo as the Mining Co. said it was prepared to wait for a Foxdale–Douglas quotation via the suggested Ballacurry Branch. The IOMR emphasised its enthusiasm for the Branch as local residents had long sought a station at Ballacurry. If the mine's traffic was lost, the sand business would go with it.

On the aforesaid 17th November, consternation reigned when news broke that a new company would promote a railway between St John's and Foxdale, and that six of the MNR Board members were behind it . . . clearly because the MNR itself was in no financial position to raise further funds to build such a line in its own name. J.T. Clucas, a member of the IOMR Board, was a prominent promoter 'and its Engineer was already on the ground'; Clucas was confronted by his IOMR colleagues and denied all knowledge. This made the Ballacurry Branch scheme all the more imperative but Pender cautioned that in its 'enfeebled state', even the IOMR might not receive much financial support from the public . . . 'the action of the Ramsey directors is detrimental to both companies'.

The FR Minute Book gives the inside story.† A first meeting of directors (Messrs C.H.E. Cowle, J.T. Clucas, W.B. Christian and J.R. Cowell) had taken place 'in Ramsey' on 15th November, with John Cameron in attendance, and the Company was registered on 16th November. Christian and Cowell had already been over the ground with an Engineer named Forman and his firm, Formans & McCall had been instructed to prepare a preliminary survey for £80. Next, Farrant (a director absent from the inaugural meeting) was made Chairman, with Cowell as Secretary (pro tem). No time was lost; on 4th December Forman's survey was adopted and on 15th December it was concluded that 'a separate engine would be needed to work the Foxdale traffic'. Three days later, John Beckwith, Chairman of the IOMMC was asked to meet a deputation at St John's 'to see if the Mining Co. would take an interest'. On Boxing Day, the Capital was increased to £13,000 by the issue of 1,000 new shares @ £5 each. The same day, Forman recommended the work be let out in small contracts under one supervisor. It had been a very short period of gestation!

With Pender's hesitation in mind, the General Purposes Committee considered applying for authority to work the competing Foxdale Railway

---

*There was a link between this enterprise and Dumbell's Banking Co. Ltd.
†Tower Collection.

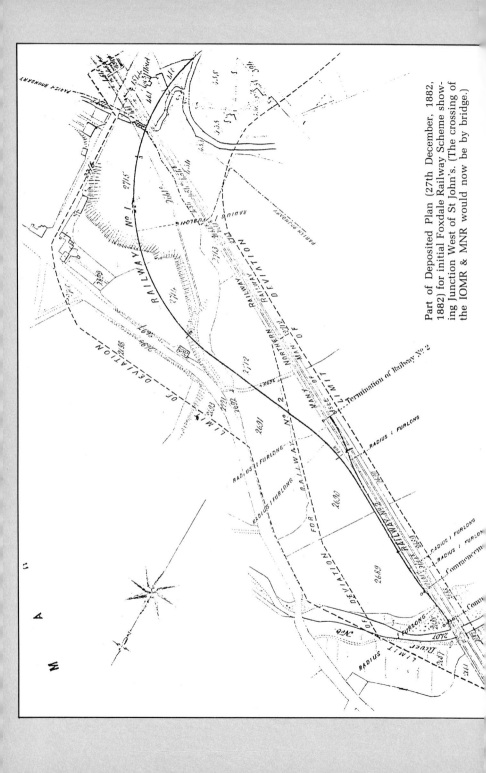

Part of Deposited Plan (27th December, 1882, 1882) for initial Foxdale Railway Scheme showing junction West of St John's. (The crossing of the IOMR & MNR would now be by bridge.)

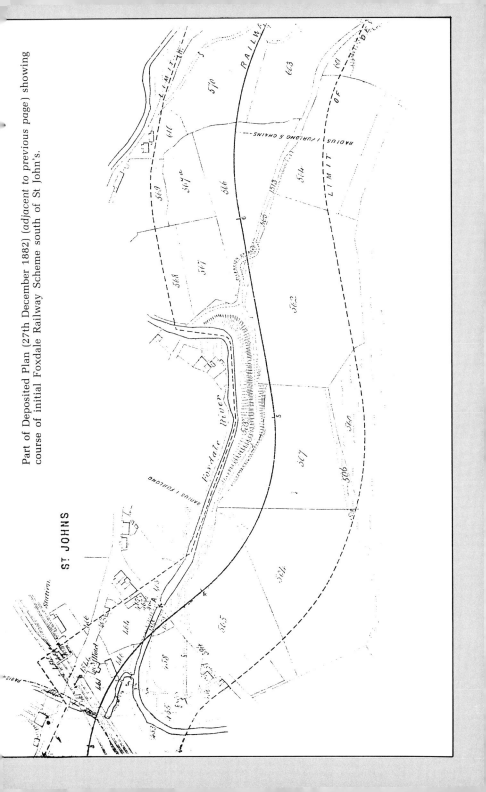

Part of Deposited Plan (27th December 1882) (adjacent to previous page) showing course of initial Foxdale Railway Scheme south of St John's.

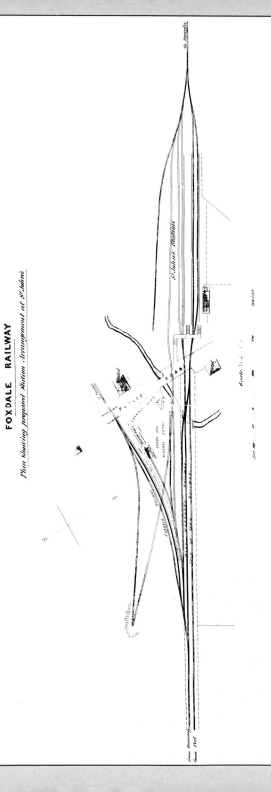

'Proposed Station & Station Arrangements at St John's – Foxdale Railway' (note abandoned & replacement siding to sandpit).

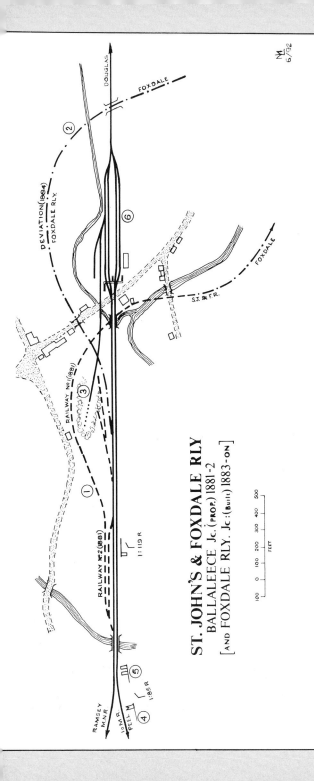

ST. JOHN'S & FOXDALE RLY
BALLALEECE Jc. (PROP.) 1881-2
[AND FOXDALE RLY. Jc: (BUILT) 1883-ON]

ST. JOHN'S: railway junction proposals 1881–2–3 [etc.]

1. 1881 Foxdale route Survey (deposited 12/1882)
2. 1883 Ultimate route Survey (deposited 12/1884)
3. Sandpit Siding: later revised and to be served off Foxdale Railway
4. Up St. John's Distant (220 yds.)
5. Up St. John's Home
6. St. John's IOMR & MNR Joint Station

scheme by acquiring running powers over it. Wood did not agree as such permission would enable the MNR to acquire running rights between St John's and Douglas, and more would be lost than losing just the Foxdale traffic. Furthermore, the IOMMC had said it would only use the intended IOMR line if the rate was equal to that of the MNR. Clucas had put his shirt on the MNR, which, it now appeared, had three surveyors of its own out on a course and was likely to win the day, (in the event of the two schemes competing in the Keys), with the undoubted influence Clucas exerted therein.

The MNR route (under a 'Foxdale Railway' banner) would leave their line below Ballaleece Bridge and cross the IOMR there; at 1 in 42, it would be steeper than the IOMR project and this might influence the Keys towards the IOMR route on the score of safety. The MNR case would be underpinned by the knowledge that Foxdale paid out £2,000 in wages monthly, and Ramsey tradespeople were determined to have the lion's share of it. The IOMR was fearful that the Mining Co. might renege on its verbal assurance that it would prefer to use the IOMR rather than the MNR yet Pender was hopeful that if the Press took up the matter, Douglas tradesmen would rally to support the IOMR scheme which if it failed, would lose them much business. Other assets in the IOMR favour would include its proximity to the Townsend Mines, that at 2 miles 5 furlongs 5 chains it would be 2 miles shorter than the St John's route, and the Foxdale to Douglas distance would only be 9½ miles.

In December, notices (as required by Tynwald) were sent to landowners, appeared in newspapers and were pinned to church doors to the effect that the IOMR intended to build a new railway 'from Ballacurry to Foxdale'.

It was calculated that to build a first-class IOMR branch line with 56 lb new steel rails would be useless unless the North Quay Tramway 'to the Steam Packet Shed' was made at the same time. Together they would cost £12,136; should the MNR be empowered to work the Foxdale Line, its trains would connect with those for Ramsey and not Douglas, so passengers also would be lost to the IOMR. In 1881, 7,395 persons travelled to Douglas from the Foxdale district at an average fare of 1s. 0d. It was believed that by making the line, retaining and increasing mineral and passenger traffic, the IOMR would gain about £1,200 a year i.e. sufficient to pay 5 per cent per annum on cost of building the Branch.

Sheward was opposed to the building unless the IOMMC guaranteed an annual payment for a number of years: only then did it appear that the MNR had offered to build a line free from any such guarantee . . . another unwise decision. On 9th January, 1883, Wood admitted to Rixon his fears that the line would not pay; he warned that the MNR intended to run their line into IOMR metals at Ballaleece on the Peel side of St John's station 'but what for I cannot tell except they wish to obtain running powers over our line'. [Probably with the longer-term intention of obtaining running powers into Douglas.] It also transpired that they wanted to 'poach' part of St John's IOMR station and as Wood pointed out, there would have to be an extra 'Staff Station' at the point of junction: so great was the MNR challenge that 'it was backing it by bringing witnesses from Scotland'! (The proposed

St John's layout arrangement was that the entering Foxdale Line would cross the MNR Ramsey Line on the level and make a junction with the IOMR Peel track.)*

On 14th February, 1883 the MNR Board advised the IOMR they had no intention of modifying their layout at St John's so as to eliminate a proposed junction with the IOMR.

In order to avoid a break in the narrative we have advanced to February 1883 so a return must now be made to 1882.

The IOMMC now made things more difficult by saying the proposed IOMR charge of 1s. 0d. was too high, they wanted 'proper stores' erecting at Foxdale free of charge and a telegraph along the line would be necessary: it would have to be worked by the IOMR. Unless these conditions were met, no Agreement could be reached.

The IOMR Board Meeting of 26th January, 1883 concluded that the revenue from a Foxdale Branch would be insufficient to pay working expenses etc. and the Bill was withdrawn. Meanwhile The Foxdale Railway Company's scheme (the MNR-inspired project) would be opposed as regards its junction with the Peel Line, and an IOMR Bill as regards the North Quay Tramway was to be prosecuted. This decision, almost entirely by the Chairman and London Board's influence, angered many Island shareholders who approached the local directors to build a Foxdale Branch on their own, but the matter died there.

The General Purposes Committee made an inspection of the whole Railway and agreed that many curves needed relaying; more of those on the Port Erin Line would be replaced with steel rails. (There were fewer curves on the Peel Line.) The footbridge crossing at the Nunnery was to be made an underpass.

Railway-owned horse delivery carts were based at Douglas and handcarts were used at provincial stations until business required a horsecart; at some stations the handcart survived to the end; thus Tommy Cregeen, handcarter at Port St Mary (an ex-fisherman) was known to the Author's family for two generations. His work involved considerable mileage between boarding houses and station during the season. Ultimately the horsecarts were sold and motor lorries employed.

So much of the latter days of 1882 had been taken up by Foxdale affairs – and were to continue into 1883 – that a general reference to lead mining in the Island is helpful. Mining had been taking place for centuries before a railway came and was concentrated mainly in the Foxdale and Laxey areas. The working and prosperity of the mines was spasmodic, companies working the same sites coming in and going out of business. Thus in 1811, Woods states the Foxdale mines were closed but from the middle of the nineteenth century however, lead and silver-lead mining in the Island had grown to outstanding importance. The Isle of Man Mining Co. lacked a convenient sea outlet for its Foxdale output. Laxey was more fortunate, having a small port on the east coast adjacent. The existence of rail-borne transport from Foxdale mines to quayside was a critical factor in the early 1880s, and stemmed from potential arrangements between the Mining

---

*The Deposited Plans lodged at the Rolls Office 27th December, 1882 show a crossing by bridge.

Co. and the MNR in early November 1882; whilst lead would form the staple tonnage, sand and gravel, granite, silica and spar traffic was also envisaged.*

To close the year, a peep into Wood's diary shows that on 31st January the Duke of Edinburgh visited the Island and late trains were run for the Illuminations: the MNR put on an 8.14 pm to St John's which returned from there are 11.20 pm, giving connections by IOMR to Douglas; who said the Victorians retired early to bed? The Ramsey Regatta on the 12th July was a wretched day and the six carriages loaned from IOMR to MNR were not used. During the autumn, Specials were run for The Salvation Army, YWCA and Bethel School.

1883

We must look back a little into 1882 to set the stage for 1883; Greenbank was to the forefront from November, pressed by London for a quick survey of the Ballacurry–Foxdale project in order to give the Mining Co. a quotation for continuance of their working arrangement. He was certain that none of the IOMR locomotives was suited to so steep a line and put it to Rixon that a special one might have to be bought for the work . . . it would 'give a better service than the MNR could'. At the same time, the sight of MNR surveyors (for at this juncture, the MNR was prepared to build St John's to Foxdale itself) on its proposed course, forced him into an attempt to read 'the enemy's plans'; he would have given his right arm to know what was in the mind of the Mining Co. and which Railway Company they would support. He had obtained a copy of the MNR surveyors' work and noted that there would be a Foxdale Line station at St John's at the point where it *bridged* the IOMR. The course would have to pass the rear of The Central Hotel on an embankment 30 ft high . . . 'not very nice for the occupants . . . the Hotel will be 'done', it is only 5 ft from Hotel wall to the foot of the embankment'. The MNR would now abandon its existing station at St John's and erect an interchange one at Ballaleece Junction instead '. . . that won't please the locals', wrote Greenbank.

The title 'The Foxdale Railway Co. Ltd.' was that taken by the new company which had first come to light on 17th November, 1882; with a Board comprised almost wholly of MNR directors, it took early steps to explain to the IOMMC that it was actually that same promotion as had been made in the name of the MNR, but under a new name, and that legislation was being sought to build the line which the MNR would work on behalf of the FR. Application by the FR for a Bill was referred by Tynwald to a committee which met on 20th February, 1883, and this in turn recommended that leave be given to introduce the Bill. In an extraordinary additional development, the MNR shareholders agreed to lease the Foxdale Railway for fifty years as from 5th January, 1885 . . . and at a time when not a

---

*For extended reference to mining see THE INDUSTRIAL ARCHAEOLOGY OF THE ISLE OF MAN. Chapter 4. [David & Charles Ltd: 1972.]

yard of track had been laid. The MNR would provide the rolling stock and take 50 per cent of the FR's gross receipts.*

An Extra Ordinary General Meeting of the IOMR was held at the Registered Office (St George's Street) on 18th January

> to consider application about to be made to the Legislature by the Foxdale Railway Co. Ltd. for powers to construct a Railway from the line of the MNRCL, across this Company's line to Foxdale in the Parish of Patrick, and give powers to Directors of this Company to take such steps as . . . and if thought necessary to construct a branch line to Foxdale from a point on this Company's line between Douglas and Peel.

So reported the SUN.

The paper continued:

> The Chairman thought that the manner in which the FR Co. proposed to do it was objectionable in itself . . . that Company was really the MNR . . . he did not say they had no right to make a railway but thought they were coming out of their territory. At present the IOMR had the Foxdale traffic and the Foxdale Railway was commencing the fight . . . it could be shown the railway would not pay . . . he believed the intention was to work the MNR and FR together for the benefit of Ramsey and he would recommend the IOMR to make a line to Foxdale for themselves.

Formans & McCall,† 160, Hope Street, Glasgow, were chosen as Engineers to the FR, Charles Forman having close involvement with the birth of the FR scheme. He was to play a prominent role in a Committee of Enquiry held before the House of Keys on 12th and 13th April. Opposing the project the IOMR complained:

1. There would be a second and separate St John's station on the Foxdale Line, connected by footpath to the IOMR station lying below.
2. The IOMR/FR Ballaleece Junction would create a steep fall in the IOMR Peel Line and there was danger that an Up train from Peel, stopped at that Junction, might fail to restart on the 1 in 85 here: the IOMR maintained that this was the worst place for a junction as trains from Peel frequently loaded to 100 to 110 tons, and exceptionally, 130 tons.
3. Should a station be erected at Ballaleece, the IOMR would find itself with two stations within ½ mile . . . if its own Ballacurry Junction–Foxdale plan had gone ahead, that junction would at least have been on level ground.
4. The layout on the Deposited Plans involved facing junctions which were objectionable.
5. Defending their position, the FR pointed out that Foxdale traffic, now brought to and from St John's by road, seriously interfered with goods traffic there – principally in sand which accounted for about half the business at St John's.

At the IOMR, AGM on 2nd March the Chairman, John Pender, MP, made no secret of what he thought of the MNR/FR alliance and its lack of

---

*See Appendix 1885 for summary of Agreement.

†FORMANS & McCALL (usually Formans & M'Call). Business founded by James Richardson Forman, a Scots-Canadian from Nova Scotia in 1828. Responsible for many of the early Scottish lines. Name adopted as above when Charles de Neuville Forman MICE became a partner in 1875: born in 1852 he was never robust and died of consumption in 1901.

Both before and after the Foxdale Railway, the firm were Engineers to the Kelvin Valley, Glasgow Central, Strathendrick & Aberfoyle Lines, and, in the late 1880s, the West Highland and Invergarry & Fort Augustus Railways. Its close links with Scotsmen engaged in railway-allied businesses was of vital importance to the Foxdale Railway.

commercial sense*; the MNR, AGM in the same month, disclosed some cunning manipulation with the accounts, not to the complete agreement of the MNR auditors, Turquand, Youngs & Co.† Hitting back, the MNR Chairman, J.T. Clucas, made characteristic criticism, coming from a staunch Manxman who considered remarks made from the mainland were quite unacceptable. He pointed out that Pender was in no position to comment, what with the IOMR's worn-out iron rails, its flimsy timber stations and 'little huts' for gatekeepers. Pender might have retorted about poor financial returns and the feeble MNR locomotives!

We must move on to 1st May when the FR Bill had its first reading in Council – complete with the offending layout at Ballaleece at that juncture – when, on 10th May, the Governor presiding, he read a telegram from Pender pointing out that the layout there would not be acceptable 'to any responsible railway experts in England': Pender asked for adjournment until the Governor had given the matter further consideration. The Governor was relieved of an embarrassing position by recommending that Col Rich pronounce on the matter on his forthcoming visit. Pender's view was upheld – Rich condemned the layout, the Bill was amended, passed by the Keys on 29th June, but it was to be 12th December before Royal Assent was received. In its re-cast form, the Foxdale Railway had junction with the MNR not the IOMR at Ballaleece; however, it might extend its system from St John's to St Mark's, Castletown or Ballasalla after suitable notice. The fact that, to the advantage of the IOMR Rich had damned the intended junction at Ballaleece, did nothing for his reputation in the eyes of Greenbank as to the 'laying out of the Foxdale Railway . . . I was not much impressed with the gallant Colonel's evidence, though I admit he is an authority on junction signals etc.'#

Now, back to the existing MNR line. A stopping place at Orrisdale was not a success and was reduced to the status of a request halt. A station, nominally for Peel traffic and where the Peel–Ballig road passed over the line, was begun at Poortown Bridge on 31st March and opened on 28th June with three trains in each direction. The time involved by travelling between Peel and St Germain's (previously the nearest stop for Peel) made the 1⅜ mile walk from Peel to Poortown (as it was first dubbed) a time-saving

---

*See extracts from speeches at IOMR AGM (16th March, 1883) in Tower Collection.
†Currently also auditors to the IOMR.
#At the height of these Maytime altercations, Greenbank was neglected; on 14th May he wrote to Wood saying 'What is being done about the Foxdale affair?' A week later, he must have seen the elevation drawing for the proposed FR overbridge, for he writes again pointing out that with only 4 ft 6 in. clearance from the outside rail to the arch of the bridge, the IOMR signal will be obscured and the MNR will be obliged to erect and fund a repeater on the station side. 'Rich should have drawn attention to this'.
On 30th May, he told Wood he was 'delighted with the news contained in his letter of 28 May . . . I would have given something to be present when Col Rich gave his evidence'. He regretted the IOMR had been put to so much expense to defend its interest. 'The Foxdale people . . . had better adopt the route suggested by me . . . and approved by Col Rich . . . I will make them a present of the idea . . .'
Greenbank's final disclosure was that Thomas (of all people) had been unofficially permitted – and with Greenbank's knowledge – 'making drawings and taking out quantities of bridges etc. with a view to attacking Formans estimate' and had sent a note of his expenses to Wood. Greenbank had warned Thomas against doing this when there was no certainty that the subject of Estimates would come up or not. All of which hints at a feud between Formans & McCall and Thomas.

alternative to the rail journey and change of company trains at St John's. In consequence St Germain's, a station more useful for its possession of a passing loop than as a centre of population, declined almost into oblivion; and it never recovered.

The Ramsey Harbour line was completed and goods sheds and coal stores added at both Kirk Michael and Ballaugh: some loops were extended. New drains had to be dug at the unstable section of line at Gob-y-Deigan. The shareholders were told that until the Foxdale Railway actually became fact, an Agreement between the parties involved would route IOMMC business over the MNR metals only as between St John's and Ramsey.

It was necessary to give new fireboxes to both original locomotives and it would be interesting to know why this was necessary after such a short life? Once again the summer traffic was disappointing 'due to want of hearty co-operation on the part of the IOMR': passenger journeys were 167,913 and 69,514 train miles run.

Looking back to January, it will be noted that the Extraordinary General Meeting of the IOMR had given the Board approval to build the Ballacurry–Foxdale branch and the North Quay Tramway – fresh powers and Capital were to be raised also. By February, the London directors had stamped on the Foxdale idea, 'income would be insufficient to pay working expenses.* (Greenbank's estimate was £10,900 to build a railway or £2,136 for a tramway.) The determination to oppose the Foxdale Bill shown at that meeting had, as described earlier, but limited success ... at least, IOMR metals would not be invaded. This left the North Quay Tramway, and on this ambition was placed:

> A tramway along the North Quay has been under consideration for many years ... not only with the idea of going along the Quay, but to the new street and Victoria Pier so as to enable the people of Ramsey, Peel and Castletown to go by train direct to the boats.

The new street – a matter as yet undetermined – was still a dream and until its position was settled, nothing could proceed. The newspapers warned that if Douglas did not move in this matter, the MNR's new rail connection at Ramsey could decimate the Douglas sea trade. No real progress had been made by the year end. The Governor intervened when the planners opted for certain demolitions and recommended the new street be related to a tramway: the Governor thought the IOMR should contribute towards the cost.

Accordingly, the General Purposes Committee met with the Town Commissioners; the Committee was already angered by the Commissioners whom they had addressed on the subject twelve months before, and were still waiting for an acknowledgement. Enquiry of the Harbour Commissioners brought a negative result also and the familiar '*deja vu*' situation prevailed whilst conflicting loyalties sabotaged intelligent development. The MNR Chairman, with the advantage of a spectator, said 'the fact remains there IS a tramway in Ramsey and not in Douglas and it is likely there will not be a tramway there for some time, perhaps not at all on the North Quay'.†

---

*Manx Museum: R/168/3 Proposed Foxdale Rly. 1883. See *also*: Estimates of costs, tonnage and additional motive power: Tower Collection.
†Manx Museum: R/58: Drawing of relative gauges IOMR and MNR Tramway Co. for North Quay Tramway (Dec. 1883).

Some insight into the Harbour Board's view of the Tramway comes from its Minutes:

> 9th February, 1883. A deputation from the Town Commissioners waited on the Board . . . with reference to the proposed Tramway along the North Quay . . . the deputation pointed out with reference to the Tramway that it would be inadvisable to permit the line to be laid close to the mooring posts as it would in that position interfere with the discharging of vessels and that in their opinion the part of the Quay below the Market Place was too narrow to allow of the line being extended down there.

There were naturally daily working arrangements with the MNR (quite apart from the scheme whereby the IOMR had operated that Railway between 23rd September and 6th November, 1880), and it was imperative to have good relations on traffic, booking, rating and above all, a procedure for St John's station. The strained relations between the two companies had compelled the MNR Board to seek assurances that such would continue to be good. George Sheward was adamant that no new scheme should be made for a period of less than seven years and throughout 1883, the IOMR Board refused to re-consider the existing arrangements until the result of the Foxdale Bill was clarified. On 1st May it was agreed that they continue as they were but, following another hiccough, the IOMR insisted that unless a three-year period could be agreed, the scheme would cease on 1st November, 1883. After MNR refusal to accept this, saner counsels prevailed and, with six months's notice either side, existing arrangements were to continue until 1st May, 1885; so the cat and mouse situation continued. Relations between Ramsey and the London IOMR Board were strained but on the Island itself, the operating departments were on better terms.

A man was caught by his coat as a train was leaving Peel; his hand was injured and two fingers had to be amputated. More severe flooding in the south of the Island damaged the river bridge at Castletown in October; this would be a frequent happening. Over at Ballasalla the operators of the lime works, Jefferson & Moore, reported a busy time, sending 200–300 tons weekly from there by train.

Both at Douglas and Peel, new work was in hand and outside the station at the former a new street to serve the railway station caused the demolition of seven public houses!

In April, the IOMR asked the Secretary to call upon the Midland Carriage & Wagon Co. Ltd. regarding ownership of three wagons 'in our possession, belonging to Davis Meadows'. In the same month, James Moore was 'painting the small carriages and locomotive No. 1'. In May, the MNR asked for reductions in through fares and were refused. This was not only a MNR experience as traffic on the South Line was diminishing, so fares were lowered; numbers still went down so fares were raised again . . . Fares between Douglas and Ramsey were 4s. 0d. Return (1st class) and 2s. 6d. Return (3rd class), considerable sums in those times.

On 7th June, the first train from Peel to Douglas ran the whole distance without changing the Staff – driver J.G. Smith, guard Cowen and Station Masters Flux and Boyne were blamed – Smith was already under notice to leave the Company's employ and other than he, the remainder was fined 5s. 0d. each.

Later that summer, Castletown was in the news when the earth closets at the station were to be among the first converted to water treatment. The other news was of trouble with boys from King William's College who were attempting 'to enter the train in motion – on many occasions the Station Master had had to complain of the conduct of College boys to the Headmaster. It is difficult to prevent the boys being injured'. Not so a young girl who fell from the train between Port St Mary and Colby in August; her grandfather jumped out after her.

A supply of 50–60 tons of steel rails 28 ft 4 in. long from the West Cumberland Iron & Steel Co. Ltd. @ £4 15s. 0d. per ton on quay at Workington, was bought for laying on curves. The Barrow Haematite Works made another delivery, the cost being £7 per ton landed on the Island.

There was an increase in salaries commensurate with the growing business of the Company and monthly figures were: Wood £33 6s. 8d., Hunt £16 13s. 4d. and Thomas Stowell (chief clerk) £10 0s. 0d.

On 26th October, driver Murphy brought a train from Port Soderick to Douglas with the wrong Staff and so was given the option of a fine or being reduced to fireman for a period.

At Peel, the 'old dilapidated building hitherto used as an engine shed' was to be replaced. In November the SUN reported that 'men have laid down rails to the new shed and re-arranged the points'.

December storms at Peel destroyed the goods shed utterly and the roof of the engine shed was blown away; neither could be used. The engine shed was beyond repair so its walls were demolished and a new building 60 ft long was to be substituted. (Greenbank had warned that these timber buildings were ten years old 'and cost more money as time goes on; they are not capable of resisting storms'.)

Sand traffic from St John's now diminished sharply with the completion of the new promenade at Douglas. The heaviest goods traffics were in bricks, cement, stone, sand and lime; lower tonnages covered lime, marine stores, iron and timber and manure.

Each year the IOMR prepared figures to demonstrate which line earned the most revenue and that to Peel continued in the forefront, though in later years it would be utterly overtaken by the South Line. In 1883 receipts were between Peel Line 53 per cent and South Line 49 per cent.

Once again there are some nice entries in Wood's diary:
July: Several Specials for sports etc.; often no passengers, only the bandsmen.
28 July: Special working for Foxdale Pay Week, 15 coaches.
30 July: Special train for Port St Mary concert: only 5s. 0d. taken.
28 August: Port Erin sports: best day. Receipts £400.
25 Sept.: Maguire's Minstrels at Port Erin. A very good day.
28 Sept.: Port Erin damaged by floods.

At the year end, Hunt the Locomotive Superintendent, retired.

Something can be added to the Foxdale Railway picture by dipping into the Minute Book. In view of the time the Legislature was involved with the Bill, the Plans (original and amended) etc., meetings were down to three during the year. In January, J.C. LaMothe showed his antagonism to fellow-director J.F. Gill and threatened that, unless he (LaMothe) obtained a share of the promotion, he would withdraw his support for the scheme. Outbursts to this effect came more than once, in the second naming Gill as his opponent for the business. At the first AGM (May) no shareholder turned up and the meeting was adjourned for seven days. By the Board Meeting on 3rd November, Forman's patience had worn so thin that he said 'if the Company has made no further progress towards a railway he would render his account'. Replying, the Board invited Formans & McCall to come to the Island and 'test the route proposed by Colonel Rich – could Forman suggest a cheaper route?'

1884

The year began by the MNR having second thoughts about their mutual Agreement, and sending the statutory six months' notice to terminate: the revised arrangements had only been in force for less than a month. They also wanted a reduced rate for bricks despatched from Sulby Bridge station to Douglas if more than 500 tons were consigned in twelve months; the existing rate was 2s. 10d. per ton; also the 4s. 5d. per ton rate for potatoes from Ballaugh to Douglas abased.

Reconsideration of the new Peel engine shed brought agreement that it should be as that at Port Erin . . . (the exact style etc. of the original shed at Port Erin is not known). A site preferred meant moving the road 'which the Harbour Commissioners and Town Authorities would not allow', so it remained where it was.

A reply from the Midland RC&WCL re Bruce, Davis & Co. Ltd. (a slightly different title than the one used in the enquiry) confirms three wagons were either on hire or purchase by stage payments to them from the builders, and that the former were still owed an undisclosed sum. The IOMR was willing to purchase the three for £132 on 'condition the Midland paid a debt of £ (unreadable) due to the IOMR by Davis & Meadows,* and if the latter will forego their claim for the use of three wagons for the last three years . . .'. Into this can be read that the Railway had had the use of the open wagons for which the owner or lessee had no use. Currently the IOMR was short of wagons, as will be seen. The deal was concluded, the wagons becoming part of the stock, carrying Nos. M5, M6 and M7.

The matter of the latent Douglas & Laxey Railway's joint use of Douglas station came to the attention of the Governor who, uninvited, submitted his personal recommendations as to how the IOMR might set about the alterations. He was told (in the most polite way) to submit a set of Plans and Estimates for consideration.

Five hundred tons of steel rails were to be ordered from the Barrow Steel Co. Ltd. @ £4 18s. 6d. per ton, f.o.b. Barrow: some of it was made into new pointwork for Douglas.

*Mona Chemical Co. Peel (ceased by 1884) trading as 'Bruce, Davis & Co.' (owner: Dumbell's Banking Co.) – 'Tar Products, Sulphate of Ammonia, Tar & Patent Black Varnish, Naphtha, Creosote, Torch Oil, Duck Oil, Pitch etc.: special attention given to laying Asphalte Paths, Damp-proof floors etc.' [Brown's Directory, 1881.] (Did they operate the Gas Works?)

It had been a dreadful winter and the traffic in lime had been reduced almost to nothing. In February, the rain dried up and all farmers began to want lime simultaneously: although normally there was sufficient stock of wagons, now there was an acute shortage. Three more were ordered, however it was considered 'imprudent to buy more for the demands of a few weeks'.

In March, Rixon, who had been considering the North Quay Tramway problems, proposed that it should be built and maintained by the Government and a toll charged for its use; an annual sum of £400 might be contributed by the Railway. The General Purposes Committee submitted the idea to the Governor, Spencer Walpole, who had had opportunity by June to re-examine the Quay Tramway position. He rejected the IOMR offer of £400 per annum as 'too small' and the IOMR countered by asking him what was his idea of a fair figure?

On 30th March, a child ran in front of the train at 'Bell's Crossing' (i.e. Ballacraine) and was killed. At the Enquiry the jury thought that the gates should have been manned (this was an attended crossing, with gates closed across the railway).

Plans were prepared for a new entrance at Douglas, while additional cartage business brought the need for extra horsepower and a new stable was built beside the Douglas Workshops. This was not all. The comfort of passengers was also to the fore and water-served conveniences ('so very much required') were to be put up using timber, at Port Soderick, Santon, Ballasalla, Colby and Port St Mary by Charles Kaye (Gelling & Kaye) at a cost of £27 each, 'excluding pumps'. The same contractor was to build a crossing cottage at Level, near Colby (so-called after the nearby mine adit), and the cost was £126. Excavations on the north side of Douglas yard were completed and a gatekeeper's house built at Ballastrang by Gelling & Kaye to save 7s. 0d. in gatekeeper's wages.

The Foxdale Railway promoters had thought they had appeased the IOMR when they altered their plans by diverting their line to cross the IOMR at St John's by a bridge on the Douglas side. Comment was: 'The IOMR dissents from their proposal'.

Between Castletown and Douglas, a pig died in the brake van and the newspapers gave good coverage of the event.

A request from the Harbour Commissioners for a piece of land owned by the Railway at Peel Harbour gave the Railway the chance to put the Commissioners 'on the ropes'. They would agree, subject to a tramway along the Old Pier being approved, and an alteration being made at the Slip at the end of the station yard 'enabling us to lay down a tramway over the Slip'.*

Through IOMR carriages between Douglas and Ramsey became a June matter and the MNR (perhaps smarting at criticisms of their stock from the IOMR) refused to allow 'two short carriages' to run over their metals, but would allow 'one long carriage' instead. The Governor was behind the MNR 'request' which obliged the IOMR to convert 'one long 1st/3rd class for through Douglas–Ramsey traffic, the same to run against their two coaches; the IOMR will be prepared meanwhile to run one of the MNR coaches through to Douglas on the first and last trains if same be found upon

---

*Manx Museum: R/219 Proposed West & East Quay Tramways, Peel. (Greenbank) 4/1884.

inspection by Mr Hunt to be in a safe and proper condition' (a reference to unsatisfactory couplings and wheel profiles) '. . . MNR to make no charge for the mileage'. Until conversion of the 'long carriage' was complete, the IOMR was to make available one short 1st class and one short 1st and 3rd class, or one long 3rd.† Ultimately Hunt permitted MNR coaches Nos. 2, 3, 4 to run on the IOMR, and through working began on 11th May.

In the same batch of interchange, the Governor now felt he was unable to make any suggestions as to the amount the IOMR might contribute towards the North Quay Tramway . . .! Like a bad penny, the matter of the North Quay Tramway kept on turning up. The IOMR Board had debated the matter from every angle and by October, put forward some specific proposals stating it would run from the station at the foot of Bank Hill, to 'Fleetwood Corner'. The IOMR

> would construct and maintain it and would work it with what is known as a noiseless, smokeless, steam tramway locomotive engine . . . which would prevent the Tramway from becoming a nuisance . . . dangerous to ordinary road traffic. The Board would give a piece of land to the town near the end of Athol Street at the station which would widen and improve the street, if the Town Commissioners allowed it to build the Tramway.

The Company had prepared the Governor for this positive approach by emphasising the 'wholly discreditable' present arrangements; their most optimistic dream was to connect the station to Victoria Pier, with a branch to the Steam Packet Co.'s office and the Red Pier, with sidings along the edge of the Old Harbour and for the line to be of a standard to carry the IOMR trains throughout. They also sought an extension of the 'passenger tramway from Loch Parade to Douglas station'. It was their earlier opinion that the Government should install it and charge tolls for its use, but (as abovementioned) the final draft commended construction by the Railway . . . it was probably realised at this later stage, that involvement of the Government was a recipe for further delay and excuse on the score of cost.

The new MNR layout between MNR and IOMR at St John's allowed connection between the two systems in the MNR yard by means of the sand siding which was the property of the IOMR. In a bid to make life a little more difficult for the MNR the General Purposes Committee decreed that the ability for MNR vehicles to run onto IOMR metals by this siding was a danger to the IOMR and proposed to remove the siding. When this matter reached the London Board, the Chairman (John Pender) ruled against this being done.

Castletown station was now fitted with gas lighting, supplied from the local Works. In September George S. Gell applied to the Harbour Commissioners to 'lay lines on Castletown Quay and up to the station'. The Harbour Commissioners were not going to be goaded by the IOMR concerning a tramway at Peel and would not permit one, preferring to buy land to make approach for a new bridge. Kaye* finished the crossing house at Level.

†The definitions are as given in the Minute.
*Gelling & Kaye (Joiners & Builders), Circular Road, Douglas. [Brown's Directory. 1881.]

Close attention was being paid to fencing repairs on the IOMR as these had become old and vulnerable. Wood was alerted by a threat that the Railway might have to pay full rates on its properties which would follow a new valuation. Fortunately the matter was resolved by allowing 'Lunatic Asylum rates on railway property'.

In November the newspapers published frequent letters about the unsteady riding and 'oscillation' of the 'short carriages' and Hunt was called in to report. He felt they were 'safe enough if maintained in proper and safe condition' and was instructed to devise a method to make them steady and avoid oscillation. 'Would any alteration impair their use in heavy traffic?' they asked. The Secretary wrote to Metropolitan, who recommended an alteration in tyre profile. The view of the General Purposes Committee was sceptical . . . 'the plan was far from perfect'. However, the Chairman had decreed that a number of carriages should be allowed as a trial, and one was fitted with thicker flanges. The Board bore in mind that they had 20 sets of new wheels and axles on order to the existing profile. (It would be early 1887 before any more steps were taken to eradicate this behaviour.) During 1884 only 6 per cent of passengers travelled 1st class, yet it was this class of traveller who complained most frequently.

All this railway construction had sown seeds in the mind of other entrepreneurs and by September, word had gone about that a party was planning to take a railway up Glen Helen. Wood brought the matter to the attention of George Sheward in London. Sheward was then ill and confined to bed (he died on 2nd November) but suggested that if the promoters should make an informal approach to Wood which would involve the IOMR having to agree to build and operate such a line, then Wood should mention the matter to Goldie-Taubman. Sheward would be agreeable to build and operate on a percentage basis. The matter then rests until January 1885.

Out on the IOMR, Wood's diary again gives pleasant references to daily goings-on and extracts (verbatim) include:

16th February: Steamer into Peel. Special left 10.40 pm.
Easter: Splendid days and good trains. Late working 10.50 pm. Douglas–Port Erin: good train.
22 April: Dramatic entertainment at Douglas. Trains leaving for Douglas after nine, leaving there at 10.40 and 10.50 pm.
26 June: Bazaar at Crosby. Train not guaranteed: Committee had to pay 5/1d. – trains only realised 34/11d.
10 July: Douglas Flower Show. Rained all day: trains poor.
14 July: Ramsey Regatta – lent Ramsey Line six short coaches.
26 July: Foxdale Pay Week – late Specials. Rained all day. Very few passengers on Specials.
31 July: Foresters Demonstration at Ramsey.
3 August (Sunday): Poor day. Bishop on Douglas Head. Receipts less than in 1883. No use.
7 August: Ramsey Agricultural Show. Douglas–Port Erin 4 am. Special returns with stock for Show – Special then leaves St. John's for Ramsey 7.15 am. Cost £3 for this early train. Very unsatisfactory – our receipts down and owing to MNR Coy's trains, our trains were delayed. Late Special from St. John's 58 mins. late . . . in future we should not wait for Ramsey train if more than 10 mins. late. It would be as well to run a Special at night to Port Erin if cattle offering.

12 August: 512 travelled on Special Peel–Ballasalla @ 10d. return (childrens' outing).
20 August: Church School Peel–Douglas 1.15 pm @ 6d. return. 673 persons travelled. All parties satisfied.
26 August: Opening Peel Church. Late trains poor.
19 September: Amusements at Falcon Cliff. Late Specials leave 11 pm guaranteed £5.
7 October: late workings for Gaiety Theatre – IOMR to pay Mr. Elphinstone 1/- for Pit and 2/- for Stalls: he guarantees £8 per train. Very poor trains: theatre did not attract people – too late in season.
Christmas: Douglas Dog & Poultry Show. Exhibits carried free at owner's risk. Not equal to previous year.*

During heavy rain and wind in early March the cutting at Gob-y-Deigan was filled by a landslide; the line was completely blocked and road vehicles connected trains on either side of the obstruction. The line was closed from 3rd to 5th March.

The MNR, AGM in April was notable for the frayed tempers of those present. Apart from the IOMR which was targetted for loss of business, the number of road vehicles had 'reached immense figures'. The 'complete repair' of locomotives Nos. 1 & 2 cost £1,001, the first major overhaul since the line was opened. For the first time, bridges, viaducts and all woodwork were painted or tarred as required. A rosy picture was painted of an Agreement between the IOMMCL, FR and MNR to convey IOMMCL goods which, until completion of the Foxdale system, would be limited as between St John's and Ramsey. They had reduced their fares to attract business but the IOMR refused to do so – in the end they had to comply. The Company was anticipating a reduction in wages paid to the IOMR staff at St John's as their share of the cost; soon the MNR would have its own station there, and the Agreement about joint working could cease. The matter of building a branch to Peel was aired. There then followed a row about Free Passes which had spiteful overtones, and there were threats of resignation from Board members who invited their critics to take their places if they thought they could do better. Tempers then cooled.

The IOMR, AGM displayed behaviour of similar type. Underlying all was the vexed question as to whether the Railway was being managed from London or the Island, 'by Englishmen or Manxmen?' There was anger at the MNR for giving notice of the termination of joint working at St John's, the site of Castletown station, and the failure of the North Quay Tramway to progress.

It is opportune to visit St John's to examine progress of the MNR's new station which would in due course, be the commencement of the Foxdale Railway. The contract for the St. John's work had gone to William Murray of Aberfoyle, known to both Cameron and Forman. He began work immediately after receiving it on 12th May; on 17th June he obtained an additional contract for the station house and locomotive water tank's supporting brickwork, but a temporary timber shed had to suffice for the opening station as there was no time for anything better in brick. In 1881 the unfinished station site lay athwart the IOMR's siding into Dumbell's sandpit

---

*Railway matters apart, the diary is first-class material for a study of the social habits of those times.

(the 'St John's Sand & Gravel Co.'). Murray took matters into his own hands and without a 'by your leave', removed the siding and laid in the station tracks. A new connection had to be made from the MNR run-round (IOMR correspondence on this subject has yet to be traced!) Business began at the new terminus from 1st July but of course, through working and the IOMR joint station working arrangements continued as before.

At Ramsey a lead store was erected for the convenience of the IOMMCL: being found too small it was enlarged early the following year. On the far (north) side of it the unused ground up to the river bank was infilled, levelled off and became a saw mill and timber yard. It was necessary to embank the river to prevent erosion.

Three sidings now feature in MNR traffic matters; that at Ballavolley* was in operation and the Highway Board made arrangements for the MNR to put in a siding at Poortown to serve the Board's quarry from which road-stone was obtained. It was the following year before the siding and high level loading bank were complete; stone was carried @ 1½d. per ton/mile if over 2,000 tons were conveyed per annum.

Ballakillingan was the home of E.C. Farrant, a MNR director who requested a siding for his estate purposes at Lezayre; up until then loading/unloading of wagons took place whilst they stood on the main line. Traffic was mainly of incoming lime. Anticipating these extra tonnages, the Board sanctioned purchase of eight low-side open wagons in March; they were similar to those of the same purpose on the IOMR.

Materials for the Foxdale Line were noted arriving at Ramsey in mid-April and in May by the SUN's reporter . . . 'Rails are of a heavier kind than those at present in use in the Island . . . the new station at St John's is to be commenced at once . . . hoped to be ready for 1st July'.

The Foxdale Railway Prospectus of July was noted by the SUN and that its directors† occupied similar positions on the MNR

> The district is not very populous but it has been estimated that the annual traffic now existing may be relied upon in coal, lead and timber for the mines . . . is about 12,890 tons annually . . . arrangements have been made . . . to convey the traffic for 12 years . . . worked by the MNR.

(The account was somewhat fictitious.)

The 'existing traffic may be relied upon' proved – as with many mining ventures – to be ill-timed for in September the MNR was told by John Beckwith, Chairman of the IOMMCL that due to a continuance of low demand, the Mining Co. was unlikely to invest in the Railway. This awesome news was made all the worse for the Foxdale Railway Co. who had committed themselves to building a railway without substantial safeguards. John Pender of the IOMR must have had a quiet chuckle . . . needless to say, no mention of such setback appears in the MNR Minute Book. Once again the MNR, AGM had to be put back a week as there was no quorum on 13th June; the recalled meeting saw three directors and three shareholders present, other than those 'in attendance'. It was agreed at that gathering that all MNR shareholders should be sent a copy of the Prospectus and this had some effect, a shower of small shareholders, mainly from Ramsey itself, taking up shares in small lots of threes and fives.

---

*see SRN 51 page 11. Siding laid 1882.
†J.T. Clucas, E.C. Farrant, W.B. Christian, J.C. LaMothe, C.H.E. Cowle, J.R. Cowell.

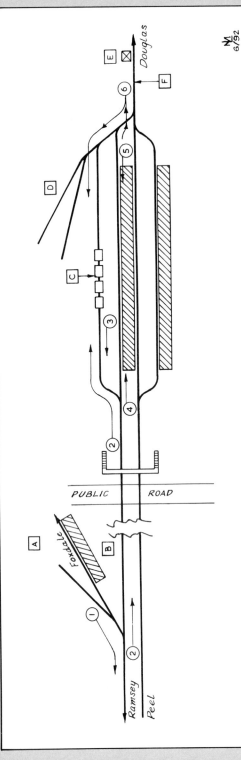

ST. JOHN'S: Rich's sketch to show dangerous shunting movements (1884)

A. St. John's 'new' station
B. St. John's 'new' station Foxdale Branch platform
C. Wagons to be taken to Douglas
D. Sidings
E. Signal Box (MNR)
F. 'IOM Coy's train* stopped here and then pushed back onto Through Coach and next onto wagons'

1. MNR locomotive draws Through Coach from Foxdale platform†
2. MNR locomotive propels Through Coach onto rear of wagons in error
3. MNR locomotive draws Through Coach away from wagons, sets back,
4. and propels Through Coach into IOMR platform and detaches
5. Whilst this movement taking place, IOMR Peel – Douglas train propelled back into platform to attach Through Coach‡
6. IOMR locomotive, train and Through Coach draw forward to F, reverse and push back onto rake of wagons which are then attached. Train then leaves for Douglas, leaving MNR locomotive awaiting next duty

*from Peel – J.I.C.B.
†Locomotive presumed to be at Ramsey end of Through Coach.

During 1884, MNR passenger figures dropped to 173,484 with 69,169 train miles, but the Annual Report showed a nice increase in mineral tonnage (mainly ex-Foxdale) to 19,211. November saw a sad accident when a little boy jumped onto a carriage coupling at Ballaugh; the train jerked when starting, throwing him off and under the wheels.

At the Foxdale Board Meeting on 10th October an anxious representative from Andrew S. Nelson & Co. (of Glasgow: Engineers' Agents), and Hurst, Nelson & Co. Ltd.* who had supplied 300 tons of steel rails delivered to Ramsey in August and ordered the previous May, pressed for payment: if not forthcoming, interest would be charged. However, he made a peace-offering by adding that if Nelson & Co. was favoured with the order for chairs and fastenings, and the promise of prompt payment conditional that the Company would take the rails in the next ten days (they were temporarily in the care of Formans & McCall), they would waive the interest. It was not a happy Meeting; LaMothe, Gill and Christian resigned and Robert Scott, J. Cottier and William Kitto (Manager of the Foxdale Mines) took their places on the Board. By 30th December some of the cost of the steel rails was still outstanding and the MNR was owed for carriage of rails and sleepers between Ramsey and St John's, and the owners of the CLOFFOCK had not been paid for shipment. As yet, with no contractor assigned to the construction, Forman suggested it would be possible to find contractors who would invest up to £7,000 in Stock; Formans & McCall were then instructed to obtain tenders which stated the amount of Stock an intending contractor was prepared to take. Meanwhile, the IOM Banking Co. issued overdrafts to meet the parlous cash-flow position.

The Government Director of the MNR inspected it on 12th October and wrote:†

Sir,
I inspected the Manx Northern Railway on Thursday last and found the line in good order. Many of the sleepers are partly decayed and it will probably be necessary to renew the greater part of them in the next two or three years.

I observed that the Company are using a new station at St John's which I presume has been made in connection with the new Railway to Foxdale.

The manner of working the through carriages from this station to the Isle of Man Railway's stations at St John's is dangerous and very inconvenient to the passengers.

Six shunts were made at St John's with the through carriage in which I travelled from Ramsey to Douglas. The diagram attached# will show how this was done.

Two of these shunts (Numbers 2 & 3 on the diagram) were I presume made by mistake: but it is by such mistakes that dangerous accidents occur. All shunting operations are dangerous to the passengers, therefore there ought to be only one shunt to transfer one or more coaches from the Railway of one Company to that of the other.

I believe the IOMR Co.'s train was moving back when number 5 shunt on the Diagm. was being made with the Manx Northern Railway Co.'s Carriage & Engine. This is particularly dangerous. I have known many very serious accidents occur by such shunting operations and one serious accident would be very prejudicial to the interests of the Manx Northern Railway Coy. I would therefore suggest your special attention to this matter. In my opinion it would be far better to discontinue

---

*Forman was responsible for bringing in Nelson.
†Original in Tower Collection.
#see previous page

the through traffic and to give the Isle of Man Railway Co. notice, that the junction between the two Railways at St John's will no longer be required for the service of the MNR, than to continue to incur such risks.

I would at the same time reiterate what I have urged from the commencement viz. the desirability of both Cos. working in unison and of continuing to use the IOMR station for both the Ramsey and Foxdale traffic.

I think the IOMR Co. must now see the desirability of arranging this with the MNR Co. as combined working would be far better and cheaper for both Companies.

In any new arrangement the MNR might very properly insist on having a man of their own at St John's to see that the Coy's interests were properly attended to by the Station Master and employees of the IOMR Co.

This Company derives considerable benefit from the traffic which is carried over the MNR and should be prepared to do that Coy's work at St John's thoroughly well at a small cost, and it is certainly in their interest to do this and not oblige the MNR Co. to take their traffic away from the IOMR Co.'s station at St John's.

I have the honour to be Gentlemen,
Your obedient servant
F.H. Rich: Colonel (Royal Engineers).

Two more letters follow and their message is clear!

Letter from Rich to Clucas (Chairman MNR)*

17 Queens Gate Terrace.
13 October, 1884.

My dear Mr. Clucas,

When I returned to Douglas on Thursday last I spent 2½ hours with Mr Wood in talking about the two Companies working in unison and how it would be to the advantage of both.

I was particularly induced to do this considering what appears to me, the very dangerous manner in which you are now working the through traffic at St John's. The delay would usually be considered objectionable, but when I tell you that very many of the Railway Accidents that cost the Coys a good deal of money occur in shunting, you will understand the risks you are running: that last winter the Great Western Rly. Coy turned over and damaged 3 coaches at the platform at West Drayton when making a shunt from the Down line to the Up line, and the London & North Western coach in which I was travelling was thrown over on its side in Tredegar station under similar circumstances. Both these accidents were caused by trains having been moved before the points were in the proper position . . .

(Rich recommends Cameron to talk to Wood and set down in writing the result of the interview so that there is no mistake in what Cameron reports to the MNR Board. Rich also recommends Clucas' attendance at the IOMR Meetings (he being a Director of the IOMR also) when anything relating to the MNR is discussed) . . .

> I believe that the IOMR Coy see plainly that in trying to hurt the MNR Co. they have only been hurting themselves and that if properly managed that they will work more harmoniously in future.
>
> I told Mr. Wood that I thought the through traffic had better be given up rather than continued to be carried on in the inconvenient manner that it is now done

---

*Original in Tower Collection.

and that if discontinued, the Junction at the Douglas end of St John's station would no longer be of use to the MNR and that I should advise that Coy to give notice of surrender. The MNR Co. could leave all through Goods & Mineral traffic in the IOMR Co.'s yard for that Coy to take on, in the manner that might seem best and as the law requires: but I suggested that expenses would be saved and the interest of both Companies would be promoted by the common use of Old St John's Stn. at a fair price. The Board should be careful not to anger the Common Public, if it can be helped, by becoming Coal Merchants.* The law in England does not allow this.

Yours sincerely,
F.H. Rich

1885

The IOMR was feeling the loss of the IOMMCL traffic; by now only all boxes and parcels were consigned to Douglas; the IOMR/IOMMCL special rates were discontinued, and what was the IOMR loss was the MNR's gain.

Creggan's Lime Quarry at Ballasalla approached the IOMR for a branch line into their premises; Greenbank surveyed but found that the point of the junction would increase the main line gradient there to 1 in 80 – the Board would not countenance this. Creggan wanted to erect kilns for burning the lime between the railway and the Silver Burn but could find no site for them. A tramway to either Ballasalla or Castletown would have suited him. A second request brought the same answer from the IOMR but Creggan came back with his own plan for a line into Castletown; this was acceptable, subject to the main line and tramway being kept no less than 7 ft apart where the two lines ran alongside each other into Castletown yard. The junction was to be under IOMR control, all traffic would have to be consigned for IOMR and the trackwork must satisfy Greenbank. The IOMR was 'prepared to lend sufficient old iron rails for the tramway'. And there the matter ends; there is a suggestion that Creggan could not obtain a wayleave over the intervening land.

In March 1885 – nothing having been done to this end – G.H. Wood wrote to the Douglas Town Commissioners reminding them of an application by the Railway Company for liberty to lay down a railway to the North Quay, 'between the railway station and the Fleetwood Corner' to which they had not replied. The Railway had sent Plans 'some time ago'. The outcome was a meeting between the Board of the Railway and the Douglas Town Commissioners Improvement Committee.

The legal advice given to the Douglas Town Commissioners was that their Act gave them no powers to give the IOMR permission to lay a tramway and the Legislature would have to sanction that power. Greenbank was summoned to re-cast his Plans once more – he can by now have considered

---

*Author's note: Coal merchanting – several MNR Directors were involved.

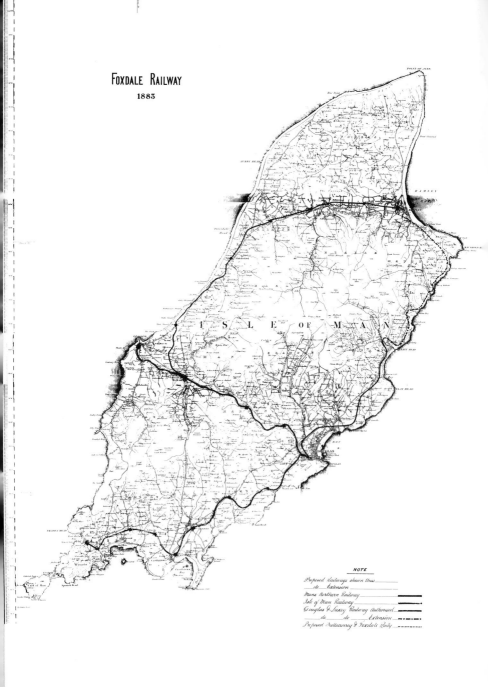

all the options but the determination of the IOMR Board is notable.*
Greenbank did his survey as far as 'The Fleetwood Corner'. The Governor
now backed the idea subject to the IOMR paying an annual rent of £25; at
that stage the Commissioners put their scheme for a new street from Victoria
Pier to the Market Place before the Legislature and the tramway plans went
into storage.† (Whilst on the Island, Greenbank was also to inspect the
overbridge which the Foxdale Railway had thrown across the IOMR at St
John's.)

James Kissack wanted a siding into his stoneyard at Castletown and was
told he could have one if he paid for the installation ... nothing further was
heard from him. Over at Peel the new Locomotive Shed was completed.
Meanwhile the High Bailiff was attempting to encourage a steamer service
between there and Belfast, and the Peel authorities wanted the matter of a
suitable quay tramway re-opening (the attempt of 1884 has already been
described). The IQMR was not prepared to reconsider the subject without
the certainty that such a service would continue, and on a cost-shared basis.

Now to Douglas where in the late summer, the long-deferred objective of a
new station was sanctioned. Initially (at a cost of £50,000–£60,000) an
adjacent property was to be purchased and then, a new building thereon
would house the general office, Station Master's office, waiting rooms,
booking office and refreshment room, the only condition being that building
should not take place during high season. The matter had been precipitated
by the Company receiving notice to quit their existing rented offices. Such a
building would be on the site 'of the proposed extension to Victoria Street'
so perhaps the dream of the North Quay Tramway was fading.

The IOMR, AGM was told that further gatekeepers' cottages were to be
built, that Ballasalla cattle pen and loading bank was complete and more
steel rails were on order. It had cost £199 5s. 6d. to convert a 2nd class
carriage into a composite for the Ramsey through traffic; three more open
wagons had been delivered.

Complaints about the rough riding of the IOMR coaches reached a pitch
where something had to be done at least to appease the 1st class passengers,
and the answer was to convert a 2nd class bogie vehicle into a 1st and 2nd
class composite.

The IOMR mail contract was renewed for a further seven years @ £325 per
annum.

During August, Henry Hunt, the IOMR Locomotive Superintendent,
'resigned', and Joseph Sproat, Locomotive Foreman since February 1875,
took his place 'for the time being'.

We may turn to Wood's diary again to see how he saw IOMR affairs during
1885.

   25th February: Circuit Convention, Castletown.
   21st March: Concert, Douglas. 21 passengers on Port Erin Line and 47 on Peel.
      Trains did not pay.
   Good Friday: Special from Peel at night: 22 coaches and could have done with 2
      more. Rest of Easter traffic very bad – wet and stormy.
   9th April: School of Art Concert, Douglas. Poor trains.

---

*IOMR files contain a drawing of the Wisbech & Upwell Tramway track with McKee's System of
chair and check rail (drawing dated July 1885.) Also Greenbank's North Quay Tramway Cross
Section (drawing dated August 1885.)
†Manx Museum: R/12 of July 1885.

14th April: Amateur Dramatic entertainment at Douglas. Port Erin train good. Peel train poor.
15th April: Gordon's Entertainment at Castletown. Special: Port Erin–Castletown, poor train: not worth running.
5th July, Tynwald Fair: St Thomas Band of Hope. 100 children and 8 adults to Port Soderick @ 5d. return.
21st July: Wesley School. Peel–Port Erin @ 9d. return. Very complex workings. 950 travel.
26th July (Sun.): Bishop at Peel Castle. Very poor, Special left Douglas 2 pm.
30th July: Castletown Agricultural Show. All went well up to departure of cattle train, 22 mins late due to late arrival of No. 24 train (9 mins) and difficulty in coupling up and getting cattle train onto siding. No. 23 train 23 mins late leaving Castletown and arrived 34 mins late at Douglas. No. 26 left Douglas 46 mins late. Mr Callister is to blame for the first delay through not coupling up his train properly at Douglas and allowing the van to become detached in Nunnery cutting.
5th August: (Herein are some driver's names listed) – Morrison, I. Beard, McDonald (shunting engine). Murphy, Kendall, Skircs (sic), Wade, Cusson, Clucas, Shires, I.B. Smith.
28th August: Tooles' Theatre. Good train from Douglas 10.50 pm, best we have had on the Port Erin Line for a long time.
2nd September: Ballasalla Athletic Sports.
14th October: Peel Lifeboat demonstration. Good day.
Boxing Day: Ordinary Market Day Train from Ramsey will not run (dep. Ramsey 8.25 am).
29th December: Pantomime, Douglas.

A fatal accident to the Colby Station Master on 17th December clouded the IOMR events for the year. He was hand-shunting a cattle truck onto the rear of the 1 pm train and allowing it to run by gravity. Apparently he misjudged its speed, jumped on the handbrake and was still standing on it when the truck came into sidelong contact with the train, both moving in the same direction at the time. The Station Master was thrown under the moving vehicles. Albert Kelly, the guard, had started the train 'to go over the points as usual to pick up the wagon. The Station Master and a little boy had started to push it along the siding before I started the train, and both were moving in the same direction towards the points . . . I saw the wagon was likely to collide with the train before the train had passed: I called the Station Master to jump off but he did not. The wagon struck the last coach and was derailed and the Station Master fell beneath it. He was much injured and said 'The Lord have mercy on me', twice. Some people from the train took charge of him'. Patrick Murphy was the driver: had not seen the accident 'as there is a curve in the line passing over the points'.

To complete railway matters for 1885, we turn to a proposed Glen Helen Railway, the Douglas, Laxey & Ramsey Railway, the MNR and the Foxdale Railway under construction. A letter from Pender to Goldie-Taubman in January adds an air of mystery to the Glen Helen proposal. He stressed that the utmost secrecy must be observed, especially over Clucas in whose presence the matter should not be mentioned . . . 'because there is a scheme on foot to go to the MNR if we decline to make a junction on their line . . . and I imagine join us about Union Mills and this might prove dangerous if only as to running powers'.

News reached the Press much later in the year when the SUN reported on 25th July that this Glen Helen Railway scheme was the fruits of an undertaking, The Manx Brick & Tramway Co. Ltd., which had been formed with wide powers in the previous March. It was permitted not only to engage itself in building materials but to carry on transport businesses, piers and vehicle building. By the end of 1885, something under £1,000 towards progress had been raised by its promoters who were largely in the Douglas region. A railway up Glen Helen from Ballacraine on the IOMR was the subject of their tramway petition in that July, the line to be worked by tramway-type steam locomotives, suitably encased so as not to affright passing persons and animals. On 24th October, the route was described as from Ballacraine level crossing, across the Neb river by bridge at Ballig and then along the highway towards Glen Helen; the rail tops would be flush with the road surface. The Legislature was cool towards the proposal and leave to introduce a Bill was refused.

The MB & T Co.'s tramway scheme was based on tourist traffic and that 44,000 people had visited Glen Helen the previous year. The rolling stock would only be 6 ft 4 in. wide so as to be acceptable on the roadway; the estimated traffic per month was 200 tons of coal and 1,000 bricks. A Plan and Section (undated) by Herbert Hall, Engineer of Villiers Chambers, Douglas, shows the proposal leaving the IOMR from an area south of Ballacraine crossroads whence the tramway would join the road up Glen Helen and run up the centre of it. Here the road was 27 ft – 31 ft 6 in. wide: at Ballig the road was only 22 ft wide. To cross the river and streams, the tramway was to use the road's bridges. Ballig was ⅛th mile north of the brickworks and stood on the right hand side, and there would have been a tunnel under the road where the brickworks to brickpits line ran. Beyond, at The Temperance Hotel, was the sharpest curve of 6 chains radius. The line would not have actually entered Glen Helen but terminated at Swiss Cottage near the 'Glen Helen Grounds' at the foot of the Glen; it would have been 2 miles 3 furlongs long. There would have been a northbound uphill gradient of 1 in 18 and 1 in 20 at Ballacraine crossroads. Apart from the end termini which lay on sections off the road, the whole route was along the highway.

[The subject may be conveniently concluded for 1885 – 7 by adding that by November next year (1886), the Company was now allied to the MNR which was offering it a line from near Poortown station rather than that the tramway should stem from a point on the IOMR; the threat of such a link might enable the MNR to bring pressure to bear on the IOMR; costings were prepared in January 1887 but no more was done. Poortown was renamed Peel Road in May.]

Now to St John's to see how the Foxdale Railway was progressing. By the end of February work was advancing nicely, according to the SUN whose correspondent must have been blessed with good imagination as a contractor had not been selected at that time. The Foxdale project was encouraged by the knowledge that on 3rd January the MNR had made Agreement* to work the line for the next 50 years: Cameron, Manager of the MNR, would manage the FR too, and the MNR would operate the system for

---

*Manx Museum: R/181 and R/187 (these are identical).

55 per cent of the gross receipts. The MNR also gave a conditional guarantee to make up FR receipts (should they fall short) to a figure which would enable 5 per cent to be distributed on the Paid-up Capital. The latter amount, it was confidently expected, could be earned by carrying the Foxdale traffic, but only as to 45 per cent of receipts.

In February 1885, Formans & McCall chose Hugh Kennedy & Son, Partick, Glasgow, as a suitable and most competitive contractor: arrangements with them were concluded on 31st March and a contract signed on 14th April.

On 20th June, Kennedy offered £120 'for the locomotive at Peel as it stands on the ground' (Harbour Board Minutes) and the offer was accepted. Thereafter Peel would rely on the locomotive powers of its steam crane which had disgraced itself in the January by falling into the water. It was sent to Stothart & Pitt Ltd. of Bath for repair.

The first sod of the Foxdale Railway was cut at St John's on 13th April; 'Formans & McCall of Glasgow will have the work under their superintendence' wrote the TIMES. Equipment for Kennedy was arriving in the Island during April: A.S. Nelson & Co. Ltd. had already sent steel rails (value £1,271 14s. 7d.) and chairs (the latter a heavier type than that being inserted into MNR track) and payments due for these and to the contractor were placing a heavy burden of debt on the FR who arranged an overdraft on the IOM Banking Co. The two stations were to be at Lower Foxdale (latterly called Waterfall) and Foxdale: John Glen of Kilsyth, Stirlingshire (a mining town), obtained the contract for the buildings* @ £315 ... but not until February 1886.

In April, it was intended to give the order for fishplates, bolts and spikes to Nelson also, but payment for the rails was a problem and Formans & McCall 'took them in' temporarily and reimbursed Nelson; this embarrassed the FR and prevented an order for the fishplates etc. which in turn obstructed track laying. Sleepers of larch were to come from P. McGregor & Co., Kirkintilloch, Glasgow, 7 ft × 8 in. × 4 in. @ 1s. 3½d. each. [The geographical proximity of suppliers for the Foxdale Line is noteworthy.] On 30th April, the Agreement by the MNR was signed and, in June John Wark was engaged as Inspector of the Line @ £6 4s. 0d. a month to supervise the contractor's work. A list of shareholders at this date reflects the almost-total support of Ramsey residents.

The new railway would require a much more powerful engine than existed on the Island already and it must have occasioned no surprise when the order went to a Glasgow firm, Dübs & Co., Polmadie, Glasgow, in June. On 19th December, the SUN said,

> Ramsey. A very large engine for the Foxdale Railway came by steamer FENELLA from Glasgow yesterday morning: weight 22 cwt.† It is in parts on the steamer and will be put together on the quay.

During the first week in January, their correspondent wrote

> We have had the pleasure of viewing the new engine recently built which has just been erected in their workshops at Ramsey ... it is chocolate colour ... guaranteed to take a gross load of 150 tons on a gradient of 1 in 50 at a speed of 35 mph ... which will be used principally for the Foxdale traffic.

---

*'station work' in the Minutes.
†obviously a featherweight! This should read '22 tons'.

Plate 56: A 'might-have-been'. Using the North Quay beside the Inner Harbour at Douglas, the long-debated extension tramway would have run to piers where the steamers berthed. *Collection J.I.C. Boyd*

Plate 57: Another 'might-have-been'. Peel Harbour with the original station in the centre distance. There was a First World War tramway along the eastern quay (*left of picture*) and a projected tramway on the western (*right of picture*). The former was lifted after the War, and the latter was never built. The two pictures on this page sum up the absence of vital sea/land links by which the Isle of Man Railway was always disadvantaged. c1903. *Manx Museum*

Plate 58: The Foxdale Railway began with a junction off the Manx Northern Railway's line into St John's. Here the photographer is standing on the main Foxdale Line; St John's (Foxdale) station is behind and the turnout from the MNR can be seen ahead.
Collection J.I.C. Boyd

Plate 59: Looking in the opposite direction to the picture above, we see that the Foxdale track has become chaired. The station is hidden by the hedge on the right, and the water tank base has lost its tank: the St John's–Castletown road bridge crosses the line and the pointwork just beyond leads into sand and gravel pit sidings.
C.E. Box

Plate 60: Before the official opening, the Inspection Train ran up to Foxdale with MNR No. 4 and the Foxdale Railway coach. The personalities are (*left to right*): John Cottier (FR Director), C.H.E. Cowle (FR Director), Charles Forman (Engineer), J.T. Clucas (FR Director), J.C. LaMothe (MNR Director), Col F.H. Rich (Inspector appointed by the Governor), Hugh Kennedy (Contractor), Capt. William Kitto (Mine Captain & Foxdale Mines Manager), J.R. Cowell (FR Director), Bob Thompson (guard), John Cameron (Manager). Engine driver was Jack Kneale and (holding handrail) William Kelly (fireman).
S. Boulton

Plate 61: Foxdale station after the workings had been taken over by the IOMR. The engine is No. 4, by then allocated to Ramsey and working chimney-first out of there, attached to an ex-MNR six-wheeled carriage and 'The Foxdale Coach'. The engine's rear carries a bucket, the large lamp (often seen on Foxdale workings) and has rear steps on the beam ... purpose unknown. The Station Master carries the Staff.
E.H. Quilliam

Plate 62: Douglas workshops; office on left, packing stacked against lefthand wall, wheel lathe in the distance.

Plate 63: Further inside the building shown in the previous view, the wheel lathe, pillar drill and stationary engine are prominent. Beyond the far doorway (*right*) the locomotive boiler for the stationary engine can be seen. *C.E. Box*

Plate 64: Before regulations required walls to be whitewashed annually, No. 8 (?) stands over the pit; it is shedded away from Douglas and would enter that station chimney-first. *F. Moore*

Plate 65: The boiler unit has been parted from the frames of No. 8 (now running chimney-first from Douglas), the former running on a homespun trolley carried on wooden-centred coach wheels. Note how much of the equipment has remained in use from earliest times. 1931. *C.E. Box*

Plate 66: The same scene as the above picture, but viewed from the west end of the shop. *C.E. Box*

Plate 67: Douglas, with the railway station (centre right), Inner and Outer Harbours beyond, and the Nunnery Estate in the foreground. The railway station has not yet been outraged and the Steam Packet Company's ships at the piers show no evidence of the 'floating garage' era yet to come.

Manx Technical Publications Ltd

Plate 68: A closer view of the Douglas terminus at 7 am on a Sunday morning, forty years ago.
J.I.C. Boyd

Plate 69: Douglas, looking east in April 1960. The demands of the timetable are slight and the only sign of life is No. 11 simmering outside the workshops. Note the two water columns and coaling platforms, to allow two engines to be serviced at once.
J.I.C. Boyd

Plate 70: This scene commemorates two events: the completion of the new Nunnery Bridge and the delivery of bogie coaches F24, F25, F26 – both occurring in 1896. Members of staff and labour force, recruited to fill the train, lean from the windows. The bearded figure in front of the first coach is G.H. Wood; the engine is No. 2 DERBY.

Manx Museum

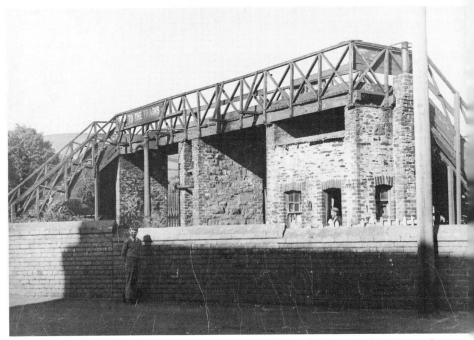

Plate 71: A bridge of different character was the footbridge at St John's, seen here from its southwest side. It was demolished in 1945.   *J.H. Flower*

Plate 72: Yet another bridge; a St John's-bound train crosses the ex-MNR viaduct at Glen Wyllin pleasure grounds on 2nd June, 1952, headed by engine No. 3. The cattle vans and open wagons converted to carry sheep, reflect the importance of this traffic on the North Line; it *is* a Monday!   *J.D. Darby*

Plate 73: No. 1 of 1873, still in original form with small side tanks, outside the Douglas running shed. The newly-built carriage shed appears in the background.
F. Moore

Plate 74: No. 2 stands beside the coal stack, Douglas; the inked lines marking the cab handrails were to emphasise a feature in a letter to the makers.
F. Moore

Plate 75: No. 3; it, and Nos. 1 & 2 were landed on the Island in 1873.   *F. Moore*

Plate 76: In 1901 No. 4, employed on the South Line, and shedded at Port Erin, was running chimney-first into Douglas. Nos. 4 & 5 of 1874 were slightly larger than the first three engines, having larger side tanks and coal bunkers for their employment on that more heavily graded route.   *F. Moore*

Plate 77: No. 7 of 1880 is ready for the 'right away' at Peel. Detail differences from its predecessors include the positions of name and maker's plates, and the moving of the sandbox from the footplate to a position forward of the tank; the injected water now enters the boiler through the first ring. Wooden brake shoes still persist.
F. Moore

Plate 78: No. 8 of 1894 was the only new engine delivered to the IOMR that year. A detail difference now introduced was the wheel and handle on the smokebox door, in place of double handles. St John's: at the Peel platform. *Oakwood Press*

Plate 79: No. 9 of 1896 was the last of the near-original design and marks a watershed in IOMR locomotive policy. Here it stands at the east end of St John's station in July 1933, very little different outwardly from the day of delivery. *H.C. Casserley*

Plate 80: No. 9 again, seventeen years later than the above (Monday 10th April, 1950) behind Ramsey carriage shed at the coaling stage. Practically the only difference is in the canvas 'dodger' on the cab; in this picture it is fully 'set' against the weather.

J.D. Darby

Plates 81 and 82: Nos. 10 & 11 were the pioneer machines of a new 'big engine' strategy. With bigger boilers and water tanks, and longer wheelbases, they were built to maintain better timekeeping on the South Line where traffic was heaviest and increasing annually. There was competition on the North Line from the electric railway to Ramsey, plus a need to replace MNR engines. When Nos. 10 & 11 arrived, they would assist the IOMR to work the newly-acquired MNR system.

Collection J.I.C. Boyd and C.E. Box

Plate 83: A driver's view of things as in 1873 on No. 1 SUTHERLAND. This is a righthand drive locomotive – the reversing quadrant with its notched plate (*right lower*) and above, the double-wheeled control for the righthand injector. Prominent is the regulator handle with blower valve below, and below that, the firehole door; flanking the blower valve are the two water gauges, their cover glasses missing. The only strange fitting for the 1873 driver would be the vacuum brake equipment (*upper right*).

J.I.C. Boyd

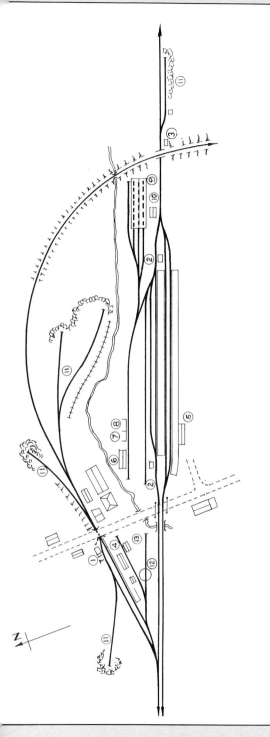

ST. JOHN'S: as closed (signalling omitted) [1968]

1. Water tank, Foxdale Branch (disused)
2. Water tanks
3. Water tank
4. Foxdale Branch station (disused)
5. IOMR station building (adjacent platform added after 1886)
6. Goods Shed (demolished)
7. Goods platform
8. Cattle Dock
9. Carriage Shed
10. Signal Box
11. Sand and gravel pits
12. Turntable
13. Maintenance Yard and Store Sheds

Trials began in January. Anticipating the heavier traffic, chairs were inserted into MNR tracks at Gob-y-Deigan and Orrisdale – the wooden keys were outside the rails.

It was clear as 1885 drew to a close that Kennedy would not meet their contracted finishing date of the year's end.

The MNR's year was no better than that on the IOMR: the latter blamed the weather and a lack of money during a short season, the former the 'Agricultural Depression'. Despite the through carriages now running between Ramsey and Douglas, passenger figures dropped further to 164,834 and the mineral traffic of 24,884 tons was thanks largely to Foxdale traffic between St John's and Ramsey; in the previous year it had been 19,211 tons and trains had run 77,927 miles. Certain improvements continued to take place and at Sulby Glen a corrugated iron goods shed was erected by Waddell Bros. of Sulby Bridge.

So to conclude the year; after lying fallow, the Douglas, Laxey & Ramsey scheme re-appeared when new Articles of Association were drawn up in August. On 17th November, Chadwicks, Boardman & Co. of 64 Cross Street, Manchester, issued a Prospectus but money perhaps after all, was 'scarce' (as Wood put it), and the dream faded for lack of support.

Summary of form of Agreement approved by the Governor 6th January, 1885 as between Manx Northern and Foxdale Railway Companies.*

1. Agreement to extend for 50 years.
2. MNR at own expense to provide locomotive power, rolling stock and plant. To pay all wages, keep accounts etc.
3. Service to be two passenger trains daily in each direction, save on Sundays.
4. MNR to pay FR 'A yearly sum equal to 45% of such (gross) earnings, to be considered as due on 31st December each year'.
5. MNR to fix Tolls, which are to be considered as 3 miles only.
6. Station for joint use at St John's, with cost borne equally by the two Companies.
7. Foxdale Railway to provide a station at Foxdale ('and at least one station between St John's and Foxdale, such stations to include all necessary buildings and conveniences to be approved by the Governor').
8. Within five years of the opening of the FR to traffic, at the option of the MNR, the FR may become amalgamated with the MNR on terms viz.

> The MNR to pay the FR a sum equal to the paid-up Capital with interest thereon @ 5% per annum from opening of FR to traffic but reduced by the amount of dividends etc. etc.

Summary of Agreements between MNR, FR & IOMMCL dated 3rd May, 1884 and 14th September, 1885.†

3rd May, 1884
1. MNR/FR, when FR completed, to carry IOMMCL trucks or wagons, and IOMMCL agree to send such goods as far as they have control of the carriage . . . for 12 years from date of opening.
2. At Ramsey, the Railway Co. is responsible for taking to or from vessels in the Harbour.

*Original in Tower Collection.
†Full original in Tower Collection.

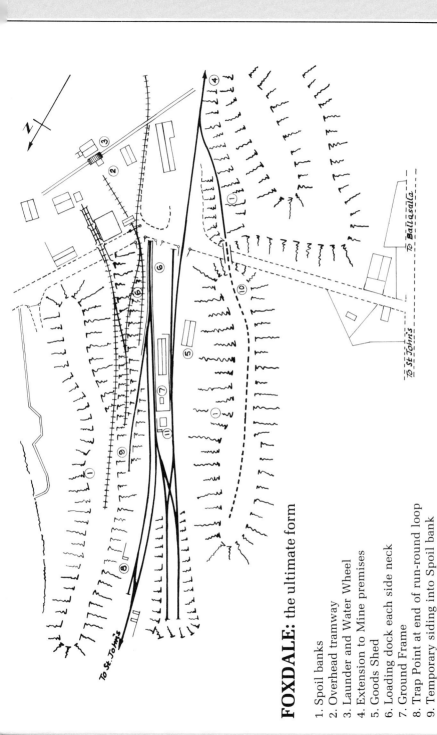

FOXDALE: the ultimate form

1. Spoil banks
2. Overhead tramway
3. Launder and Water Wheel
4. Extension to Mine premises
5. Goods Shed
6. Loading dock each side neck
7. Ground Frame
8. Trap Point at end of run-round loop
9. Temporary siding into Spoil bank
10. Site of abandoned Tip Line on Spoil bank
11. Water Tank

3. At Foxdale, the Railway Co. is responsible for taking to or from the coal and lead stores (or as may be arranged).
4. IOMMCL to load and unload trucks at Foxdale.
5. At Ramsey, Railway Co. not responsible for placing goods on vessels but MNR to provide reasonable accommodation at station for temporary storage (other than coal) which cannot immediately be forwarded to Foxdale.
6. MNR to provide small office for IOMMCL at Ramsey station.
7. At Foxdale, the Railway Companies to provide lead store convenient for being served by a siding, and a coal store to hold at least 1,000 tons.
8. No requirement falls on IOMMCL to use MNR/FR for business linked with Douglas.
9. IOMMCL to pay 2/6d. ton between Foxdale and Ramsey Harbour.
10. Until Foxdale Rly. is open, St. John's to be the railhead; meanwhile MNR to build temporary stores for IOMMCL ores and coal at Ramsey station: the ores to be in bags, not loose. IOMMCL to pay 1/10d. ton between St. John's and Ramsey Harbour.
11. Should MNR become bankrupt (or), or Foxdale Railway not be built within 18 months, IOMMCL may terminate this Agreement.

14th September, 1885 (with reference to the 1884 Agreement)
1. Temporary stores for coal and ores at Ramsey station to continue, but MNR may have use of the lofts.
2. FR released from the obligation of making coal stores at Foxdale, but IOMMCL will build them on FR property, the FR to provide a siding, the IOMMCL to convey the necessary land for same. Spoil for ballast may be taken from spoil banks, excepting those containing mineral substance.

(There were subsequent alterations and extensions of time to this Agreement.)

1886

The disposal of horse manure from the streets was a problem that faced all towns (Douglas was no exception) and the IOMR carried it regularly to St John's for the use of farmers, but now the quantity had become so large that the Douglas Town Commissioners were considering the purchase of their own railway wagons and setting up a depôt at St John's. The IOMR was prepared to co-operate on this idea and would convey the manure @ 4s. 9d. per wagon so long as each wagon held no more than 6 tons; the wagon design would have to be approved by the Company.

The Peel brick-making concern alongside the railway station had a siding put into their premises and a loading bank for bricks set up at St John's.

Down at Ballasalla, Thomas Moore of the Turkeyland Quarry, aware of the Creggan plan for a tramway to the IOMR, decided such would also be helpful for him; his line would have a junction near Ballawoods level crossing where the main line was on a gradient of 1 in 80. Again, the General Purposes Committee turned down the idea but Moore was given leave to run his branch into Ballasalla station, on the same provisos as they were prepared to allow Creggan into Castletown (see 1885).

At the beginning of the year, Sproat's appointment was made permanent and at the same time, London sent over George Armstrong* of Wolverhampton following a meeting between Wood, Rixon, and Armstrong (at his residence) on 19th February, to inspect the locomotives and rolling stock on their behalf. His observations (dated March and April) contained some wider suggestions:

1. That turntables at Douglas, Peel and Port Erin be considered to obviate frequent reversal of engine tyres.†
2. The original 4-wheeled carriages be close-coupled in pairs to improve their rough riding quality, and new axleboxes fitted; one pair to be fitted first. He offered to send Joseph Armstrong‡ to see the result.
3. A wheel lathe to be installed in Douglas workshops (was not there one already, or was it eliminated from Trevithick's recommendations to save money?).
4. All bridges of timber baulks to be replaced by iron girders.

Further problems between the couplings of MNR and IOMR stock were to delay summer traffic interchanges at St John's and the IOMR blamed the MNR 'who had not altered as per Hunt's instructions'. James Cowle, the Douglas architects, were consulted by the IOMR and thereafter were to work on behalf of the Company for many years. Their drawings for Douglas (dated 18th November, 1886) are for a one-block building abutting the platform and not alongside the adjoining Bank Hill. The space between Bank Hill and that building would be used for road carriages and cars to turn and is presently thus. There was later amendment to give more space for sidings at a total cost of £2,500.

A youth was caught changing the points in front of a moving engine at Peel and was prosecuted. The original timber roofs of the buildings at Union Mills and Santon 'were in a bad state' and were replaced with corrugated iron sheeting. When a porter forgot to open the crossing gates at St John's, a train ran through them in the dark. Though they had not built a tramway, the MB&T Co.'s business was booming due to demand in Douglas, and the IOMR brick tonnage rose sharply; the boom was not to last. On the last Sunday in February the Island was hit by violent snowstorms: on the Monday morning trains were embedded at Ballasalla, Santon and Orrisdale on the MNR; at the latter the drift was 9 ft deep, and the engine put up for the night at the crossing house (the paper does not mention the fate of the passengers). A rescue engine from Ramsey also stuck in 11 ft of snow but 'The Heavy Engine CALEDONIA (bought for the Foxdale Railway) did good work with the snowplough'. There was no change for the better on Tuesday so at 6.40 am CALEDONIA set out from Ramsey with 'the small snowplough' but was brought to a stop before Ballaugh in a drift 400 yards long, 3 ft deep on one side and 7 ft on the other, in cutting. Ballaugh was reached at 9 am and the gates lifted off their hinges to allow the engine to pass: here it took water and left for Orrisdale at 10 am where the cutting was filled with snow at an average depth of 8 ft for 700 yards. With pick and shovel the line was cleared, CALEDONIA 'was shackled to her two unfortunate sisters who had

---

*George Armstrong (1822–1901) Northern Divisional Locomotive Superintendent, Great Western Railway, Wolverhampton. (Retired from Stafford Road 1896). Brother of Joseph Armstrong.
†A quotation from Cowans, Sheldon & Co. Ltd. was submitted.
‡This would be 'Young Joe', a son of Joseph Armstrong who had died in 1877.

been out all night and Ramsey was reached at 2 pm'. At 3 pm another move was made to reach the southern cuttings between Bishop's Court and Kirk Michael, where due to continual drifting, there was snow over 6 ft deep for 400 yards. The plough reached that part of the train left at Michael on Monday and returned with some passengers who had been left there on the previous day. It was a difficult journey and Ramsey was not reached until 7 pm.

On Wednesday, matters became worse and running was restricted between Ramsey and Kirk Michael; on Thursday a gang cleared Kirk Michael–St John's but by 1 pm there was a mile of drift between Kirk Michael and Glen Mooar, in places 11 ft deep. At Gob-y-Deigan, there was drifting of 200 yards at an average depth of 7 ft and a further 400 yards at Knockharry Farm; the cuttings at Lhergydoo and St John's were now blocked. The plough engine bucked the snow and threw it over the fences '... two hundred men could not have cleared it in anything like the time' and the engine was used cab-first for the work as it was proved that when running chimney first, it was lifted off the track as the pony truck derailed. (This account is mainly from the newspapers, and was typical of many another severe winter.)

On 10th April Thomas Kelly, a MNR employee, was riding on a wagon whilst shunting, and was 'caught between it and a stack of coals'; he was off work for some time.

We may view IOMR events from the pages of Wood's diary again:

> 11th February: Odd-fellows' Ball, Peel. Train left Peel at 11 pm. It paid us.
> 4th March: 'Messiah' at Douglas. Snow spoiled these trains.
> 11th May: Queen's visit to Liverpool. Last train leaves Douglas for Peel at 11 pm. Very poor trains – only eight passengers from Port Erin and twenty from the rest.
> 11th June: Opening of Rosemount Wesley Chapel. Night trains guaranteed by the Committee.
> 1st July: St George's Band of Hope. Port Soderick and back 4d. return. 183 children: £3 1s. 10d. Paid same day.
> 5th July, Tynwald Day: Poor day but worse for MNR. Only £65 taken.
> 23rd July: Opening of Pier at Ramsey. Special train from Douglas to St John's at 12.10 pm returning at 3 pm. Special train from Douglas at 11 pm returning at 11.50 pm. This was the best day for MNR but bad for us as we did very little on Peel or on Port Erin Line. There should have been a train from Douglas at 11 pm. The 12.10 am ran empty nearly. Coach off road at St Germain's at night.
> 25th July: Bishop in Peel Castle. Church Anniversary. Special train will leave Douglas for Peel at 2 pm. Return from Peel at 5.15 pm.
> 29th July: Ramsey Regatta adjourned – wet day – late train from Ramsey had only two passengers.
> 3rd August: Castletown Regatta: seven engines in steam.
> 2nd and 6th August: Bank Holiday and Ramsey Cattle Show. Six engines in steam.
> 19th August: This was a grand day: receipts whole line £322 net. (£242 last year)
> 31st August: Second Regatta Castletown. Another good day and worked well up to No. 9 train when Kendall's engine failed the crossing at Ballasalla.* Caused 15 minutes delay for rest of day.

---

*Frequent use of 'Kendall's Sunday' or 'Shire's Sunday' to denote timetable and driver on duty, e.g. Christmas Day is always run to the same timetable as 'Shire's Sunday'.

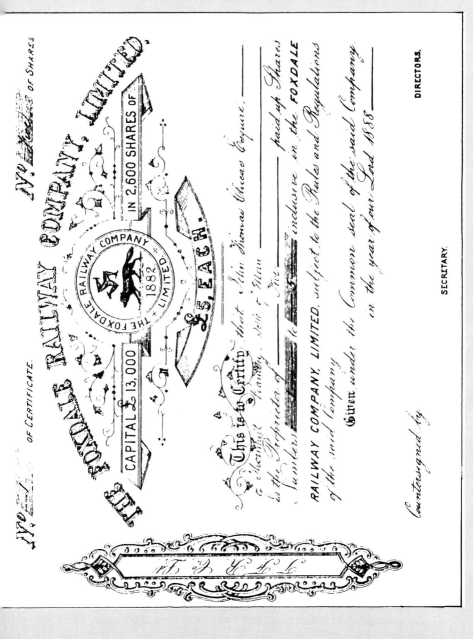

28th September: Opening Masonic Lodge Peel. Poor train from Peel at 11 pm.
9th December: Brass Band Contest at Douglas.

After the detail of the diary, IOMR matters seen through the Annual Report have a somewhat dead ring; they included the acceptance of James Cowle's drawings for the Douglas station building and the seeking of tenders for same. Enquiries about the North Quay Tramway showed that nothing had been done and the town authorities had made no decision; 'They don't seem anxious to create new streets'. This was much in the mould of the Manx character. Trade depression was hitting business again; competition from ships round the Island and road transport, together with extra attractions in Douglas keeping visitors there, not forgetting the Liverpool Exhibition and the failure of the fishing season, had made 1885 poor and this was continuing into 1886. Half of the Railway's mileage was now in steel rails and when complete, would save c.£1,000 per annum. Shareholders were directed to the contents of the Armstrong Report.

Greenbank was called back to inspect the IOMR in early 1886 and reported on 31st March. It was his first inspection since the contractors ceased their period of maintenance in early 1875 and by and large he was delighted with what he found: 'the line has been well looked-after'. Knowing all its weaknesses he discovered they had been tended, watched and righted. His main criticism was that the track still held 68,000 sleepers of the W&S period – about half the total. The greatest problem was the spreading of gauge on curves but a ⅜" thick steel plate set in a notched recess in the sleeper top and between it and the rail, would solve the trouble. Where timber baulk bridge spans survived, they should be replaced by iron girders. There were signs of decay along the ground line of wooden buildings, the Ballastrang crossing lodge had not been fully painted and the wooden booking hall floor at Douglas was wearing thin. He had much praise for management and employees.

It was evident in the first week of January that 'construction of the Foxdale Line was far from satisfactory', according to Forman. Work on the viaduct over Foxdale River, south of St John's, was so badly done that masonry would have to be taken down because a pier (then 22 ft high) was unsound and the contractor had refused to start again. Materials to build the embankment over the IOMR at St John's would be taken from ground belonging to Dumbell's Banking Co. where the FR was given right to remove all gravel and sub-soil from the top of the sand 'in the fields between the two lines'.

Although 1,175 FR shares had been taken up, many 'holders' had not yet paid their calls – this problem would become worse. Kennedy, the contractor, became more stubborn and began to build on the condemned viaduct work. Signs of financial stress became apparent when Formans & McCall and Kennedy both agreed to take part-payment in shares and, in order to compromise, directors, contractor and Forman met at St John's on 8th February. In consequence, payment to Kennedy would now be made into the National Bank of Scotland to the credit of a joint account held in the names of J.T. Clucas and Hugh Kennedy & Son 'until the line is ready for goods traffic'. The amount was £1,048.

It is not revealed where FR Board Meetings were taking place but the first AGM was held at the Post Office, Ramsey in March – certainly 'neutral ground'. Waddell Bros. of Sulby Bridge were altering the stables of the Junction Hotel, St John's to allow the Foxdale Line to pass over the site; a new boundary fence and the removal of a sandbank were involved. The order for chairs had gone to A.S. Nelson & Co. who threatened legal proceedings if their rails, released by Formans & McCall, were not paid for; they would press not only for payment but interest too. They would overlook the matter if they were given the order for chairs, fishplates etc., and paid for the rails immediately. The blackmail must have worked as the chairs were shipped by the WIZARD, whose owners now joined the long list of creditors. Forman put it about that the line would be ready by May. Turquands, Youngs & Co. were to be appointed auditors.

In May, it was reported that the river bridge was still not built to specification or contract and, to secure it from fracture, a wall and wing walls must be built around an abutment up to 12 ft from the girders ... or the whole thing taken down – so much for May completion! In June, the tender of Stevens & Sons for signal ironwork was accepted and Glen was to provide the woodwork for them. By July, so great was the delay that Forman was told to take steps to remove the contract from Kennedy (as provided in the Agreement) and complete it by direct labour. At this stage, it appeared that Glen's contribution to Waterfall* and Foxdale stations was limited to the buildings only; 'roads, platforms and sidings were to be let to an independent contractor, William Murray, for £50'.

It was easier said than done to be rid of Kennedy (or did the Scotsmen close ranks in the face of the Manx?) Certainly Kennedy was not ousted, for in March, and again in August, he applied to the MNR for their locomotive to be returned for his use to expedite the work. This was agreed, and the hire charge was £392 17s. 2d. for the engine (MNR No. 2): the driver's, fireman's and cleaner's wages were an extra charge. Certainly the vertical boilered engine from Peel Harbour must have had limited power at this site; it is known that it visited Ramsey from time to time for routine maintenance and repair, and would 'coal up' from MNR stocks. It may have been used as a form of 'taxi' for Cameron's inspections. Wagons were also loaned for Kennedy's use.

Forman's now made charge for all the extra work and visits they had had to make. The Postmaster General interrupted things and offered to construct and maintain a line of telegraph on the same terms as he did for the MNR; he was told to mind his own business; the MNR terms were excessive. Glen had not been paid and was given one of a series of Bills at three months to keep him sweet.

Irregular mineral trains had run unhappily amongst the unfinished work from June. Ultimately the line was complete allowing regular non-passenger trains to run from 14th August. A special working to convey shareholders to Foxdale (where the opening was marked by Mrs Clucas who was handed the Train Staff on arrival), ran on 16th August and the official service began the next day but a published timetable showed a daily service of five passenger

---

*'Lower Foxdale', 'Hamilton Waterfall' were names considered but discarded: both titles 'Waterfall' or 'Waterfalls' persisted thereafter.

THE ISLE OF MAN RAILWAY

Foxdale Railway
COMPANY, LIMITED.

OPENING OF A NEW
RAILWAY.

This Line has been passed by the Government Inspector and will be OPENED for

Goods and Passenger Traffic
ON AND AFTER
SATURDAY, 14TH AUGUST.

·Visitors should not lose the opportunity of visiting the Mines at Foxdale, which are the most extensive and largest producing Mines in the United Kingdom. This Line passes through a beautiful Glen, and a grand view can be had from it. Mount South Barrule, the second highest Mountain in the Island, is within easy reach of the Terminus of this Railway, where a splendid VIEW of the SURROUNDING COUNTRIES—England, Ireland, and Scotland, can easily be had on a clear day.

Trains will run as Under :—

Fares from St John's	STATIONS.	WEEK DAYS.
Single Return 1st 3rd 1st 3rd d d d d 4 2 5 4 6 3 9 6	St John's dep. Waterfall ,, Foxdale arr.	a.m. a.m. a.m. p.m. p.m 8 54 10 10 11 20 2 50 6 40 9 2 10 18 11 28 2 58 6 48 9 8 10 24 11 34 3 4 6 54

Fares from Foxdale.	STATIONS.	WEEK DAYS.
Single Return 1st 3rd 1st 3rd d d d d 2 1 4 2 6 3 9 6	Foxdale dep. Waterfall ,, St John's arr.	a.m. a.m. a.m. p.m. p.m 9 49 10 50 11 50 3 52 7 46 9 52 10 54 11 54 3 58 7 52 10 0 11 2 12 2 4 6 8 0

Through Bookings of Goods and Passenger Traffic between Stations on this Line to all Stations on the Manx Northern Railway. For Rates, &c., apply to the undersigned, or to the respective Station Masters.
(By order)
J. CAMERON, Secretary and Manager.
Ramsey, August 12th, 1886. [434n

A Misleading Announcement!

trains daily from 14th August! The inaugural train was hauled by CALEDONIA in charge of John Kneale, driver, and William Kelly, fireman. The SUN (14th August) gives a flavour of the previous few days:

> The line was inspected by Col Rich on Wednesday . . . formal opening . . . train leaving St John's at 2.41 and returning from Foxdale at 5.48 pm. Shareholders and wives are entitled to free conveyance and Mr Kitto (General Manager of the Mining Co.) and Mrs Kitto issued invitations to lunch on the occasion . . . shareholders living in Ramsey will have free conveyance by the Northern Railway but we have not yet heard that a similar privilege is to be accorded on the Douglas line.

Rich was paid £72 10s. 3d. for his services and Hugh Kennedy & Son allotted 498 shares.

Arrangements were altered and the SUN's forecast of one train became two trains. The first special left St John's during the morning, another one following it to cope with the overflow. At Foxdale, the specials were met by a deputation of officials including officers of both Foxdale and Manx Northern concerns. Captain Kitto, principal of the IOMMCL*, thereupon handed the Single Line Staff to Mrs Clucas, wife of J.T. Clucas (the local member of the House of Keys) and asked her to declare the line open.

The Foxdale Brass Band led a procession to Brookfield (the residence of Louisa Ann Bawden) where lunch was served to 150 guests on the lawn; unfortunately, the meal was unfinished when heavy rain began to fall and the speeches – which were cut short because of the weather – were made under umbrellas with suitable references to the climate. [There was considerable embarrassment between the Railway Companies and the Mining Co. over the catering arrangements for which thorough preparation had not been made.] Eventually, the rain became so drenching that everyone crowded into the house, and the Toast List was completed. One speaker said that they hoped shortly to proceed with a southward extension from Foxdale to join the Port Erin Line of the IOMR. (This branch may still be seen as 'projected' on maps published before World War I.) The extension would cost £20,000 to £25,000 and all Islanders were called upon to support the project. It was pointed out that even if the lead deposits failed there were other minerals which could be exploited. Possibly traffic would develop to the extent where it would be necessary to convert the branch to double line.

Captain Kitto's speech referred to his hope that one day all the lines in the Island would be operated by one company. How ironic that almost twenty years later it would be the failure of the Mining Co. which in turn would bring the Manx Northern to its knees and the fulfilment of the Captain's wish in quite an unlooked-for way.

[The rosy mood of optimism on the opening day was typical of the spirit which had pervaded the Foxdale and Manx Northern promoters. True, the past record of the mines was an excellent one. It is understandable that those nearest to the undertaking were quite sanguine in their prophesies. No one was to know that the mines would fail not because the lead gave out but because through economic and political causes it would become un-

---

*Registered as a Public Company 1856. Into Voluntary Liquidation 24th April, 1911. Final Meeting 4th June, 1917.

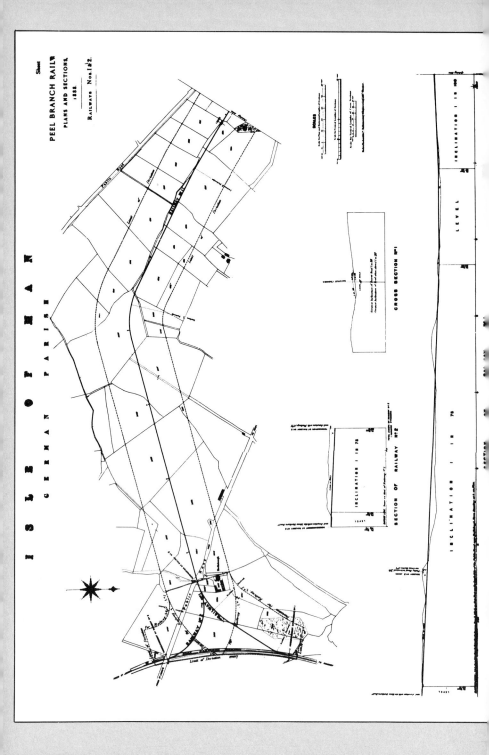

Sheet No 2.

PEEL BRANCH RAILWAY.

PLANS AND SECTIONS,
1888.

RAILWAY No. 1.

SCALES

Scale for Plan and Horizontal Lengths of Sections

Scale for Vertical Lengths of Sections

Scale for Vertical Lengths of Cross Sections

Maclure Macdonald & Co. Parliamentary & Engineering Lith. Glasgow.

ISLE OF MAN

GERMAN PARISH

RAILWAY No. 1

Ballawattleworth

Peel Cathedral

SECTION OF RAILWAY No. 1

INCLINATION 1 IN 100   LEVEL

TOTAL LENGTH OF RAILWAY No 1
1 MILE 2 FURLONGS 7·33 CHAINS

remunerative to mine *any* minerals at Foxdale, or for that matter anywhere else in the Island.]*

In September, Kennedy threatened to take matters to court if the cash held in the Joint Account with Clucas was further withheld; after all he had completed the railway; it was agreed to release it.

Out on the Foxdale system, removal of mine spoil began almost at once, the opportunity of cutting down the size of the tips and reducing the area occupied by them, now became an important aspect of the branch traffic. It seems there was usually a customer for the spoil, and removal took place until 1911 when working there ceased. (It resumed 1936–43 for other reasons.)

Within a month of opening Foxdale residents were complaining about the train service; it was angled towards Ramsey rather than Douglas and *they* wished to go to Douglas. Independently-minded Foxdalites preferred the Douglas shops and showed it with their feet, walking to St John's as in the past 'rather than be subject to the tyranny in Ramsey's favour'. If they were obliged to use the train, it was necessary to leave Douglas as early as 4 pm to make the connection at St John's. Timetables were now headed MANX NORTHERN & FOXDALE RAILWAY COMPANIES LIMITED.

A Special General Meeting of the FR was held on 27th November to enable the Company to raise money by mortgaging the railway up to a sum of £6,500. [The ultimate cost of finishing the railway would be over £30,000 or £12,500 more than estimated.] Much land taken for the railway had not been paid-for as yet; T.C.S. Moore was given £251 11s. 6d. for the five acres of land 'lying between the IOMR and FR to save his further exorbitant demands' (the precise area is not clear).

Leaving FR matters for a while, another inopportune and improvident scheme had surfaced shortly after its opening. The SUN had heard rumour of it in April and suggested Peel businessmen were about to build a railway from Peel to connect with the MNR at Peel Road (ex Poortown). The idea had been mooted by LaMothe of the MNR at that Company's 1886 AGM in March and (with ear to the ground) on 22nd May the paper said 'almost immediate steps will be taken to construct a line from Poor Town into Peel ... on completion of the Foxdale Railway ... greatly needed'.

The promoters met in Ramsey on 30th August, deciding to take up shares themselves, and with Robert Scott of Bowdon, Cheshire as Chairman, a Company was formed and registered on 2nd October under the Companies Act 'deciding to go on with constructing the line at the earliest date'. Other directors were H.T. Graves, John Corrin, J.R. Cowell, J. Cottier, J.C. LaMothe, the first two being of Peel and the other three were now well-known characters in the MNR business. Formans & McCall had already completed a survey and the Peel terminus was to be close to the new church; an opening date for early the forthcoming summer was envisaged. Capital was £5,000

---

*ISLE OF MAN MINING CO. LTD. – Stock Exchange Year Book 1886 *page 329*.
Directors: J. Beckwith (Chairman), H. Churton, T.H. Dixon, C. Townshend, F. North, A. Potts, Sec. R.L. Barker.
Offices: St. Werburgh Chambers, Chester.

£10,000 in Ordinary Shares, £7,000 in 7½ per cent Preference Shares, £10,000 in 6 per cent Bonds. Results 1884–5 sufficient to pay 2 years Preference dividends and 5 per cent Ordinary capital.

in £5 shares and title, Peel Railway Co. Ltd. 'to connect between Peel and the Peel Road station (formerly called Poortown) on the Manx Northern Railway and elsewhere in the Isle of Man'. Ambition is clearly hinted. (The affair will continue to lie almost dormant until 1890; dissolution took place in 1923 – not a yard of rail was laid.)

Railway euphoria did not end with the Peel promotion; the lure of extending the Foxdale Line southwards down to join the Port Erin Line of the IOMR was irresistible '... the directors are determined not to stop at Foxdale and Formans & McCall are making a survey to Kirk Santon ... a well-maintained service between north and south is greatly needed'. 'Transmission of lime now goes via Douglas and is so costly as to take away the marginal profit ... cartmen, once employed in carrying coals at present out of work ... can cart from the kilns to Foxdale'. (The second quotation accepts the usefulness of the railhead at Foxdale without a linking railway.) The north/south link was attractive because it passed largely through the property of J.T. Clucas whom it was known was sympathetic to the scheme.

A current editorial congratulated the people of Peel 'wider awake than ever' not only for their dream of a railway but the hope of a steamship connection with Belfast – they had approached Sir Edward Harland there to lay information before the Belfast Shipping Co. The Island's Railway Bubble was now at its largest, but the burst was not as yet.

At St John's a new through-running line of the MNR parallel to the IOMR's line to Peel, was laid during the year, enabling one level crossing instead of two at St John's to be used. The former track (1881) was lifted either side of the crossing, leaving a siding on each flank. The costs of moving and increased facilities at the IOMR station (an island platform and footbridge, not at first envisaged but provided later) were shared, the IOMR paying £300 and the MNR £1,300. Platform roofs were considered but never erected.

The Annual Report for the MNR gave 171,080 passenger journeys but a fall in through bookings. Foxdale traffic was 22,281 tons and train mileage 92,686. It was necessary to renew a large number of rotten sleepers (only seven years old). £158 7s. 1d. was due to the FR out of the profits of carrying its traffic, being the contribution required to pay 5 per cent on its share capital; as the MNR had only earned £150 10s. 9d. for that business, the loss was immediate and would continue to be a growing millstone around the MNR's neck. It had been necessary to extend the Ramsey engine shed to contain the fourth engine (CALEDONIA) and to pay for the chairs to strengthen the track in places.

There was now more profitability on the MNR mail contract than previously, due largely to determined action on the part of Manager Cameron and a good example of a David and Goliath situation. The north of the Island was agog on 22nd July, when the new Queen's Pier at Ramsey was opened. The Bishop (Lord Bishop Hill) performed the act in the absence of the Governor; he had travelled in his own 'Through Coach', namely A12, the 'Governor's Saloon'.

Scottish relations were further emphasised when Nelson was instructed to order a suitable carriage for Foxdale purposes. The Oldbury Railway

Carriage & Wagon Co. Ltd. executed the order* for a guard's composite bogie carriage. It carried MNR No. 17.

During August, the MNR was involved in providing a 2 ft gauge tramway from the Highway Board's quarry at Poortown; it was laid alongside the road and then dropped steeply onto a high-level loading bank at Peel Road station, being about 300 yards long. The content of tramway wagons (mainly granite for road surfacing) was tipped from above into open wagons on a siding below. Half a dozen skip wagons were supplied through A.S. Nelson & Co. Ltd., the business being handled by the MNR. Horsepower was used on the tramway throughout its life.†

1887

The Armstrong-suggested trial of the IOMR close-coupled short carriages was promising and in February Wood recommended that five more pairs be so treated; the results were good enough for a decision in November to convert the remaining thirty-eight to close-coupling @ £34 a pair. The Oldbury Railway Carriage & Wagon Co. Ltd. would supply five sets of ironwork @ £16 10s. 0d. a set and then twenty-five pairs in all would be done for a cost of £830 12s. 3d. and this would be charged to the current year's working expenses. The growing number of carriages created a further fire risk and it was agreed that a second Carriage Shed would be prudent.

Lace's Brickworks, Ballaleece,* requested a siding into their premises.

News reached Douglas that the Station Master at Crosby was now the Sub-Postmaster as well. He was permitted to accept this rôle, so long as it did not interfere with his railway duties.

St John's was the scene of a mishap on 19th April. A combined Peel and Ramsey train (ex-Douglas) came to a stand before entering the station as usual, and the Ramsey coaches were detached and left in charge of the guard; the Peel portion in front, drew into the station, leaving the Ramsey coaches, engineless, on the running line. The MNR engine (due to back onto the Ramsey portion) called the signalman for the road and began moving towards its train: thus far was the customary movement. But the guard of the Ramsey carriages had released his handbrake and the signal box was manned by an inexperienced porter: by now the train was moving smartly downgrade towards the oncoming engine . . . there was considerable impact and all the 'thirty-four people in the Ramsey train were severely shaken'. The matter was duly reported to the Governor, according to law.

Irritation caused by the accident and additional train movements gave birth to a letter from the Chairman (John Pender), wherein the IOMR pointed out to the MNR the time lost to IOMR trains 'shunting your trains into your separate station at St John's'.

---

*Oldbury Railway Carriage & Wagon Ltd., Birmingham. A reconstruction of The Railway Carriage Co. of Birmingham.
†A note concerning the pointwork for what became the IOMR siding here, will be found regarding the Knockaloe Branch (*Volume II*).
*Apparently a branch of their Peel premises.

The MNR investigated the St John's collision and refused to accept responsibility for it. Irritated by this, the IOMR Board was ready to suspend the facility of booking passengers off its system onto the MNR.

Manx Line Steamers, incorporated earlier in the year, was to run a service both between Douglas and Ramsey and in opposition to the IOMSP Co.: it asked for an express train from Douglas to Ramsey etc. and the free conveyance of luggage from boat to station. The IOMR would consider such a train but could not carry luggage free; they emphasised that when they had power to lay a Quay Tramway, this problem would cease. The MNR also wished to support the MLS and co-operation was agreed; passengers proving they had left the Irish Sea boat were allowed Douglas–Ramsey–Douglas tickets at single fare. Sailings commenced in June for the high season only.

In June consideration was given to a supply of water for locomotives at Port St Mary instead of as currently, at Port Erin. This was because of supply problems and local complaints. IOMR employees had asked for time off to celebrate Queen Victoria's Golden Jubilee, but it was not granted. The IOMR was on the 'receiving end' of a stream of complaints over the absence of any proper arrangement for carrying luggage between steamers and station so in September they contracted with a carter specifically for this duty. Further consideration for passengers was shown when an order was given to apply mouldings to all 3rd class carriages for £45 in all; next, the thirty-eight short carriages (twelve had been close-coupled) were on the agenda yet again; was this balance worthy of the £199 10s. 0d. which Oldbury would charge for 19 sets of materials? It was, and the work was done during the ensuing winter.

By now 27 miles of the railway had been relaid with steel rails, exceptions being in station limits, and 600 tons of new rails needed to be bought to complete this transformation, but such a quantity in one purchase would have been financially unwise: orders were spread from now onwards. At Douglas an entrance was to be made from Athol Street, and more land had to be bought for the new additions of the yard; the Carriage Shed, goods shed and Workshops, on the brink of being enlarged/rebuilt for so long, and agreement for this to be done confirmed once more in September, the following year the whole matter (as yet not started) was deferred once more and would not begin before autumn 1888! Down at Port St Mary William Costain occupied the crossing cottage there and decided there was business to be done if he built a small refreshment room on a plot of land across the tracks from his residence. It was accordingly rented to him for 14 years on condition he built such a place, maintained it and delivered it up on expiry of lease.

By the year end, Enos Lace's main brickworks at Peel was extremely busy; 300,000 building bricks were sent to Port St. Mary @ 2s. 4d. ton carriage and a similar tonnage to Castletown @ 2s. 7d. (reduced to 2s. 0d. if Lace sent more than 4,000 tons per annum). Ashbury was given an order for 12 new 'box wagons' @ £43 5s. 0d. each, specifically to carry bricks and stone. Such quantities reflected the amount of local building expansion; it was cheaper to buy local bricks than ship them into either port from Connah's Quay – (up to the 1930s Port St Mary was receiving bricks etc.

from North Wales by schooner). Building of the Port St Mary refreshment room was not so spectacular; Costain, only seven weeks from receiving the go-ahead, had re-assessed his finances and the Company had agreed he could build 'only part of the refreshment room' – the result must be left to imagination! In general, leases of refreshment rooms must have been a hazardous undertaking for the lessees who came and went with rapidity.

The Isle of Man Railway Act became law this year and it authorised the Company to omit the word 'Limited' from its title, and increase its borrowing powers and issue Perpetual Debenture Stock in place of the terminable Debenture Bonds already existing.

The main new building at Douglas (offices above, refreshment room below)* was in an advanced state of construction. As to rolling stock, by the year end fifty four-wheeled carriages had been close-coupled and the first replacement of a locomotive boiler and firebox had been ordered from Beyer, Peacock @ £403 13s. 3d.

Though the current bright spot on the IOMR was the brisk building materials' traffic on the Peel Line, two grey clouds were all too near. One was the threat of another new rating system which would hit the Company hard and the other was a daily steamboat between Douglas–Ramsey and Liverpool–Ramsey which was taking the edge off the tourist traffic.

Again, a peep into Wood's diary gives a more intimate picture of IOMR activities:

> Easter Monday: Steamer round the Island cut railway business: MNR connections at St John's were 40 minutes late.
> 21st June: Jubilee demonstration at Castletown.
> 27th July: Ramsey Regatta did not do much for the MNR.
> 30th July: Volunteers in camp at Union Mills.
> 4th August: Douglas Agricultural Show. Banking engines used on late day trains both to Port Soderick and Union Mills. Late trains very good.
> 2nd October: End of summer season . . . a remarkably good one. We have had heavy trains . . .
> 23rd December: 'At Home' at Bishop's Court. Only 36 passengers.
> 25th December: Operated as 'Kendall's Sunday'.
> St Stephen's Day: A very good day.†

Of the Foxdale Railway's extension southwards, very little is heard during the year; one newspaper reported a firm of Bristol engineers surveying from Foxdale to Ballasalla, whilst another report said that the 'Ballasalla Extention' (sic) was in abeyance. In March the Manx newspapers began to reveal rumours concerning the Island railways and on the 26th, the SUN had simply, 'the Chairman (of the MNR) said there had been negotiations with a view to amalgamating with the Southern Railway Company'. Added was, '. . . Progress of the Peel Line has been arrested owing to the Peel projectors asking for a large guarantee to which the MNR would not agree'. At the MNR, AGM the Chairman admitted things were not as bright as they might have been, blamed the 'agricultural depression' and the late opening of the Foxdale Line after the season had ended. Due to wet weather, a large number

---

*Manx Museum: R/147/8. Plans of Douglas Offices. 1/1887.
†Note that a train service was operated on both Christmas and Boxing Days: this was normal on almost all railways in those times.

of MNR untreated sleepers had had to be renewed. Many shareholders were dissatisfied and the Chairman remarked he found his position far from 'a bed of roses'.

And what justification was there for talk of amalgamation (or 'Forman's Scheme')? On 25th February, Greenbank asked Wood 'what the local directors felt about it?' He added, '(or rather what the Major thinks – the others do not count)'.† 'The more I think of it the more barefaced swindle does it appear . . . the assurance which would place the ordinary shares of the Foxdale in priority to those of your Company is astounding . . . project is not conceived in any spirit of common fairness'. A letter from him the next day to Rixon said 'it is proposed to *take* from the IOMR and *give* to the other two Cos. . . . amount appears to be £1,906 per annum . . .' And again, to Wood on 3rd March: 'I was far too liberal in estimating Foxdale profit @ £400 per annum; half that sum would have been quite enough'. Forman envisaged a single railway company with a capital of £561,425.

Writing on 21st March, Greenbank told Wood it 'was no wonder the health of the MNR Chairman is not in a satisfactory state' as he had read in the TIMES that morning that the published accounts of MNR and FR showed the MNR had worked the FR for nothing yet paid £7 16s. 4d. for the privilege of doing it. He pointed out there were nothing in the MNR accounts about the 'bogie carriage' they had bought, nor did it appear on the stock returns (it was actually a FR-used vehicle: Author). He thought the auditors' reports for each company were highly suggestive of all sorts of things. Rixon wrote the same day '. . . the Northern accounts are deplorable . . . what right have they to exceed their borrowing powers?'

Behind the scenes, Charles Forman was now in secretive and direct touch with Wood, Rixon and the IOMR Chairman, Sir John Pender. Supplied with figures by the IOMR, he now had material from the three operative railways, albeit the MNR/FR figures would reveal their arrangements for but a short period. On 10th March, he discussed how strongly he felt that a saving to these Companies would follow 'an amalgamated management' and that he held a mandate from MNR and FR directors to negotiate on their behalf.* Some members of the IOMR faction took legal opinion; this was that 'the scheme is on the principle of all take and no give'. By July the heat had gone from the idea; Rixon summed it up, 'the amalgamation of two concerns should lead to economy is a commonsense view which recommends itself to any business mind, but in our case we should have been landed with an incubus we should never have been able to shake off'.

In between-times Rixon had been considering the cost of IOMR stations and he was worried that the enlargements at Douglas meant they had now spent more than had the MNR at Ramsey. He was cynical about the value of the other stations on the MNR '. . . what are they?' He continued '. . . there is one station I should like to know about very much and that is the new one including the land at St John's . . . has the land and the cost been paid for by either railway company?' (i.e. MNR and Foxdale). Rixon was the typical lawyer, reminding his client of issues which might not seem relevant.

---

†Major J.S. Taubman.

*Other accounts state his negotiations were not known to the 'Island-based directors' (of the IOMR) – this would be nothing new! See also Greenbank–Rixon correspondence (Feb. 1887) in Tower Collection.

Moving to the Foxdale Railway; the AGM called for on the 3rd March was adjourned to the month end — the usual trouble was the indifference of shareholders and the failure to find a quorum. On 22nd March the Board was told the Isle of Man Banking Co. would not allow any further withdrawals on the already-overdrawn account . . . no wonder Forman was covertly recommending amalgamation. A special Board Meeting at 8 am took place on 12th April to consider a claim by the contractor which would be heard in Glasgow; a deputation was needed to go there to meet the Arbitrator. When it returned, (the matter in question being the Foxdale River viaduct) they reported that no progress could be made as there were discrepancies over the measurements of the faulty masonry. By now the FR was so far behind with its payments that creditors were threatening legal proceedings by every post.

In May the IOMMCL was urged to take up shares to assist the FR's parlous finances — another special Board Meeting was called as Scott was expected to be in Ramsey at that time . . . it was but rumour and underlined the pathetic position.

On 9th June, a FR Extra-ordinary General Meeting had to be called (Cowell was made Chairman). Enlargement and modification of the existing powers was sought under the FR Act 1884, especially regarding the issue of Debenture Stock. Attempts were made to hold Board Meetings on 4th and 21st July. On 18th August (with Farrant in the Chair) Kitto proposed Scott as Chairman. Farrant became Vice Chairman and Kennedy the contractor was put on the Board in place of Clucas and Cottier who had resigned. Formans & McCall were instructed to inspect the line now that Kennedy's year of maintenance was over. On 1st September the Board Meeting failed to take place (no quorum). They met on 14th November; Cameron of the MNR was made Secretary and notices were to be sent to shareholders to pay their calls within seven days or face legal proceedings. It had little effect as many involved had accepted shares in lieu of cash for land sold for the line.

Now back to Glen Helen: Plans & Section for a Glen Helen Railway* are undated but marked as 'MNR proposal': no Engineer's name is given. In this instance the line would have left the IOMR/MNR by a facing junction on the Douglas side of St John's, run round the back of St John's station (north side) and travelled along the east bank of the Neb above Ballig. A 30 ft span ('as at Quarter Bridge on the Peel Railway') and another of 40 ft span would be needed between St John's and Ballig to cross the river twice. A ruling gradient for most of the distance was 1 in 77 and the high road in St John's village would have been crossed on the level. Stations were to be at Ballig and Glen Helen and the length would have been 2 m 3 fur 7 ch.

The MNR, AGM (10th March) was reminded that all trains ran mixed; passenger journeys had dropped again and were now 167,254. This time the IOMR was not blamed — it was steamer competition. There was a slight decrease in mineral tonnage but the Board was still pressing for running powers through to Douglas. Trains had run 98,852 miles. Optimism was shown for the potential attraction of the district of Foxdale and tourist traffic from that source should increase. The following week the HERALD

---

*Manx Museum: R/110, R/111, R/112.

reminded its readers that the Foxdale Railway was now open to traffic '. . . many lovely spots can now be more easily reached' – (and it might be truthful to have added, some particularly dreary mining sites as well).

Money difficulties dogged the MNR throughout the year and financial links with the original Government support found no friend in the Governor Spencer Walpole, (who had replaced Loch in 1882):* he had made difficulties when Clucas, faced with the deterioration in income, applied for Government aid; Walpole rejected the MNR accounts and disapproved its Agreement with the FR and, under his influence, the Government guarantee on the 'B' Preference share was held back. The MNR then took proceedings against the Government. In the midst of all this, Greenbank's comment on J.T. Clucas' health had been apt, for Clucas died on 14th June. He was the father of the MNR and its constant champion. In the event, the MNR was obliged to make alterations to its 1886 Balance Sheet – there was much more detail to the affair than space allows herein.

With Rich's backing, the MNR now suspended winter Sunday trains as they were profitless; the Company could no longer play the Fairy Godmother rôle. When the decision reached Government ears the Company was told it was mandatory to provide them and Rich, as the Government Director, found himself between the two factions, finally having to advise the MNR to re-commence Sunday trains on 18th September. The affair was another shining example of the difference between the IOMR and the MNR, the latter tied to the Government's Apron Strings.

The IOMR met the Post Office objections to the number of letters consigned by train, by tying them up in bundles with string, and sending them as Parcel Post!

1888

The Island's holiday traffic was growing and each of the three railways should have been sharing in the business. It was obvious by now that the IOMR covered the routes most likely to show profit, and the MNR had not produced the potential which was expected of it; moreover, it was prey to east coast shipping competition. The Foxdale was as yet an unknown quantity but from correspondence exchanged between members of the IOMR administration, to be tied to a doubtful company like the MNR would sooner or later bring the downfall of both.

Letters to the press continued to criticise the tardy running of the IOMR trains – perhaps it was the improved smoothness of the running of the four-wheeled stock in pairs, or the better ride of the bogie vehicles? Speeds could be much improved, was the common cry. 'As regards smartness . . . it might be stated that Major Spittall's trap beat the train to Peel by 15 minutes'. In Easter Week complaints about overloading were penned and when 3rd class passengers sought places in 1st class compartments, those IOMR travellers

---

*Spencer Walpole (1839–1907) son of Horatio Spencer, one time Home Secretary and Chairman of the Great Western Railway 1862–66. Spencer Walpole, ex War Office and Home Office; to IOMR 1882–93. Knighted 1898.

who found them in MNR stock attached to the train 'were sought out by the IOMR staff to seek out the excess ... in the enemy's carriages'.

Thieves found railway stations a useful source of income and they were not apprehended after burgling Crosby (twice), Union Mills, Sulby Bridge, Lezayre and St John's.

At the March IOMR, AGM, it was suggested a line to Laxey be proceeded with, but the Chairman did not think it would be a success '... the comparative failure of the Foxdale Line had cast a damper on the scheme'. This arose due to a partial re-hash of the earlier dream for a railway from Douglas to Laxey, using the IOMR Douglas station, which re-appeared as the Douglas, Laxey & Snaefell Railway Co., with again the possibility of sharing Douglas station and being worked by the IOMR. Work on the enlargement of station buildings was already proceeding and the appearance of another railway brought building construction to a temporary halt. A complete transformation of the 1880/1 layout was already in hand, for whatever the outcome of an incomer, it was essential for IOMR development.

It is not entirely clear as to what stage work had reached when it ceased but two iron Carriage Sheds @ £525 each were ordered and, when the new trackwork was finished later in the year, Thomas Silcock (P.W. Inspector) and John Clague (his assistant), received cash bonuses for an exceptional effort.

To increase the area for further extensions at Douglas in the future, excavation was carried out on the north edge of the station. Further land was bought from Taubman for £1,087 for the intended additions were only deferred — everything depended on the accommodation needed for the DL&SR ... if ever! Meanwhile, a large crane was urgently needed for Douglas goods yard wherewith to lift large blocks of stone from wagons: to meet the need, a 2 ton crane was borrowed from the Workshops (see 1889).

Again with further business in mind, an order for another boiler and firebox went to Beyer, Peacock.

Mr Greensill, whose advertisement had appeared on the reverse of IOMR tickets, died during the year and no further similar advertising was done. Income from this source had been £52 per annum.*

A subsidy, to obviate threats from Douglas–Ramsey–Douglas steamer competition and shared by IOMR and MNR, was paid to Isle of Man Tramways Ltd. for running a horse bus between Douglas promenade, pier and railway station for twelve weeks during the summer season. A fare of 1d. in each direction was charged but traffic was disappointing. There was also a subsidised service between Upper Douglas and the station by the Isle of Man Omnibus & Cab Co.; this was a purely IOMR arrangement. The MNR now wanted to employ their own carters between pier and Douglas station on behalf of passengers to and from their Ramsey through carriages, and to charge nothing for the service. The IOMR employed two porters with handcarts for this purpose, and would not countenance any MNR representation. A small charge was made.

The IOMR Minute Book reveals many examples of the conservatism of the Company: being satisfied with their product, The Rhymney Iron Co. of South Wales supplied steam coal for locomotives at this period, and did so for almost half a century.

*Thomas G. Greensill, 78 Strand Street, and Marina Road, Douglas. (Dispensing & Family Chemist).

For a second season, railway business was hit by steamers operating under what the Islanders called 'Manx Line Steamers' but what was actually the 'Isle of Man, Liverpool & Manchester Steamship Co.' (registered in Liverpool) who operated two ships built by Fairfield Shipbuilding Co. of Glasgow. They sailed between Liverpool and Douglas, and between Liverpool and Ramsey. The MNR also wanted the IOMR to reduce fares to combat the small ship MANX FAIRY operating a daily coast service between Douglas and Ramsey with fares 1s. 6d. Single and 2s. 0d. Return. Both railway companies believed the ship was being illegally overloaded and it had been shown that in bad weather those who arrived by it and wished they hadn't, would return to Douglas by train, alternatively, if the weather was good, those who came to Ramsey by train might decide to return by sea. Last minute problems arose when after a fine morning, when Ramsey was full of visitors who had come by sea, an unexpected change in the weather took place and prudent seafarers crammed the last train to Douglas to the chagrin of those who had booked Douglas–Ramsey–Douglas railway tickets. The IOMR did not believe in reducing fares, rather they hoped the steamship competition would be shortlived. It was. Registered in 1886, the concern was in voluntary liquidation by November 1888 and the ships were bought by the IOMSP Co. on 23rd November for £155,000.* Unfortunately for the railways, the IOMSP Co. then took up the Liverpool–Ramsey service.

The Governor returned to railway affairs in August; he had studied the working arrangement between MNR and FR (January 1885) and recent discussions regarding an amalgamation had reached Government Office. The Governor liked the idea of one company and one management to be achieved either by simple amalgamation or by one company working the two others for a proportion of the gross receipts, or one of the following:– 1) a fixed annual sum, 2) a percentage of net profits of the whole combined system, 3) a fixed sum per train mile, 4) as one company, being paid the actual cost of working by the other two concerns. He put it to the IOMR as the senior body and the ideas were vetted by the General Purposes Committee and reported to London. London thought that the Foxdale Line had not operated for a sufficiently long period for it to be assessed; further, no dividend had yet been paid on the Ordinary Shares of the MNR and taken together, it would be difficult to arrive at an amalgamation valuation. Meanwhile, the General Purposes Committee approved of the idea for the IOMR to work the other railways. To follow this matter, we move to December when we find Wood writing to the Governor; 'the subject is a lean one getting leaner . . . and the offer would endanger our shareholders . . . £55,000 would be needed to pay MNR/FR debts, but as a basis for working these lines, the IOMR would suggest a sum of £6,400 per annum'.

On 4th September, IOMR carriage F5 left the track at Ballastrang level crossing when the wooden centre of the wheel on the leading bogie, disintegrated, and shattered when the tyre separated from it. The cause was the heating of the tyre from rubbing of the brake blocks and its subsequent expansion. In consequence, forty-four 'new improved wheelsets for brake composite carriages' were ordered.

---

*PRINCE OF WALES, length 330 ft, beam 39 ft 1 in., 1,568 tons, 25 knots, 1,546 passengers, 69 crew. Sold to Admiralty 1915.
QUEEN VICTORIA, ditto. (both cut up in Holland, early 1920s).

Few steel rails were laid this year due to poor weather, but a better price was obtained for the old iron ones: in two years all the iron would have gone. And rail-wear would lessen now that 25 four-wheeled carriages were close-coupled.

For the first time traffic on the Port Erin Line grew to the point where it drew business away from the Peel Line, mainly due to the attractions of Port Soderick and the high bookings there. Brick and sand tonnages reached their highest level though the rates were low; 17,200 tons of minerals were carried in 1887.

Sproat had to write to Beyer, Peacock concerning 'the four Abyssinian Tubewells which the Directors have put down'. The supply was for the Beyer, Peacock engines but a test of the water found it to be very salt; he sent a sample to Manchester for the maker's chemist to analyse. (The reply is not traced.) It must be recalled that the position of the wells was in the site of the former bed of the estuary of the two rivers which at that point would be tidal; the wells were probably sunk into ground which was salt-saturated.

Relations between IOMR and MNR were slightly warmer and the practice of exchanging Free Passes was resumed.

As ever, Wood's diary for 1888 gives the IOMR Manager's view of things:

> Easter: There must always be room in our last two trains from Peel to accommodate passengers off the MNR at St John's.
>
> 12th April: Miss Wood's concert, Peel Church. 100 returned to Douglas – paid well.
>
> 27th June: Special Port Soderick–Port Erin return train cost 30/-: 108 children.
>
> 2nd August: Ramsey Cattle Show: Agricultural Society paid £6 for Specials. Trains got very late . . . working altogether unsatisfactory on account of crush on MNR line through their taking schoolchildren from Foxdale and Peel – caused delay to Ramsey trains. Ramsey Coy. short of coaches although we lent them three.
>
> 5th August (Bank Holiday): Very good day. Four engines in steam. Lucky we had the extra engines.
>
> 6th August (Bank Holiday): Six engines in steam but wet, and not needed.
>
> 7th August (Bank Holiday): Six engines in steam. Good day.
>
> 8th August: Many carried to Port Soderick only – several Specials there. Six engines in steam.
>
> 26th August: Port Soderick is the favourite place for visitors.
>
> 4th September: Ballasalla Sports Day. No. 3 train on Ballastrang level crossing when bogie wheel on F5 broke (wooden centre gave way). Trains delayed an hour . . . very poor day.
>
> 20th September: Peel Regatta. Too late in season. Peel Line very poor. Port Erin Line good at night.
>
> 29th September: Season ends. Whit–September weather was bad. Steamer sailings were altered and consequently we were compelled to run too many trains.
>
> 8th–9th November: Bad weather – steamer forced to land at Port Erin. IOMSP Co. was charged £6 and £5 for Special Trains.

The drive for a Peel Railway came from Cresswell Tayleur, a Peel businessman. By March Charles Forman had completed his re-survey for the route and a Registered Office had been established at 6 Crown Street, Peel. It was intended it would have a guarantee from the MNR as had the FR. Unfortunately, at this time Tayleur was taken ill and the urge for progress disappeared.

Financial troubles dogged the Foxdale Railway; at the AGM (29th March) it was noted that Scott and Cottier had resigned from the Board on 13th March and with Clucas dead, there were three vacancies which J.M. Cruikshank, Charles B. Nelson and Thomas Kneen filled. The MNR's arranged contribution (£423 5s. 9d.) was earmarked for a dividend but doubts were expressed on the legality when the FR was still in debt and the matter was sent to the Attorney General for an Opinion. The Company was again directed to the matter of unpaid land claims, and in consequence appealed to its Bankers for help to that end. Away from this side of affairs, as a railway it was carrying out its duty without attracting much comment. A bystander on the lineside would have remarked on its mixed trains, and an intelligent observer that traffic to Foxdale was largely in coal for the boilers, most wagons returning empty for the lead output was waggoned away in small sacks of high value. The solitary passenger coach might be strengthened by a second on Market, Pay etc. Days but otherwise it was as a lackey to the mines and the Company must have been in high glee to be so served without investment of its own in the undertaking.

The problems of the MNR had become so exhaustive that it might clearly be overlooked that the Company was operating a railway as well as battling with its expenses. Early in the year the cost and necessity of re-sleepering imposed a double burden, and although the AGM was told income was never better, the Bank overdraft was considered by the Government to be an unauthorised debt and legal proceedings against it were still incomplete; and no one would come forward to take up more shares. On the matter of powers to run into Douglas, nothing had been prosecuted: the meeting was told that for the MNR 'to be in Douglas, was as if in an enemy's camp'. The SUN recorded that the Legislature would be given an application for such Running Powers ... 'MNR officials enjoy no standing in Douglas'. A proposal to run an IOMR train through from Douglas to Ramsey in 60 minutes was rejected by Wood 'who doubted it would be possible to run a train at over 20 mph' (he must have meant the average speed).*

MNR dividends had fallen to nothing i.e. 4 per cent (1885), 2 per cent (1886) and nil for 1887.

Other aspects of the MNR, AGM included the apparent anomaly of Nelson taking a seat on the Board in place of Clucas deceased; his past record had sometimes been in opposition to the MNR e.g. he had backed the MNR contractor Grainger in his dispute with the Company. Now things were different and his directorship was an appointment to the advantage of both. Nelson's link with the Foxdale and Kennedy had helped the Foxdale position also in its financial difficulties with the contractor. It might be emphasised here that Col Rich, the Government Director, enjoyed perpetual membership of the Board.

The MNR felt itself further encouraged by a desire of the good people of Ramsey to raise the 'watering place' image to the status of the town and a

---

*A draft of through booking arrangements MNR/IOMR (26th November, 1887) is in Tower Collection.

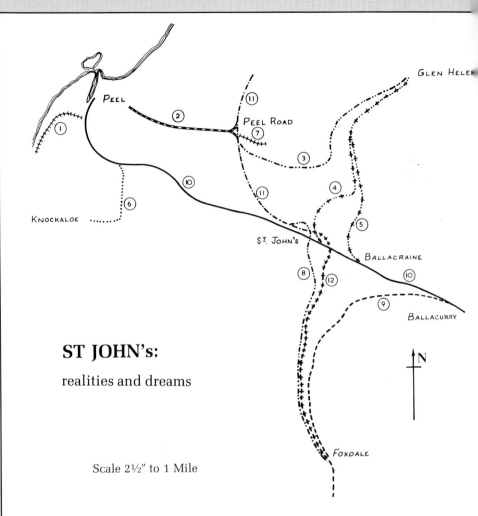

ST JOHN's:

realities and dreams

Scale 2½" to 1 Mile

1. Corrin's Hill Tramway c.1860
2. Peel Branch Railway* 1888
3. Glen Helen–Poortown Branch (MNR)* 1886
4. Glen Helen Railway (Fell)* 1888
5. Glen Helen Railway (MB & T Co.)* 1885
6. Knockaloe Camp Branch (HM Govt) 1915
7. Poortown Quarry Tramway 1884
8. St. John's–Foxdale extension (MNR)* 1882–3
9. Ballacurry–Foxdale Branch (IOMR)* 1882
10. IOMR: main line Douglas–Peel 1873
11. MNR: main line St. John's–Ramsey 1879
12. Foxdale Railway 1886

Original Foxdale Railway proposal (188 omitted for the sake of clarity.

*Lines not built.

considerable building programme was in being, bringing added business to the railway – so useful in fact, that when the building boom ceased there was a sharp drop in railway income.

Income from Foxdale Railway sources was £1,169 3s. 6d. and the mineral tonnage was 25,637; 175,158 passenger journeys had taken place and train mileage was 96,486. Despite the auditors' recommendation, no renewal fund had been set up.

A local enterprise was to operate a small steamer between Douglas and Ramsey; this was the Mona Steamship Co. Further, some Ramsey people were considering the charter of another small ship (HERALD) to make connection with Douglas-based steamers and take passengers to and from Ramsey in competition with the railway service.

Cameron of the MNR was an opportunist for any traffic the MNR might create. As 1888 was the year of the Glasgow Exhibition and with its Scottish links long established, Foxdale 'gravel' (spoil in the main) was shipped from Ramsey for both the Exhibition and for pathways in municipal parks. The long-term prospect for public parks did not materialise as the authorities did not favour its quality.

The Glen Helen Railway schemes, which first came to light in autumn 1884, may have been considered to be dead, but they were brought before the IOMR again in January 1888, when Wood and George N. Fell, Civil Engineer (1849–1924),* were in correspondence and conversation over a plan prepared by Fell. Fell was no stranger to the Island, having surveyed for a steam-worked mountain railway in 1887 as part of the Douglas, Laxey & Snaefell Railway. Fell submitted his Glen Helen plan in late 1887 (his backers are not named) and in January 1888 was pressing Wood to learn if the IOMR Board had considered it and would be willing to operate for a percentage of gross receipts? 'Until this is known, I would be unable to lay it before my financial friends'. On 24th February he wrote again giving some detail which shows various differences from the 1887 plans which carry no name. Length would be 2¼ miles and gauge 3 feet. It would leave the IOMR on the west side of St John's and 'cross the public road 150 yards from the bridge over the IOMR'. It would then be carried on a light trellis iron viaduct† . . . for about a mile . . . so crossing over roads instead of on the level. It would pass close to Glen Helen Brickworks where there would be a siding. The terminus would be in the field adjacent to the Pleasure Grounds. The gradient would not exceed 1 in 50 and the cost £10,000 excluding rolling stock. 'Would the IOMR be willing to work it for 50 per cent total receipts and what rebate would be allowed on passengers carried to Glen Helen?'

Nothing more is heard.

The position vis-a-vis the MNR and FR Companies was regularised by an Act during 1888: 'Limited' could be omitted from their titles (etc.).

John Pender, Chairman of the IOMR received a knighthood.

---

*Son of John B. Fell, originator of the Fell centre-rail system for mountain railways.
†Here Fell enclosed a photograph of the 1880 timber viaduct on the North Devon Clay Co. Ltd.'s 3 ft gauge Torrington & Marland Rly. for which his father, J.B. Fell, was responsible. [A similar viaduct appears on one of his Snaefell schemes.] Ref: THE LOCOMOTIVE MAGAZINE: (1913, page 167.)

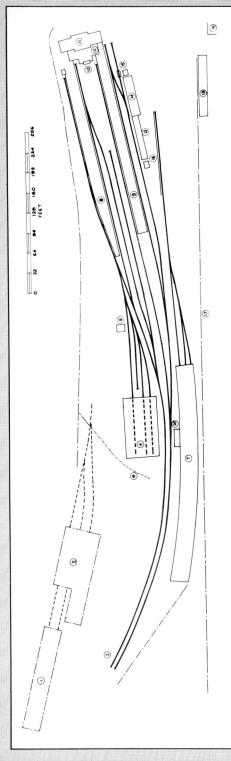

DOUGLAS: Greenbank Plan to accommodate DL & SR traffic, being an enlargement of existing station. 1889

1. ⎫ Possible sites for Workshops etc.
2. ⎭
3. Main Lines (no connection shown)
4. Locomotive Shed*
5. Guards' Room
6. River boundary
7. Carriage Shed*

8. Peel Line platform
9. Port Erin Line platform
10. Bookstall
11. Station building
12. Concourse
13. Goods platform
14. Goods Shed
15. Weighbridge

16. Goods Office
17. Ropewalk's wall
18. ⎫ Quiggin's premises
19. ⎭
20. Signal Frame

*'To be taken down'.

(Note omission of crossover between Lines, and no link to Carriage Shed.)

1889

It was inevitable that the Douglas Workshop crane, which had been 'borrowed' to lift stone blocks from wagons in the yard which were to be used in the lengthening of Douglas Pier, would not return! The Workshops would require a proper replacement, and preferably one of heavier type: a new one was ordered in February. Out in Douglas station itself, its frontage began to take on the appearance which survives to this day and the entrance from Railway Terrace, Peel Road and Athol Street was opened with its impressive flight of stairs. Before Easter, the strip of land which lay between the station and Quiggin's ropewalk was taken in (ultimately Quiggin's boundary would lie much further to the south thus freeing the railway from the narrow neck of land between the existing ropewalk and the 'cliff-face' on the north, more land being excavated on the north edge to this end) but further station and workshop developments were still held back awaiting the outcome of the proposed DL&SR scheme; also there was anxiety to avoid the creation of a curved platform. That these were still in abeyance at the year end is evidenced by Greenbank's drawing for a new layout* prepared in November, and an alternative of even greater sophistication, with a special area for the incomer having its own platform.

The building boom around Douglas continued at first but the end was in sight; loaded wagons were now detached from the train at Quarter Bridge (no siding facility here) whilst lime, bricks and shingle were unloaded on the level crossing, giving rise to loud complaint from road users '. . . a station should be built there'.

The attitude of Chairman Major John S. Goldie-Taubman at the IOMR March AGM was reported with droll sarcasm by the newspaper:

> . . . he has never displayed his peculiarities as a public speaker better than on Tuesday when he presided at the meeting. I have seen a few similar gatherings and had the pleasure of listening to such insignificant Railway Managers as Sir Edward Watkin (etc.) all Chairmen of leading English Companies. They were not without fault but could not get within miles of the respected Chairman of the IOMR; to spread out a huge sheet of paper on a desk, enumerate rapidly a lot of figures extracted therefrom, with lowered head and in a confidential tone of voice addressed to the table over which he leaned without rising to his feet – that may be the Chairman's view of how best to discharge his duty to the shareholders, and explains the position of their property, but I hope he has the monopoly . . .

In June, July and August, a steamer was operated by the Peel & North of Ireland Steam Ship Co. between Peel and Bangor, Co. Down, in conjunction with the train service, and through tickets were available from IOMR stations. No profit was made.† Initially, MONA'S ISLE (1882) was chartered from the IOMSP Co. and later PARIS (1875), an ex-London, Brighton & South Coast Railway steamer.

Douglas Town Council must have been upending its 'Pending File' for it found a drawing submitted by the IOMR linked to the rebuilding of Douglas station and showing a proposed extension line to either The Battery or Victoria Pier, which embodied a gradient which the Council considered too

---

*Manx Museum: drawing seen in 1973 but not located in 1992.

†The next year the IOMSP Co. ran a steamer between Peel and Belfast in July and August. Similar ticket facilities were offered and train times changed to meet IOMSP Co. needs.

steep for safety. So the whole dusty subject of a quay extension came to the fore again only to lie fallow once more. (Two years later (1891) the Council was told 'the railway has been trying to build such a line for the past sixteen years without success'). And so the matter has rested from that day to this. It was still to the forefront in 1948 when considered amongst the priorities for increasing the Island's tourist numbers – a train alongside the ship would have been an irresistible attraction.

By the year end, the Douglas building bubble had burst; the town was now 'overbuilt'. Many shops and new houses were unoccupied and the IOMR began to feel the loss of business carrying lime, sand and bricks which had enjoyed a three-year honeymoon. During the previous year, the 'Glen Helen Co. and Mr Enos Lace made bricks near St John's' and they were supplied with 'a great deal of coal' by rail. The fall in income was replaced by two new sources, firstly, from Castletown in the form of stone from Scarlett, and secondly, from the quarry at Poortown (on the MNR) which travelled over the IOMR from St John's. This material came into Douglas, destined for both the new Harbour works and the Town Commissioners.

At this period, the IOMR's General Purposes Committee was meeting weekly.

Wood's diary reveals one or two items of new interest:

16th March: Football at Castletown. 400 passengers.
7th August (Bank Holiday): Best day we have had – receipts £311.
2nd September: Oldham Wakes. Six in steam. 10.35 am ex-Douglas had 19 on for Port Erin and 6 for Port Soderick.
5th September: Thick fog delays all trains.
30th September: Showery weather. Suits the railway.

To complete the IOMR picture; express trains were run in high season between Douglas and Ramsey with three intermediate stops. Five minutes were allowed at St John's and the running time was 65 minutes. A train hit a cow at Santon and it effectively derailed part of it; the fate of the cow is not recorded!

There is as little to report about the Foxdale Railway as to the line itself. The special Board Meeting in the Law Library, Douglas, in the presence of the Attorney General on 25th March, was to discuss the vexed question of whether it was lawful or not to pay a dividend when the Company was in debt. So indifferent to their shareholding were its owners, that only one shareholder attended its 5th June AGM which was consequently adjourned for one week. The same non-event then repeated itself and the meeting was adjourned indefinitely.

A deputation was sent to Glasgow to see if the former FR contractors, Kennedy & Son, would 'assist the Company to their own benefit'. What a turn-around in the face of financial collapse! The deputation had met Kennedy on 1st April but returned 'with little hope of extracting the Company from its financial embarrassments'. More gloom threatened when Dumbell's Banking Co. gave notice of their intent to bring the financial failings of the FR before the Court. It was no wonder that the shareholders had lost interest; they had been prepared for the worst when asked if the Company should carry on operating. The directors held subsequent meetings on 2nd and 8th November, also on the 10th December to consider various 'schemes of arrangement' which might be interpreted as throwing in the towel if this was thought prudent. Unpaid landowners were issuing summonses and Thomas Kneen (an advocate) was asked to appear in Court in the interests of the Company. Discussions occupied hours and ended with agreement that a deputation should go to the Isle of Man Banking Co. 'to arrive at some scheme which would meet both concerns'. Money due from the MNR would be pressed-for, and used to pay landowners. The inevitable end to the patience of landowners, still owed for the value of their holdings sold to the nascent railway, resulted in four summonses and the resignation of Kneen, but the Board refused to accept the resignation.* In December several landowners arrested the monies due from the MNR to meet the value of the land taken from them.

Needless to say, Foxdale traffic in 'tourists' hardly existed: there were some suspicious entries when the figures for passenger journeys (8,599) and tonnages (12,182) were the same as for 1888 – these were in fact, lower than 1888 which were 11,763 journeys and 14,152 tons.

The MNR Board members were not satisfied with their Free Passes over the IOMR which only covered the stretch between St John's and Douglas; 'the IOMR seldom use the MNR Passes but the MNR frequently use the IOMR'. [The MNR showed their true colours when, on an occasion before Passes were granted, they had attended a joint meeting in Douglas at the request of the IOMR faction, they asked for a refund of the IOMR fare . . . and were given it.]

Business on the MNR was falling; though more through passengers had appeared, the mineral traffic tonnage was lower at 23,817 tons due to the building recession which was not the prerogative of Douglas but had hit Ramsey also. Nevertheless, Foxdale takings were slightly up at £1,169 3s. 6d. and train mileage was up at 94,590.

The main developments in Ramsey had been to the north of the existing town, on the land beyond the Sulby River, and were at their height in the late 1880s. Two features were (and remain) prominent, firstly the Mooragh Estate and Park with its boating lake, and secondly, the provision of a large swing bridge to connect the town with this north shore development; the bridge was the work of the Cleveland Bridge Co. To facilitate F. McCulloch, the contractor for the development, a contractor's tramway was laid down.†

It is tempting to linger over the financial problems of the MNR which stretched throughout 1889 and, although they form the principal anxiety of the proprietors they are unlikely to be the most sought-after subject in a railway history: suffice to say that the January lawsuit between the MNR and the Government was only partially successful for the MNR who approached the Governor in February 1890 and were recommended to apply for further financial powers which would give preference to those obtaining already . . . yet further into the mire did affairs sink. The MNR made it clear that if such powers were not granted, they would seek legislation to give them running rights into Douglas over IOMR metals – it was the only saving grace they could seek.

*Kneen became a Director of the FR in 1888.
†Hendry, page 57.

DOUGLAS: Greenbank's alternative 11 January 1890 Plan to accommodate DL & SR if required: replaced by Plan approved by Board on 4 November 1890

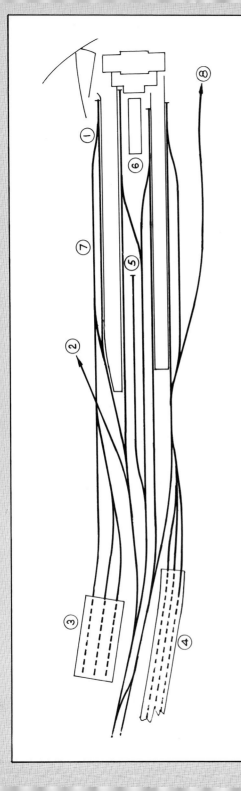

1. 'Horse Dock'
2. To 'Goods Depot' (presumably DL & SR)
3. Locomotive Shed & Workshops (IOMR)
4. Carriage Shed (IOMR)
5. 'Carriage Siding'
6. 'Porters & Urinals'
7. This side of station to be used by DL & SR trains: north face island platform to be named 'Laxey Platform'
8. Proposed line to Harbour

Plan signed by H. Greenbank and G.N. Fell.

Plate 84: Sharp. Stewart's official photograph of Manx Northern Railway No. 2. The nameplate NORTHERN has not yet been affixed.
Collection J.I.C. Boyd

Plate 85: Now with some subtle differences from the previous illustration, No. 2 stands at the head of a train (but not coupled to it) at Ramsey. The tank-top tool box is prominent, brake rodding is now outside the wheels and the blower fitting is behind and outside the

Plates 86 and 87: The other two MNR locomotives were MNR Nos. 3 & 4; No. 3 became IOMR No. 14 and was long-lived. It is seen here in the 1930s at Douglas. No. 4 (which became IOMR No. 15) was built for working the Foxdale Railway's mineral traffic but spent the greater part of its working life on other duties.

C.E. Box and collection J.I.C. Boyd

Plate 88: IOMR four-wheeled coach No. B4 of the initial batch of stock. It was intended to be a 2nd class carriage but was relegated 3rd.

Plate 89: Seen at Peel in 1913 is FENELLA attached to F33 and B2. F33 was the first of its type. B2 was paired to C6 (*off the picture*) and in 1912 that pair was put on a bogie frame; this was only the second occasion when a pair had been so treated, number F55 being given. From a carriage history viewpoint, the picture is doubly interesting.
Manx Museum

Plate 90: F6 of 1876 was the last of a batch of bogie coaches delivered to the IOMR by Brown, Marshalls & Co. Ltd., being the first bogie coaches supplied to that Company.
Manx Museum

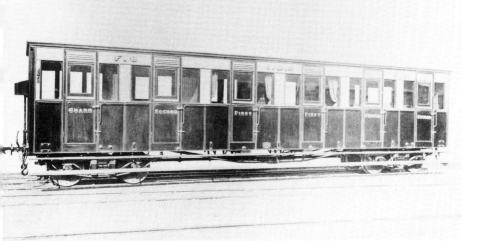

Plate 91: F1 in Douglas in the early 1970s demonstrates the care and attention given by the railway workshops to such 1876 vehicles. *J.I.C. Boyd*

Plate 92: F62 in the bay platform at Port Erin, shows how the 'pairs' were mounted on Metropolitan-supplied bogie underframes. Some had the gap between them cosmetically covered in to make them more weatherproof, but not this example. The lefthand body was B1 (3rd) and the righthand A1 (1st) i.e. in each case the first-delivered vehicle. Note the longer body of the latter; they were put on the underframe in 1926, one of the last three to be so treated. July 1933. *H.C. Casserley*

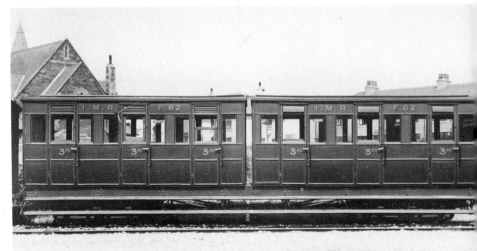

Plate 93: F15 in the splendid colours of the early 1930s – white upper and purple lower panels, light grey roof and gilt lettering shaded vermilion. The 1st class compartments are curtained. Douglas. July 1933.   *H.C. Casserley*

Plate 94: In 1950, F15 had recently been overhauled and repainted in all-red, but the 1st class curtains had disappeared. Peel. April 1950.   *J.D. Darby*

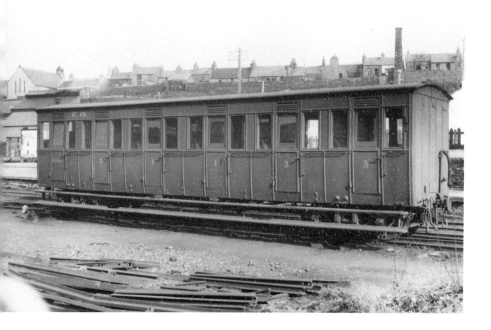

Plate 95: In August 1947 F24 and F33 had received post-war furbishing and were among carriages in a two-tone brown paintwork, not unlike that used on certain stock in the 1920–30s. Douglas. *J.I.C. Boyd*

Plate 96: Initially the IOMR's brake and luggage vans were of the four-wheeled variety as was all the other stock. These vans, given the prefix 'E' to the number, were never 'paired'. They had a mixed life, some ending up without their chassis as goods warehouses at stations. This is E5 (the lookout ducket has been removed from the righthand end) at St John's in 1931. *C.E. Box*

Plate 97: Of the saloons, much was expected but in traffic their reception was mixed. Engine drivers did not like them because of the weight; passengers did not like them because they were stuffy. F35/36 were restored for the Royal Train in 1972: here is F36 at the Centenary celebrations of 1973. To improve the riding the original diamond frame bogies have been replaced. Douglas. *J.I.C. Boyd*

Plate 98: Whether the Foxdale Branch was operative or not, 'The Foxdale Coach' (as the staff called it) stood for weeks at a time in St John's yard.

Plate 99: 'Luggage in Advance' was a system whereby railway passengers might consign their luggage beforehand by rail, so that when they arrived at their destination, it was awaiting them; the only condition was that they held railway tickets for that journey. Two large vans were built to meet this popular service; this is F28. St John's. July 1957.   *J.I.C. Boyd*

Plate 100: N42 (originally MNR No. 3) was one of the six-wheeled carriages built for the opening of the Manx Northern Railway; there were 3rd class compartments at each end and a 1st class section in the middle. The nearest compartment had been altered to 'Guard' by giving it a handbrake and small ticket rack; a small window was fixed in that end. MNR six-wheeled vehicles were only used by the IOMR when under stress; this one and its fellows stood inside or around St John's carriage shed for their latter years.   *J.I.C. Boyd*

Plate 101: This is MNR No. 8 as built, and reproduced from an illustration in an early RAILWAY MAGAZINE; originally finished in varnished teak, this and other six-wheeled stock was given a 'near LNWR' livery (white upper, and purple lake lower panels). In July 1905 it was badly damaged in a buffer stop collision at Douglas, and withdrawn. Ramsey c1898.
Courtesy Railway Magazine

Plate 102: Hurst, Nelson-built bogie carriage for MNR, one of two supplied for through Ramsey–Douglas services and in many ways more superior than contemporary stock on the IOMR: F37, ex-MNR No. 16 of 1899. Douglas.
Collection J.I.C. Boyd

Plate 103: H41, standard pattern of open goods wagon, IOMR. St John's. April 1960.
J.I.C. Boyd

Plate 104: M56 of the series originally termed 'ballast wagons', being two-plank dropside vehicles with fixed ends. This example is one of the second batch, known as the 'Improved' type, with two-wheel brake gear. St John's. March 1962.   *J.I.C. Boyd*

Plate 105: There was once a requirement for six bolster wagons, used mainly for carrying long timber. Four came from Metropolitan in 1874 and two were built in Douglas in 1910. L4 (seen here in August 1947) was scrapped in 1959–60.   *J.I.C. Boyd*

Plate 106: In July 1972 most of the surplus goods stock had been cleared from the provincial stations and brought back to Douglas goods yard where it mouldered to the end. This fish wagon once carried barrels, baskets, boxes or crans of herring; the fish was shipped by the Steam Packet Co. to Liverpool Market for sale each morning.

J.I.C. Boyd

Plate 107: Castletown goods yard always contained a goodly assortment of vehicles, many of them in connection with Brewery traffic, coal, vegetables, bagged lime and fertiliser. A certain amount of coal was brought to the harbour by coastal steamer and carted to the Castletown station for distribution by railway. 1952. *J.I.C. Boyd*

Plate 108: There was still a useful cattle traffic in 1947; here in Douglas yard are three Douglas-constructed vans on former coach chassis, the nearest is K26 built in 1923. The last van is an original, unroofed. *J.I.C. Boyd*

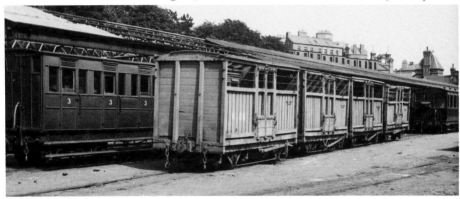

Plate 109: This well wagon was built at Douglas in 1936 and used mainly to carry the mechanical excavator about the system; it worked at the St John's sand and gravel pits, in removal of the Foxdale mines' spoil and at the Douglas coal stack. *J.I.C. Boyd*

Plate 110: The MNR received eight wagons from The Swansea Wagon Co. in 1884 especially for the Foxdale mines' traffic; they were similar to the dropside 'M' series wagons on the IOMR but owing to errors by the makers, they gave considerable problems. This is Mr34, ex-MNR No. 28 at St John's in April 1960. *J.I.C. Boyd*

Plate 111: In the same month as the previous illustration, Hr45 (with homespun extensions to carry sheep or pigs which could be loaded via the drop-door) lurked among the wounded wagonry in the cripple sidings at Douglas. With part of the headstock rotted off, the end was inevitable; it was the last of a series carrying MNR Nos. 37–42, becoming IOMR Hr40–45. *J.I.C. Boyd*

Plate 112: E1, ex-MNR brake van (this should have been Er1), formerly MNR No. 19 of 1895 and relegated to goods work from 1940. Port Erin. May 1953. *J.I.C. Boyd*

Plate 113: A poster of the 1910 period. *Collection J.I.C. Boyd*

In April, after continuous rain, the unstable portion of MNR line at Gob-y-Deigan collapsed for a considerable length, but, by immense efforts over Easter, Cameron put in a temporary connection and by May, a permanent line was re-established.

In September, the MNR was again trying to obtain concessions from the IOMR. There was no connecting winter train at St John's for the MNR afternoon service and they wanted to run a complete train from Ramsey into Douglas (locomotive included) to facilitate those 'wanting to do an afternoon's business there', and return. In reply, the IOMR criticised MNR time-keeping; if the arrival time of an MNR train at St John's could be guaranteed, the IOMR would put on an extra connection for the cost of wear and tear but under no circumstances could MNR trains run over its metals. To improve performance, the IOMR suggested that MNR trains avoid picking up and setting down wagons in this instance. Some more brotherly arrangements were already in force at St John's as to save time, certain MNR trains now ran direct into the IOMR station.

At the resumed Second Hearing of the MNR Finance Bill on 31st October, Cowell was reprimanded for bringing in the Governor's name but he insisted that in respect of Government support for the Company, it was that body 'which had broken faith' ... such was further delay that a Second Reading was not received until 17th December. More problems would follow in the ensuing month.

1890

During the year, a new waiting room was erected at Ballabeg and, after another storm damaged Peel goods shed, yet more extensive repairs were made at a cost of £35. Patience at the Douglas end was exhausted; it seemed unlikely that a 'Laxey line' (by whatever title) would come into existence, despite consultations which had dragged on from the previous January, so the piece of land allocated for its station was earmarked for the building of the IOMR's new Workshops; such were commenced towards the year's end. There was still some doubt as to where the IOMR's new Carriage Sheds would stand but ultimately echoes for a Laxey Railway died away and these Sheds also were begun; gates, railings and walls were put up, the last-named 'to stop people throwing stones'. Shrubs were planted.

Beside the railway line at Santon, during the hot July weather, a bullock was driven wild by the heat: jumping onto the line, it 'charged' an oncoming train of ten carriages, brake van and wagon. The engine pushed the bullock for some distance, then ran over it; it then derailed the first bogie of the leading carriage in which there were twelve passengers. The third coach, 'one of the short twin-carriages', was also derailed but no one was injured and it appears the engine remained on the track.

A new Rule Book was issued in July, and Ballasalla received a new locomotive water tank. The next month James Cowle & Son were engaged to build a gateway and shop at the corner of Athol Street, at the summit of the new stairway.

The earlier enquiry by Douglas Town Commissioners, concerning the carriage of manure, returned again in differing form; the Commissioners now asked the Railway Company to install a siding and loading bank at Santon to enable stones to be taken from there to Douglas. The IOMR quoted for 5–6,000 tons of stones per annum for 4–5 years @ 1s. 3d. per ton, reducing to 1s. 1d. per ton if this tonnage was exceeded; wagons were to be unloaded immediately on reaching Douglas. The Railway would need to buy extra land for this purpose. A short time later the Commissioners widened their enquiry 'in case manure was carried' (this suggests such traffic had not yet begun) confident that both manure and stones would be accommodated in the same siding and loading bank. It was explained to them that the height for one would be unsuitable for the other and 'a manure siding would be objectionable to passengers'.

The age of the early IOMR carriages was now beginning to show; despite frequent maintenance, their roofs were leaking and body-sag on the first bogie carriages was put down to 'the frames getting weaker, and it is more difficult to screw up the tie rods into a firm position'. Joseph Sproat put in a plea for more locomotives and carriages; did he know that Wood would be telling the shareholders that profits were now greater than before?

And so to Wood's diary once more:

> 3rd April: Late trains delayed 45 minutes to suit Prince of Wales' steamer.
> Easter Monday: Horse races in Douglas did us harm. Last train to Ramsey leaves Douglas at 11 pm.
> Whitsuntide Sunday: Shuttle service to Port Soderick.
> Whitsuntide Monday: Five in steam. Good day. Shunting engine double-headed 5.10 pm train and returned with six wagons of straw (a straw Special ran again on 27th May).
> 28th May (Whitsuntide): Five engines in steam.
> 1st July: Peel–Belfast steamer begins. Fourteen passengers.
> 8th July: Queen's Promenade opened. Did pretty well.
> 4th August (Bank Holiday): Splendid Day. 10.35 am Port Erin left Douglas with 29 vehicles and two locomotives – banking engine brought back 10 vehicles.*
> All trains banked up to 3.30 pm and then banker ran to Ballasalla to bank all UP trains save the last. Six locomotives in steam. 10.35 am to Peel had banker to Union Mills.†
> 5th August: Port St Mary Regatta. Seven locomotives in steam.
> 7th August: Belfast–Peel steamer delayed, train left Peel an hour late: MNR passenger at St John's kept waiting for it. Good day for Ramsey Company.
> 11th August: Considerable banking trains both lines. Six locomotives in steam every day.
> 28th August: Trotting Matches. Bellevue.
> 30th August: Belfast steamer ends. Pretty well on the whole. (2,852 passengers bring in £241 12s. 10d.). We are £1,256 better than last year. Short of coaches in August. Peel steamer needs night train to meet it. Unsettled weather has been good for the railway.
> Christmas: Poor. People seem short of money.

---

*Presumably the ten carriages were run to Port Soderick only.
†Note the Port Erin Line's demand for engine power over Peel Line.

The MNR Bill was ultimately passed but not signed until March; it was widely accepted that it was more to restore the credibility of the Government than for the good of the MNR. This did nothing to simplify the complex financial position into which the MNR had sunk, and the details were not divulged to shareholders before the 1890 AGM on 13th March. Shareholders present at the meeting were unwilling to vote a remuneration to the directors for their services and the newspaper was critical of this lack of appreciation. The MNR being now enabled to issue additional Stock in the title of 5 per cent 'C' Stock but market forces were against their placing and the matter left aside until money was cheaper.

An important source of tourist traffic on 24th July was to benefit the railway until recent times – this was the forming of a syndicate to operate pleasure grounds at Glen Wyllin, situate just south of Kirk Michael station and below the viaduct there. It was linked to Kirk Michael station by footpath only.

The TIMES for 23rd August had a paragraph headed:

> MNR Speed-up. A MNR train travelled between St John's and Ramsey on August 20th in 32 minutes. Nothing serious resulted from this recklessness.

(The distance being 16½ miles the average speed was only 32 mph – well within the capacity of the locomotive; complaints about dilatory running on the northern line were commonplace.)

Meanwhile, Foxdale matters had almost disappeared from sight. There had been no shareholders' meeting since the suspended 1889 AGM called for 5th June and it would seem that MNR interests in it had accepted it was only a matter of time when, there being no obvious remedy for its bankrupt state, it would fold up. As a railway of course, it continued to function. It was said that the locals never used the railway, it was too expensive and they preferred to walk to and from St John's.

The FR Board met on 11th February, only to suggest that a scheme of liquidation should be prepared for the next meeting. Possibly the news of this had leaked out and created the anxiety of creditors to obtain their money before the thing collapsed and thereafter meetings were almost confined to the problems of presenting accounts which satisfied the auditor. Information for them was still incomplete when the Board held its last 1890 meeting on 13th June.

If the Foxdale Line was dying and the MNR fighting to save its own life, then the 'Peel Branch Railway' scheme had almost totally expired. (It was not finally dissolved until 1923 when it was stated the creation had lain dormant since 1890.)

One would feel that the effect of these dismal disclosures would be to pour a cold douche on current dreams of a railway(s) up the east coast, yet a London-based proposal took shape in the following May!

1891

On the IOMR, most of the spectacular work was being done at Douglas, though bad weather was slowing down its progress. The station staff there must have lived in a perpetual melée of alterations and there was no prospect of peace when the Cowle plans of 1888 were taken off the shelf and dusted, and the new booking hall, parcels and Station Master's offices were begun. The new building soon advanced to the position where the roof was ready to go on. Down in the west yard, the old, small and inefficient Workshops had been demolished and the new ones were ready by the spring, occupying a similar site. The new goods shed (by James Cowle @ £825) was ready save for its loading platform at the same date, and a 'Carriage Paint Shop' came into being. The unfinished gateway and steps into Athol Street were not complete until mid-year.

New trackwork was to continue but needed Greenbank to come over and supervise the work; meanwhile the job was postponed whilst the outcome of a Manx East Coast Railways Co. Ltd. (registered 2nd May for a line Douglas–Laxey–Snaefell Summit) was in the air.*

A tender of £805 by Dutton & Co.† of Worcester for signalling work was accepted, this included interlocking and provision for a signal box. Further urinals would be built by B. Finch & Co. for £117 and a clock from Smith & Sons of Derby for £48 would grace the cupola over the Athol Street gateway. 'Thomas Smith' of Rodley, Leeds, supplied two watercranes in August.‡

Less spectacular was the erection of an oil store, large water tank house and a store for permanent way materials. Decisions taken concerning the two iron Carriage Sheds in 1888 had after all, been part of developments held back (though at one time they were excluded from delay). Now it was decided they would not be needed until completion of all other work as that would leave no available land for them. (In the event it was considered that a single Carriage Shed (to house 61 carriages) from Main & Co. of Glasgow @ £1,150 would be preferable. It was almost ready for use by March 1893 and was 320 ft long.)

It was not a good summer but as was previous experience, it gave the Railway more traffic at the expense of road and steamer competition. The year 1891 would see a threat to the IOMR from a proposed Douglas–Castletown coastal steamer owned by the Mona Steam Ship Co., now the possessor of two vessels: luckily this service did not materialise but the MNR was hit again by that concern's Douglas–Ramsey sailings. A reduction

---

*Registered Office: 20 Athol Street. No work done. Company dissolved 12th October, 1923.

†Dutton & Co. Ltd., (originally Dutton & Co.) set up in 1888 by Samuel Telford Dutton who was formerly with McKenzie & Holland, and operating from a works on McKenzie & Holland's doorstep, a 'wholly new establishment set up by signalling engineers for the purpose of manufacturing railway signalling equipment . . . undertook a certain amount of engineering work'.

[J.F. Pease & Co. Ltd. took over Dutton's assets in 1899: in October 1901 McKenzie & Holland took over signalling assets of J.F. Pease & Co. Ltd.]

‡'SMITHS of RODLEY' founded in 1820 at Rodley, Leeds by David Smith and two partners. Amongst the first steam-crane builders in Yorkshire but made other lifting machinery, stone-cutting machines etc. after a move into engineering in 1840. Notable for their excavators' involvement from 1885 at Cardiff, Preston and Barry Docks, and Manchester Ship Canal. Many overseas contracts. (More recently, part of the Thomas W. Ward Group.)

in Douglas–Ramsey fares requested by the MNR was given a positive response so more visitors used this route . . . a sign of the growing number of tourists each year. A new form of business arose in the carriage of mine arisings from Foxdale conveyed to Douglas for use in concrete foundations.

Between 1st July and 7th September the IOMSP Co. resumed its daily sailings between Peel and Belfast.

Horticulture was not confined to Douglas station alone – the Station Master at Union Mills was praised for his floral efforts and it was suggested an annual prize be given for the best station. The matter of a Douglas Harbour line was given an airing again.

A delicate situation – so familiar on the limited Manx boundaries – arose when Taubman 'closed one of the arches of the Nunnery Bridge' which spanned the River Douglas on his estate.*

The Board received a Memorial from the inhabitants of Port St Mary who saw what was happening at Douglas with some envy, and related this to their own wooden shanty called 'a station'. They asked simply for 'increased accommodation' and received a favourable hearing.

A visitor who made notes of a journey between Douglas and Port Erin this year commented, 'very amusing to see the women pointsmen employed on the railway'.

Again, we may peep into Wood's personal diary for his view of IOMR affairs:

> Whitsuntide: Timetable now needs five engines in steam.
> 23rd July: Marine Drive opened – inward bookings good.
> August Bank Holiday: Open wagons attached to trains for large quantities of luggage.
> 2nd August (Sunday): Bishop on the Head† and new Drive kept people in Douglas.
> 3rd August: Mainly short travel to Port Soderick for the Drive. Poor weather.
> 4th August: Bishop's Court Garden Party. Barrow steamer ran down a boat at Port Soderick.
> 6th September: Belfast 2,776 passengers = £281 10s. 6d.‡ Special train each day, ends today.
> 30th September: Straw traffic from Castletown ceases: receipts for goods down. Passengers up £262 3s. 2d.#
> 7th December: Floods 4 ft deep over meadows beside railway at Belle Vue.

The MNR figures for 1891 showed 182,689 passenger journeys with more through bookings, and mineral tonnage at 22,080; trains had run 95,427 miles. Due to an increased number of clergy meetings, stops at Bishop's Court had risen. Though the Foxdale Railway (see on) would go into voluntary liquidation later in the year, the MNR was obliged to continue its obligations to carry its traffic until the end of their Agreement. At the AGM on 10th March, it was explained that the 'C' Stock had not attracted buyers because, in the event of liquidation, its holders would not have had preferential treatment. The previous year had required expenses to re-timber Glen Wyllin and Glen Mooar viaducts, plus track and locomotive repairs.

---

*These arches were on the banks of the river; the railway was carried over the river (72 ch from Douglas) by 2 main spans of 24 ft girders with a 6 ft central pier. There were side spans each of 10 ft. [Drawing: Manx Museum.]

†i.e. Douglas Head – open air Sunday service.

‡These were figures for the period of operation of the steamer.

#Passenger figures for whole of high season only.

The Company was looking for buyers to lift it from its financial plight; the IOMR had been approached but would not be tempted and after clandestine meetings with the Governor, a Government purchase of both MNR and FR was considered, the former to receive £85,000.

The year 1890 marked the point of no return for the Foxdale Railway. In early March the Bank threatened legal proceedings if the debt due to interest on the Debentures was not paid at once. Large sums were due to Nelson for professional services. The next month the Governor suggested (as just mentioned) that the Government might take over both MNR and FR, the offer of £8,000 being made for the latter. A MNR Board Meeting on 16th April flatly rejected it and called for a meeting with the Governor in order to parley and obtain an increased figure.

The Governor wrote to the MNR on 22nd April (but not apparently to the FR) refusing to increase 'his' offer, and a meeting with the Government Director of the MNR (Col Rich) was sought in London. In the High Court of Justice, before His Honour (Deemster) Sir W.L. Drinkwater the suit of the IOM Banking Co. to recover principal and interest on their 5 per cent Debenture Bonds was a formality (29th June).

But the doom of the Foxdale Railway was at hand; its Directors were currently C.B. Nelson, J.M. Cruikshank and J.R. Cowell; Kitto* and Kneen had resigned. The meeting on 30th June, held in Ramsey railway station, was chaired by Nelson in the absence through illness of Cowell. Nelson explained† that as a carrying company the mining traffic was very satisfactory but that tourism and general passenger traffic was far below expectations (SUN, 4th July) – he gave a succinct account of affairs now past, how Kennedy had taken £4,500 in shares in lieu of payment and how his contract for £12,000 had become a cost of £15,300 due to alterations and having to cut through rock. Land which had been valued at £1,500 had in reality cost £4,000. The Company had expended large sums on engineering, overtime, sleepers, rails and building St John's station and sidings. Hire of a locomotive during construction had amounted to £7,578 so that instead of the line being constructed for £19,500 it had cost far more.‡ Now there was a bank overdraft of £6,060 and currently they owed £17,676. 'It is a most regrettable state of affairs, due entirely to increased cost of constructing the line'. He explained that he and J.M. Cruikshank had come into the business after the above debts had been incurred and it had been an arduous job trying to keep the ship afloat.

Nelson waxed long and detailed after the exposition, explaining the Agreements with the MNR and IOMMCL, the latter to pay the FR 2s. 6d. per ton for their traffic between Foxdale and St John's. The Agreement with the Mining Co. for 12 years, still had 6–7 years to run. The original directors who incurred the construction debt were each personally responsible to repay it. At this stage, unusually for a FR meeting, a shareholder suggested he and his fellow shareholders should help to meet the debt and the Chairman said it was not the intention that 'these gentlemen should bear any personal responsibility'. The meeting was followed by an Extra-Ordinary General Meeting which agreed to postpone it until 7th July in the hope that

*Following retirement from the IOMMCL in 1890; his son W.H. Kitto succeeded him at the mine.
†'In an exhaustive speech' (Minute Book).
‡About £26,878 in fact.

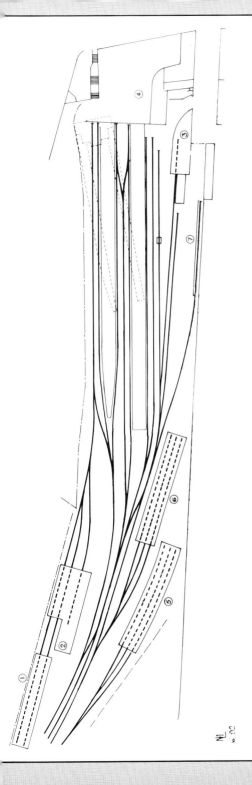

DOUGLAS: Greenbank's final Plan of 26 August 1891
[The two 3-road Carriage Sheds were not prosecuted but one large Shed was delivered at the end of 1892]

1. New Carriage and Paint Shop (1891)
2. New Workshops, etc. (1891)
3. Goods Shed (less platform) complete (1891)
4. New building in work (1891)

5. ⎫
6. ⎭ Carriage Sheds (not erected)
7. Sunken Siding

(Note re-position of platforms cf. original station)
[Signals not shown on original.]

Cowell would be fit enough to occupy the chair. On 7th July there was no quorum!

Much of the foregoing appeared in the SUN and the TIMES added a little detail, outlining the sympathy Nelson had expressed for the contractors . . . 'the price was the subject of a prolonged struggle in which Mr Kennedy succumbed to persuasive powers brought to bear on him, and was induced to take part payment . . . in shares'. [Kennedy & Son were suing for £4,563 owing as contractors.]

Cruikshank, a MNR Director, also took his cards – at least in part – away from his chest: 'the MNR is working the FR at a certain percentage and the result is that the expenses of the FR have never been more than £40 per annum . . . the MNR is floating and making good headway . . . the FR ought to be a good investment at £14,000 because in practice the MNR have paid 5% on that amount'. It was wise to wind up otherwise a certain 'creditor suing the Company was likely to win and in order to ensure that other shareholders received fair play'.

It is opportune to mention FR figures for 1890 revealed at the AGM: tonnage had been up at 12,963 and there were 6,686 passenger journeys, a fall. It would be superfluous to mention that no dividend was declared. The train service had now dwindled to two mixed return workings each day (not Sundays).

The adjourned EGM held on 14th July (Cowell still away), agreed to wind up the Company, the three directors becoming the liquidators. (The next AGM of the Company would not take place until 25th January, 1906!) Regrettably, the Court had upheld both Kennedy & Son's claim and that of the IOM Banking Co. and, to these two was added a third of earlier date referring to land and sand from the property of Dumbell's Banking Co. at St John's. The matter of the FR was, from beginning to end, simply due to under-capitalisation.

1892

At a time when new building and the development of Douglas both on land and seafront, was taking place, it possibly occasioned little surprise that the IOMR station there was also undergoing a transformation. The original site and layout was being abandoned completely, and virtually over the top of portions of it, a new station was arising. The AGM was told that 'the entire of the station's track layout has been reconstructed, and the new signalling and interlocking has been installed'. A useful verandah roof now projected towards the new platforms, cantilevered from the new booking hall building. Every track had been lifted and platforms repositioned, without cessation to the running of trains. The work was a monument to Thomas Silcock, the PW Inspector, who had started work on the Island with Watson & Smith and remained with the IOMR afterwards.* His deputy, John Clague, had also been with the Company since 1873 – their service was typical of the loyal support of almost every employee.

---

*A bad leg eventually caused his retirement in 1894.

The magnificence of the new arrangement, set off with the completion of staircases, walls, railings etc. up the side of Bank Street, certainly put Douglas into a class of its own; it could not be bettered by any other terminus of a narrow gauge railway in these Islands. Lying incongruously alongside (disused) was the wooden station building of 1873 and, in February, it was offered for sale where it stood. Ultimately, the Douglas Recreation Ground committee bought it for a pavilion for £135 and some weeks later, purchased the bookstall for two guineas. The station shop was quickly let, and the shortcomings of the Abyssinian Wells being proved, water was now taken from the river in Taubman's land on the basis of 15 years @ £20 per annum. This was led up into two tanks on top of the new tank house. Nor was this all, for combined with the carriage paint shop, a carpenter's shop arose.†

Early in the year, the possibility of a short branch into Port St Mary village was discussed but did not reach the surveying stage. It was also suggested a station be provided at Belle Vue and if this was satisfactory, another at Quarter Bridge might be built. No action was taken on these three ideas.

Dutton's work on Douglas signals was complete by April but the two distant signals (one on each line) were out of sight, so electrical repeaters were affixed to each and the instruments placed in the handsome new cabin. The Post Office was contracted to install and maintain them. The old double-arm semaphore and open ground frame disappeared.*

During the year, land for a Station Master's house and a goods shed at Castletown was purchased. Richard Gibbins & Co. of Birmingham received an order for an 8 ton 'Travelling Crane' for use at breakdowns and it cost £265. The Government issued instructions in July that all cattle wagons must be whitewashed within.

The IOMSP Co.'s Peel–Belfast daily sailings ran from the 1st July to the 3rd September and brought some useful traffic. Steamer sailings of a competitive kind from the Mona Steam Ship Co. continued to eat into Douglas–Ramsey traffic ... the steamer only charged 2s. 0d. return and the MNR, thinking it was better to join rather than fight them suggested a circular trip involving IOMR and steamer, but the IOMR would not encourage the steamer in any way. The ship carried 200 passengers and, as remarked earlier, frequently overloaded. Those who feared the return journey by sea would cram the last train from Ramsey and the IOMR view was that it was 'taking enough risk already with MNR booking arrangements', a vague term to cover all inadequacies of the MNR real or unreal as seen from Douglas. The hesitation on the part of the IOMR to grant MNR directors a Free Pass over the whole IOMR system still festered, though this had been laid to rest over two years previously.

The most exciting day of the year for the IOMR, was due to a midnight stranding of the IOMSP Co.'s MONA'S ISLE# which ran into a cleft in the rocks off Scarlett Point and held fast. Two ladders were lashed together and enabled the passengers to walk ashore, almost dryshod; this was on 6th September.

---

†Manx Museum: R/105.
*Manx Museum: R/103 Signal diagram.
#MONA'S ISLE III (largest on IOMSP Co. at the time). An iron paddle steamer launched 1882 from Caird & Co. Speed 17½ knots. Twin funnels. Length 338 ft. Beam 38 ft 1 in. Gross Tonnage 1,564. Sold to Admiralty 1915: used as net-layer off west coast of Ireland.

Wood's diary has a nice reference. Some further points from that journal include:

> 1st August: Storm. Belfast steamer could not land at Peel but went to Douglas. (Some entries now have frequently: 'Fine day . . . traffic bad'.)
> 6th August: 600 passengers on Special train Peel to Douglas off Belfast boat.
> 27th August: Special from Foxdale for Douglas Exhibition @ 9d. return. We ran Specials to and from St John's.
> 29th August: Passengers off Workington steamer arriving Ramsey travel to Douglas by MNR/IOMR
> 7th September: MONA'S ISLE on Scarlett Rocks at night; passengers taken to Douglas by Special in morning, coupled to No. 7 train which went out from Douglas empty. Many people went to Castletown to see steamer. Traffic good. Six engines.
> 8th September: Another grand day – passengers rushing to see MONA'S ISLE. Good bookings to Castletown.
> 9th September: Steamer got off. Traffic very quiet.

The March 1892 MNR, AGM was a dismal affair – there was nothing to cheer at all. The Governor was irritating them again, requiring the Company to pay a dividend and so reduce the amount to be found from Government sources. There ensued another period of financial wrangling, one result being that Nelson, wearing too many hats, was relieved of being liquidator of the FR by the Court. Another Bill, to meet the current debts, was left abandoned before it was enacted, it being feared that its result might be worse than before . . . 'better the devil you know'. Resumed financial discussions, involving Col Rich and the auditors, failed to progress the impasse, the auditors making it clear that dividends should not be paid whilst debts stood at such a high figure. Hoping that their (Turquand's) opinion would carry weight, they were pressed by the Board to stress it before the powers-that-be.

Traffic on the line was rather better than 1891 but a new boiler had had to be bought for No. 1 engine and the cost of one for No. 2, due for delivery in the spring of 1893, would have to be met. Depression in the Ramsey building business was given as the reduction in mineral tonnage.

1893

As the '90s progressed, the overall picture of the Island railways was one of the growth of the IOMR against the stagnancy of the other companies: how right were the earliest prognostications as to where the profitable lines would run and how interesting it is to speculate how things might have been had the IOMR had sufficient capital from the beginning to build the Ramsey Line!

Nevertheless, 1893 was to see a hiccough in such developments, for a 22-week strike of cotton operatives and a long summer strike of coal miners hit the very visitors on which the Island relied. Virtually every visitor arrived in Douglas and that town was anxious to retain their custom and prevent its guests from wandering the Island in search of amusement elsewhere. So rapidly was the magnetism of Douglas itself growing that the railways admitted that more people 'were staying in town, and competition from coastal steam boats was stronger than ever'. Both major railway companies feared the threat of new Douglas–Laxey electric railway which would 'be an extra attraction' next year.

The IOMR, true to form, was ready to meet these challenges by aggressive marketing: they owned presently 51 four-wheeled carriages and 12 bogie vehicles which could be made up into 'five moderate trains'. There were seven steam locomotives. The drawback to Port Erin Line services was the existence of Port Soderick – already, the South Line was drawing business away from the Peel Line and management was aware that the short haul up the steep bank from Douglas, only to deposit a proportion of passengers at the first station (i.e. Port Soderick) was not as profitable as it might be. If separate shorter trains could be run between Douglas and Port Soderick, and with the benefit of extra carriages and one more locomotive for that purpose, a new South Line timetable would enable some excessively long trains (with three locomotives) to be taken off. It was the current practice to detach the emptied portion of such trains on arrival at Port Soderick, and return it with the third locomotive to Douglas.

Management calculated that four separate trains would in future be needed for the South Line: the maximum load for one engine was 15 short coaches and double-heading was a frequent practice in high season. Two hours and ten minutes were needed for a train to run to Port Erin and back, including taking water at Port Erin. On return to Douglas, that train must take on coal and water and 'cannot be ready to start again for Port Erin in less than about 2 hr 20 min. from starting its first trip'.

There was much concern about the layout at Port Soderick station and the number of trains using it at busy times, especially the 'turn backs' which appeared twice or more daily: 'there is a very dangerous entrance at the Douglas end of the station . . . we have facing points leading out of the inside of a sharp curve on top of a bridge and high embankment . . . through which we have to send heavy trains consisting of 32 well-filled coaches . . . some improvement at that station is necessary'. In short, management asked for six extra bogie coaches, one bogie composite brake coach and another locomotive so as to be able to run an extra Port Erin train out of Douglas at 10.20 am and 2.40 pm 'to avoid the necessity of running heavy and unwieldy overcrowded trains up the steep incline . . .'.

Things were not so busy on the Peel Line, where management did not think extra trains were necessary. Wood forecast that uncertainty about the 'future of the Ramsey Line . . . would prevent (the Board) . . . from concluding what might be required if the IOMR ultimately became owners of that line'. He added estimates for providing this extra stock.

Prices had fallen below previous purchases and this was a good time to buy, Wood reminded the directors.

[We spent some time demonstrating the forward-looking mood of the IOMR in a year when things had not been at their brightest. How in complete contrast was the position with the MNR still battling with the Government as to whether it should retain its resources and pay off its debts (as the Board thought it should) or 'go under' and pay some sort of dividend at the Government's decree. Little needs to be said of its lackey, the bankrupt Foxdale.]

Let us now see how 1893 progressed for each. The IOMR started in optimism but ended with disappointment. Nonetheless, Wood's enthusiasm for the future gave birth to orders for seven new bogie carriages and a new locomotive by the year's end. The total cost of £1,090 was to be met by an issue of Debenture Stock. These were on top of a new boiler and firebox ordered for No. 2 in February. As the wheelsets on the old carriages were worn out after twenty years of use, replacements were ordered. It was stressed the new Workshops would now cut down the expense of repairs.

Problems with Taubman: the footpath near the Nunnery Bridge and its attendant foot/occupation level crossing were solved. In Douglas station, new cattle pens and a loading bank appeared, plus a new entrance at the foot of Bank Hill. The new Carriage Shed was in use; it had four tracks within it. Castletown also received a loading bank.

It was the policy to provide station staff with uniforms according to their rank (see photograph of original Douglas station,) so the interpretation of a Minute deciding to give Station Masters a uniform might apply to the provincial stations? Clothing was bought by tender from Island suppliers and extreme conservatism was shown in the ordering thereof, year after year.

The Belfast–Peel sailing featured again during the summer; from time to time passengers on the Special Train which met the ship and who were destined for the MNR, failed to alight at St John's and were carried on to Douglas. The IOMR accepted some responsibility for this and compensation payments became a regular feature to those who had spent an unintentioned night in Douglas.

There was an accident at St John's on 9th November with tragic consequences when MNR wagon No. 5, loaded with sand, was being shunted for attachment onto the IOMR train for Douglas. Albert Kelly, the booking clerk in charge of the movement, and substituting for the Station Master who was away, ran in front of the moving wagon and was fatally injured; he died in hospital during an operation. He was but a lad. The wagon brake was faulty and had no effect on the speed of the wagon. He had tried to run round the moving vehicle to use the brake on the other side, but tripped over the rail and fell in the wagon's path. Funeral expenses were paid by the IOMR and there was great sadness in the village.

On 8th December, another accident took place during the shunting movements between IOMR and MNR trains. The TIMES (12th December) said that

> after the 11 am train from Douglas to Peel had reached St John's and as usual had dropped the through Ramsey coaches and brake van to be picked up by the Ramsey engine ... the MNR engine stopped at the tank to take water. The guard of these coaches, to save time, let his carriages run slowly down the incline to meet it ... meanwhile the engine, filled with water, had started for the points with the result

THE PEEL RAILWAY COMPANY, LIMITED.

The Company is Registered under the "Companies' Act, 1883," which limits the liability of the Shareholders to the amount of their Shares.

Provisional Directors:

J. MYLCHREEST, Esq., J.P., Whitehouse, Michael, Member of the House of Keys, *Chairman*.
JOHN JOUGHIN, Esq., Member of the House of Keys, Peel.
E. T. CHRISTIAN, Esq., Peel, Chairman of Town Commissioners.
THOMAS KELLY, Esq., Merchant, Peel.
THOMAS CLAGUE, Esq., Merchant, Peel.
WALTER CANNELL, Esq., Bank Manager, Peel.
JOHN C. LAMOTHE, High-Bailiff, Ramsey.

Solicitors:

Bankers:

ISLE OF MAN BANKING COMPANY, LIMITED, Douglas, and its Insular Branches; and their London Agents, THE LONDON AND WESTMINSTER BANK, Lothbury, London, E.C.

Secretary:

JOHN CAMERON, Railway Station, Ramsey.

Registered Office:

RAILWAY STATION, RAMSEY, ISLE OF MAN.

THE PEEL RAILWAY COMPANY, LIMITED.

ISSUE OF 1,000 ORDINARY SHARES OF £5 EACH.

10s ON APPLICATION, 10s ON ALLOTMENT, AND 4 CALLS OF £1 EACH.

FORM OF APPLICATION FOR SHARES.

To the *Directors* of THE PEEL RAILWAY COMPANY, LIMITED.

GENTLEMEN,

Having paid to the* _____ the sum of £ _____ , being the amount payable on application in respect of _____ Ordinary Shares in the above Company, I have to request that you will place my Name for the same upon the Register of Shareholders in the said Company; and I undertake to accept such Shares, and to pay the same or any less number that may be allotted to me.

Usual Signature _____

Name in full _____

Address in full _____

Profession, Trade, or Occupation (if any) _____

Date _____

N.B. In the event of a less number of Shares being allotted than that applied for, the sum represented by such short number will be immediately returned.

THE PEEL RAILWAY COMPANY, LIMITED.

The following Receipt is held by the *Applicant* as a *Voucher until the Certificates are issued*.

RECEIPT.

ISSUE OF ORDINARY SHARES.

_____ 189

Received from _____ on account of the Peel Railway Company, Limited, the sum of £ _____ , being amount payable on application in respect of _____ Ordinary Shares in the above Company;

_____ Secretary.

that both met midway with a terrible crash. The brake van was shivered into splinters but no harm was done to the rest of the stock. The guard only saved himself by a timely jump and is practically prostrated.

Engine NORTHERN was involved and its buffer beam was smashed.

The IOMR took a different view of the matter, later reporting that they now possessed one less passenger brake van; 'this is the van the MNR's men destroyed for us on 8th December ... gross carelessness'. This demonstrates the current state of feeling between the companies.*

The Douglas signalling was now up-to-date, but what of it elsewhere? Plans were set afoot to improve that at provincial stations but for the time being, the Staff & Ticket system of working the single line was considered to be adequate.

In August Ballasalla yard was altered and the new layout was to remain in this form until after World War II.† Layout changes were also made at Union Mills, and more would follow in 1907.‡

Now to Wood's diary for a more intimate insight on IOMR affairs:

> 26th May: Late train for Ramsey Volunteers – a dead loss.
> 5th July (Tynwald Day): Guard Morrison slipped off van step on last train to Peel and hurt right leg badly.
> 19th July: Peel Church choir to Douglas and back. 27 @ 10d.
> 3rd August: Kermode forgot to mark 7.40 am as Cattle Train (Castletown Cattle Show) – last year it was at Ramsey.
> Bank Holiday Monday: Specials to Port Soderick. Seven in steam.
> 8th August: 10.35 am to Port Erin. 32 coaches + 3 engines to Port Soderick. 11 coaches and engine returned; engine became banker to Crosby. Seven in steam.
> 21st August: (as 8th August).
> 29th August: Too fine a day for the railway. Dublin and other steamers got the people. Port Soderick traffic low. Poor year for railway: the steamers have hit us.

On 25th March, a circular of even date appeared from Ramsey over the names of LaMothe and Cowell, calling for a meeting of the Peel Railway Co. Ltd. at the Peel Castle Hotel in Peel on 5th April next. It drew attention to the fact that the directors and shareholders were now desirous of proceeding with the scheme, based on the earlier survey# of Formans & McColl, and that a return of 5 per cent was guaranteed by the MNR ... LaMothe had been prospecting for coal in the north of the Island 'and its discovery is likely to become an accomplished fact'. Just how that would turn the MNR/Peel venture into profit would appear as baseless as all that had gone before. The meeting was called to appoint a new directorate and was ill-attended, blame being placed on the MNR for by-passing Peel in the first instance, Peel having a population only 100 souls less than Ramsey's (which was 5,000). There would be a triangle of lines at Poortown on the MNR where the Peel Line would branch off; it would terminate near the new Cathedral and Court House at Peel and cost about £5,000. There would be a falling gradient of 1 in 75 from Poortown (Peel Road) westerly, followed by a short level

---

*The van was IOMR No. E1 and the IOMR charged the MNR £41 9s. 2d. for reparation.
†Manx Museum: R/122.
‡Manx Museum: R/4a.
#Manx Museum: R/169 of 1888.

section, another fall of 1 in 100 and then a final level to the terminus which would be on the heights above the old port. With a length of only 1 mile 2 fur. 7 chains there would be only the slightest curves, save on the triangle where 2 chain curves would exist on either chord. Tayleur, the original promoter, had died and it proved impossible to obtain a copy of Forman's original survey from the Trustees so Forman supplied a copy: attempts were made through the MNR Manager Cameron to find a financial supporter, without success.

The MNR's March AGM was given the news about LaMothe's search for coal at Point of Ayre and heady suggestions as to what profits that might bring to the MNR; the meeting was almost obliged to declare a dividend in order to appease the Governor again, even though there was an overdraft of close on £4,800. There followed the familiar farce of attempting to raise money by existing legislation, a proposal to introduce a new Bill for the purpose, and the decision to withdraw it after all. Though through passengers increased again, journeys were down to 176,790 and freight traffic down to 21,053 tons. Train mileage was up at 93,461 and two new goods wagons were added, both built at Ramsey.

1894

Tenders for the supply of IOMR carriages came in early February and turned out to be somewhat different than appeared in Wood's records of the previous autumn. The order went to Metropolitan in March and was for 'seven new long coaches' i.e. three composite 1st & 3rd class, four 3rd class and a brake van to replace that destroyed in the recent St John's accident. That was to cost £141 10s. 0d. and the IOMR Minutes gave the MNR contribution as £45 which was not the figure given by the MNR. On the other hand, E1's wheels and ironwork were to be kept for incorporation into a goods van.

The new engine on order from Beyer, Peacock would become No. 8 and the name was now chosen, FENELLA. A new boiler and firebox for No. 5 was ordered (£408 10s. 0d.)

Other matters noted at the IOMR, AGM was the annual decrease in fish traffic, and the increase in business on the Port Erin Line in contrast to the Peel route. Stations which were still laid in iron rails (the main lines were all now in steel) were almost fully relaid in steel and a new water tank had been erected at Port Erin. Port Soderick station was to be 'improved' at a cost of c.£1,800. The new Carriage Shed at Douglas was extended so that it spanned the river which was ducted beneath it.

The year was not spectacular for the IOMR, yet it may have been the first when momentous problems were not affecting business.

The Belfast–Peel sailings resumed at the end of June and continued to the end of September; the IOMR directors exchanged Free Passes with the MNR following the business brought about by the Belfast steamers.

Flood troubles began on 7th November and the SUN wrote:

> Heavy rain swept away several bridges, two in the grounds of Belle Vue . . . roads and pathways from the Nunnery to Pulrose were impassable and the fourth structure was the railway bridge; soon after 11.30 am the massive central pier* was swept away (30–40 ft long and 10–11 ft wide), completely gone. The bridge itself, [a two-span plate-girder structure of iron] did not suffer. Taubman was summoned and with railway officials declared the bridge unsafe to run trains across. Passengers had to walk across and were then conveyed by another train to Douglas . . .

All this occurred on 7th November, and for some days the shuttle service either side of the bridge continued. Ultimately, new girders of 80 and 85 ft. span would replace the old structure. No sooner had replacement work begun, than Major Taubman was on the warpath complaining that the new bridge was being assembled on his land without permission (and he was the Chairman of the General Purposes Committee!). When the new girders had been positioned (but before the bridge was ready) carriages were propelled from Douglas and pushed over at reduced speed, the engine remaining on the Douglas bank as Greenbank had instructed that no train must come to a complete stand until the bridge was finished. The theory of this arrangement was excellent but in practice it was found that when the engine stabled on the Port Erin side of the river had attached these carriages, it could not haul them up the gradient from a standing start. To overcome this, a second engine was permitted to cross the unfinished bridge from Douglas and thereafter all trains were double-headed to Port Soderick. Even after completion on 15th November, Greenbank imposed a speed restriction on the bridge. [It was Wood's practice always to walk up to the Nunnery Bridge after heavy rain.]†

A lull in the weather was followed by a severe storm which struck on 22nd December, damaging the goods shed roofs in Crosby and St John's; three signal posts were blown down.

The MNR was given a little breathing space and hoped that relations with the Government might improve consequent upon Spencer Walpole's departure and the appointment of Sir West Ridgeway as Governor, but 1894 saw its now familiar impasse over money, whether to pay a dividend it could not afford and offend one party, or withhold the dividend and displease another. The Manager, Cameron, was despatched and interviewed Rich and Turquands in London; a number of directors followed. The Annual Report compromised; there was enough money to pay something but it would not be distributed until outstanding debts were paid. This went some way to make everyone happy, save the shareholders who saw it as a strange financial balancing act (certainly not in an accountancy sense). Passenger figures for 1894 were down to 170,221 journeys, with freight at 21,088 tons; miners' strikes in the mainland had influenced the orders for coal in the Island whilst the IOMMCL had increased its purchasing so as to have c.1,200 tons of coal on hand in case of trouble. This made tonnages over the Foxdale section somewhat variable from year to year, but not so much as to vary the tonnage figures alarmingly.

---

*Actually, that on the Douglas bank of the river.
†See also SRN No. 11 *page 12* (which also states repairs were never fully completed as a decision was made to replace the bridge: no documentary evidence has yet been seen to this effect.)

1895

The year began with extreme weather, and blizzards were to block all railways in the second week of January and first in February. The MNR suffered worst, with a train snowed up for 40 hours at Ballahutchin. Castletown was without mail for four days.

A new electric railway (initially the Douglas & Laxey Coast Electric Tramway Ltd.) opened briefly on 7th September, 1893 as far as Groudle, re-opened to Groudle on 12th May, 1894 and Laxey on 28th July, 1894.* Wood had predicted beforehand how badly this would affect their bookings; however when it came to December 1895 both the Electric and IOMR systems could look back on an excellent season, largely due to more stable conditions on the mainland and therefore more visitors. In fact, the newcomer was unable to cope with the business 'the electric tramcars ... simply unable to carry all the passengers offering for conveyance' and there was already talk of a tramway from Douglas to Kirk Braddan, parallel to the IOMR.† Worse, this might be extended to Peel! Wood wrote ruefully, 'people seem ready to lay down tramways whether they will pay or not'. [From 30th March, 1894 the D&LCETy Ltd. changed its title to the Isle of Man Tramways & Electric Power Co. Ltd.]

The new Parish Church at Kirk Braddan (built in 1876 to replace the historic one rebuilt in 1773) was already exercising the minds of the IOMR to provide a train, although it was to be 1897 before the new church was formally opened; existing outdoor Sunday church services were attracting visitors who walked the 1½ miles each way from Douglas. Though the IOMR Board said 'it would not pay', it was sympathetic to 'a platform ... at small cost' near the church ... 'but the landowner is greedy over cost'. [Open-air church services during the summer were originated in June 1856 by Bishop Powys.]

The Company was less sympathetic to a demand from residents for a stopping place 6½ miles from Douglas about halfway between Crosby and St John's; 'agitation is being got up for a station'. Doubtless these requests came from those who saw how flexibly the tramcars stopped on the new east coast line and expected the IOMR to do likewise.

Crowded trains and tardy running on the IOMR were targets of visitors' complaints. Such weighed against further stopping places as passengers complained there were too many already ... worse, the level crossing site

---

*A summary of east coast proposals (each followed by page reference to Pearson) would be:

January 1874.	Wm Lewis scheme for a Douglas–Ramsey railway seen as an extension off the IOMR Douglas–Peel Line (page 334).
March 1882.	Douglas, Laxey & Ramsey Railway Co. Ltd. Steam-worked (page 334).
1887–9.	Surveys for Douglas, Laxey & Snaefell Railway. Application for Douglas–Laxey section only. Plans dated September 1888. Steam-worked (pages 149 and 335).
1890.	Douglas, Laxey & Maughold Head Marine Drive & Tramway Co. Ltd. (no details motive power). (page 335).
post-1890.	Douglas, Laxey & Dhoon Railway (page 336).
1891.	Manx East Coast Railways (revival of DL&SR of 1887–9). Electric working assumed (pages 134 and 335).
March 1893.	Douglas & Laxey Coast Electric Tramway Co. (construction March 1893 as between Douglas and Groudle Glen) (pages 131 and 133).
November 1893.	Douglas & Laxey Electric Tramway Act 1893 (pages 131–140).

†Pearson (page 342) gives dates 1895–7 and proposals for a horsedrawn tramway along a widened road as far as Kirk Braddan.

chosen for the foregoing request was on a gradient of 1 in 165, an abhorrence to Greenbank. Nonetheless, the IOMR Board was in an unhappy position – if they did not erect extra stopping places they might be at the mercy of the proposed electric tramway scheme to Peel.

Other IOMR matters included the replacement in April of the Nunnery bridge with lattice steel girders, supplied by The Phoenix Foundry Co. for £550. In July, the purchase of 'square sleepers' is noted for the first time in the Minutes though it is presumed that the first steel rails may have been laid on them at an earlier date? Delivered at Douglas, square ones were imported for 2s. 8¾d. each and halfround at 1s. 6d. each.

Sailings between Peel and Belfast had resumed on 29th June and ended on 9th September; special trains were still run if required to connect with late arrivals. The local Harriers'* organisation must have been able to exert some influence on the IOMR for they were granted free travel for a second season 'in cattle trucks only'; but at the year's end passengers were to be given better accommodation than for the previous year . . . seven long bogie carriages and a new locomotive were ordered for the Peel services, following Wood's October Report to the General Purposes Committee – his annual duty at the end of the summer season. For £415, No. 7 would be fitted with a new boiler and firebox from Beyer, Peacock. Port Soderick station was to be taken in hand and James Cowle was to design a building for it at a cost of £1,054 – even then, there was no house for the Station Master.

A further word about Port Soderick whose business was due to heavy advertising by the IOMR. The existing siding was inadequate for a quick turnround of short Douglas to Port Soderick workings, and the layout was improved by the installation of a loop in 1894–6. The need for this improvement was accelerated by the incorporation of the Douglas Southern Electric Tramways Ltd. on 21st October, which was to build and operate a tramway from Douglas Head to a point above the cliffs at Port Soderick; up until this time, the Port had only been accessible by a road leading from the station, giving the IOMR the monopoly of the traffic (the Tramway was opened on 16th July, 1896).#

By far the most important event on the Island this year, was the opening of a Fell centre-railed 3 ft 6 in. gauge electric railway from the Douglas & Laxey system at Laxey to the summit of Snaefell which, at 2,036 ft, is the highest mountain on the Island. Although not competing directly with the steam railway enterprises, it drew visitors to another competitive attraction. A private group, The Snaefell Mountain Railway Association had obvious personal links with the MNR; the Association commenced building the line in early 1895 and progress was rapid enough to allow an opening on 21st August the same year.†

To facilitate construction, the Association hired MNR No. 4 CALEDONIA @ £20 per week; it was shipped from Ramsey in the PORPOISE and used by dint of laying a temporary third rail; the raised central Fell Rail was not, of course, in place at this period. Two open wagons from the same source came with the engine.‡ (Further details Volume III). In this regard, the use of a

---

*Isle of Man Harriers formed 1868: a cycle race against a Douglas–Peel train took place – the train lost. Joint meetings with horse races at Braddan Race Course.
#The long and complex gestation period of this undertaking is given in Pearson (page 306-on).
†Pearson (pages 149, 151, 157).
‡Pearson (page 154).

steam locomotive pre-dated the extension of the electric railway from Laxey to Ramsey when no less than three locomotives, each from a different source, were in use. Cameron of the MNR was to act as Consultant to the Snaefell concern and later, the aforementioned Ramsey extension.

Not all, but most of what has been said about 1895 pre-dated Wood's Annual Report to the General Purposes Committee; this reveals more about IOMR affairs and the personality of the man than any other records (his diaries for this period have not survived). As each season ended, he cast bread upon the waters to tempt the Committee into consideration of the following year. He began by seeking ways of improving winter traffic returns but did not enlarge on this. For the IOMR, the season had shown a 6 per cent rise on 1894 traffic and this was better than any year (except 1887/8) when different companies competing for the Island's steamer business had brought sea fares down to a level when the country was overrun with visitors. The current visitor figure was c.26,000 for 1895, but the IOMR had not had its fair share of that increase due 'to a new mode of travel', namely the electric railway. There were more road conveyances and extra steamers now sailed round the Island and across to opposite shores of Wales, Scotland and Ireland. The opening of the Snaefell Line would be more injurious too, as would the extension of the electric railway to Ramsey. If the IOMR's trade had been affected, how much more so had been that of the MNR – it was shocking that there were directors of the MNR amongst the promoters to extend the Laxey Line to Ramsey . . . the season had shown that 743 less passengers had booked Douglas–Ramsey (thus were Wood's comments).

Wood conjectured that one answer would be to improve the Peel Line service; if seven carriages and another engine were bought (approximate cost £4,114), Peel could enjoy in 1896 the same increased services which Port Erin had had in 1895. The original short 1st class carriages were, due to their age, being demoted to 3rd class . . . 'our new Firsts are much superior'. He recommended the purchase of four bogie carriages having six compartments, the inner four being 1st class, two 3rd class six compartment and one 3rd composite with guard's brake/luggage compartment, seven vehicles in all. An engine from Beyer, Peacock would cost £1,130 (last time £1,090). [That Wood succeeded in his plea for this stock has already been noted.]

Now to affairs on the MNR during the year. As mentioned, the blizzards of the early year hit the railway very hard; the employees were only too familiar with those sections of line where snow blockages would occur and wires would be down. There was no precursor to the snowstorm on 5th February however, when over the whole Island, three trains were stranded. During the following night the drifts built up to heights of 20 feet: three MNR engines were stuck in the Ramsey yard. They were released with difficulty, and with snow intermittent, and under the personal drive of Cameron, sometimes fifty men time and again showed their ability to keep the north line fitfully open. Their efforts became a byword. As to those who braved the risks of making a rail journey, it was found better that they should travel in covered goods vans rather than in the carriages which with their low footboards were more vulnerable to damage. Services did not begin to recover until the middle of February. Very properly, Chairman LaMothe at the MNR, AGM on 15th March, gave high praise to his Manager for his courage and leadership during the exceptional weather of the previous month.

Further financial juggling, in association with the Governor, Sir John West Ridgeway, brought a pitiful monetary benefit to the MNR, but it was a close-run thing, being accomplished on the eve of his posting to Ceylon; consequently the wooing of yet another Governor (Lord Henniker)* had to begin from 24th January, 1896 when on that same day, the MNR followed the conventional railway custom of providing a Special Train for His Excellency. Every penny saved was vital to the MNR; the 1895 season had been pretty disastrous. Passengers were well down and freight tonnages had fallen. The summer was poor and the counter-attractions of coastal steamers and novel electric railways kept visitors off the steam railways.

As to the Foxdale Railway, its future was to be assisted by the Railway Regulation Act which was passed in May 1896, but which had started its painful journey as a Bill before the Council in January of 1895 to allow the FR to be sold. Attempts were made to widen the powers of the Act to allow freedom of buying and selling of railway undertakings but in the event, the selling of such was restricted to any company in liquidation only.

In the last month, the ghost of the Peel Branch Railway re-appeared in different form when C.B. Nelson† (a man of many hats and now prominent among the east coast electric railway faction) applied to the Highway Board for leave to build a tramway on the Poortown Road from the MNR station into Peel. The last documentation is dated October 1897.

In the latter years of the century, the Ramsey Steamship Co. operated two steamers (LANCELOT and FAIRY QUEEN) making two return trips Douglas–Ramsey daily, calling in at Laxey and Dhoon Glen.

1896

At New Year a deputation called on the IOMR management to ask for a station at Ballacurry to serve the Greeba district. It will be recalled that Ballacurry was the intended junction for a Branch to Foxdale, proposed in 1882. Stations were also under consideration at Kirk Braddan (see previous year) and Quarter Bridge. At Greeba, the profitability of a stop there 'depended on the deepening of the Corvalley Mines' (Ref: 298796) rather than passengers and the matter of Braddan was still one of obtaining the necessary land at a sensible price. Eventually the Greeba scheme was dropped, the English Board of Trade making a decision for the IOMR (for which they hardly disguised their thanks) on the score that the gradient was objectionable and they would require to have the line doubled at this section. Farmers who wanted a siding there were turned down. It proved impossible to buy land at Quarter Bridge and so it was left ultimately, for Kirk Braddan to have a stopping place.

---

*Lord Henniker. (Henniker-Major) 5th Baron Henniker: succeeded to title in 1870 and was four times a Lord-in-Waiting to Queen Victoria. Died 1902.
†Charles Banks Nelson, Manx Advocate.

Port Erin and Port St Mary stations were reviewed; at the former the original stone building was inadequate and it was decided this year to demolish it, but a replacement building in brick was not ready until 1904, so demolition could hardly have begun at once. Port St Mary's wooden shed with corrugated iron roof was to go and be replaced by a handsome red brick structure (of similar parentage to that at Douglas) and would also receive a passenger platform and goods shed. The old station at Port Soderick was demolished as the new one, with licensed refreshment room, was under construction. It was ready in March.* A platform would be provided on the Down side, flagged with stone from Hipperholme, Yorkshire. The AGM was told it had cost £1,100 but that it was 'not a very beautiful or ornate structure'.

To improve the image, c.1,400 trees were planted at IOMR stations and many remain today to enhance the scene. In March the big sandpit behind the Foxdale Railway station at St John's closed; this was one of many occasions when the fitful working of such places experienced a temporary closure.

In April a further locomotive was ordered from Beyer, Peacock to be called DOUGLAS, No. 9, and in the late year two large bogie luggage vans were delivered from Metropolitan, especially for dealing with the 'Passengers Luggage in Advance' scheme (currently the Railway was handling 150–200 'boxes' per day and the vans could be used as lock-up warehouses to store goods 'on arrival from the Packet' until sent forward).

The IOMSP Co. operated the summer Peel–Belfast service again and Free Passes were issued by the IOMR between Douglas and St John's (only) to The Mona Steamship Co. When the season ended, management's attention was drawn to 'irregularities in working Castletown Loop' which proved to be a labour-saving system whereby the Station Master allowed trains to use whichever side of the passing loop suited his ends ... his attention was drawn to management's disapproval!

The Douglas Southern Electric Tramways# line had opened on 7th August and, as anticipated, much traffic was lost to the IOMR which had upgraded its Port Soderick station in readiness. The TIMES for 6th June reported on the new station:

> ... the new building has 120 ft frontage and is 32 ft high. There are two storeys, the upper one supply a residence for the Station Master ... also a new approach road from the glen ... special sanitary arrangements have been made ... a retaining wall 120 ft long, 12 ft high and 6 ft thick had to be built at the back to keep the high land from slipping ... the Station Master's house is entirely separate from the station, the entrance being at the back on the high land ... trees have been planted by Messrs. Fell & Co. of Hexham ... James Cowle is designer and builder of the station which is erected of rubble stone from the Howe Quarries.†

There were changes on the IOMR Board when Sir John Pender died on 7th July, 1896:‡ he had been associated with the IOMR from the first and provided for its early financial needs. He was replaced by Sir J.S. Goldie-

---

*Manx Museum: Drawing R/119.

#Pearson: Chapter 12.

†Whilst an operative building of the IOMR, the station had no mains water or electricity.

‡The worthiness accorded to any deceased member of the IOMR organisation was reflected in the amount spent on a wreath.

Taubman as Chairman and the vacancy was filled by Thomas Fisher of Castletown ... the Board was now moving visibly towards its Island base.

At the IOMR, AGM, certain shareholders condemned the 3rd class carriages; they had bare seats 'and cushions were needed'. Another voice 'strongly advised the directors to take into consideration the wisdom of altering catches on carriage doors which were productive of much swearing'. Earlier complaints about winter travel were reduced by buying second-hand footwarmers from mainland railway companies which had installed carriage heating. (The continued purchase of the same into post-World War I times created much correspondence from the Manager to English companies; management rather prided itself on bargain purchases in this regard.)

At Crosby, the loop was lengthened but heavy alterations were deferred until September 1907 when a new building was put up on the original goods shed site, the yard enlarged and the whole layout moved towards the south.* It was necessary to build a new culvert beneath these extensions; 'hitherto there has been great risk and delay here'.

The 1895 MNR passenger figures showed a decrease (170,221) with an increase to 21,088 tons of freight. Train mileage was 92,619 but of course the clearance of snow in the first part of the year had added to actual non-profitable mileage. Overall, it had been a better year but there was a sense of foreboding as the electric railway would sooner, rather than later, enter the streets of Ramsey. In this respect it is of passing interest to find that Fell was again involved in the promotion – perhaps the last steam railway envisaged for the Island? – for a Laxey to Ramsey rail link ... not in fact, an extension of the existing railway.†

1897

The land having been purchased at a reasonable price, a small 'platform' (ground level) was put up at Braddan Bridge, virtually for the exclusive use of the Sunday Church services. The National Telephone Co. was given permission to erect poles alongside the Port Erin Line. Deliberations on the type of bricks to be used in the new Port St Mary station caused some reversed decisions; at first it was to be of red bricks from North Wales, but this was altered to grey bricks from Glenfaba, Peel.‡ In the event, red bricks (possibly from Acrefair?) won the day and the Peel bricks were confined to the interior. James Costain was to build.

'The new Foxdale station at St John's' was contemplated this year for through traffic and a proposed fast train service between Douglas and Ramsey to meet the challenge of the new electric railway; authority for the work was found in an Agreement between the Foxdale Railway (then in voluntary liquidation) and the IOMR dated 27th December, 1895. The cost was £248 14s. 4d. with half being paid by each company. Despite its grandiose title, it was merely to be a ground-level platform sited immediately east of the Foxdale Line's junction with, and north of, the

---

*Manx Museum: Drawing R/120.
†Pearson: *page 336.*
‡appears in 1894 as Glenfaba Brick Co. (Rates Book). Bricks made here since 1866.

MNR. In consequence, the 'temporary' stopping place (used since 1881) on the west side of the road crossing would then be abandoned, and allow the MNR to discontinue the extra stop at their own St John's station, a procedure which, for certain Ramsey-bound trains, had meant setting back into the Foxdale Branch station to attach wagons/coach bound for Ramsey. It would be beneficial to westbound trains which, whilst standing at the 'temporary' station, were blocking the level crossing. [This new 'platform', actually constructed by the MNR after a haggle with the IOMR who claimed to be the owners of the land – but were not – opened in July the following year. It was almost immediately found to be too short! It was destined to have a brief life and was closed in 1905 when the MNR ceased to operate as a separate undertaking. In 1925, it was cleared to make way for a siding and turntable. It appears that the Foxdale Line station closed in deference to the new platform which was then used by both MNR and FR workings, the latter having to reverse direction at the junction.]

The effect of the new platform would herald not the introduction of one through single coach between Ramsey and Douglas but whole rakes of MNR sixwheelers. When the Douglas-bound portion of the MNR train arrived at St John's, its engine would run ahead and reverse out of the way: the IOMR Peel–Douglas train, which had arrived earlier in St John's, would then back down onto the MNR carriages, couple up and proceed to Douglas. In this wise the procedure of train marshalling at Douglas was born. The west-bound train would be made up of two rakes, the heading one for Peel and the hinder one for Ramsey. At St John's they would be divided, the Peel portion would run ahead and another engine be attached to the Ramsey portion which was left behind. Thus a ghost of the former companies persisted until the end of that railway system. To eliminate confusion by passengers, destination boards with a scarlet background were hung on the horizontal handrails of the luggage vans attached to each set (whilst standing at Douglas).

The electric railway on the east coast was creeping inexorably northwards towards Ramsey (the completed section would open to the public on 24th July, 1899) and 'opposition was now of a most formidable character' wrote the newspaper, which seems rather pointless now that the horse had bolted! The IOMR especially, was fearful of the personalities common to both The Isle of Man Tramways & Electric Power Co. Ltd. and the MNR, and that the former might make a bid for the latter and make a rail link between the two termini in Ramsey. From that stage, anything might happen and the nightmare to the IOMR Board was the spectre of the electrification of the MNR from Ramsey to St John's and worse, of an electric railway parallel to their own between St John's and Douglas – physically, such developments were quite possible. Once in Douglas, connection with the horse tramway could be made and, if electrified, the nightmare system would re-join its point of departure at Derby Castle at the north end of Douglas promenade.

The spectre of such brought the IOMR to conclude that only a more efficient service would answer and Greenbank was called over to survey and cost for doubling the line between Douglas and Peel. This instruction was extended to the whole system, but when he reported that Douglas to

Port Soderick *alone* would cost £16,000, 'of course, this puts it entirely out of our power'.

Some of this anxiety is reflected in a letter of December from Rixon to Wood. Rixon deplored the loss of Sir John Pender as 'being a lion of a leader' and added his own fears about the possible sale of the MNR to the electric undertaking. He fears that Bruce (Chairman of Dumbell's Banking Co.) may have made private deals with MNR shareholders in order to give him control of the MNR, and wishes it could be contrived to obtain a list of MNR shareholders without alerting Cameron to what was in the wind. Rixon makes the extraordinary suggestion of 'laying down an electrical plant for the Peel and Ramsey . . . it would be a good thing . . . it would involve a double line but better that than be crushed without a fight.' He continues that Bruce is rumoured to be contemplating an electric line between Upper Douglas and Glen Helen, Rixon being put in mind of it by the poor Glen Helen results for the previous year which he thinks could have been improved by a railway link. He thinks the attempt to build such a project by Bruce, would be one of his 'most likely lines of attack'. [Rixon admits that he prefers to take a belligerent role in all such circumstances, rather than to hang back and await developments. (He suffered from constant gout which may have made him aggressive.)]

The Peel–Belfast sailings resumed in high summer and The Mona Steamship Circular Tour, begun in 1896, was repeated again. Among the peripheral personalities linked with the IOMR were a number of Licensed Porters; besides those at Douglas, two were attached to Port Erin station. These porters would meet passengers off the boat at Douglas and found plenty of customers due to the amount of luggage brought over in those times. The porter would load baggage etc. on a handcart, and make certain the owner had noted his licensed number shown on an enamelled plate affixed by leather strap to his arm. He could be trusted to ensure that baggage was stowed in the correct luggage van and would then confer with his employer at the door of the compartment. (Like other visitors, our own family used the same porter every year and formed a useful rapport with him.) Such was the growth in business that in this year, Port Erin porters were made up to four; their engagement was subject to meeting train arrivals only, and being subject to the orders of the Station Master. At Douglas, luggage porters worked independently of railway-based instructions.

The issue of Free Passes was strictly limited and the facility quickly withdrawn at times when relations between parties were fraught . . . needless to add, it all depended on whom you were, and the IOMR Chairman's Huntsman and the District Nurse were among the favoured.

A keen-eyed newspaper reader noticed that the IOMR timetables read:

```
Douglas to Port Erin ...............Up trains
Port Erin to Douglas ...............Down trains
Douglas to Ramsey .................Down trains
Ramsey to Douglas .................Up trains
```

He wrote to the SUN and asked why one line differed from another: the answer remained a mystery.

The attractions of the newly opened tramway from Douglas Head to Port Soderick were all-compelling and Wood calculated that in the season the IOMR bookings were down by £510 10s. 0d. from this cause.

For the MNR, 1897 was to prove an even more unhappy year. Only eight shareholders attended the AGM on 19th March; ordinary passenger journeys were down by over 11,000 but 3,724 school excursionists had been included in this figure; tonnages were down to 19,659 and train mileages less than 97,962; it was decline in every quarter and not surprisingly, most noticeable in the number of through bookings Ramsey–Douglas. The Annual Report reflected the Chairman's warning that considerable renewals of track and rolling stock were now needed after twenty years of usage; as on most railways there were stretches of low lying line where drainage was slow and this applied especially along the Sulby River length which was subject to flooding. Not only did sleepers suffer but mud etc. in the ballast made that ineffective also.

1898

The year 1898 began with the alarming news for the IOMR that the IOMT&EPC Ltd. (operating the electric railway, Douglas to Ramsey) was negotiating to purchase the MNR. This sent the IOMR Chairman (Sir John Goldie-Taubman) hotfoot to see the Governor. There is no denying that he was an excellent advocate for the Company and, after some cunning discussions with all interested parties and not a little diplomacy, it was agreed that the IOMR should also put itself forward as a bidder, and the MNR was asked to place a value on its undertaking to that end. [In discussions it was revealed that it was the MNR which was trying to sell itself and not the reverse; the IOMR remonstrated with the MNR complaining that the latter should have offered itself for sale on the open market.] On 3rd February, the MNR tendered itself to the IOMR for £72,500, an answer being required before the month end. Documents involved in the proposed deal confirmed that the electric railway *was* ready to electrify the MNR and build a tramway from Douglas to St John's, so supporting the IOMR's earlier fears.* It was still being put about that the electric railway was the prime mover and a brief newspaper announcement in February showed the strength of that rumour saying 'The Electric Railway have withdrawn their offer for the Ramsey Line'.

Captain Richard Penketh died on 24th February, 1898 having been on the IOMR Board since March 1877.

We may turn to actual events and not intentions: on the IOMR Port St Mary station (with platform) was building throughout the year, the work being delayed three months. It would cost of £1,677 2s. 10d. There was urgent need for a goods shed here for as soon as the station was sufficiently ready, commodities were stored in the waiting rooms so that there was little space for persons. At Crosby, the extended layout was not ready until the autumn.

---

*Pearson: *pages 176–7.*

On 5th July, the Peel–Belfast steamer resumed.

The IOMR could no longer resist an outcry for a degree of comfort in its spartan 3rd class compartments and cushions would be provided. G.D. Peters & Co. was given an order for 100 cushions but when they supplied a further 300 in November, they had raised the price from 27/- to 35/- each.

It was put forward that smarter running on the Peel Line, which might lessen competition from the coast railway, could be achieved if 'Electric Train Tablet apparatus at some stations' was installed. The idea would require an Agreement with the Post Office over the supply of poles and wires, but this was not forthcoming. 'An alternative and more favourable arrangement with the National Telephone Company might be found'.

Wood was now nervous about the intended extension of the Douglas boundary which, if carried out, would embrace some of the furthermost buildings at the station, importantly the Carriage Shed and Workshops which would have rateable values placed on them instead of being free from the charge as at present.

On 18th August, a train entering Castletown loop was derailed as the points had not been closed properly – it was the duty of the Station Master to ensure that point blades had been fully moved – so passengers had to use road vehicles for the remainder of the day. The impact of a carriage falling off the track dislodged a roof lamp which fell on a passenger who successfully claimed £1 2s. 0d. for a new pair of trousers.

In the autumn tenders were submitted as below:

	Metropolitan RC & WL	Brown Marshalls & CL	Birmingham RC & WL	Ashbury RC & IL	Oldbury RC & WL
8 box wagons	£58 5s. 0d.	£62 5s. 0d.	£64 0s. 0d.	£66 10s. 0d.	£73 0s. 0d.
2 cattle wagons	£72 0s. 0d.	£77 15s. 0d.	£83 0s. 0d.	£82 0s. 0d.	£90 10s. 0d.
2 covered wagons	£73 15s. 0d.	£78 10s. 0d.	£79 0s. 0d.	£86 10s. 0d.	£91 10s. 0d.

the order going to Metropolitan.

With help from the Insular Government the IOMR arranged for the Postmaster General to remove the Single Needle Telegraph instruments in November and the telephone took their place. Free Passes were exchanged with the IOMT&EPCL; some influence must have been brought to bear when the Royal Society for Prevention of Cruelty to Animals was given a *First Class* Pass.

Though passenger traffic was feeling the competition, the freight side of the business was holding up and the end-of-season Report wrote of large tonnages in bricks, cement, stone and sand ... though admittedly some of this was to build Port St Mary station.

Sir John Stenhouse Goldie-Taubman, a man of many roles besides being Chairman of the IOMR (and Speaker of the House of Keys) died on 9th November, 1898 and at the March 1899 AGM, Dalrymple Maitland and W.A. Hutchinson were appointed to the Board.

This was a turning point of greater significance than it first appears. Dating back to the first promotion of the Company and the shortage of funds which limited its progress, it had always been hoped that finance might be found within the Island and direction of the Railway Company might remain a Manx affair. The necessity to bring in 'outsiders' brought to the Board a mixture of Manx and London interests and complications, and did not always lead to harmonious relations. By the end of the 1890s this irritant had been rectified.

The year began badly for the MNR: on 13th February, the Chairman LaMothe died and William Todhunter* became Acting Chairman. It was an unfortunate time with negotiations for sale on hand and as February passed into March it was clear the IOMR was not going to make a purchase.

Another nail to add to the coffin of the MNR was the announcement in the Annual Report for 1897 that Cameron, who had been with them since the start, and Secretary & Manager since 1880, would be leaving to take up the post of Manager on the new Blackpool & Fleetwood Tramroad Co.† (opened July 1898). [He had, in fact, been permitted on occasions during 1897 to leave the Island to monitor the building of that line.]

On 24th February, Cameron's own choice to succeed him was named as George John Fleming of Belfast, who had at one time been a partner in Brebner & Fleming who subcontracted part of the MNR construction, and thus again underlined the personal alliances of this strongly Scottish support. It is recalled that when Cameron left for the Fylde, a number of men went with him, (not all from the MNR); his leadership was thus underlined.

The COURIER of 4th March recorded the presentations made to Cameron, and his initial appointment to oversee the building of the western portion of the MNR at the age of 19½. No opportunity was lost to advertise the suppliers of the gifts '. . . tea service supplied by V.C. Joughlin of Parliament Street,'‡ etc. '. . . smart waitresses and the dinner altogether reflect the highest credit on Miss Sutcliffe's management'.

Fleming and family sailed in from Belfast on 13th March and conferred with Cameron who had come over from England for the handover. So Sunday passed. On Monday, Fleming's wife could not rouse him; he had died following a heart attack. It was as if the MNR misfortunes had no end. Todhunter had completed his caretaker task in the MNR Chair and C.B. Nelson had taken it at the MNR, AGM on 11th March (i.e. before the abovementioned event) so Nelson was obliged to send for Cameron's return to assist him in finding another appointee. On 31st March David McDowall became Fleming's successor. A Caledonian Railway employee, he was contacted through Charles Forman (Formans & McCall) and was able to take up his duties on 12th April.

The MNR Agreement with the IOMMCL including transport charges was due to end and it was left to the new Manager to arrange its successor. The Mining Co., captive in the matters of railway transport, set out to bluff the Railway Co. by threatening to use steam traction engines and trailers instead. In the end, agreement on price was attained.

The Island Railway Companies and Steam Packet Co. came together to entertain a Conference of Railway Clearing House Superintendents and

---

*Merchant & iron-founder of Douglas.
†Incorporated by Special Act 1896: purchased by the Corporation of Blackpool on 31st December, 1919.
‡Parliament Street, Liverpool.

Goods Managers in Douglas during early July, and combined Free Passes were provided for the pleasure of delegates.

Traffic figures for the MNR were again dismal; all figures showed a fall in numbers and the effect of electric railway competition heralded worse to come.

1899

The first important landmark for the IOMR was the March AGM: shareholders were told that £300 had been put aside for a goods shed at Port St Mary, and such had begun. Plans were to be prepared for survey of a branch from Peel to Dalby, and though these were overdrawn on the One Inch to One Mile Ordnance Survey map, they were pigeonholed at that stage.* Peel traffic was good as the Peel–Belfast ship was bringing business. As the year wore on, inroads made by the electric railway continued but such was the increasing popularity of the Island that the IOMR's traffic improved despite them.

An excellent publicity booklet was put out by the IOMR, BEAUTY SPOTS OF MANXLAND, and showed generosity of treatment to its competitors; for instance to the MNR; 'parties can be set down near the caves at Gob-y-Deigan by giving notice to Station Masters . . . (parties) can romp about and enjoy themselves'. Due to a number of accidents to children falling out of doors whilst investigating their curious locks, a long-term plan would replace the originals with 'Matthew's Patent Door Catches'.

The gatekeeper's hut at Four Roads was of typical 1873 form found elsewhere on the IOMR, a small stone hut with wooden door, window(s) and fireplace, stoutly built but very basic. For £205 it was agreed to build a proper cottage there. (The 1873 building still stands in 1992, as does the cottage, re-roofed, and now a private dwelling.)

Wood had heard of a 'new type of carriage now being used in Jersey' and would investigate. He was to enquire about lighting carriages by electricity and one may ask how many of these ideas would have been so urgently prosecuted if competition from the east coast line was not forcing the pace?

The year was also a landmark within the Douglas offices when the first typewriter was acquired. Towards the year's end the shortcomings of Castletown became acute and to keep commodities out of the weather and secure, a goods shed was to be built. (Up to this time there had been sufficient accommodation within the stations themselves for goods storage but quantities had grown and goods sheds were urgently needed at many stations.)

Alongside Douglas station, on the southern edge, neighbours Quiggin & Co., ('The Isle of Man Ropery') built a six foot dividing wall which still stands.

Surprisingly, the IOMR bought 5,000 half-round sleepers from a regular London supplier, Burt, Boulton & Haywood. In April, the Port Erin

---

*Manx Museum: R/168/1–2.

Commissioners made a curious complaint concerning the noise made by the night-time water pump, used by the overnight cleaner when filling the water tank which supplied the locomotives; legal steps were threatened but the Board ignored the warning saying 'this had been taking place for the last 24 years without complaint'.

Improved arrangements were made for luggage coming off the train at Douglas and destined for the steamer. For an extra charge of 2½d. for cabin trunks, portmanteaux, etc. and 1d. for small items, they would be brought onto the deck and placed with their owners.

St John's was the scene of a collision on 6th July, when a train bound for Peel overran the station and made sidelong contact with a Peel to Douglas train which had stopped there without fully clearing the points at the west end. The Government Enquiry revealed some idea of the composition of the trains involved; Douglas–Peel, 17 carriages + brake van; Peel–Douglas, 18 carriages + brake van. Both enginemen were fined 10s. 0d. each (i.e. about 30 per cent of their weekly wage).

Throughout the year, the IOMR was under pressure from the MNR to reduce its Ramsey fares; the MNR considered the electric railway was doing everything to bring it to its knees. As such requests from the MNR had been a regular feature for the whole of its existence, the IOMR gave their familiar answer, 'No'. To maintain a stranglehold, the electric system lowered its fares again in July (not for the first time) and the steam railways were forced to answer by doing the same. It was obvious this was ruinous to all.

It was a wonderful year for weather, thus accounting for the higher traffic figures of the IOMR. Fire appeared, of two varieties; a controlled version when Peel station became lit by gas, and an uncontrolled version as fields and haystacks were set ablaze by hot cinders from engine chimneys. Recompense was expensive!*

Wood's diary is on hand for 1899; this time there are a few phrases which crop up frequently, such as 'too much wind ... no visitors about ... gloomy ... dead loss ... did no good ... Friday is a bad day for Tynwald Fair Traffic ...' All these refer to Special Workings which turned out to be unprofitable. This second series of diaries gives most detail at the Bank Holiday periods. One such in November is Hollantide (originally the Fair Day when farm labourers were hired for the ensuing year†) and is a Manx Bank Holiday.

> 13th November: (Hollantide) Extra trains.
> Christmas: Gas Works accident affected our receipts.
> New Year's Eve: This was the best year in the history of the Company; trains often sent out in duplicate.

Finally, there is almost a memo to himself, 'signal in rear means Train Following – "I am on Ticket" '‡

The MNR, AGM took place on 16th March when the concern of the meeting was the low income per train mile; the IOMR was said to be twice their own. Now, the MNR had always prided itself on low running costs

---

*The Peel event must have been a re-conditioning of the existing system.

†held in the Adelphi Hotel yard, Douglas.

‡This refers to the operating practice of hanging some form of signal on the rear of the last vehicle of a preceding train if another is to follow in the same direction; the practice may stem from this period and be the consequence of having to run trains in duplicate, as Wood mentions.

compared with similar lines, but if trains were running without a paying load of passengers, such statistics were useless. The meeting was reminded of the age of all the equipment and fended off criticism of the antique and filthy carriages. During 1899, passenger figures would be down to 159,542 journeys with an extra 3,205 carried on school excursions: freight was up to 23,959 tons and train mileage was up at 102,331.

McDowall gave an interview to THE RAILWAY MAGAZINE which appeared in July thus putting the MNR to the forefront of notice in those times. The article gives some misleading figures but is notable for the publicity given to a small company. Other narrow gauge concerns covered at this time were the Cork & Muskerry, Corris, Snowdon Mountain, Clogher Valley and Festiniog Railways.

The new MNR manager showed his motivation in the form of the new broom sweeping clean – pots of shrubs, tubs and face-lifts through new paint were included in a well-meaning cosmetic exercise. This does not suggest that such coats of paint hid the defects. Even some of the 3rd class now had cushions ... but then, the IOMR was doing the same against a common 'enemy'.

The Island is notorious for its strong winds and on 3rd November a typical mixed train (brake van, three six-wheeled coaches, open wagon and goods van) was hit by a ferocious gust which derailed two coaches and blew the vulnerable van at the tail onto its side at Ellanbane just outside Ramsey. For a time, trains were worked either side of the fallen. The newspapers were in praise for the alacrity in which the half-dozen passengers were taken forward to Ramsey on the engine ... there would be little room on that footplate!

To feel the pulse of the Manx railway companies, it is essential to read the private letters which, in the case of the IOMR, were exchanged between Wood, Greenbank and Rixon who shared many confidences. For instance, in the matter of promotion on the Board ...

In January, W.B. Stevenson made it known that he thought HE ought to be made Chairman at the AGM in March as he was then the longest-serving director and held the largest stake in the Company. His friends were recommending him to resign his seat if not elected and unfortunately John Denison Pender did not particularly want the Chair. Wood being the man he was, had persuaded Maitland to join the Board in Taubman's place the month before the AGM; P.V. Luke, a London director, was to be asked if he would accept the Chair as Pender was apathetic about it, but by some mischance, the invitation was never sent ... In the same exchange of letters between Rixon and Wood, their anxiety to promote Hutchinson in opposition to Sir John Goldie-Taubman, is clearly illustrated. With the AGM approaching, the pair was intent to enact the king-making themselves, present a firm proposition to the shareholders and underline that 'local shareholders ... preferred Hutchinson'. During the correspondence Goldie-Taubman obligingly died in the November, and they had the satisfaction of seeing Hutchinson duly elected to the Board at the 1889 AGM.

Wood looked upon Nelson of the MNR as a cunning operator. In April, word got about that 'Nelson of Ramsey is promoting an amalgamation' of the

MNR with the other two railways, 'and is creating ill-feeling amongst the tradespeople of the Island'. Nelson, being a director of Dumbell's Bank, caused Wood to write, 'What effect will this have if customers remove their accounts from Dumbell's?' Wood is careful to explain to Rixon that he does not want to be personally involved in the foregoing, 'and take the blame if wrong'.

During November it was common knowledge to the General Purposes Committee that there were doubts about the financial soundness of Dumbell's Banking Co. and the credit standing to the IOMR was reduced accordingly.

Way back in 1891, the IOMR Board had debated whether to buy the buildings (property of Quiggin & Co.) which lay at the foot of Bank Hill. If another buyer was to purchase, the Railway might be cut off from access to the North Quay, but if the IOMR was to buy and demolish it, 'then if ever a tramway is extended to the station a portion would be needed'. Quiggin had attempted to sell for £4,000 in 1891 but could not get that figure; in January 1899 this old warehouse was put up again at that price, and in May the IOMR bought and demolished it.

1900

The new century did nothing for the Isle of Man, rather the reverse. It had been rumoured in November 1899 that affairs at Dumbell's Banking Co. Ltd. (established 1874) were not all they should be and on Saturday 3rd February at 10 am came the shattering news of its failure. 'The entire Manx community has been taken by surprise ... it has brought ruin to tradespeople and a very large number of others in the Island, and completely paralysed every description of business'.* The immediate cause was the calling-in of a loan from Parr's Bank on 1st February. This disaster has already been chronicled elsewhere† and was to affect Manx business for more than one succeeding generation. Fortunately for the IOMR, the loss was a mere £30! The IOMR&EP Co., its business completely interwoven with that Bank,‡ dismissed 100 quarry workers (at the Dhoon Quarry) on the same day. The affair bankrupted the IOMT&EP Co. which had been operating some suspicious accountancy practices.

The intention to rebuild Castletown station and provide a goods shed, taken the previous year, was deferred – costs were too high, but £104 3s. 3d. was spent on further second-hand footwarmers and new cushions.

The dangers of having raised platforms at some stations and not at others was emphasised when a woman fell from the train at Port Soderick (where a

---

*The Author knew several families of respectable upbringing, who were still living on meagre incomes thirty years later and displaying a noble front to the world.
†THE DUMBELL AFFAIR (Connery Chapell).
‡The IOMT&EP Co. had obtained a loan of £65,000 from Dumbell's who had, in fact borrowed that amount from Parr's Bank. To bolster the image of Dumbell's, its Chairman (Alex Bruce[+]) had been paying dividends from capital. Since 1896 the IOMT&EP Co. (with Bruce as Chairman) had also paid dividends 'other than out of profits'. See also Pearson, pages 128, 187–9.
[+] Alexander Bruce was Manager of Dumbell's Banking Co. He came to the fore following the boom year of 1887 together with men of more or less standing, including some in the Keys. They 'launched several big ventures'. Bruce evolved his own scheme for an electric railway north out of Douglas and made rapid progress due to his connections with both technical and financial sources.

platform was already provided on the Down line only). Until now, ground level platforms had sufficed (even) at Douglas, but without further delay, the permanent way gang for that station commenced to build two long and wide raised platforms at a cost of £505. There being no siding at Union Mills, one was to be installed 'for local lime and heavy traffic' (this is something of a mystery, for according to the Minutes, one was added in 1881) . . . the work was not effected until 1906–7[#] so perhaps it was another matter of cost whilst the 1881 work continued in use. At Port St Mary, James Costain completed the new goods shed and the SUN reported the opening of the 'new station' there on 10th March. Perhaps seeing all these improvements, letters now appeared in the Press demanding a goods shed at Port Erin.

Sabotage was suspected when stones were found in the point blades at Port Soderick during March and it was expressed that it might have been done by someone with a grudge rather than through mischief. One of a Station Master's duties was to check points were set correctly before signalling an incoming train; William Boyde, officiating here for the past twenty-seven years, must have ruminated over the incident as he resigned later in the year.

The privilege of free travel for the Harriers has been noted. The Isle of Man Hunt Committee now pressed the IOMR for concessions and were granted free travel for their hounds in winter months only, starting in October.

Even before the season ended, it was obvious that the Island was expecting to experience the worst year it had known. The Dumbell failure had affected every undertaking 'and would be so for years to come'. One result was the sudden and almost complete suspension of all building work, with resultant loss of brick etc. traffic. The added expense of South Wales steam coal for locomotives, as used by the IOMR, had brought up costs considerably, it being £1 10s. 0d. per ton on Douglas quay. The same company's older engines were in need of new water tanks and cylinders: locomotive manufacturers were busy, and Beyer, Peacock needed 4–5 months for delivery of a set of tanks and a pair of cylinders, costing £177 fob Liverpool.

The matter of carriage accommodation was investigated. Since the IOMR opened, an average of 7.75 per cent of persons used 1st class yet oddly during a poor year, this rose to 9 per cent.

A sum of money was set aside for equipping both IOMR routes with the Electric Train Staff.

All the Island railways squeezed as much from the visitors as they could extract . . . it was long the custom to drop fares for the winter and attract local people to use the railway at bargain rates so at the end of 1900 season the electric railway dropped its fares sharply to draw Ramsey business away from the steam lines, obliging both to do the same in October.

The second momentous event of the year gave little surprise to the IOMR. The MNR and FR together asked it to make an offer for them, a sum of £60,000 being suggested, subject to approval by the Government and various parties. That approval was obtained without difficulty, for the parlous state of the applicants was notorious. The fact that the IOMR was not tempted by this idea is explained by a daring scheme conceived by Pender (or was it

---

[#] A loop, concrete platform and siding with access road were provided in 1906–7 – was there not a loop already – or just a siding?

Rixon? . . .) for the IOMR to buy both the electric line and the MNR 'at a fair price, and so rid itself of severe competition and the risk of the electric line being extended to other parts of the Island'. He warned 'that the electric tramway is likely to fall into the hands of Debenture holders and they would then be stronger and more dangerous competitors'. He added, 'some curves are dangerous when the trams run off at great speed as they have done on several occasions . . . as the Company controls the press, it has been kept out of the papers'. Continuing, 'The Foxdale Agreement is the stumbling block to the MNR and the only answer is the liquidation of the MNR . . . there has been a great falling off of bookings to Ramsey due to electric competition . . . the liquidator of the Foxdale Company wants to sell the Railway'.*

A meeting of interested parties was to be held.

In November, word came from the three MNR directors, saying they would not sell out to the IOMR for less than £75,000, only to receive in reply 'that the IOMR has no further interest in buying the MNR at that price – it is not worth more than £60,000 to us'. By December, the IOMR Board felt it was supported in that decision by the disclosure that the MNR had issued £40,000 in Debentures and had current debts of £7,466; they stressed the age-long problems of dealing with that Company – 'We have been trying to get a Traffic Agreement for years'.

Rixon's letters to Wood (June–December 1900) reveal the depth of his involvement in the proposed purchase of the MNR and FR and, at the same time, their detail shows how limited is his knowledge of the Island and its way of thinking. He and Wood constantly threaten to cross over and see each other, but it is Wood who is usually sent a telegram to come to London at short notice, and be prepared to stay there a week at a time. Occasionally Wood puts his foot down, and writes he is 'off to Scotland', or that he can be contacted at his family home, Beaumont, Slaithwaite, near Huddersfield.

In June, Rixon stresses the need to keep negotiations on a private basis and asks Wood, 'what extra capital would be needed to lay out the Ramsey line and rolling stock to develop the undertaking . . . and the cost of doubling the line out to St John's?' In August, he advised Wood that 'negotiations have opened'. In November, he was being somewhat hard on Wood as 'being unduly nervous about an extension of the Electric system' etc. He emphasises the effect the failure of Dumbell's Bank will have on the availability of money in the Island, and waxes at length on the world political situation, to demonstrate how difficult it would be to raise money in London to make purchase of the other Railways. News must have reached him that the wet weather had adversely affected the solidity of MNR civil engineering works, and how essential it was to close the deal before things became worse.

Finally, he congratulates the IOMR Co. on 'its escape from heavy loss . . . almost a miracle' i.e. the small amount involved in Dumbell's collapse.

As the year ended, the London directors had the reconstruction (sic) of

---

*Manx Museum: MD529: copies of correspondence.

Castletown and Union Mills* before them and, in reply to enquiry, the General Purposes Committee advised the shelving of Union Mills but the prosecution of Castletown. The Chairman, intrigued 'by the use of open carriages on a Jersey railway' was still awaiting a satisfactory explanation from the Manager . . . 'he wished to further the idea'.† The Peel–Belfast boats ran as usual, and in season two trains served Kirk Braddan on Sundays only, together with the 10.00 am Douglas–Ramsey train on weekdays. However, there was no return working for the last-named!

Some further excerpts from Wood's diary:

> Easter: Extra Ticket Collectors Union Mills at night, and extra Booking Trap at Douglas.
> 27th June: Booksellers' Convention in Douglas.
> 18th July: Garden Party at Bishop's Court – trains delayed there.
> 18th August: Visitors are not here: traffic very low.
> 24th August: 10.40 am to Peel and Ramsey delayed at Union Mills. Ramsey coach and two cattle off the rails – fault of wheel and brake block of Ramsey coach.
> 29th August: Fire on Douglas Head diverts traffic from the railway.
> 18th October: Traffic low. People short of money.

The position of the MNR was worse than ever; passenger journeys had fallen to 151,862 plus 3,190 due to school excursions. Minerals were 23,959 tons and train mileage 97,650. Through passengers were down also. However, the SUN recorded the arrival of 'two new bogie carriages by Hurst, Nelson of Motherwell with bodies mounted on rubber blocks and having a double floor in the 1st class, the space in the 'sandwich' being filled with sawdust to deaden sound. 'They are electrically lit on Stone's system'. Its reporter was one of several invited to participate in an evening excursion in the carriages to demonstrate the superior fitments and lighting: earlier in the day the same vehicles had made their first visit to Douglas (their purpose was as Through Carriages), clearly to make the IOMR envious; that Company had nothing to match them.

The MNR, AGM was on 15th March, with Nelson, the Chairman; his colleagues, like himself, had become men of distinction in the Island but this was not to say the directors of the IOMR were not of the same standing, for the importance of 'good connections' in that small community was overriding. The meeting was notable in that 4 per cent interest was to be distributed on 'B' Shares and, for the first time, the Government guarantee of £1,000 was given to the Company. But Nelson had also been a director of Dumbell's and in mid-summer was found guilty of falsifying accounts and served a prison sentence in England.

Personal tragedy seemed to be the lot of the MNR as McDowall, a sick man, died in England on 26th October and the Company was obliged, yet

---

*Manx Museum: Colour-wash sketch of June 1900 and drawing for Union Mills building (two storeys) in 'Port Erin' style for £1,034 (undated).
†The Jersey Railways & Tramways operated a bogie saloon (origin unknown) with end balconies; a number of similar coaches was built by the Bristol Wagon Works Ltd., Lawrence Hill, Bristol, (later Bristol Wagon & Carriage Works Ltd.) and for which an official photograph exists, with dropped balcony ends running on diamond-framed bogies, some of which had the ends enclosed later: also a bogie saloon with clerestory roof built by themselves in 1907 (No. 11). Any one of the foregoing might have sparked-off the enquiry. [The IOMR's first saloon carriages appeared in 1905: see Volume III.]

again, to seek out a new Manager. This they found in another Scotsman, one James MacMillan, a Traffic Inspector from the Caledonian Railway in Edinburgh. He took up the reins on 17th January, 1901.

Finally, the IOMR Board noted with regret that income might be trimmed still further as 'the purchasers of the Calf of Man intend running a steamer between Douglas and Port Erin next year, calling at the Calf. It will hurt us'.

1901

On the IOMR the coming year was to be most noticeable for station improvements; improved lighting was needed over the new platforms at Douglas, and other stations without raised platforms and lighting were to be considered for it. Early in the year, there was a *volte face* over the June 1900 decision regarding Castletown, the whole scheme was deferred in preference to the complete rebuilding of Peel which, it was felt, would be more profitable. There would be a diversion of Mill Road to give more space for the station between road and river bank. Third thoughts about Castletown then obtained, and Cannel & Corrin of that town would build a new goods shed (to cost £297 12s. 0d.) to replace that of 1881; the latter had become too small and currently goods were being stored in the Ladies Waiting Room, the occasional entrance of workmen in that demesne being somewhat embarrassing to its legal occupants. Next year the station building, (saved from demolition), was given a wooden verandah at the front to increase its covered accommodation.

The usual trouble spots along the IOMR closed the Peel Line after heavy rain and the River Glas flooded. Quarter Bridge, Union Mills (submerged over one foot deep), and Ballaleece suffered their annual douche, a bridge buttress at the foremost was so badly damaged (a cumulative effect over the years) that the bridge itself needed replacement – the work extended into 1902. (It had been decided that the new bridge* should be a single lattice span 'instead of four so as to increase the water space'. The redundant girders were put into a new bridge 'on the Douglas side of the existing bridge' at Union Mills (i.e. that at Snugborough) to prevent the retention of flood water behind the railway embankment there.) In some places, ballast had been washed away leaving the track suspended in the air.

Other IOMR items included the Peel–Belfast sailings (mentioned annually if only to recall their importance to the Peel Line), and the installation of telephones to every station by The National Telephone Co. Ltd., thus dispensing with the telegraph. At Ballacostain on the Port Erin Line the Douglas Rifle Club had a Firing Range; it approached the Company 'for reduced fares and the means to reach the Range' and were told that although it 'would not discount reduced fares', trains could not be stopped near the Range, 'It is unsafe and inconvenient to stop trains out of course'.

In March the IOMR was approached by the MNR suggesting a junction between their running lines be made at St John's and sited 'opposite at Peel end of station in order to do away with signalman at the cabin at the

---

*Manx Museum: R/76.

Douglas end'. [At that time there was no rail connection between the two Companies, west of the level crossing.] The MNR suggested one man could thus attend to signals, points and crossing gates if the link was near the gates ... they proposed a scissors crossing. (Under its Act the MNR had made the existing junction at their own expense and to IOMR design, and were required to work and maintain the junction signals at their own expense: the IOMR had always paid the signalman's wages in full, being refunded by the MNR.) The IOMR objection was that there would be another set of facing points in the main line if a scissors crossing was permitted – no doubt Col Rich would require further equipment at some cost. So the IOMR did not agree.

[In September Douglas Corporation made an offer of £50,000 for the town trams.]

Wood's diary casts a personal light on IOMR events:

14th April: Prince of Wales arrived 3.55 pm and caused delay to 4.10 pm and 4.15 pm trains.
Good Friday: Traffic spoiled by Laxey Sports.
25th April: Football Cup Tie at Peel.
9th May: Concert at Douglas for benefit football players injured at Peel(?!).

(Here, Wood makes comment on 'traffic spoiled' from time to time by IOMSP Co. Day Excursions 'taking the people' to Glasgow, Dublin, Belfast.)

12th July: The new tramway*, charabuses and steamers spoil our traffic.
23rd July: IOMSP Co. guarantees Special Trains @ £7 each, no less on Tuesdays, on both our Lines to accommodate Dublin Steamer. Today they produced £1 9s. 11d.
3rd August: Extra train to Port Erin 3.45 pm to accommodate opposition steamer. (Took care to run best coaches on Port Erin Line that day.)
18th October: Floods. Union Mills to Quarter Bridge impassable. Bridges at Quarter Bridge, Snugborough and Ballaleece damaged. Passengers taken by road between Douglas and Union Mills. Quarter Bridge propped up. Landslips on Port Erin Line.
21st August: Wheel of MNR coach off at Ballacraine, delayed one hour.
1st October: From today, Special Trains to carry Mails from steamer†.
12th November: (Wood notes repetition of situation as on 18th October.)
St. Stephen's Day: Year ending quite good. General depression throughout Island.

Let us look at MNR affairs; 1901 was a more encouraging year – passengers were 154,336 journeys to which were added 2,872 in school excursions, minerals 21,506 tons and 94,109 train miles had been run. During the last two years, it had been possible to add £1,805 to the renewal fund. The Company lost another director when J.R. Cowell, financially involved with the Foxdale Railway, Snaefell Mountain project and the IOMT&EP Co., was unable to counter his losses and was made bankrupt on 4th October. He thereupon resigned his public offices, and from the MNR on 4th November. It was yet another instance of the loss of personality which dogged the MNR's history: Cowell had been on the MNR scene for two decades.

---

*This was Douglas Marine Drive Tramway: Douglas Head to Port Soderick.
†The introduction of Special Mail Trains led to the additional operating rule concerning boards on the last vehicle of trains indicating Special to follow.

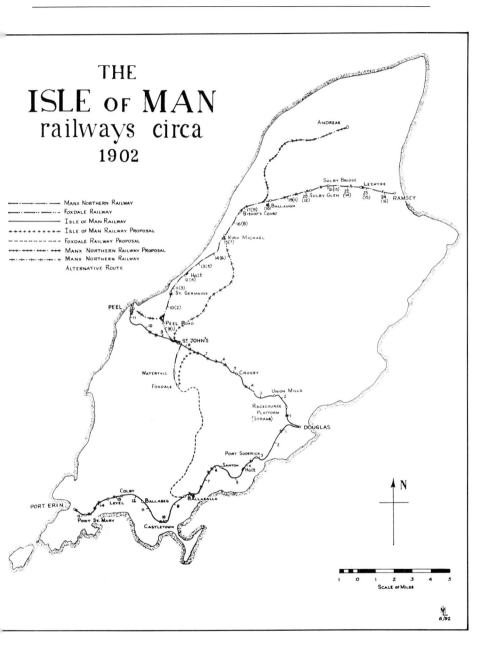

The price of lead ore had held up well but wide fluctuations now appeared to the extent that in the following year the IOMMCL would be showing a loss.†

THE RAILWAY MAGAZINE for February made reference to the change of managership on the MNR and gave this advice '... This small undertaking should be amalgamated with the Isle of Man Railway, of which it is practically a branch, and dependent on it for its connection with Douglas.' And it was wise counsel.

1902

The earlier enquiry from the Douglas Rifle Club produced a low earthen platform at Ballacostain during the first weeks of the New Year and this was followed by an Agreement with the Club that, on Thursdays and Saturdays, trains would stop at 'Ballacostain Platform' for the Range close by.

Trials had been taking place to find a substitute illuminant for the oil lamps of the carriages. Acetylene Gas was considered and thought undesirable and after further enquiry, J. Stone & Co. of Deptford was given an order to light two trains ('six ordinary + two bogie coaches* = 10 coaches') for £274 per train. The management was so confident about the correctness of the decision that instructions were amended to 'three trains of twelve coaches'. Finance for this improvement was taken from the cash reserve put aside to purchase a Single Line Tablet System: this was no longer considered necessary as 'the telephone system was serving well to control traffic'. So, for the winter of 1902, three trains were lit electrically.

A decision to rebuild Port Erin station to G & WR Kay's design was taken and a raised platform was already being built, to extend as far as the unhelpful level crossing which crossed the layout there (cost of building itself was c.£1,500). Beyond the crossing, ground level would continue. This work continued into 1905. The Port Erin Commissioners insisted that the new building should stand further from the road.

Out on the east coast, the bankrupt electric railway was re-established as The Manx Electric Railway Co. (incorporated 12th November, 1902) with Ernest Shenk acting as nominee for the purchaser.# The IOMR Minute Book

†U.K.: LEAD ORE PRODUCTION & PRICES

Year	Production in metric tons (1,000 tons)	Prices per ton in present currency
1890	34.1	£13.00
1895	29.5	£10.33
1900	24.8	£16.72
1905	21.0	£13.50
1910	21.9	£12.72
1911‡	18.3	£13.75
1912	19.5	£17.65

‡IOMMCL went out of business.
Source: WORLD NON-FERROUS METAL PRODUCTION AND PRICES (Christopher J. Schmitz)
*A bogie coach was always calculated as two vehicles.
#See Pearson Chapter Eight for extended details.

discloses a cheeky offer from the MER to buy the IOMR; the Board disregarded this as impertinent.

Nothing had yet been finally arranged for the rebuilding of Peel station 'traffic does not increase as one would wish and therefore there is not much encouragement for large expenditure'. A plan was prepared to add a second floor to the existing building and enlarge the accommodation of the ground floor and Greenbank's layout plan included some essential extra land for which an excessive price was asked. The level crossing needed improvement. Torrential rains fell in the middle of April, but they were a few days too late to save the large wooden refreshment room there ('shed' would have been a more exact description) which went up in flames, a conflagration noted for its complete destruction of the building.

Further rains on 27th April brought the customary flood to the unfinished new Quarter Bridge which caused the cessation of trains, so cars ran between Douglas station and Braddan Bridge, carrying 10 persons each and costing 20s. 0d. each per day. The span from The Phoenix Foundry for the bridge was on hand, being of lattice construction, 92 ft total length to span 86 ft and weighing 30 tons. The flooring was to be of G.A. Hobson's Patent as used for the decking of the Liverpool Overhead Railway† (and already on the Nunnery Bridge). This replacement was one of the most difficult the IOMR had to tackle, and was not completely finished until 1903.

The IOMSP Co.'s steamer from Dublin was frequently late in berthing and in April arrangements were made to run Special Trains when this occurred, the SP Co. to pay the cost. At the same period, J.W. Corrin was engaged to put up the wooden verandah on the front of Castletown station for £134. This would carry the balcony, supported on eight pillars. Nearby, the goods shed was completed. St John's received a cattle pen.

In connection with the Coronation of King Edward VII on 26th June, a request was made for extra trains at midnight; this went unheeded and the last working was at 11 pm. At the end of August the new King and Queen visited the Island and though they travelled on the MER, neither IOMR nor MNR was utilised. [The Royal couple went by road from Ramsey to Peel, calling in on the Bishop of Sodor and Man at Bishop's Court.]‡

This summer the Peel–Belfast service did not operate.

Wood's Annual Report to the IOMR Board emphasised the great falling-off of traffic on the Peel Line. St John's and Peel stations were showing the greatest drop in returns and he put this down to the effect of Dumbell's failure which had affected that part of the Island more than any other. He bemoaned the reduction in business, both farming and commercial, which was well into a second year. The IOMR was collecting a small tonnage of gravel and sand from the Foxdale Branch. The Port Erin Line was in the ascendant compared with the Peel. For some years a coastal steamer operated between Liverpool and around the ports of the Island omitting Peel; during 1902 it had served Peel also and poached a considerable amount of traffic from the railway. Wood deplored the regular annual losses in goods traffic tonnages, for which he blamed an increasing number of coastal vessels.

---

†THE LIVERPOOL OVERHEAD RAILWAY. (C.E. Box) *pages 22–23.*
‡Pearson. *page 195.*

Later, consideration was given to track levels at Quarter Bridge; the new bridge had a decking 6 in. higher than its predecessor and Greenbank arranged to have the whole line back towards Douglas as far as Pulrose level crossing, (about ¼ mile)) raised by 18 in. This had a beneficial effect to prevent flooding again.

As the year closed and nothing having been done about refurbishing Peel, Wood was informed that Peel Gas Works, standing on land adjacent to the station, was built on wooden piling to offset the unstable nature of the land. He had ascertained that when the site for the station was chosen, it had had to be filled with large quantities of sand from the nearby sandhills 'down to a great depth'. Currently the harbour wall beside the station was collapsing.

Twenty thousand less visitors had come to the Island than in 1901 but he hoped the Royal visit in August would draw the attention of many people to its existence.

The Company had paid Ordinary Shareholders a 5 per cent dividend for some time but the Board was now cautioned about the 30-year age of its rolling stock; further, there were still eight wooden stations which would ultimately require renewal. A reserve was agreed upon for this purpose, and for extending the carriage lighting.

Now to the more personal entries of Wood's diary:

Easter: Golfers' Specials to Castletown a failure.
8th May: Church Sunday School Teachers' Excursion to Bishop's Court.
26th June: Coronation delayed owing to King's illness but Specials on all lines. Finished at 1 am.
3rd August: Horse Races at Strang spoiled our day.
14th August: Horse Races at Castletown – splendid day. Return train due Douglas 6.25 pm required two engines + twenty-eight bogie carriages. 811 passengers.
15th August: Quiet day. Cars carried the people.
25th August: King & Queen from Ramsey to Bishop's Court by car, then to Peel and Douglas (they left Douglas by Electric Car).
29th August: Steamer for Dublin Horse Show. Late trains ran.
8th September: Lord Raglan arrives by EMPRESS QUEEN, takes 3.25 pm to Bishop's Court.
30th September: Very moderate season. Peace rejoicing at end of Boer War, and Coronation were drains on pockets and left less for seaside pleasures. No Belfast traffic this year. King & Queen will bring Isle of Man to notice.
Christmas Day: Boy fell into the river at St John's, through railway bridge.

The IOMR was concerned about the numbers of 'an improved method of road transport', namely the motor vehicle, which were appearing on the Island and touting for visitors. Cameron, (lately MNR and now Secretary & Manager of the Blackpool & Fleetwood Tramroad Co.) was running 'Chars-a-banc' (*quote*) and recommended the petrol car which he felt had a great future; his company's motorbus with 19 passengers and petrol @ 11d. per gallon, was giving 12 mpg on the level. [He reckoned that good weather was all that holiday transport required, and deplored the lax way in which the IOMSP Co. was running the Fleetwood–Douglas steamer, a useful source of traffic for the B & FT Co.] This marked the beginning of a period when, for the next two years, the IOMR made enquiries about road buses, steam rail-motors etc. with the conception of tours to Glen Maye and Glen Helen, and a linking service between Port Erin and Foxdale. A considerable weight of correspondence was created.

So to the MNR; the March AGM faced a financially bleak prospect, for the Island's recession showed no promise of hope. The late J.T. Clucas had held the MNR Debenture Bonds from day of issue and after passing into the IOM Bank, they were due to expire at the end of the year. A fruitless effort to place them elsewhere was met by private discussions with the Governor, Lord Henniker, to see what financial re-arrangements could be worked out. Another of those cruel blows then hit the Company: Henniker had gone to London for the Coronation and died there unexpectedly, postponing some promising progress and, yet again, requiring the Company to woo another Governor. It should be added that the MNR had never defaulted on its Debentures which were of course, a prior charge. There were 157,117 passenger journeys made, with 3,122 journeys by schoolchildren in addition: 21,577 tons of minerals had been carried and 94,218 miles run.

1903

During February a typical delivery of rectangular-section Baltic Redwood sleepers arrived for the IOMR per the agents, Burt, Benton & Haywood of London, being 6 ft × 9 in. wide × 4½ in. deep, creosoted @ 1s. 9¼d., delivered to Douglas. In the same month the Board agreed that the Saloon Carriage used by the Governor, should be paired with an up-dated 3rd class vehicle and mounted on a common frame; the work was complete by early 1904 at a cost of £74 7s. 10d. and used thereafter for premier and secondary dignitaries, the retinue travelling in the conversion. The pair was dubbed 'The Governor's and The Keys' and by the early 1930s was frequently used on the South Line's Douglas-bound trains linked to steamer departures. Enthusiastic for its difference, the writer's family was disappointed in it as the seating and windows did not suit small boys who wished to lean out of windows! (*Details in Volume III.*) And thus the last four-wheelers were paired.

The same meeting decided that the coaches which ran through to Ramsey should now be given electric lighting as a priority; the IOMR could not afford to be upstaged by the MNR's new vehicles which were superior in this and other respects (and again, were commonly sought out in a train, giving a better and more comfortable ride).

A momentous event took place on 29th April when George Henry Wood retired and was given a seat on the Board. He had been Secretary since 1871 and Secretary & Manager since 1876. A Yorkshireman from Huddersfield, he had first come to the Island to study the Manx legal system. He was given a £450 per annum pension. His position was taken by the Chief Clerk & Accountant, Thomas Stowell (who had started with the Company in 1875).

During the first weeks of the year, and before his retirement, Wood had been corresponding with Greenbank regarding the value of the Foxdale

Railway in connection with the exchange of offers which the IOMR would have to make in order to purchase both Foxdale and Northern systems. Greenbank pointed out that he had not seen the Foxdale accounts: 'they are never publicised and cannot be seen by outsiders'. He thought that the MNR owed the FR £2,766 9s. 8d., i.e. the amount due under guarantee by the MNR to the FR. 'I do not see how the MNR can extricate itself from the difficulties created by the Working Agreement without an Act ... the MNR cannot afford to lose the FR traffic'. Wood (basically an Accountant, we should be reminded) said he could understand neither the Agreement nor the Accounts (which he had managed to obtain).

Continuing on this subject; after Wood had retired, Stowell and he conferred in June on the matter of a suggested offer from the IOMR of £70,000. 'Too much', wrote Wood. However, there was an underlying fear that if action was not taken by the IOMR, the MER would make the purchase and electrify the line between Ramsey and St John's ... 'the electric company is reckless in regards expenditure'. The year wore on. Wood wrote to Greenbank again, remarking that the offer price was 'effectively now down to £67,500'. Rixon was playing his usual role on behalf of the London directors but his illness in the autumn delayed decisions. Wood was anxious that the IOM Bank, with its creditor position with the MNR, would take action before negotiations were completed; 'the IOM Bank is leading the field ... it is all Bank'. 'The IOMR would have to raise capital if it seriously wanted to buy the lines'.

This was a year when many of the events affecting the IOMR happened in the latter half; on the 26th July Mrs. Mary Ann Corlett was struck by the 8 am train from Douglas at Ballastrang level crossing, and killed. This elderly lady was acting as a crossing keeper for her daughter Mrs. Cornish, and without the knowledge of the management. At the inquest, the jury recommended 'better signalling arrangements' and the IOMR agreed to make enquiry into 'improving appliances for pulling up trains'. As was required, the Governor was informed; he wished to know how it was the train ran through the gate signals showing danger and, in due course, required a report on how the Company was meeting the jury's recommendation. As a result, five level crossing cottages (names not stated) were to be given 8-day timepieces costing £2 5s. 0d. each.

A less injurious accident took place on 30th November when No. 7 TYNWALD passed signals at Douglas and was derailed. The driver had a poor record and was dismissed; his fireman was demoted to cleaner.

To curry half-day closing business in October/November, an experiment of issuing return tickets at single fares was tried with such success that it was repeated in March/April 1904.

Delays were holding up work at Port Erin. The old station had been demolished but the Port Erin Commissioners had not yet passed the plans, so in September a temporary building in the new foundations appeared. Moore & McArd were able to start the new building in October. At Crosby a cattle dock was set up and both Port St Mary and Castletown were given gas lighting.

By the year's end, one quarter of the IOMR carriage stock was fitted with electric lighting but such was the extra power required from the locomotives to drive the dynamoes under the coaches, that coal consumption increased markedly; to meet this, one carriage was taken off every rake of vehicles. More footwarmers were purchased.

Despite his retirement, Wood continued to keep his diary in 1903. Thus:

> Whit. Sunday, 31st May: Thomas Stowell took over management this day.
>
> 26th June: Fatal accident at Ballastrang level crossing.
>
> 6th July (Tynwald Day): Every vehicle out and 'B' vans packed with people. Trains lost time due to ticket collecting.
>
> 11th July: Break down of MNR coach when near Closemooar by late train out of Douglas.
>
> 1st August: 600 Volunteers to Peel by Special Train 8 pm 22 coaches + 2 locomotives.
>
> 3rd August: Bank Holiday: 800 Volunteers from Peel. All stock save 2 coaches out. (Camp all week at Peel, including Cadets). Ended best week IOMR Co. ever had. Receipts £2,033 11s. 11d.
>
> 9th August: Regulars camping at Milntown.
>
> 11th August: Port St Mary Regatta – 2nd best day ever. Had all vehicles out. Seats put into large luggage vans. Tickets collected at Colby. Trains passing at Port Soderick – one of engine and 22 coaches had difficulty in passing another of two engines and 24 coaches. In future, no trains must pass here with more than 22 on.
>
> 30th September: Ends best season Island ever had. Railway receipts £2,202 13s. 4d. over last year. Probably result of Royal visit.

(Wood adds a note to the effect that the new Governor had been installed at Castletown on 16th October, 1902, and had called for a Special Train on several occasions since then.)

We may now turn to Stowell's first Report to the Board, which gives further insight into IOMR affairs:

> Land was purchased at Ballabeg on which to erect public conveniences and at Port Erin 'to obtain greater depth of platform and give the Commissioners a strip 4 ft wide to widen the road'.
>
> At Peel, trial bores were to be made to ascertain the nature of the ground. If unsuitable, a new building would have to be of wood and zinc as presently, but being 31 years old, the existing one was unsafe.
>
> Visitors to the Island numbered 390,357 of which 22,359 had landed at Ramsey rather than Douglas. The season had been good for the railway: it was dull and cloudy and this had robbed the road competitors of business. Moreover, it was the wettest year since 1877. Tynwald Day had been the best day ever experienced – other records were made which demonstrate the IOMR was a carrier of no mean ability despite its narrow gauge, and had lifted itself from the definition given to it by Vignoles in 1872.*
>
> In August Bank Holiday week 26 Specials were run. Those using 1st class had risen to 8.35%. As between any two stations, traffic between Douglas and Port Erin had risen the most.
>
> There was a lack of better-paying tonnage in goods traffic, that is an absence of groceries, furniture, draperies, etc. which formed such tonnages but an increase in bricks, stone, sand and gravel, the last two coming from Foxdale. The IOMR was also having to compete with even more sailing and steam vessels plying between the mainland and Peel, Castletown and Port St Mary.

*See statistics at end of chapter.

The public was crying out for new stations at Ballasalla and St John's, 'complaints are loud and long about the former'. 'A covering of a portion of Douglas station is very much wanted', (but the Board felt that a verandah at the front would have to be adequate for the moment, and that platform coverage would be too expensive at present). A gatekeeper's cottage was to be built at Four Roads.

Perhaps with the recent conversion of the Governor's Saloon into a 'paired' bogie vehicle, Stowell's last comment was, 'A Company of this stability should possess a modern Saloon Carriage'. Maybe he was thinking of a Directors' Saloon?

Behind the scenes, discussions on the purchase of the MNR and FR by the IOMR continued and were brought to a conclusion before the IOMR, AGM on 27th February, 1904; thereat the Chairman remarked '. . . (the bringing of the MNR and FR) under one ownership . . . was started as far back as when Sir Spencer Walpole was Governor and my late father, Chairman of the Company'. During 1903, meetings were to extend into July, culminating in a London meeting with representatives of the three companies. Agreement was reached, but an Act of Tynwald was needed and IOMR shareholders would have to ratify.* The Chairman did not expect to make much profit out of either lines and bringing their standards up to those of the IOMR would be expensive: the IOMR did calculate that their working expenses would be covered.

Carried away by the euphoria of amalgamation, some shareholders recommended electrification of all the steam lines as the way forward.

And how were matters looking on the MNR? The Board had made a provisional contract for the sale of the undertaking to the IOMR on 26th February. The Annual Report outlined the various debts owed by the concern, and the half-cost of the new Foxdale station at St John's (sic) owed to it under the MNR/FR Agreement of 27th December, 1895. Certain sums had been put aside to meet some of its financial obligations.

All this followed fruitless negotiations with Lord Raglan† earlier in the year, as no one was willing to take up any new Debenture scheme the Company might dangle before the public: the IOMR took the initiative on 16th March to meet with a sale in mind. The MNR's selling price was recommended by Col Rich but, as already mentioned, it was not acceptable to the IOMR. Delays frayed MNR nerves; the IOM Bank (which had received its Debenture interest without fail for 23 years), was now liable to foreclose and put the Company into liquidation. In April, the Company appealed to the Governor, anxious to obtain a loan to secure its independence. The Governor however, was firmly behind an amalgamation, and resistance to the inevitable took place on 2nd June when the MNR agreed to sell out; the MNR shareholders would have to accept the offered figures, but this seemed only to be a formality. In the event, the breakdown was:

MNR	£60,000
FR	£7,000
MNR stores	£500
Total	£67,500

*IOMR Co. Minute Book for 1903 pages 294–95 gives details of a Scheme of Arrangement.
†Lord Raglan was Governor 1902–19. Born George Henry Fitzroy Somerset 1857. Joined Grenadier Guards 1876. ADC to Governor of Bombay 1880–83; served in Afghan War before appointment to the Isle of Man.

This was the figure suggested by Wood earlier in the year, but MNR agreement on 28th July to these sums was not given until all its other avenues had failed. The Company had fought to the last with its back to the wall.

The IOMR lost no time in making provision for its extra duties and in fact, in some ways it had already infiltrated into the MNR to such degree as to make the transfer less momentous.

1903: Record traffics IOMR

Tynwald Day (6th July)	took	£452 00s. 0d.
August Bank Holiday Week	"	£2,033 00s. 0d.
Month of August	"	£7,836 18s. 11d.

August Bank Holiday Week   carried 54,503 passengers.
train mileage 4,340 miles.
Receipts – 112.456d. per mile or
£75 6s. 4d. per mile of rly.
Gross profit per railway mile 96.456d.
Working expenses per mile 16d.

1904

Despite heavy expenditure to come in the purchase of the other two railways, (for which appropriate steps to meet it were in hand), improvements on the IOMR continued. 'Seven incandescent lamps' were set up in Douglas station, and rustic trelliswork (then all the gardening rage), was spread daringly about Port Soderick station – it was already 'going wild' on certain MER stations. Collisters had finished the crossing cottage at Four Roads for £217; it was more of a bungalow than a 'cottage' (and today remains a substantial private residence).

People were currently excited by the prospect of car racing being held on the Island, although 'trials' would be a more apt definition. They took place on 14th May and were organised by the Royal Automobile Club after a special Court of Tynwald was held on 4th May to permit it.* The Governor backed this promotion heavily, and approached various organisations for a donation towards its cost. Anxious as everyone was, to 'keep sweet', the IOMR sent the sum the Governor suggested, *viz*, £25, and was much peeved when the 'Races' did little or nothing for traffic on their railway!

Booking clerks might be excused for being confused by the constant changes of fare structure which characterises the whole history of the IOMR. Detail would be tedious, but a good example takes place in the spring of 1904 when it was arranged for fare reductions during March/April as normal traffic would be light; instead, the return halves of Seven Day Tickets were made valid for a month (and receipts dropped smartly though more passengers travelled).

The Governor was 'sticking his oar in' again in May, suggesting the level crossing at Foxdale should be replaced by a bridge; whatever the legal

---

*THE ISLE OF MAN (Canon E.H. Stenning) *pages 319–20.*

niceties were, he was firmly turned down. From the same month the Port Erin Commissioners would supply the water to the station and Engine Shed, and so relieve the IOMR from pumping water from their well every night.

At St John's, in anticipation of extra vehicles being required to work the MNR section, and the withdrawal of the existing MNR coaches, a large corrugated iron Carriage Shed was to be built, so relieving pressure on Douglas and Ramsey Carriage Sheds. When new carriages arrived, they could be put under cover at once, so saving them from the ravages of weather and salt spray. Drawings were prepared for enlargement of the Douglas Workshops.†

On 7th July, a train ran through the crossing gates at Ballastrang and demolished them; it would appear there was a hoodoo on this place! Cattle traffic on the IOMR came entirely from Ramsey where the weekly Monday Mart created the business; the MER had its eyes on this traffic and built a 'cattle car', running it at unremunerative rates to secure the business and this hit IOMR receipts very hard.*

The Isle of Man Railways Act 1904 was passed on 24th May, allowing, among other things, for the IOMR Capital to be increased by £80,000, this to be covered by the creation of 4 per cent Perpetual Debenture 'A' Stock. The Company's Capital would now be £380,000. The completion of purchase of the MNR and FR was now held up by the illness of the FR liquidator. Under the Act, the IOMR was given wide power, which included the operation of road vehicles.# The above situation had not come about without the inevitable hiatus when in April the MER made a second attempt to purchase the MNR 'which was drifting into the hands of the IOMR' and which had been working it since February with Government approval. However, when the MER invited MNR representatives to a meeting to discuss the matter, the latter failed to turn up. It was rumoured (there is no documentary foundation) that at this stage the IOMR panicked lest the MER overcame the MNR's reluctance to parley, by offering them a still higher bid, but on 18th April the situation calmed when the MER withdrew from the contest.‡

The IOM Bank transferred £20,000 in Manx Northern Railway Mortgage Debentures to the IOMR.

In late April the IOMR had 'done its sums' over the MNR and submitted:

Cost of MNR and expenses	£70,000
2 new locomotives	£4,000
6 new coaches	£3,500
(St John's) carriage shed	£1,000
new goods vehicles	£700
	£79,200

plus repairs to existing stock, dismantling MNR platform at St John's, remedial work on unstable ground at Gob-y-Deigan, repairs to buildings and fencing (the latter very poor), new sleepers and fresh ballast, installation of electric lights etc. in all coming to £12,375.

---

†Manx Museum: R/13.
*Pearson: opp. page 196 No. 12 Cattle car c.1909.
†Apparently the first instance in the British Isles of a railway being permitted to operate buses.
‡Pearson: pages 205–6.

We take up the IOMR again; Port Erin was now to have a red brick wall surrounding it, with ornamental railings atop. Post Office mails were bringing in £325 per annum, and as the year progressed, there was a considerable increase in fish traffic (in barrels). Peel station was to receive heavy repairs – rebuilding would be deferred whilst money had to be found for railways' purchases. Further, Port Erin traffic continued to show greater increases over the Peel Line.

When the season ended, 738,719 passenger journeys had been made (another record) but they had travelled shorter distances as money was tight. The building trade slump continued but more of the better class of goods traffic improved the income of this section. The Kirk Braddan services showed a useful increase too.

At this stage, 59 coaching vehicles 'equal to 76 short coaches had been fitted with electric lighting'.

Reference to the loyalty of IOMR servants will be mentioned elsewhere, but a good example was to be found in William Lowe, the Traffic Inspector, who had worked regardless of his own health for many years, and died in 1904. It was the practice to appoint the Douglas Station Master to the vacant post, and hence George Watterson took up the mantle.

Whatever form the Rifle Range platform took (opened only two years previously), it must have been inadequate, as a 'new' one was opened in April, and a fresh Agreement made with the Rifle Club.

Anticipating the operation of the MNR section, the IOMR placed orders for 'two larger engines' from Beyer, Peacock, having a Douglas–Ramsey Express in mind to combat the MER. Eight 'corridor bogie coaches' (in practice, of saloon type) were ordered from Metropolitan; they were to be ready for the August 1905 traffic.

Wood still continued to keep a diary and we have his personal view of 1904:

> 12th May: Motor Speed Trials at Douglas. Inward trains only moderately patronised.
> Whit. Monday: Station set up at Milntown for Volunteers' Camp.
> 23rd May: There are 600 men at Ramsey. Ran Special Trains @ 1s. 6d. return. Trains poorly patronised – prefer to travel by Tramway.
> 30th May: Specials all week have been poorly patronised and hardly paid their way. 3,000 men in Camp.
> Tynwald: 5th July: All stock out. One train had five brake vans full of people standing.
> End September: End of second best season ever – visitors down – less money.
> 14th November: Hollantide Fair Day.
> Christmas: One of the worst had.

So to railway matters in the north; Sir John D. Pender and his Lady decided to sample the railways so much in the news and did a 'round trip' in late February, travelling north by MER to Ramsey, thence by MNR section (worked by IOMR at this date) and IOMR to Douglas. The COURIER (4th March) waxed, 'the party had every opportunity of viewing the beautiful scenery; Sir John and Lady Pender especially enthusiastic in their admiration'. However, the weather was not all that bright. After chairing the

IOMR, AGM, 'Sir John and his spouse left Douglas in their yacht, MARETANZA'.

The same paper's Editorial maintained: 'We must be thankful for the outcome of meetings . . . one railway company is enough on a small island: better quarter of a loaf than no bread at all for MNR/FR shareholders. The MNR has always been a series of trials, difficulties and uphill work, minus any tangible financial benefit to those long-suffering shareholders'. And that summed it up!

The MNR had made one last attempt to create more traffic by proposing an extension of the Quay Tramway to a point opposite the Ramsey Custom House, but they had been prevented.

Spurred by the takeover, a correspondent to the COURIER (18th March) said he hoped 'petrol driven railway carriages would enable outside villages and towns along the railway to have connection with the steamers' . . . he hoped the new management would do this 'before buses step in and lift southern passengers from the Landing Pier at Douglas and set them down at Port St Mary . . . an hour's wait at Douglas station for passengers coming off the steamer is one way of choking off visitors from holidaying in the Island'. ('A lover of Manxland'.)

Now to the MNR; the Governor agreed the Government guarantee should be honoured up to 22nd September (being the actual date of expiry). The AGM was a dismal affair on 17th March with the sale of the undertaking and the need for an EGM to agree to same, permeating the atmosphere. The gathering was short. Sale of the Foxdale Railway had been approved by the Chancery Court on 6th April.

The Governor was prepared to question the IOMR's estimate of expenses which they considered were essential to bring the MNR into an appropriate condition; he had before him Col Rich's opinion of the Railway which did not tally with the figures required by the IOMR. Rich said he had inspected the MNR on 6th May:

> and found the permanent way and rolling stock in good working order. This railway was well ballasted before it was opened, and has been well maintained since. The steel rails that were originally laid on it have proved to be of excellent quality. They show little sign of wear . . . if well maintained will last for many years.* The fences have always been weak . . . the works are in a better state at present than when the line was opened for traffic, except for the ordinary wear and tear of iron girders and rolling stock.

A compromise was reached on the cost of bridge repairs, and the final £20,000 of the 'A' Debentures would be realised only with Government agreement.

Nominally, IOMR working of MNR/FR trains began on 27th February but in practice the trains were operated by the MNR on its behalf until 19th April, 1905 . . . a sensible arrangement until new IOMR rolling stock arrived. Meanwhile, the 'new' St John's MNR interchange platform was abandoned and later demolished. The IOMR took over;

> 4 locomotives: 15 carriages: 2 brake vans: 36 wagons (according to the list given at the IOMR, AGM). (SUN 19th March).

---

*This was true – some were never replaced.

Remaining on the Northern Line, a stange business occurred at Kirk Michael as the 9.19 am for Ramsey approached. A billposter named Galbraith, travelling in the guard's van with guard R. Thompson, was almost hit by a bullet as the train passed under the road bridge at Cronk-y-Voddy. The bullet hit the window and shattered it; Galbraith instinctively put his arm to his face and was covered by broken glass. The guard had noted a man standing on the bridge with a rifle in his hand. It was averred that had it not been for the thickness of the window glass which diverted the bullet, Galbraith would have been seriously injured. The matter caused great unease in the district; was it linked to the IOMR takeover?

Acknowledgements

The Isle of Man Railway has engaged my interests since I was a child; I mention this that I may not overlook its many staff and employees who, though now beyond recall, met my earliest appetite for knowledge and enabled me to write the earlier editions of this title.

The following have come to my help in the present volume:

Jeremy S. Wilkinson – Wilmslow
Alastair Lamberton – Laxey
J. Douglas Darby – Brooklands
Charles E. Box – Liverpool
Frank Smith – Bolton
Miss Ann Harrison – (Public Records Officer) Douglas
Tony Beard – Douglas
Julian Edwards – Lezayre
Colin Goldsmith – Douglas

I owe a special debt of gratitude to Brian Crompton for his support, to the Staff of the Reference Library, Manx Museum, Douglas, to the Management of Isle of Man Transport for anticipating the needs of an author, and no less to my wife who has assisted with research and used her considerable experience in the drudgery of preparation.

After the untimely death of John M. Lloyd, I am grateful to Michael Morton-Lloyd for stepping into the breach with such enthusiasm and preparing much new drawing work.

To those whom I have failed to name individually, my grateful thanks and the hope that they will judge this memory of them to be wholly acceptable.

Sources

Primary
    Government Office papers
    Railways' Minute Books
    The Tower Collection
    Diary of G.H. Wood
    Isle of Man Public Records Office

Secondary
    Isle of Man Harbour Board
    Castletown Town Commissioners
    Attorney General's Chambers records
    Isle of Man Land Registry
    Royal Military School of Music
    Wakefield Libraries
    Derby Libraries
    Glasgow District Libraries
    Leeds Leisure Services
    Sheffield County Council
    Suffolk County Council
    Quiggin & Co. Ltd.
    Bradshaw's Railway Manual (annual)
    Field notes by R. Shepherd, Ian Macnab, L.T. Catchpole and Frank Hewitt
    STEAM RAILWAY NEWS (IOMR Supporters' Association)

Newspapers

MANX SUN	1826–1906
ISLE OF MAN TIMES	from 1861
ISLE OF MAN EXAMINER	from 1880
PEEL CITY GUARDIAN	from 1882
RAMSEY COURIER (now ISLE OF MAN COURIER)	from 1884

Bibliography

STATUTES OF THE ISLE OF MAN	Manx Government
HISTORY OF THE ISLE OF MAN RAILWAY	Ian Macnab
ISLE OF MAN TRAMWAYS	F.K. Pearson
MANX NORTHERN RAILWAY	P. & P. Hendry
INDUSTRIAL ARCHAEOLOGY OF THE ISLE OF MAN	Various
ON THE ISLE OF MAN NARROW GAUGE	J.I.C. Boyd
ISLE OF MAN – PAST & PRESENT	George Woods
ISLE OF MAN – MEMOIRS OF A GEOLOGICAL SURVEY	G.W. Lamplugh
ISLE OF MAN	E.H. Stenning
THE ISLE OF MAN	John Quinn
BRITISH STEAM LOCOMOTIVE BUILDERS	James Lowe
A BIOGRAPHY OF RAILWAY ENGINEERS	John Marshall
THE LIVERPOOL OVERHEAD RAILWAY	C.E. Box
THE CENTENARY OF THE ISLE OF MAN STEAM PACKET CO. LTD.	P.W. Caine
ATLAS OF THE ISLE OF MAN	George Woods
THE DUMBELL AFFAIR	Connery Chapell
ISLAND LIFELINE	Connery Chapell

INDEX

Subjects which occur frequently in the text are not indexed e.g. individual station names, individual locomotives etc. Such will be indexed (where more appropriate) in Volumes II and III.

Accidents and Incidents 50, 54, 63, 64, 65, 66, 67, 72, 75, 78, 82, 83, 84, 90, 92, 105, 110, 114, 122, 128, 132, 136, 137, 140, 145, 158, 159, 161, 167, 172, 179, 190, 197, 207, 218, 219, 232, 235, 236, 238, 248, 252, 255.
Acts 21, 60, 95, 100, 106, 156, 192, 201, 226, 252.
A.W. Adams (IOMR Advocate) 36, 56, 94.
Advertising and Publicity 69, 74, 128, 144, 234.
Agreement
  IOMMCL + MNR 157, 176, 178, 233.
  IOMR + MNR 116, 127, 139, 160.
  MNR + FR 164, 173, 174, 176, 197, 214, 248.
Amalgamation of railways 192, 193, 194, 197, 236, 237, 238, 239, 250.
Armstrong
  George 27, 179.
  James 27, 30, 54.
Ashbury Railway Carriage & Iron Co. Ltd. (see Rolling Stock)
Attempts to build a railway 17-on.
Avonside Engine Co. Ltd. 117.

Ballabeg (need for a station, et seq.) 75, 83, 88, 90.
Ballacraine ('station' at) 90, 91.
Ballacurry (request for station: see also Greeba) 147, 226.
Ballaleece 145, 152, 156.
Ballast Pits 82.
Ballavolley Quarry Siding 165.
Ballymena, Cushendall & Red Bay Railway 35.
Banking Co.
  Dumbell's 182, 204, 214, 237, 238, 239, 240, 245.
  Isle of Man 212.
'Barrow Haematite Co. Ltd.' 159.
Beadle, Major-General J. 106.
Belle Vue Racecourse 54.
Beyer Peacock & Co. Ltd. (see Rolling Stock).
Billown Quarry & Branch (proposed) 73, 169, 178.
Blackpool & Fleetwood Tramroad Co. 233, 246.
Block System 65.
Boyde Bros. 109, 116.
Braby & Co. 57.
Brakes, defective carriage 88.

Brebner & Fleming 109, 118, 233.
Brick Traffic 159, 160, 178, 191, 198, 203, 232.
Brick Works
  Lace's 190, 191.
  Manx Brick & Tramway Co. Ltd. 172, 179.
  St John's Brick & Tile 67.
Brick Work's Siding (Peel 1886) 178.
Brown, Marshalls & Co. Ltd. (see Rolling Stock)
Bruce, Davis & Co. Ltd. 160.
Byelaws (IOMR) 50.

Cameron, John 122, 129, 140, 147, 173, 194, 222, 225, 233.
Car Racing 251.
Carriage Sheds 86, 109, 121, 122, 139, 190, 191, 196, 207, 210, 218, 221, 252.
Cartage (station, pier, luggage etc.) 69, 153, 161, 191, 196, 230, 235.
Castletown (diversion of railway) 13, 36, 48, 56, 65, 74.
Castletown Quay Tramway (proposed) 14, 162.
Castletown station – rebuilding 241, 245.
Cattle traffic 88, 120, 215, 252.
Class, changes in passenger 106, 136.
Clucas, J.T. 29, 67, 80, 99, 117, 121, 145, 147, 156, 172, 173, 182, 189, 194, 195.
Coal
  locomotive 65, 67, 131, 196, 238.
  mining 68, 222.
Competition (IOMR)
  MER 226, 253.
  Road 101, 105, 123, 182, 246, 254.
  Ship 123, 182, 196, 197, 210, 215, 242, 245.
Competition (MNR)
  MER 226, 228, 234, 239.
  Ship 123, 182, 194, 195, 196, 197, 215, 226.
Complaints
  re IOMR carriages 49, 63, 78, 80, 91, 99, 136, 163, 171, 232.
  re Watson & Smith 67, 74, 80, 81.
Constructional problems
  FR 182.
  IOMR 48, 58, 68, 69, 75, 76, 81.
Contractors
  FR 174.
  IOMR 35, 67.
  MNR 116, 120, 121.

Contractors' locomotives 43, 46.
Corvalley Mines 226.
Costain, James 228, 238.
Cowell, J.R. 140, 147, 194, 220, 242.
Cowle, James & Son (Architects) 207, 224.
Cranes, Travelling, Workshop, Yard 196, 203, 215.
Craven Bros. (see Rolling Stock)
Cregeen, Daniel 56, 110, 143.
Creggan's Lime Quarry (see Billown Quarry)
Crosby, layout alterations 228, 231.
Cruikshank, J.M. 212, 214.

Dalby – proposed railway from Peel, 234.
Davis & Meadows 158.
Deemster (Sir William Leece Drinkwater) 40, 212.
Delivery of Rolling Stock to Island 55, 56, 61, 74, 75, 116, 118, 119, 129, 137, 174.
Deviations, Trevithick's recommended 64.
Directors
    FR 147, 159, 160, 167, 212.
    IOMR 63, 236.
        unexpected visit 1873 58.
    MNR 102.
Donations by IOMR 136.
Doubling of line IOMR (proposed) 229, 230
Douglas & Laxey Coast Electric Tramway Ltd. 223.
Douglas & Peel Railway Co. Ltd. (1862/1864) 17, 18, 19, 21, 22.
Douglas Bay Tramway 143.
Douglas, developments and extension of facilities 111, 128, 132, 138, 143, 144, 158, 161, 171, 179, 191, 196, 203, 210, 214, 215, 218, 238, 241.
Douglas, Laxey & Ramsey Railway Co. Ltd. 143, 144, 160, 176, 224.
Douglas, Laxey & Snaefell Railway 201.
Douglas, piers and harbours at 48.
Douglas Quay Tramway (proposed) 48, 49, 57, 65, 68, 99, 128, 136, 143, 146, 153, 157, 158, 161, 162, 169, 171, 182, 203, 204, 237.
Douglas Recreation Ground 215.
Douglas Southern Electric Tramways Ltd. 224, 227, 230.
Dübs & Co. Ltd. 174.
Dutton & Co. Ltd. 210, 215.

'Ebbw Vale Steel Co. Ltd.' 136.
Edward VII, King, Royal Visit 245.
Electric lighting of carriages 240, 244, 246, 247, 249, 253.
Employees and Staff relations 82, 132, 135, 137, 253.

Employees: lack of experience 67, 91.
Excursions, road: Peel–Port Erin 127, 128.

Fairlie, Robert F. 28.
Fares* 89, 125, 129, 158, 235, 238, 248, 251.
Fell, George N. 201, 228.
Fencing 40, 46, 57, 67, 74, 88, 101, 138, 162.
Festiniog Railway 28, 121.
Finance
    FR 147, 167, 174, 182, 188, 193, 194, 199, 205, 209, 211.
    IOMR 34, 36, 40, 54, 55, 63, 64, 67, 73, 76, 77, 83, 91, 105, 125, 157, 252.
    MNR 93, 94, 99, 100, 101, 102, 103, 108, 110, 116, 140, 156, 189, 193, 195, 199, 205, 209, 212, 221, 222, 231, 240, 247, 250.
Finch, B. & Co. 210.
Fish Traffic 102, 127, 221, 253.
Fleming, George John 233.
Floods 72, 73, 78, 114, 222, 231, 241, 245.
Footwarmers 228, 237, 249.
Forman, Charles 147, 193.
Formans & McColl (or) 147, 155, 160, 167, 174, 183, 188, 194, 220.
Foxdale Branch (proposed IOMR) 145, 146, 147, 152, 153, 154, 155, 157.
Foxdale Mines Traffic 27, 30, 81, 88, 105, 145, 146, 147, 169.
'Foxdale Railway' – proposed 145, 146, 147.
Foxdale Railway
    sale of 254.
    southward extension 156, 185, 189, 192.
Free Passes and Gold Passes
    IOMR 54, 72, 122, 127, 145, 198, 205, 215, 221, 227, 230.
    MNR 122, 164, 198, 205, 215, 221.
Furness Railway (1867 proposal) 17, 22.

Gas lighting 69, 73, 88, 91, 162, 235, 248.
Gelling & Kaye (builders) 46, 54, 64, 116, 122, 161, 162.
General Purpose Committee, formation of 40.
Glasgow Exhibition, gravel for 201.
Glengarrif Land & Development Co. 35.
Glenfaba Deviation 65, 73.
Glen Helen 91, 92, 94.
Glen Helen & MNR 173.
Glen Helen: railway proposals 163, 172, 194, 201.
Glen Helen Slate Quarry 49.
Glen, John 174, 183.
Glen Wyllin 209.
Gob-y-Deigan 129, 131, 157, 164, 207, 234.

*Selected references only.

INDEX

Goods Sheds 86, 105, 106, 135, 157, 176, 210, 215, 231, 234, 237, 238, 241.
Goods Trains 78.
Government Director/Inspector (see Rick, Col.)
Governor's Saloon Carriage 247.
Grainger, J. & W. & Co. 103, 108, 109, 115, 120, 122, 123, 140.
Grant-Dalton, M. 109, 121.
Great Manx Railway (1845) 17.
Greeba, proposal for stopping place 128, 223, 224.
Greenbank, Henry 38, 48, 100, 128, 144, 145, 146, 154, 156, 169, 222, 229, 247.
Greensills (chemists) 90, 196.
Gregory, Charles Hutton, (Sir) 64, 74.

Halstead 131, 132.
Harbour Commissioners/IOM Harbour Committee 146.
Harbour
  Douglas 35.
  Peel 137, 138.
  Ramsey 35, 131.
Harriers 224.
Henniker, Lord 226, 247.
Hobson's Patent 245.
Hollantide (Fair Day) 78, 235.
Hughes, William 132, 139, 140.
Hunt, Henry 90, 120, 135, 159, 171.
Hunt, IOM Committee 238.
Hurst, Nelson & Co. Ltd. 167.
Hutchinson, W.A. 232.

Inspections
  FR (not traced).
  IOMR 58, 61, 64, 70, 74, 76, 182.
  MNR 128, 129, 131, 132, 133, 167.
Island industries 11, 12, 40.
Isle of Man
  Extension Railway (1862) (proposed) 17, 18.
  Liverpool & Manchester Steam Ship Co. 197.
  Mining Co. Ltd. 68, 70, 71, 147, 153, 154, 165, 185.
  Omnibus & Cab Co. 196.
  Race Co. 54.
  Steam Packet Co. Ltd. 13.
  Tramways & Electric Power Co. Ltd. 229, 237.
  Tramways Ltd. 196.
Isle of Man Railway (1864) (proposed) 17, 21.
Isle of Man Railway Co. (1845) (proposed) 17.

Isle of Man Railway Co. Ltd. (1857) (proposed) 17.
Isle of Man Railway construction 39, 43, 46, 47, 49, 51.
Isle of Wight Railway 46, 65.

Jefferson & Moore's Quarry 110, 158.
Jersey, open carriages on Railway 234, 240.
Junction, Peel & Port Erin Lines, alteration of 73.
Jurby, 101, 102.

Kay, G. & W.R. 244.
Kennedy, Hugh & Son 174, 182, 183, 185, 194, 204, 214.
Kirk Braddan Church, Sunday train services 223, 240.
Kirk Braddan, request for station 226, 228.
King William's College 14, 159.
Kissack, James 90, 171.
Kitto, Capt. William 49, 146.
Kneen, Thomas 205.

LaMothe, J. C. 120, 220, 233.
Landowners and values 28, 29, 54, 110.
Laxey (IOMR proposal) 196.
Lead Mining 153, 154, 244.
Lead Store, Ramsey 165.
Lease of FR by MNR 154, 155.
Lewis, William 71, 92, 94.
Level Crossings and Accommodation
  FR 251.
  IOMR 39, 50, 59, 68, 71, 82, 83, 84, 86, 139, 161, 234, 248, 251.
  MNR 109.
Lezayre 129, 165.
Lime Traffic 87, 88, 90, 159, 161, 165, 203.
Lloyds Bonds 73.
Loch, H.B. (Sir) 20, 71, 84, 106, 115, 144, 156, 157, 160.
Locomotive, Peel Harbour 138, 174, 183.
Locomotives
  FR Special for Foxdale 147.
  IOMR Special for Foxdale (proposed) 146, 154.
  MNR Loans to contractors 109, 183, 224, 225.
  Problems with 94.
London Board, IOMR 41 etc.
Luke, P.V. 236.

Mackenzie, W.S. 40, 48, 50.
Macmillan, James 241.
Mails, carriage of
  IOMR 48, 68, 72, 77, 88, 171, 253.
  MNR 140, 189.

Main & Co. 210.
Maitland, Dalrymple 232.
Manure Traffic 178, 208.
Manx Brick & Tramway Co. Ltd. (see Brickworks).
Manx
  East Coast Railways 210.
  Electric Railway 244.
  Fishing Fleet 101.
  Line Steamers 191, 197.
  Northern Railway
    Agreement with FR to work 152.
    construction 103, 108, 109.
    creation of 92, 93, 94, 99, 100, 102, 103.
    problems with navvies 103, 109.
    purchase by IOMR 231, 233, 239, 248, 250, 254.
    supposed take-over by IOMT & EPC Ltd. 229, 230, 231, 248, 252.
Metropolitan Railway Carriage & Wagon Co. Ltd. (see under Rolling Stock)
Midland Railway Carriage & Wagon Co. Ltd. 158, 160.
Mona Chemical Co. (see Bruce, Davis & Co. Ltd.)
Mona Steamship Co. 201, 210, 215, 227, 230.
Mooragh Estate and tramway 205.
Moore, Thomas (Turkeyland Quarry & Branch; proposed) 178.
Moore & McArd 248.
Murray, William 164, 183.
McDowall, David 233, 236, 240.

National Telephone Co. 228, 232, 241.
Nelson, Andrew S. & Co. 167, 174, 183, 190.
Nelson, C.B. 199, 212, 215, 233, 236, 237, 240.
Nunnery Bridge 211, 221, 224.

Oldbury Railway Carriage & Wagon Co. Ltd. 189, 190.
Opening
  FR 183, 184.
  IOMR 61, 62, 63, 68, 76.
  MNR 120.
Operating
  IOMR 50, 76, 86, 87, 167, 168, 169, 217.
  MNR 118, 120, 121, 125, 140, 167, 168, 169, 195.
  Rules IOMR, for working MNR 120, 123.

Pearce, Martin 139.
Peel
  destruction of engine shed/goods shed/refreshment room 159, 207, 245.
  diversion of railway into town 101.

MNR - lack of proximity and consequence 101, 143.
Quay Tramway 49, 57, 65, 161, 162, 171.
station rebuilding 241, 245, 246, 253.
Peel and N. Ireland Steam Ship Co. Ltd. 203.
Peel Railway Co. Ltd. 188, 192, 198, 209, 220, 221.
Peel Road (Poortown) 156, 165, 173, 220, 221.
Pender, John (Sir) 36, 155, 193, 201, 227, 253.
Permanent Way
  FR 174, 183.
  IOMR 99, 101, 111, 182.
  MNR 135, 176, 189.
Personal Relations 233.
Phoenix Foundry, The 43, 224, 245.
Platform awnings, shelter, etc. 128.
Poortown Quarry & Tramway 165, 190.
Port Erin
  extension of line to landing stage (proposed) 20, 49, 69.
  Harbour Works 20, 35.
  locomotive water supply 252.
  new station 227, 244, 248, 253.
Port St. Mary
  new station 211, 227, 231.
  Tramway (proposed) 215.
Port Soderick
  lack of shelter 85.
  new station 128, 221, 224, 227.
Promotion
  FR 145, 147, 152, 154, 155, 156, 161.
  IOMR 27, 29.
  MNR 92, 93, 94.
Prospectus
  FR 165.
  IOMR 27.
  MNR 96, 102.
Provisional Committee, IOMR 29.

Quarter Bridge
  request for station 136, 215, 226.
  bridge repairs and renewal 241, 245, 246.
Quiggin & Co. Ltd. 132, 203, 234, 237.
Quotations – Rolling Stock (IOMR) 95, 99, 232.

Racecourse Platform, Union Mills 54, 65, 68.
Raglan, Lord 250, 251.
Rails
  FR 165, 167.
  IOMR 40, 43, 99, 106, 114, 132, 147, 153, 156, 159, 160, 191, 198, 221.
Railway Clearing House 233.

INDEX 261

Ramsey Harbour/Quay Tramway 103, 129, 131, 139, 146, 156, 254.
Ramsey Line, abandonment by IOMR 33, 36, 77, 84, 85, 92.
Ramsey town – developments and recession 200, 201, 205, 216.
Ramsey Steamship Co. 131, 226.
Ransomes & Rapier Ltd. 128.
Rates 162, 169, 192, 232.
Refreshment Rooms 60, 75, 82, 139, 191, 192.
Reports (and Surveys)
  Armstrong, George 179, 182.
  Greenbank, Henry 47.
  Mackenzie, W.S. 49, 50.
  Rich, F.H. 69.
  Rixon, A.W. 69.
  Stowell, Thomas 249, 250.
  Thomas, W.H. 104.
  Trevithick, F.H. 78, 81, 85, 88.
  Vignoles, H. 43–47, 49, 78.
  Watson, 51.
Rich, F.H. (Col.) 57, 61, 66, 77, 117, 128, 131, 134, 156, 185, 195, 199, 222, 242, 254.
Ridgeway, John West (Sir) 222, 226.
Rifle Range Platform, Ballacostain 241, 244, 253.
Rixon, A.W. 48, 54, 136, 193, 230, 239, 248.
Rolling Stock
  general 57, 92, 95, 106.
  FR 189, 193.
  IOMR 57, 83, 87, 136, 138, 145, 191, 192, 217, 218, 221, 224, 227, 247, 253.
  MNR 117, 118, 120, 129, 134, 140, 145, 165, 179, 240.
  shortcomings 87, 91, 92, 120, 121, 179, 190, 191, 208, 217, 218, 225, 228, 246.
Route – description MNR 119.
Routes considered 30, 33.
Royal Bengal Fusiliers 62.
Rule Book – IOMR 105, 207.
Running Powers (MNR over IOMR) 152, 194, 205, 207.

Salaries 90, 116, 159.
Sand and gravel traffic 147, 159, 198, 245.
Scarlett
  Lime Co. 88, 90.
  Stone Quarry 88, 204.
Schoolchildren's Outings 119, 120.
Scott, Robert 92, 167, 188, 194.
Sharp, Stewart & Co. Ltd. 117, 129, 135.
Sheward, George 36, 37, 58, 163.
Shipping and steamers 13, 20, 46, 91, 123, 127, 171, 189, 191, 192, 197, 215, 225, 234, 245, 246.

Sidings (IOMR) lack of 59, 82, 179.
Signalling
  improvements at Douglas 220.
  modifications MNR 140.
Signals
  FR/MNR 122, 129, 140, 183.
  IOMR 50, 75, 79, 82, 86.
Single Line Working (IOMR) 50, 59, 220, 232, 238, 244.
Skelmersdale, Lord 77, 106.
Smith & Sons 210.
'Smiths of Rodley' 210.
Snaefell Mountain Railway Association, The 224.
Snow, effects of 179, 180, 223, 225.
Special Workings (IOMR) 110, 132, 218, 245.
Spoilbanks, Foxdale 188, 211.
Sproat, Joseph 171, 179, 208.
St John's & Foxdale Railway (proposed) 145.
St John's
  joint working 122, 124, 125, 127, 158, 179, 190, 207, 229.
  junctions and alterations 111, 124, 125, 129, 139, 145, 153, 156, 162, 164, 173, 183, 189, 228, 229, 241, 242, 254.
Stacy, Davis & Co. (see Phoenix Foundry)
Stanley, H.F. (Hon.) 37, 77.
Station Masters' accommodation 215.
Stations – 'classes' and material
  IOMR 33, 39, 40, 54, 57, 64, 79, 85, 86, 179.
  MNR 109.
Stations – recommended 33, 39, 136.
Stevens & Sons. 183.
Stone, J. & Co. 240, 244.
Stone Traffic 204, 232.
Stowell, Flaxney 90.
Stowell, Thomas 247, 248.
Sulby Glen, station re-siting 131.
Sutherland, Duke of 36, 37, 38, 58, 106, 114.
Swansea Wagon Co. Ltd. 117.

Taubman – all references 33, 36, 47, 143, 203, 222, 227, 228, 232.
Telegraph 47, 48, 59, 69, 74, 77, 79, 83, 84, 115, 122, 183, 232.
Theft 196.
Thomas, William Henry 100, 103, 121, 122, 129, 156.
Through carriages 129, 139, 161, 162, 171, 176, 229, 240, 247.
Tickets 50, 115, 116.
Timber Bridges (IOMR) 182.
Timetables 59, 72, 74, 77, 78, 115, 120, 121, 125, 129, 188, 204, 214.

Todhunter, William 233.
Tolls (IOMR) 111
Tramway, Douglas Station – Victoria Pier (proposed) [see Douglas Quay Tramway]
Travelling conditions (IOMR) 81, 195, 196.
Trevithick, F.H. 72, 79, 84, 85, 87.
Trevithick, improvements required 73, 76, 77, 79, 85, 86, 89.
Trial Runs 56, 58, 59, 61, 75, 116, 118, 120.
Turkeyland Quarry (Branch proposed) 110, 178.
Turntables 94, 95, 99.
Turquand, Youngs & Co. 156, 183, 216, 222.
Tynwald Day – operating 75, 82.

Uniforms, IOMR 57, 218.
Unsatisfactory condition of MNR 239.
Urinals, want of, IOMR 77, 79, 85, 210.

Vignoles, Henry 28, 81.

Waddell Bros. 140, 176.
Wagons
  hire of 160, 183, 224.
  need for additional 89, 90, 161.
Walpole, Spencer 93, 161, 195, 197, 212.
Wark, John 174.

Water Supply (Taubman) 47, 215.
Waterlow & Sons 50.
Watson & Smith 37, 38, 40, 51, 64, 67, 73, 76, 81, 82, 105, 132, 214.
Wells, Tube 59, 198.
West Cumberland Iron & Stone Co. Ltd. 159.
West Kella 129.
Witham, Samuel & Co. 43, 83.
Wilson, W. D. 56, 69.
Winter economies 68, 88, 89.
Women, employment of 211.
Wood, George Henry 28, 33, 40, 90, 101, 116, 121, 132, 135, 144, 163, 167, 168, 201, 222, 225, 235, 239, 247, 253.
Wood, Diary of 132, 139, 154, 159, 163, 171, 180, 182, 192, 204, 208, 211, 215, 220, 240, 242, 246, 249.
Woodhouse, Henry 142, 144.
Working arrangements (etc.)
  FR/IOMR/MNR 106, 108, 115, 117, 121, 123, 124, 125, 133, 134, 135, 138, 139, 158, 251, 254.
  ending of and consequences 125, 127, 129, 139, 158, 164.
Workshops
  IOMR 47, 77, 87, 161, 191, 196, 207, 210, 218, 252.
  MNR 131, 139, 140.